# COUNTRY WALKS NEAR BOSTON

## Revised and expanded 3rd edition

## by Alan Fisher

## RAMBLER BOOKS

### Baltimore

COUNTRY WALKS NEAR BOSTON, 3rd edition

by Alan Fisher
Maps and photographs by the author

Rambler Books
1430 Park Avenue
Baltimore, MD 21217

---

Printed in the United States of America

THIRD EDITION

---

Excerpts from *Oakes Ames — Jottings of a Harvard Botanist*, edited by
his daughter Pauline Ames Plimpton and published in 1979, are
reprinted by permission of the Oakes Ames Orchid Library, Harvard
University, Cambridge, Massachusetts, USA.

---

ISBN 0-9614963-7-1

On the cover: the Blue Hills Reservation, one of Boston's outstanding
areas for walking.

# CONTENTS

(T) Indicates sites that are reachable by public transit.

MAP 1 — Orientation

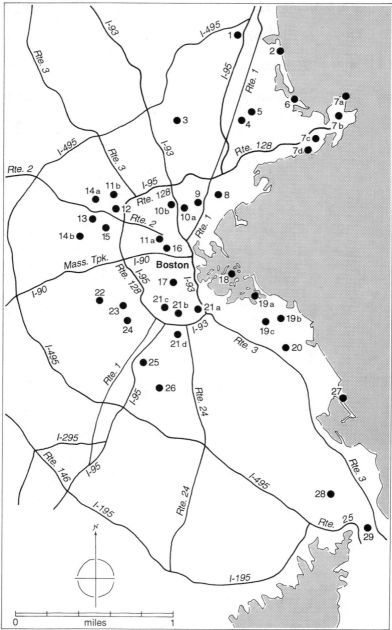

# PREFACE

THIS BOOK IS FOR PEOPLE who want an outing in a country setting without wasting half the day getting there and back. If you live in the Greater Boston region, the excursions described here are close at hand. The parks, refuges, reservations, state forests, and other sites cover the gamut of the region's landscapes. Successive visits during different seasons — to see the changing foliage, views, flowers, and birds — provide an added dimension of enjoyment.

**Automobile directions:** Because readers will be driving from different places to reach the sites described here, the directions sometimes outline several different avenues of approach. Necessarily, there is much repetition, so focus on the set of directions that applies to you and skip the others. Also, you may find it helpful to use **Map 1** at left in conjunction with each chapter's more detailed map or inset showing local roads.

**Public transit:** Many of the places described here can be reached by the MBTA's system of trains, rapid transit lines, and buses. Sites that are accessible by public transit are identified in the Table of Contents. Telephone **(617) 222-3200** for current information on schedules routes, and connections from your starting point. For calls from outside the (617) area, use the toll-free number **1 (800) 392-6100**.

The following people helped me with this book in various ways, including providing information, reviewing chapters, and making suggestions: Leslie Baskin, Ernest Cook, Mallory Digges, Michelle Dumas, Scott Elledge, Bob Fleming, Charlotte Goodwin, Nancy Hanssen, Janet L. Heywood, John W. Kimball, Bill Mahoney, Alan McClellen, Jr., Pamela McEntee, Geoff McGean, Neil Miller, Robert P. Moncreiff, Frederick Strong Moseley III, Holly Richardson, George B. Rideout, Jr., Jim Shea, Joan Shirley, James W. Skehan, Pamela Snow, Bill Stokinger, Jonathan Strong, and Ellenor Yahrmarkt. Many, many thanks.

Alan Fisher

# COMFORT AND SAFETY

PLEASE READ THIS. It is customary, in guidebooks such as this, to include a catalog of cautions about possible nuisances and hazards. Such matters do not make for scintillating reading, but really, I think that you will be glad to focus here on a few potential problems, so that you can avoid them, rather than remember them belatedly through uncomfortable (or even dangerous) experience. Please also read the introductory matter for each excursion before you go.

Ordinary gear for a comfortable outing includes a small knapsack containing a snack, a water bottle or juice carton, insect repellent, and an extra layer of clothing, such as a sweater or rain parka. For footwear, lightweight walking shoes are fine spring though fall, but in winter wear hiking boots that will keep your feet dry and provide traction in snow.

Some of the trails described in this book traverse steep slopes and follow the tops of cliffs, so control your children closely. Bear in mind that terrain presenting only moderate difficulty when dry can be treacherous when wet, snowy, or icy. And unlike some people I have encountered, don't undertake impromptu rock climbing, only to find yourself perched on a ledge and unable to extricate yourself.

Every year the newspapers carry stories about people who pick up a squirrel, a raccoon, or some other animal and get bitten. They then have to undergo a series of painful anti-rabies shots. Don't be one of these people; don't handle *any* wild animals. In somewhat the same vein, timber rattlesnakes are not unheard of in the Boston region. In rocky areas where snakes might sun themselves, be careful where you place your feet and hands.

During winter, all too often drownings occur when people fall through the ice after venturing out onto frozen ponds and rivers. I am sure that you have heard this before; everybody has. And yet each winter a few more people die in this manner. Don't be one of them; stay off the ice. And tell your kids.

Other sound advice that is ignored with puzzling regularity concerns lightning. If you are in an exposed or elevated area and a storm approaches, return to your car immediately. That is the safest place to be. And if lighting occurs before you get back to your car, hunker down in a low spot. Don't worry about getting wet or feeling stupid as you crouch there with the rain pouring down. Clearly it is better to get wet and yet be safe than to try to stay dry by huddling under an isolated tree or pavilion or some other target for lightning.

Where the trails follow roads for short distances, walk well off the road on the shoulder to minimize the risk of being hit by a car, and use caution, especially at dusk or after dark, where the trails cross roads. Studies show that in poor light conditions, motorists typically cannot even see pedestrians in time to stop, so your safety depends entirely on you.

Finally, one of the pitfalls of writing guidebooks is that conditions change. Just because this book recommends something does not mean that you should forge ahead in the face of obvious difficulties, hazards, or prohibitions.

ABOUT TICKS: Virtually all parks and wildlife refuges in New England now post warnings about ticks and Lyme disease. The chances of being bitten by a tick are minimal if you stick to wide, well-maintained trails. But if you walk through tall grass or brush, you can easily pick up ticks, which are active from early spring through autumn, or even during mild weather in winter. Some ticks may carry Lyme disease, which can cause swelling of the knees and hips, arthritis, and other disorders. The main carriers of Lyme disease are tiny deer ticks (about the size of a caraway seed in spring and summer, slightly larger in fall and winter). One simple precaution is to wear long pants and a long-sleeved shirt and to tuck your pant legs into your socks and your shirt into your pants in order to keep ticks on the outside, where you can pick them off. Spray your clothes, especially your shoes, socks, and pant legs, with insect repellent containing DEET (N-diethylmetatoluamide) applied according to the directions on the label. If your clothes are light colored, it will be easier to spot any ticks that may get on you. Inspect yourself occasionally during your outing and when you return to your car. And when you get home, wash your clothes and examine your body closely. Pay particular attention to your lower legs, the backs of your knees, your groin, back, neck, and armpits, which are all places where ticks are known to bite.

If you are bitten by a tick, remove it immediately. Grasp the tick with sharp-pointed tweezers, as near to your skin as possible, and gently but firmly pull straight out until the tick comes off, then blot the bite with alcohol. Some authorities say to save the tick in alcohol for identification and to make a note of when you were bitten. If the tick's mouthparts break off and remain in your skin, call your doctor to have the pieces removed. Research suggests that ticks must feed two days in order to transmit Lyme disease, so there is a fairly big margin of safety if you remove the tick promptly.

The main early symptom of Lyme disease is a circular, slowly expanding red rash, often with a clear center, that may appear a few days or as long as two months after being bitten by an infected tick.   Flu-like symptoms are also common, perhaps accompanied by headache, swollen glands, a stiff neck, fever, muscle aches, nausea, and general malaise.   If you develop any of these symptoms after being bitten by a tick, see your doctor promptly so that one of a variety of blood tests can be conducted. Don't put if off, because Lyme disease in its early stages is easily treated with some antibiotics.

# 1

# MAUDSLAY STATE PARK

Located north of Boston in Newburyport, this outstanding park has an extensive system of carriage roads and trails shown on **Map 2** on page 18. The bold line traces a route of 4 miles (6.4 kilometers) starting at the gardens developed by the prior owners. From the estate area, the route heads downstream along the Merrimack River, passing mountain-laurel groves that bloom in mid-June (but are off-limits each winter). You can return to the parking lot by the way you came or via any of several trails at a distance from the river. The route shown on the map is the most direct way back.

Maudslay State Park is open daily from 8 A.M. until sunset. Dogs must be leashed. Some of the trails and carriage roads in the estate area are accessible by wheelchair. The park is administered by the Massachusetts Department of Environmental Management. For information on garden programs, concerts, theatrical performances, and other events, call the park office at (978) 465-7223.

For automobile directions to Maudslay, please turn to page 17. Walking directions start on page 19.

---

BEFORE IT WAS PURCHASED by Massachusetts in 1985, Maudslay State Park was the country estate of the Moseley family of Newburyport. They called their 450-acre property on the Merrimack River *Maudesleigh*. The name is one of several spellings — including *Mawdesley* and now *Maudslay* — that are related to *Moseley* itself. Some variants survive as place names that recall the family origins in England, from which John Moseley emigrated to Dorchester, Massachusetts in 1638.

Five generations later, John's descendant Ebenezer Moseley decided to make his career as an attorney in Newburyport. Born in Windham, Connecticut in 1781, he graduated from Yale and then read law with three judges. In 1805, while his grandfather Caleb Strong was governor

13

of Massachusetts, Ebenezer moved to Newburyport. There he rapidly built up a large and lucrative practice and became active in politics. He was chairman of the Newburyport selectmen, a representative to the Massachusetts General Court, a state senator, and in 1832 a delegate to the electoral college. Moseley also served on numerous civic committees and local charities and was a founder, with others, of several businesses, including a mutual fire insurance company and the Institution for Savings in Newburyport and its Vicinity, established in 1820 and still going today.

Ebenezer's son Edward Strong Moseley increased the family's wealth. He joined a firm engaged in the East India trade and eventually became a large shipowner and the president of the Mechanicks National Bank and also of the Institution for Savings. His most notable charity was the Newburyport Public Library, where his portrait hangs in the main stairwell. In the 1860s Edward started buying land on the Merrimack River at the urging of his wife Charlotte, who deplored the cutting and digging up of plants at the locally-famous laurel groves a half-mile upstream from the old Amesbury ferry.

Edward's son Frederick Strong Moseley continued to multiply the family's fortune. He founded F. S. Moseley & Company of Boston, which brokered commercial paper and later engaged in investment banking. Although his principal residence was in Boston, Frederick greatly enlarged his father's Merrimack property by purchasing adjacent tracts over a period of decades starting in the 1890s. His unmarried brother Charles bought a parcel at Castle Hill, and eventually Frederick acquired that land also. At the southwestern end of the estate, Frederick built a sprawling, three-story, many-gabled house for use on spring and fall weekends and also each June before he, his wife Helen, and four children went to their summer place in Islesboro, Maine. In 1895 Frederick bought the *Dora*, an ocean-going steam yacht. From its anchorage in the Merrimack River opposite the house, the ship carried Moseley and his guests on pleasure trips in the vicinity of Newburyport. After four years, Moseley sold the vessel to the United States government, which used it for hospital service at Cuba during the Spanish-American War.

The big house at Maudesleigh was torn down in 1955, after the death of Frederick in 1938 and his wife in 1952. Today it is the grounds that continue to reflect the Moseleys' tenure. Frederick and Helen hired Charles Sprague Sargent, director of Boston's Arnold Arboretum, to lay out the estate, which included a terraced garden designed in the Italian style by Martha Brookes Hutcheson, a fruit garden of espaliered trees, a vegetable garden, and greenhouses for out-of-season flowers. Charles Gattrell, formerly the master gardener at Linsmore Castle in Scotland, became the estate's superintendent.  The Moseleys planted ornamental trees, masses of rhododendrons and azaleas, and thousands of white pines along Pine Hill Road.  They dammed a ravine to create a serpentine pond bordered by flowering shrubs; they erected masonry bridges; and they built winding carriage roads and trails that altogether make the present-day park a spectacular place to walk.  The estate also included large hayfields and cow pastures that are still maintained as meadow.  Whereas now the park staff is limited to three or four people, the Moseleys had dozens of gardeners, farmers, foresters, dairymen, and other workers, many of whom lived on the estate in several farmhouses and other quarters.

In 1927 the Massachusetts Horticultural Society awarded the Honey-well Gold Medal to the Moseleys, who opened the grounds for a day in order to benefit the North Shore Garden Club.  An account in the *Boston Herald* describes the "magnificent estate," the "gorgeous flaming azaleas," the "broad velvety lawns," the "huge banks of laurel," — and also, of course, the attire of the female guests from Boston's Gold Coast, New York, and Washington.  Wearing a "cool looking white ensemble and a broad white hat of rough straw, banded with black," Mrs. Moseley received the visitors, and Mr. Moseley "strolled through the gardens from time to time during the day."

In the recollections of Moseley grandchildren (now grandparents them-selves), different parts of the estate had fanciful names that added to their appeal as destinations for walks with Mrs. Moseley.  There was a rocky hillside called the Fairy Garden and an abrupt depression named the Punchbowl.  "We often went to Castle Hill for an evening picnic," one grandchild recalls.  "My Grandmother swam twice daily in the pool and taught her grandchildren to swim.  She also took a morning walk through the gardens with her dogs."

The last Moseley to live on the family's Merrimack estate was Fred-erick's unmarried daughter Helen Jr.  Between 1939 and 1941, Helen Jr. had a house built for herself a quarter-mile downstream from her parents' home.  One-room deep with wings to each side, it was designed in the colonial style by the Newburyport architect William Perry, whose firm worked for Abbey and John D. Rockefeller, Jr. on the restoration of Williamsburg, Virginia.  The house was called the Hedges for the plant-ings through which the entrance drive passed, as still seen today.  For much of her adult life, Helen Jr. rode her horse daily on the estate roads.  She gave a day each week to visiting at Massachusetts General Hospital in Boston, where she brought numerous patients bouquets of flowers from her gardens and greenhouses.  Helen Jr. died in 1974 and the Hedges burned in 1978.

Following the deaths of Frederick, Helen, and Helen Jr., the Moseleys' property on the Merrimack River was owned by a testamentary trust administered by Frederick Strong Moseley, Jr. and later by Frederick Strong Moseley III, who became the managing partner of his grandfather's firm. Although the land at Maudesleigh was an extremely valuable asset, nothing was done to explore selling the estate until the Internal Revenue Service ruled in 1975 that the trust, which had little income, could no longer deduct the maintenance costs as a business expense. When the trustees started considering ways to dispose of the property, local conservation groups and the city government became alarmed at the prospect of hundreds of new houses on a site that constituted seven percent of Newburyport's land area. To reduce the impact of development, the City Council imposed more restrictive zoning in 1978, and the Moseley trustees, in fulfillment of their fiduciary duty, responded with a lawsuit. A resolution of the controversy appeared to be imminent when the Massachusetts Department of Environmental Management undertook to buy the land for park use, but negotiations stretched on and off for several years. Price was only one of the issues. Just as significant was the state's inability to make a firm commitment to complete the purchase in a timely manner. Although the Moseley family liked the idea of a state park, they gradually lost confidence in the process. State officials, in turn, talked of exercising their power of eminent domain but did nothing to initiate action.

Eventually, to the satisfaction of all parties, the transaction was completed with help from the nationally-active Trust for Public Land, which served as an intermediary that bridged the gap between the standard practices of the marketplace and the state's more cumbersome procedures and budgetary constraints. Accepting the risk involved, the Trust for Public Land bought the Moseley estate outright in 1985, then sold it to the Massachusetts Department of Environmental Management in pieces over a period of years, in the end recouping most of its costs. In 1988, when land bordering the southwestern end of the park was threatened with development, the Trust for Public Land bought it too for addition to the park. And in 1991 the Trust for Public Land purchased the 300-year-old Arrowhead Farm adjoining the northeastern end of the park, to be maintained under trust ownership as an historic working farm subject to a conservation easement.

For people interested in the work of the Trust for Public Land, or in the possibility of making a tax-deductible contribution, the address of the Massachusetts office is 33 Union Street, 4th Floor, Boston, MA 02108.

A PARTICULARLY GOOD time of the year to visit Maudslay State Park is from mid-May through June, when the rhododendron and mountain laurel are in bloom. Even before the Moseleys bought the site and made their extensive plantings, the place was famous for its large stands of naturally-occurring mountain laurel. Annually from 1849 to 1870, at the peak of the bloom, Mr. and Mrs. William Ashby held literary gatherings at the laurel banks bordering the Merrimack River. Guests included William Ellery Channing, Ralph Waldo Emerson, John Greenleaf Whittier, William Lloyd Garrison, and other luminaries. In the same vein, each summer from 1910 to 1922, the spiritualist medium and theosophist leader Katherine Tingley staged outdoor performances of Shakespeare on her property at the laurel groves on the north side of Castle Hill. Today, carrying on the tradition of arts at Maudslay State Park, the Department of Environmental Management sponsors artists-in-residence who offer a variety of performances, workshops, and other events for children and adults.

≈  ≈  ≈  ≈

**AUTOMOBILE DIRECTIONS: Maudslay State Park** is located 35 miles north of Boston on the Merrimack River. (See •1 on **Map 1** on page 6, and also the corner panel of **Map 2** on page 18.) Two approaches are described below.

**To Maudslay State Park from Interstate 95:** Leave I-95 at Exit 57 for Route 113 east toward Newburyport. Go about 0.5 mile and then — after passing the fancy iron gate of St. Mary's Cemetery — turn left onto Noble Street, which is bordered by the cemetery on both sides. Turn left again at a T-intersection with Ferry Road. Go 1.5 miles, in the process forking left after just 0.2 mile and crossing over I-95, where the street's name changes to Pine Hill Road. The parking lot for Maudslay State Park is on the left, although most of the park itself is on the right.

**To Maudslay State Park from Interstate 495:** There are several exits off I-495 for Route 110. The one you want is Exit 55 for Route 110 to Interstate 95 southbound. Follow Route 110 for just 0.6 mile, then take I-95 south toward Boston. After 1.6 miles, leave I-95 at Exit 57 for Route 113 east toward Newburyport. Go about 0.6 mile and then — after passing the fancy iron gate of St. Mary's Cemetery — turn left onto Noble Street, which is bordered by the cemetery on both sides. Turn left again at a T-intersection with Ferry Road. Go 1.5 miles, in the process forking left after just 0.2 mile and crossing over I-95,

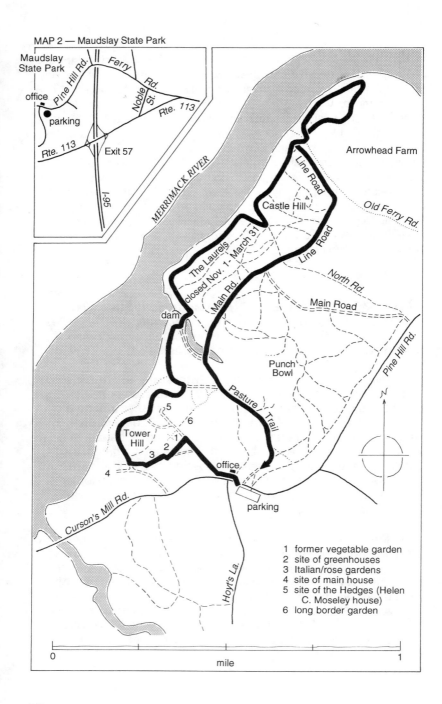

MAP 2 — Maudslay State Park

Maudslay State Park

office

parking

Pine Hill Rd.

Ferry Rd.

Noble St.

Rte. 113

Exit 57

Rte. 113

I-95

MERRIMACK RIVER

Arrowhead Farm

Old Ferry Rd.

Line Road

Castle Hill

The Laurels

closed Nov. 1 - March 31

Main Rd.

North Rd.

Main Road

dam

Punch Bowl

Pasture Trail

Tower Hill

5

6

1

2

3

4

office

parking

Curson's Mill Rd.

Pine Hill Rd.

Hoyt's La.

1 former vegetable garden
2 site of greenhouses
3 Italian/rose gardens
4 site of main house
5 site of the Hedges (Helen C. Moseley house)
6 long border garden

0                        mile                        1

where the street's name changes to Pine Hill Road. The parking lot for Maudslay State Park is on the left, although most of the park itself is on the right.

≈        ≈        ≈        ≈

**WALKING: Maudslay State Park** has an extensive trail system shown on **Map 2** at left. One section by the river is closed November through March in order to protect the mountain laurel, but this area can easily be bypassed via other trails.

It would be a shame to miss the formal gardens near the western end of the park, so I suggest that you go there first and walk northeast down the river.

**To get started,** join the trail descending behind the signboard at the end of the parking lot. With caution, cross the road and follow the shoulder left 100 yards to a gate. Turn right into the park on a wide path bordered by trees. Just before the path passes between tall hedges, turn left. At the end of the path, turn right and then left through a formal garden and out the other end.

Continue past a well and then, in 20 yards, turn right at a fourway intersection to follow a wide path through an area of rhododendrons. Continue on the broad path as it curves along the bluff, crossing ravines on stone bridges. At the serpentine pond, turn left across the dam and sluiceway, where the pond drains down to the Merrimack River.

With the river on the left, head downstream 1.5 miles. Toward the end, the trail passes an intersection with a path called Line Road, then descends steeply. Continue as the trail makes a loop before climbing steeply back to the intersection with Line Road.

To return to the parking lot, there are many trails and carriage roads through the upland. As indicated by the bold line on Map 2, one easy and attractive route is to follow Line Road away from the river and along the side of a meadow, with Castle Hill toward the right. Continue straight at each intersection. Eventually, cross a pond on a handsome bridge, then climb gradually through a large field (formerly pasture). The trail ends opposite the parking lot.

# PLUM ISLAND

Located north of Boston near Newburyport, Plum Island provides an opportunity to walk for hours along a wild beach, perhaps going as far as the glacial hill that anchors the island's southern end. The route outlined on **Map 3** on page 26 totals 15 miles (25 kilometers) round-trip. **Please note,** however, that the beach is closed from April 1 though mid- or late August in order to encourage nesting by piping plovers.

Other opportunities for walking include short nature trails that are reached via the road along the back side of the barrier island. These trails are interesting but limited in scope. If you enjoy birding, the road also provides access to several observation towers and vantage points overlooking the marsh. The Pines Trail and the observation platforms at parking lots 1 and 7 are accessible by wheelchairs.

Most of Plum Island is part of the **Parker River National Wildlife Refuge**, which usually is open daily from sunrise to sunset. An admission fee is charged. Dogs are prohibited, even if leashed. Because swimming is popular during summer, the parking lots often fill up and visitors are turned away, so you should arrive early. On some weekdays during fall and winter, the refuge is open only for deer hunting. Call the refuge office at (978) 465-5753 for information.

At Plum Island's southern end is **Sandy Point State Reservation**; telephone (978) 462-4481. It is indistinguishable from the wildlife refuge, except for the fact that the state beach is always open, even during the piping plover nesting season.

For automobile directions to Plum Island, please turn to page 25. Walking directions start on page 27.

---

LONG, NARROW BARRIER ISLANDS backed by marshes and bays are a common feature of the Atlantic Coast from New York to Florida, but in New England such formations are relatively rare. Plum Island, extending from the mouth of the Merrimack River south to Ipswich, is the biggest of our local examples.

Barrier islands are created in several ways. One sequence of events starts with massive erosion of a mainland promontory that is exposed to the full brunt of the ocean, especially in areas of unconsolidated materials. Spits of silt, sand, and pebbles develop, trailing from the eroding headland under the influence of the longshore current that is produced by waves hitting the coast at an angle. Such spits can eventually grow so long that they reach another headland or curve inland, thus nearly impounding the water behind them. When this happens, storm-driven waves and tide may rise so high on the ocean side of the sandy barrier that the sea breaks through in a new place, creating an inlet and turning the spit into a narrow island or even a string of islands. Similarly, after a storm surge has flooded a low offshore barrier and has overfilled the basin behind it, the outgoing rush of water as the tide ebbs and the wind slackens may quickly carve one or more gaps across the strand, again producing an island or several islands.

Meanwhile, as the polar ice caps and Greenland ice sheet melt, a gradual rise in sea level floods the shallows behind the barrier island, producing a bay of considerable width. Acting like a huge settlement basin, the bay may become filled in part with sediments that provide the foundation for vast marshes. A spectacular example of this whole process is the south shore of New York's Long Island, where material eroded from the exposed eastern end at Montauk has been swept westward by incoming waves from the ocean. The resulting offshore barrier stretches nearly ninety miles from Southampton to Brooklyn and is punctuated by occasional inlets that divide the barrier into islands fronting the ocean and backed by bays and marshes. Long, low islands like these are typical of the Atlantic coast southward to the Carolinas and then again in Florida and the Gulf States, where the tide rises and falls far less than it does north of Cape Cod.

In a somewhat similar chain of events, barrier islands often originate near the mouths of rivers. Even more than an eroding headland, a river continuously delivers huge quantities of silt, sand, and pebbles that are carried downstream and dumped in the ocean to produce shoals. Waves churn up the sediments and then redeposit them in a line parallel with the shore where the breakers plunge and dissipate their energy. As an offshore bar develops, more and more sand is deposited behind the bar where the waves break. Fed by the continuous arrival of sediments, the bar may eventually build upward above the level of the tides. Then vertical growth is augmented by wind-blown sand captured and anchored by grasses and other plants that colonize the new land. Dunes form and grow high above the ocean. As noted before, the gradually-rising ocean floods and enlarges the bay behind the barrier. Or, again, the bay may remain so shallow that marshes develop, augmented by sediments from other rivers flowing into the basin. This whole process is exemplified by Plum Island, trailing south from the mouth of the Merrimack River. Behind the island are broad marshes and Plum Island Sound, fed with sediments from the Parker River, the Rowly River, the Eagle Hill River, and numerous other streams. Similarly, Crane's Beach and Castle Neck stretch south from the mouth of the Ipswich River. There too the barrier island is linked to the mainland by extensive marshes fed by the Castle Neck River and the Essex River. Because of the continual input of sand from such rivers, barriers like Plum Island and Cranes Beach are able to grow ever wider and to develop multiple ridges of high dunes despite the six- to twelve-foot tidal range of northern New England. In areas where the tidal range is above twelve feet, coastal barriers are rare, small, and ephemeral.

The growth of spits and shoals and their transformation into barrier islands are processes that have actually been observed over long periods of time. A third way for barrier islands to originate is more speculative. It is possible that some long, narrow barrier islands started simply as rows of high dunes along the mainland coast. Over time these sandy ridges may have been isolated by the rising sea, which flooded the lowland behind the dunes to create wide lagoons and bays. This process could explain, for example, the Outer Banks of North Carolina in the vicinity of Cape Hatteras, where the narrow barrier islands, now spectacularly far offshore, may once have been high dunes along the coast of the mainland. This theory posits that the dunes were formed during the depths of the Ice Age, when sea level was as much as three hundred feet lower than at present because of the amassment of water in continental glaciers.

Even a cursory glance at old (and not so old) maps shows that barrier islands are constantly in flux: growing, shrinking, and changing shape. And over the longer term — at least during the period of rising sea level that has been under way since the waning of the Ice Age — many islands of the mid-Atlantic region have been migrating landward as sand is eroded from the beach and transported to the islands' back margins during major storms. One way that this happens is *washover*, which is just what it sounds like. But more common is the carving of new inlets, which typically involve the displacement of an immense quantity of sand, some of which may be swept into the bays behind the barriers. As long as the gaps remain open, which could be for a season or for years, the inlets intercept material carried by the longshore current. Waves and tide wash the sand into the bays, where it forms shoals that provide the foundation for the growth of marsh and ultimately dry land as wind and

washover bury the marsh in yet more sand. As the islands retreat, beds of peat that were formed in what was once marsh behind the barriers are sometimes exposed by waves on what is now the ocean front. Similarly, stumps from trees that once grew on the sheltered side of barrier islands have on occasion been revealed by erosion at what is now the beach. The fact that some barrier islands are retreating does not necessarily mean, however, that the bays behind them are shrinking or that the islands will one day merge with the mainland. Rather, in most places south of New England and New York — where the continental shelf and coastal plain form one continuous apron of very low gradient — the mainland shore is also retreating westward as the sea rises, so that an expanse of water and marsh between the mainland and low barrier islands is maintained.

≈      ≈      ≈      ≈

**AUTOMOBILE DIRECTIONS:** **Plum Island** is part of the **Parker River National Wildlife Refuge**. It is located 35 miles north of Boston near Newburyport. (See •2 on **Map 1** on page 6, and also the upper-left panel of **Map 3** on page 26.) The southern tip of the long barrier island is **Sandy Point State Reservation**. Two approaches are described below.

**To Plum Island from Interstate 95:** Leave I-95 at Exit 57 for Route 113 east toward Newburyport. After 2.3 miles, the road crosses **Route 1** (another good avenue of approach) and becomes Route 1A. Continue on Route 1A (High Street) for 1.3 miles, then turn left at a traffic light onto Rolfe Lane toward Plum Island. After 0.6 mile, turn right at a T-intersection and continue 1.8 miles toward Plum Island. At the first crossroads on the island, turn right onto Sunset Drive and go 0.5 mile along the edge of the marsh to the fee booth at the entrance for Parker River National Wildlife Refuge.

**To Plum Island from Interstate 495:** There are several exits off I-495 for Route 110. The one you want is Exit 55 for Route 110 to Interstate 95 southbound. Follow Route 110 for just 0.6 mile, then take I-95 south toward Boston and go 1.6 miles. Leave I-95 at Exit 57 for Route 113 east toward Newburyport.

After 2.4 miles, Route 113 becomes Route 1A. Continue on Route 1A (High Street) for 1.3 miles, then turn left at a traffic light onto Rolfe Lane toward Plum Island. After 0.6 mile, turn

MAP 3 — Plum Island

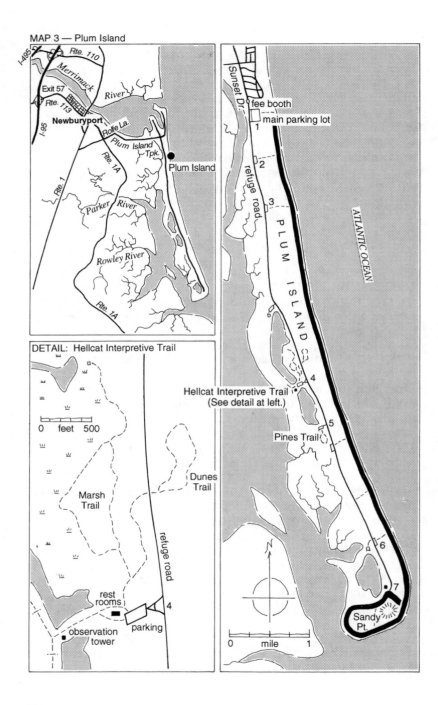

I-495
Rte. 110
Merrimack
Exit 57
Rte. 113
River
Newburyport
I-95
I-95
Rolfe La.
Plum Island Tpk.
Rte. 1A
Plum Island
Rte. 1
Parker River
Rowley River
Rte. 1A

Sunset Dr.
fee booth
main parking lot
1
2
refuge road
3
PLUM ISLAND
ATLANTIC OCEAN
4
Hellcat Interpretive Trail
(See detail at left.)
5
Pines Trail
6
N
7
Sandy Pt.
0     mile     1

DETAIL: Hellcat Interpretive Trail

0   feet   500

Marsh Trail
Dunes Trail
refuge road
rest rooms
4
parking
observation tower

26

right at a T-intersection and continue 1.8 miles toward Plum Island. At the first crossroads on the island, turn right onto Sunset Drive and go 0.5 mile along the edge of the marsh to the fee booth at the entrance for Parker River National Wildlife Refuge.

≈       ≈       ≈       ≈

**WALKING: Map 3** at left shows **Plum Island**. The bold line traces a 15-mile walk that starts at parking lot #1 and follows the beach south around the hill at **Sandy Point State Reservation** and then back again along the beach. Obviously, for a shorter walk you can turn back sooner or start at one of the lower lots that has a crossover to the beach.

Despite signs saying that hikers are permitted on the refuge road, it is a miserable place to walk. There is much traffic, and the dust on the lower, gravel-paved section is disagreeable. If you want to make use of the marshside vantage points and observation towers shown on the map, drive to them.

Midway down the island at parking lot #4 is the **Hellcat Interpretive Trail** (and also rest rooms and an observation tower). The Hellcat Trail includes two short loops: the **Marsh Trail** and the **Dunes Trail**. These trails are shown in the lower-left panel of Map 3. Both trails follow boardwalks, and each is fine in its way, but nonetheless they pale in comparison with the beach.

Still farther south is the handicap accessible **Pines Trail**.

# WARD RESERVATION

Located on the boundary of Andover and North Andover, the Charles W. Ward Reservation has about 10 miles of trails. Both of the routes described below are blazed with colored disks.

**Map 4** on page 34 shows a 3-miles route (4.8 kilometers) that provides broad views from the top of Holt Hill, which at 420 feet is the highest point in Essex County. Directions start on page 33.

**Map 5** on page 36 outlines an easy 2.5-mile circuit (4 kilometers) through the woods around Holt Hill. Directions start at the bottom of page 35.

Each map also shows the short Bog Nature Trail in the lower-right panel. Directions are on the maps.

Two booklets — one an exposition on the reservation's geology and the other a point-by-point guide to the Bog Nature Trail — are available at the caretaker's house next to the parking lot.

The Ward Reservation is open daily from dawn to dusk. It is managed by The Trustees of Reservations; telephone (978) 921-1944 or (978) 356-4351.

For automobile directions to the Ward Reservation, please turn to page 33.

---

THE DOMINANT FEATURE at the Ward Reservation is Holt Hill, named for Nicholas Holt, Sr. He was among the first English settlers in the vicinity of Lake Cochichewick, where in 1634 the Great and General Court of Massachusetts established (on paper) an inland plantation. Despite the inducement of three years' immunity from taxes, levies, and all services except military, it was not until 1641 that settlers from the coastal towns of Ipswich and Newbury moved inland to Andover, as they decided to call the place. Incorporated five years later, the new town included what is now South Lawrence and all of North Andover, site of the original settlement. As was typical in the early towns, the founders first apportioned among themselves the land near the village center. Over the following decades the outlying area — originally common land where settlers could hunt, cut wood, and graze livestock — was also parceled out.

Appearing sixth on the list of proprietors, Nicholas Holt came from Newbury to Andover in 1644. He was one of ten members of the first church at what is now North Andover Center, where he had a house lot of 15 acres and tracts of 160 and 360 acres nearby. Much more land was given to him later, and it was by one of these subsequent divisions that he acquired Holt Hill. At least part of the farm that he established remained in the ownership of his descendants until the 1870s. Then in 1917 Charles William Ward, a paper manufacturer, bought 150 acres of the old Holt property as a summer residence that he and his wife, Mabel Brace Ward, called Holt Hill Farm. Subsequent research revealed (what the Wards did not know at the time) that Mr. Ward was a Holt descendant, removed eight generations from Nicholas Holt, Sr.

After the death of Charles W. Ward in 1933, Mrs. Ward decided to give most of the Holt Hill property to The Trustees of Reservations in compliance with her husband's wish, expressed in his will, that the place be "used in some suitable manner to benefit some deserving organization." Founded in 1891, The Trustees of Reservations is the world's oldest land conservation trust, dedicated (as its statement of purpose says) "to preserving for public use and enjoyment properties of exceptional scenic, historic, and ecological value" throughout Massachusetts. For more information on The Trustees, see Chapter 24.

In memory of her husband, Mrs. Ward made her first gift to The Trustees in 1940. She then went on to purchase and donate other adjoining tracts. By the time of her death in 1956, the reservation was nearly twice its original size. Since then other people have donated more land. In particular, the Wards' grandson John Ward Kimball, who still lives at Holt Hill, has helped The Trustees to expand the reservation to nearly 700 acres, including Shrub Hill and Boston Hill to the east, Pine Hole Pond and Bog to the west, and Cat Swamp to the north. Many trails, some of them named for members of the Ward family, run through the reservation.


ONE CURIOUS FEATURE of the Ward Reservation is the radial arrangement of stones at the top of Holt Hill. These are the **solstice stones**, emplaced at the direction of Mabel Brace Ward following a visit to Stonehenge. To get oriented, north is marked by a stone pointing to the fire tower at the top of the hill. East, south, and west are shown by other short stones that are not attached to the center. Touching the center are long, narrow stones that point to sunrise and sunset on the days of the summer and winter solstices. At the summer solstice (around June 22) the sun rises in the *north*east and sets in the *north*west. At the winter solstice (around December 22) the sun rises in the *south*-east and sets in the *south*west. At the spring and fall equinoxes (around March 22 and September 22) the sun rises due east and sets due west. When the stones were installed, there were unobstructed views in all directions from the top of Holt Hill. Because of the growth of trees since then, only the winter solstice sunrise is now visible from the stones.

The precise astronomical event denoted by the word *solstice* is the two points during the year at which the sun is either lowest or highest in the noontime sky. The elevation at noon changes with the seasons because of the interplay between our planet's tilted axis and the annual revolution around the sun. In fall, the noontime elevation becomes lower day by day, and in spring it becomes higher. But for several days at the time of the solstices, there is very little difference in the noontime elevation. And so the sun is said to stand still, as indicated by the derivation of the word *solstice*, from the Latin *sol* (sun) and *stitium* (stand still or stop). Of course, the sun continues as always to move laterally with the daily rotation of the earth.


ANOTHER INTRIGUING FEATURE of the Ward Reservation is the bog surrounding Pine Hole Pond. After retreat of the last continental glacier about 12,000 years ago, the many ponds that were left behind have, of course, been catch basins for sediments eroded from the surrounding upland. Slowly the ponds have become more shallow. Some have been colonized by reeds, cattails, bulrushes, and aquatic plants rooted in the mucky shallows, and so have changed into fresh-water marshes and then into swamps. This is the usual path of transition by which ponds in southern New England become low, wet woods.

There is, however, an alternative route by which the pond is filled in, not only from the *bottom up*, but also from the *top down* — or that is, by a mat of floating vegetation that covers the pond, then slowly thick-ens and sinks. This is a bog. The process is common in coastal regions, where the climate is cool and moist, and also throughout north-ern New England.

Imagine a rock dropped at the center of a pond, so that little waves ripple outward toward the shore in concentric rings. Now picture this event in reverse, so that one after another the concentric ripples move from the shore and close in on the center. This shore-to-center motion is suggestive of the process by which, over a long period of time, con-centric rings of distinctive plant communities start at the bank of a pond and spread toward the center as the bog forms.

31

In the first stage of bog formation, the pond is ringed by such plants as cattails, cotton grass, and swamp loosestrife growing from the bank and in the shallows. Next a thin, floating mat of sphagnum moss and leatherleaf (the main bog shrub) spreads from the shore. Because of its vigorous habit of branching, leatherleaf forms a continuous tangle in which separate plants cannot be distinguished. The floating carpet of leatherleaf may be supported in part by logs that have fallen into the pond or by rafts of fallen reeds and cattails or by dense clumps of loosestrife. But for the most part buoyancy is provided by sphagnum moss growing among the vegetation. The sphagnum floats because of gases trapped within the mossy mass. The moss also forms a moist carpet where the branches of leatherleaf, as they spread out and sag under their own weight and the yearly burden of snow, become imbedded and sprout adventitious roots that further bind the mass together and establish a new locus of leatherleaf growth. As branches, leaves, and moss accumulate over the years, the mat of vegetation increases in weight and sinks lower in the water. Although the submerged leatherleaf and sphagnum moss die, the portion of the plant matrix that remains above the surface of the water continues to thrive and to replenish itself, so that the mat slowly thickens and eventually comes to rest at the bottom of the pond.

Long before the floating mat touches bottom, however, it forms a foundation for other shrubs and plants adapted to the bog environment, including cranberry, alder, and highbush blueberry. One common bog shrub is poison sumac, which has compound leaves and off-white berries during the summer and fall. (To be on the safe side, don't handle any unfamiliar shrubs.) Trees appear in areas that once were open water but now are filled with muck and partially-decayed plant debris. Tamarack — a conifer that drops its needles in winter — often is found in bogs. Tamarack roots are very shallow so as to avoid the waterlogged substrate and also to support the tree in very unstable soil. Other bog trees are Atlantic white-cedar (usually near the coast) and black spruce (commonly found in northern New England, but occurring farther south at inland bogs.)

Meanwhile, of course, aquatic plants, loosestrife, and the floating mat of leatherleaf and sphagnum moss continue to close in on the center of the pond. As tamarack, white-cedar, and black spruce in turn advance toward the center, deciduous trees such as red maple, yellow birch, sourgum, and serviceberry begin to take over near the shore. Eventually, forest will occupy the entire bog. But until it does, the bog may show a series of plant communities in concentric rings, with a small pond at the center like the bull's-eye of a target. The spot of open water is all that remains of what was once a much larger (though shallow) glacial pond or lake.

Such, at any rate, is the idealized, textbook bog. You can judge for yourself the extent to which the bog at Pine Hole Pond conforms to this model. (For the first few dozen yards, the bog boardwalk passes through an area from which trees and shrubs are cut periodically, so don't regard that as a natural anomaly.)

≈　　　≈　　　≈　　　≈

**AUTOMOBILE DIRECTIONS:　The Ward Reservation** is located 20 miles north of Boston on the boundary of Andover and North Andover. (See •3 on **Map 1** on page 6, and also the lower-left panels of **Maps 4 and 5** on pages 34 and 36.) Two approaches are described below.

**To the Ward Reservation from Interstate 93**: Leave I-93 at Exit 41 for Route 125 toward the towns of Andover and North Andover. Follow Route 125 north about 5 miles, then turn right onto Prospect Road. After just 0.4 mile, turn right into the parking lot for the Ward Reservation.

**To the Ward Reservation from Interstate 495**: Leave I-495 at Exit 42 for Route 114 heading southeast. Go 2 miles, then turn right onto Route 125. Continue 1.9 miles, then turn left onto Prospect Road. After just 0.4 mile, turn right into the parking lot for the Ward Reservation.

≈　　　≈　　　≈　　　≈

**WALKING:** There are two blazed circuits at the **Ward Reservation**: the Blue Loop and the Orange/Yellow Loop. Each is described below and has its own map. There are also white blazes for the Bay Circuit Trail, which passes through the reservation. (The maps, however, show white blazes only for one short section leading to Holt Hill, where the Blue Loop starts.)

Yet another trail is a short spur (0.3 mile round-trip) called the **Bog Nature Trail**, which is shown in the bottom-right panel of each map. I suggest that you start any outing at the Ward Reservation by taking this short trail.

**Map 4** on page 34 shows the 3-mile **Blue Loop**. The route crosses Holt Hill (the highest point in Essex county) and nearby Boston Hill, which together provide sweeping views to the south and east.

MAP 4 — Ward Reservation:  Blue Loop

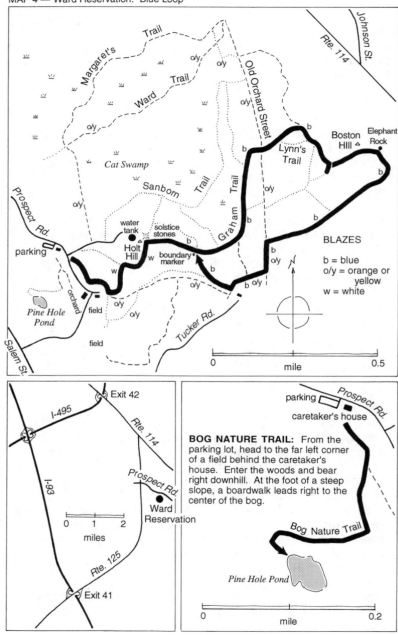

BLAZES

b = blue
o/y = orange or
yellow
w = white

**BOG NATURE TRAIL:** From the parking lot, head to the far left corner of a field behind the caretaker's house.  Enter the woods and bear right downhill.  At the foot of a steep slope, a boardwalk leads right to the center of the bog.

34

**To get started** on the Blue Loop, go first to the top of Holt Hill, where the blazes begin. To reach Holt Hill from the parking lot, follow Prospect Road uphill 80 yards. At an intersection, bear half-left across a stone wall and continue uphill between the intersecting roads. Climb through woods and an orchard, staying parallel with Prospect Road, which should be downhill on the right. Within sight of a house, bear slightly left and continue along a trail bordered by rows of trees that gradually curve right to a major trail intersection. From here, follow white blazes left along the near side of a stone wall. Continue on the broad path to the top of Holt Hill, where there are **solstice stones** that are discussed briefly on pages 30-31.

With your back to the fire tower, turn left (east) and follow a track through a gap in a low stone wall and across a meadow. As you enter the woods, join the blue-blazed trail. Pass a stone marking the boundary between Andover and North Andover and continue past trails intersecting from either side. Eventually, go straight through a four-way junction with Old Chestnut Street, which is now a woods road.

Follow the blue blazes uphill. As you near the top, the blazes lead past a short section of chainlink fence and around a plateau. Pass a trail intersecting from the right — although you may want to follow it briefly for a good view back toward Holt Hill. Continue on the blue-blazed trail past a tower, antennas, and telecommunication disks until you reach a large clearing at Elephant Rock near the top of Boston Hill.

From Elephant Rock continue straight downhill on a worn track, then curve right and re-enter the woods on the blue-blazed trail. Eventually, at a T-intersection with Old Chestnut Street, turn left between parallel stone walls. (The trail here is blazed not only with blue markers, but also with orange and yellow markers.) Follow the blue blazes as the trail turns right off Old Chestnut Street. Near a house, the blue trail turns right just after crossing a stone wall. With the wall on the right, follow the blue blazes uphill. At the boundary stone that you passed earlier, turn left to climb to the top of Holt Hill, and from there continue to the parking lot by the way you came at the beginning of the walk.

**Map 5** on page 36 shows the **Orange/Yellow Loop**, which is 2.5 miles long. When this circuit was laid out, there were not enough markers of either orange or yellow, so the two colors were used interchangeably to blaze one loop. By the time you

MAP 5 — Ward Reservation: Orange/Yellow Loop

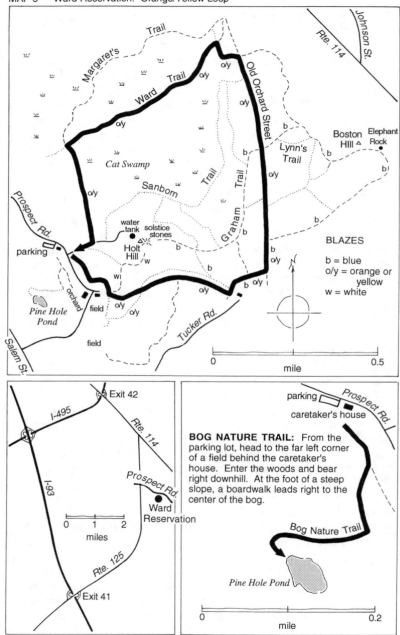

**BLAZES**

b = blue
o/y = orange or yellow
w = white

**BOG NATURE TRAIL:** From the parking lot, head to the far left corner of a field behind the caretaker's house. Enter the woods and bear right downhill. At the foot of a steep slope, a boardwalk leads right to the center of the bog.

go, the system may have been changed to just one color or the other.

**To get started** on the Orange/Yellow Loop, the first task is to go to the trailhead located part way up Holt Hill.* From the entrance to the parking lot, follow Prospect Road uphill 80 yards. At an intersection, bear half-left across a stone wall and continue uphill between the intersecting roads. Climb through woods and an orchard, staying parallel with Prospect Road, which should be downhill on the right. Within sight of a house, bear slightly left and continue along a trail bordered by rows of trees that gradually curve right to a major trail intersection where the Orange/Yellow Loop starts.

Follow the orange or yellow markers left downhill *between parallel stone walls.* Continue gradually downhill and then, at a T-intersection in front of a house, turn left uphill. At the next intersection, bear right to stay on the Orange/Yellow Loop, then turn left onto Old Chestnut Street, which now is a woods road bordered by stone walls. Pass trails intersecting from either side. Eventually, cross a small stream and then, at the top of a slight rise (opposite a trail intersecting from the right), turn left onto a narrow footpath marked with orange or yellow blazes. At the next intersection, turn sharply left onto the Ward Trail. At a junction with Margaret's Trail, turn left. Continue to a road, then follow it right back to the parking lot.

* For cross-country skiers who want to begin skiing at the parking lot, there is another (but more complicated) way to get started. From the parking lot, head to the far left corner of a field behind the caretaker's house. Enter the woods and go just 35 yards, then fork left obliquely uphill. Follow the contour of the slope through an orchard below a barn that has been converted into a house. Cross a driveway and continue straight across an open hilltop, then bear left down an open hillside. Re-enter the woods on a trail located 30 yards from the lower-left corner of the field. Turn left, pass through a gap in a stone wall, and then turn right. Before long, turn right again to join the Orange/Yellow Loop shown on Map 5.

# 4

# IPSWICH RIVER WILDLIFE SANCTUARY

Located north of Boston in Topsfield, this refuge is the largest of the Massachusetts Audubon Society's sanctuaries, comprising more than 4 square miles of woods, swamp, meadow, and freshwater marsh. For good birding and quiet beauty, there is no better place near Boston.

**Map 6** on page 44 shows a walk of 4 miles (6.4 kilometers). The route follows sinuous ridges that overlook the marshy meadows, then returns past Rockery Pond, so-named for its fantastic boulder garden planted with exotic trees and shrubs.

The sanctuary trails are open Tuesday through Sunday from dawn to dusk. The trails are closed Monday (except Monday holidays), Thanksgiving, Christmas, and New Year's Day. An admission fee is charged. Dogs are prohibited. For information on field trips, lectures, classes, guided walks, and other programs, telephone (978) 887-9264.

For automobile and walking directions, please turn to page 42.

---

IN 1643 SIMON BRADSTREET, a graduate of Cambridge University and one of the leaders and original covenanters of the Puritan migration, acquired 500 acres at what is now the Ipswich River Wildlife Sanctuary in the town of Topsfield. This occurred thirteen years after he and his wife, the poet Anne Bradstreet, arrived in Massachusetts in the first wave of fifteen ships that carried more than a thousand men, women, and children. For a few years Bradstreet was secretary of the colony. He served almost continuously in the magistracy, and late in life he was provincial governor. In 1692, five years before his death at age ninety-four, he finally relinquished all public duties.

Bradstreet's land at Topsfield was a gift from the colony in recognition of his public service. He received many such grants and eventually became one of the colony's largest absentee proprietors, developing and leasing farms. He owned land not only at Topsfield, which was incorporated in 1650, but also at the present-day towns of Ipswich, Hadley, North Andover, Salisbury, and Lynn, plus large tracts in Maine and Rhode Island. His 1689 will disposed of over 1500 acres of land in Massachusetts alone. Although the Governor sold some of his Topsfield property, the upland at Bradstreet Hill remained in the family for more than two and a half centuries. The house built by his grandson Samuel Bradstreet in 1763 is now the sanctuary office.

In 1898 Thomas Emerson Proctor, the heir to a leather-tanning fortune, bought Bradstreet Hill. At the time, he was twenty-four years old, and he lived there, a bachelor, until his death fifty years later. For his country estate he designed and planted an extensive arboretum, including not only North American trees but also exotic species from Europe, China, and Japan. Many of these trees still survive, although the arboretum has been allowed to grow wild. In 1902 Proctor hired Italian laborers to construct a fanciful arrangement of immense boulders carted in from nearby towns. Shintare Anamete, a Japanese landscape architect, helped with the project, which has somewhat the quality of a Japanese garden, complete with pond and rustic bridge. Nine years in the building, the Rockery became the center of Proctor's exotic plantings, including thickets of rhododendrons and azaleas. Proctor also constructed carriage roads and bridges that are part of the present-day trail system. He enjoyed riding around his property, which he opened to the public on weekends. In his greenhouses he raised and hybridized orchids which he sometimes exhibited under the name of his gardener.

An 1895 graduate of Harvard, Proctor was described by a classmate as showing "an excessive, but unaffected, modesty which grew on him with years." In his class reports, Proctor listed his occupation simply as "trustee." At least in name, he administered his deceased father's business interests. During his father's lifetime, he had helped the elder Proctor to acquire large real estate holdings in Boston, and the son went on to buy up about one-third of Topsfield and also parts of Wenham and Hamilton. He supported numerous local charities, usually anonymously, and gave Topsfield land for its high school, grade school, and athletic fields. He also gave money to add a wing to the Massachusetts General Hospital in memory of his father.

Two years after Proctor's death in 1949, the Massachusetts Audubon Society bought part of his country estate. Since then, pieces have been added by purchase and by gift, including 500 acres in Wenham donated by Peter Higginson. Presently the sanctuary has about 2800 acres.

BRADSTREET HILL is one of several features at the Ipswich sanctuary that are textbook examples of glacial landforms. The hill is smoothly contoured and oval in outline. Such hills are called *drumlins*. They consist chiefly of clay shaped by the last continental ice sheet that over-rode New England, as discussed in greater detail in Chapter 19. The characteristic drumlin form can best be appreciated by walking completely around Bradstreet Hill on the Drumlin Trail.

Another curious glacial landform at the Ipswich sanctuary is a long, narrow ridge called an *esker*. Typically made of coarse sand and gravel, eskers are like abandoned railroad embankments, but not nearly so straight or evenly graded. In some places in New England, eskers wind across the landscape for dozens or even scores of miles, although most are much shorter. In height they range up to about a hundred feet.

Eskers are thought to be the remains of streams that formerly flowed through tunnels within the glacial ice. As the last glacial period waned, the southernmost zone of ice no longer advanced. Instead, it stagnated. Meltwater from the surface drained into crevasses in the thick mass of immobile ice, then flowed away through tunnels. The subglacial rivers transported a bedload of sand, gravel, and even cobbles confined within the tunnels, like sediments that lie along the bottom of a culvert. Once the ice melted, these gravel streambeds simply collapsed onto the under-lying ground and survive now as long ridges that snake across the land-scape. Some eskers even run up and down low hills, which is strong evidence that the rivers were confined within tunnels through which the meltwater was pushed by higher water upstream.

Often eskers are broken into segments by post-glacial streams that cut across the ridges. This appears to have happened at the Ipswich sanctu-ary, where the esker is interrupted by a gap occupied by Mile Brook. Possibly the water from the brook accumulated west of the esker like a reservoir behind a dam or levee, then spilled over the barrier and carved a gap.

Often eskers are bordered on both sides by poorly-drained areas blan-keted with clay, sand, and rock fragments with which the ice sheet was loaded. Called *till*, this material was scoured from the earth surface by the glacier. After the ice melted, the detritus remained. It clogged valleys, producing large freshwater marshes and swamps that are flooded each spring, as occurs along the Ipswich River. Sometimes a dry route across such areas is provided by eskers on which the Indians and settlers established paths. Many eskers still have country roads along their crests. At the Ipswich sanctuary, the North and South Esker Trails follow the top of one of these gravel ridges for about a mile.

Also at the Ipswich sanctuary are scattered mounds rising abruptly from the swamps and lowland. There is some doubt about how these hillocks formed. One possibility is that sand and gravel accumulated in pockets or crevasses in the stagnant ice. After the ice melted, the material was left on the ground in an uneven heap. Such mounds are loosely termed *kames.* Sometimes kames occur as steep little ridges aligned with the old ice front. They may have originated where sediment-laden meltwater poured off the glacier. As the water spread over the flats, the current dissipated and heavy sediments settled out. Rows of alluvial fans and cones formed and merged, with the northern face heaped against the ice. After the ice melted, undulating mounds of bedded sand and gravel remained.

≈ ≈ ≈ ≈

**AUTOMOBILE DIRECTIONS: The Ipswich River Wildlife Sanctuary** is located in the town of Topsfield 23 miles north of Boston. (See •4 on **Map 1** on page 6, and also the corner panel of **Map 6** on page 44.) There is easy access from either Interstate 95 or Route 1, as described below.

**To the Ipswich River Wildlife Sanctuary from Interstate 95:** Leave I-95 at Exit 52 and follow Topsfield Road east 1.5 miles, at the end forking right onto High Street past the large white Congregational Church of Topsfield. Cross a five-way intersection to follow Route 97 south 0.6 mile to and across **Route 1**, which provides another approach.

From the intersection with Route 1, continue on Route 97 south for just 0.5 mile, then turn left onto Perkins Row. Go 1 mile, then turn right past stone gateposts into the Ipswich River Wildlife Sanctuary. Follow the drive 0.3 mile, then turn left into the parking area. If there is no attendant at the parking lot to collect the entrance fee, please pay at the sanctuary office.

≈ ≈ ≈ ≈

**WALKING: Map 6** on page 44 shows the trail system at the **Ipswich River Wildlife Sanctuary.** The bold line traces a 4-mile route that passes the area's chief attractions: the marshes (or meadows), the sinuous esker, and the Rockery. For a shorter walk, you can cut off the northern loop around Hassocky Meadow and follow just the 2.5-mile southern circuit. Some of the trails may at times be flooded, in which case a detour is necessary.

**To get started,** head directly to the Ipswich River, as follows: turn left out the entrance of the parking lot and follow the

MAP 6 — Ipswich River Wildlife Sanctuary

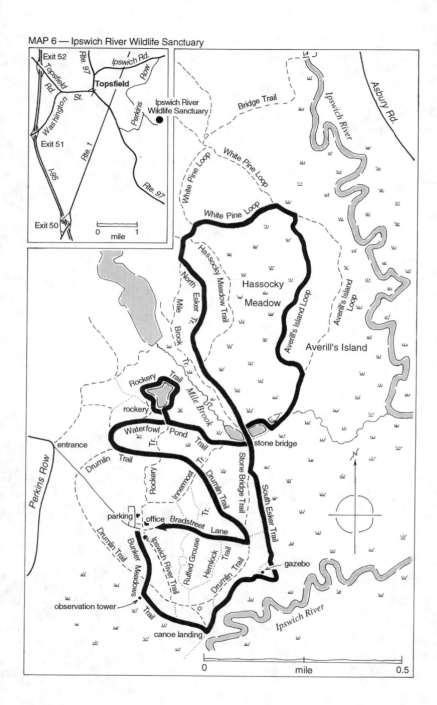

service road 30 yards, then turn right downhill on the Bunker Meadows Trail. Pass straight through a trail junction, then bear left past an observation tower. Continue to the canoe landing at the river.

From the landing, follow the South Esker Trail into the woods. With a marshy floodplain on the right (about 30 yards distant through the brush), follow the path 150 yards, then fork right obliquely downhill to stay on the South Esker Trail near the edge of the marsh. At a gazebo, fork right. Go 90 yards up to the end of a little ridge (this is the South Esker itself). Turn left and continue along the esker as it dips and rises with marsh on the right.

Eventually, turn right onto the Stone Bridge Trail. After crossing the Stone Bridge, continue straight on the North Esker Trail. Pass the lower end of the Hassocky Meadow Trail. Eventually, bear right onto the Mile Brook Trail. After a hundred yards, curve right and pass the upper end of the Hassocky Meadow Trail.

At the next intersection, fork right onto the White Pine Loop, then bear right again at two junctions to follow part of Averill's Island Loop along the eastern edge of Hassocky Meadow. Eventually, bear right between two small ponds, then left back across the Stone Bridge.

Thirty yards beyond the Stone Bridge, turn right onto the Waterfowl Pond Trail. At a four-way intersection, turn right onto the Rockery Trail. After crossing a boardwalk, circle counterclockwise around the pond. Pass through the Rockery itself and continue along the water's edge. After crossing a small bridge, turn right. At the next junction, turn right again onto the Waterfowl Pond Trail.

Pass several trails intersecting from the right, then continue straight through intersections with the Rockery Trail, the Innermost Trail, and the Stone Bridge Trail. Next, turn right up Bradstreet Lane, which leads to the parking lot.

# 5

# BRADLEY PALMER STATE PARK
# WILLOWDALE STATE FOREST

Occupying parts of Topsfield, Ipswich, and Hamilton, Bradley Palmer State Park and the adjacent Willowdale State Forest together have dozens of miles of trails. You could easily walk here all day.

**Map 7** on page 50 shows a route of 7.5 miles (12 kilometers). Two loops, one at Bradley Palmer and the other at Willowdale, are linked by a bridge across the Ipswich River. At Bradley Palmer, the trail passes through meadows and woods, with a spur to the top of Moon Hill. At Willowdale, the blazed path provides a dry route through a landscape of hillocks, hollows, and swampy woods that together typify the poorly drained terrain created when the last continental glacier melted and left behind an uneven blanket of debris.

The Bradley Palmer and Willowdale areas are open daily from dawn to dusk. They are administered by the Massachusetts Department of Environmental Management; telephone (978) 887-5931.

For automobile and walking directions, please turn to page 49.

---

BRADLEY PALMER STATE PARK and Willowdale State Forest were formerly the country estate of Bradley Webster Palmer, a distinguished business lawyer. His father was Henry Wilber Palmer, attorney general of Pennsylvania and later a Congressman. The younger Palmer graduated from Harvard College in 1888. After law school, he joined the Boston firm of Storey & Thorndike, now named Palmer & Dodge. In 1899 Palmer organized the United Fruit Company and served as its counsel for most of his life. Through his connection with United Fruit, he brought his law firm a stream of lucrative work relating to financing businesses, particularly railroads, in Central and South America. In *Palmer & Dodge: A Centennial History*, attorney Robert P. Moncreiff says, "Palmer seems to have been a quiet, even taciturn, man. He never married. . . . [H]e liked shooting and fishing and riding, but there is otherwise no record of extensive interests or involvement outside of the business world, although his activities on behalf of various governmental commissions in the First World War earned him decorations from the governments of France, Belgium and Rumania." Immediately after the war, Palmer was a member of the staff of the American Commission to Negotiate Peace at Paris in 1919. He helped prepare treaty provisions for the restoration of business relations and the adjustment of private contracts and property rights. Although Congress refused to ratify the Treaty of Versailles, Palmer's work was later incorporated into a separate treaty with Germany. Moncreiff also notes, "He is linked with Dodge in the firm's name not because he was ever its leader, but through the accident that his name stood first when Palmer & Dodge, like other Boston firms, abandoned the practice of changing names as partners came and went." (Incidentally, the country estate of Robert G. Dodge is featured in Chapter 6.)

Between 1902 and 1904, Palmer built an unusual house at Willow Dale, as he called his country estate. Designed by Charles K. Cummings, the mansion overlooks the Ipswich River near the park entrance. The master's residence, the caretaker's quarters, and the stable are arranged in one continuous structure around three sides of a courtyard. The exterior walls are constructed entirely of stones taken from old walls that formerly divided the estate's pastures and fields. The interior is paneled in oak and cherry. "[T]he "general treatment is very simple," noted the *Architectural Review* in January 1904. "Later it is proposed to decorate the plaster frieze over the wainscoting with hunting scenes, painted in oils." Reflecting Palmer's bachelor existence, the master's residence has no drawing room, but rather just an office, a library, and a dining room, plus bedrooms for himself and a few guests. Here Palmer entertained friends and acquaintances who shared his interests — and also four dozen members of his Harvard class on the occasion of their forty-fifth reunion. For his class report he wrote, "I think that there is little in my legal routine that would interest my classmates. My name has appeared twice in the public prints, once as the owner of a high-jumping horse, and again as the builder of a house made of field stones. Possibly the notoriety may not be calculated to add to the luster of our worthy class, but candor compels me to acknowledge it." The house is now leased for use as a bed-and-breakfast inn and is well-worth visiting.

In 1937 Palmer gave more than 2000 acres "to the people of Massachusetts as a place to enjoy the peace and beauty of river, woods, fields, and hills," as his deed of gift stated. A few years later, he donated more land, reserving only his house until his death there in 1946.

≈    ≈    ≈    ≈

**AUTOMOBILE DIRECTIONS: Bradley Palmer State Park** and the adjacent **Willowdale State Forest** are located 25 miles north of Boston midway between Topsfield and Ipswich. (See •5 on **Map 1** on page 6, and also the corner panel of **Map 7** on page 50.) The directions below are to the main trailhead at the state park.

**To Bradley Palmer State Park from Interstate 95:**
Leave I-95 at Exit 52 and follow Topsfield Road east 1.5 miles, at the end forking left past the large white Congregational Church of Topsfield. At a T-intersection with Route 97, turn left and go just 0.3 mile, then fork right onto Ipswich Road. Follow Ipswich Road 0.9 mile to and across **Route 1**, which provides another approach.

From the intersection with Route 1, follow Ipswich Road east toward Ipswich for 1.2 miles, then turn right onto Asbury Street. After 0.8 mile, turn left into Bradley W. Palmer State Park. After another 0.8 mile, turn right toward the pool and picnic areas, and then — in just 0.2 mile — turn left into a parking area.

≈    ≈    ≈    ≈

**WALKING: Map 7** on page 50 outlines a 7.5-mile route that includes a southern loop at **Bradley Palmer State Park** and a northern loop at **Willowdale State Forest**. The two are linked by a bridge across the Ipswich River. Obviously, each loop by itself provides a shorter walk, and for a longer hike there are many other trails shown on the map.

**To start** at Bradley Palmer State Park, locate the trailhead by the parking area. Go just 30 yards, then fork left away from a pond. Soon you will join a paved road. At an intersection where the road veers left, continue straight through a gate and out into a meadow. At a four-way intersection with a worn track, turn left and descend into the woods and across a footbridge over the Ipswich River. With caution cross Topsfield Road and enter Willowdale State Forest.

The trail system at Willowdale is so extensive that your best approach is simply to rely on the colored blazes. The route shown on the map is the Red Loop. There is also a Blue Loop and at Red/Blue Loop. (The latter has both colors on a single

49

MAP 7 — Bradley Palmer State Park and Willowdale State Forest

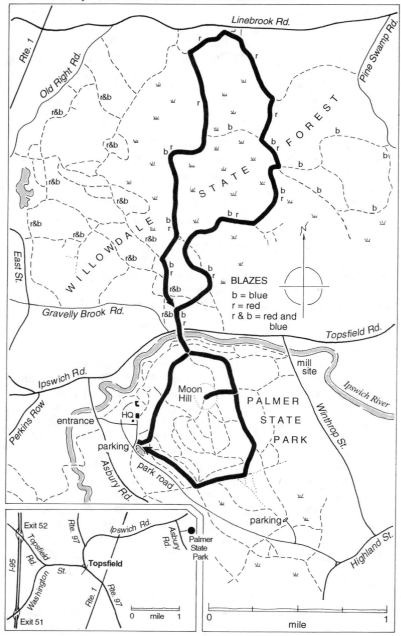

marker.) The letters on Map 7 attempt to show all three routes, which sometimes coincide. There are also white blazes (not shown on the map) delineating part of the Bay Circuit that passes through the state forest.

**For the Red Loop through the Willowdale area,** turn right at the first intersection. The red route is congruent with the blue route for much of the way to the northern edge of the forest at Linebrook Road, but the two blazed routes eventually split. Within sight of Linebrook Road, follow the red route across a large cultivated field, then to the left along the edge of a meadow and back into the woods. As you return southward toward Topsfield Road and Bradley Palmer State Park, the red and blue routes once again coincide.

Continue back across the footbridge at the Ipswich River. At the intersection in the meadow where you were earlier, turn left. Follow the main track through the meadow, which gradually curves right. Pass trails intersecting from either side. Eventually, the trail enters the woods again, then emerges at another long, open swath.

As indicated on the map, you may at this point want to turn right onto a spur that climbs 200 yards to the top of Moon Hill, where there is an immense circular clearing that shows the egglike form of the drumlin (as such glacial hills are called). From the summit, return by the way you came to the trail at the foot of the hill and continue clockwise around the loop.

As the long, narrow meadow gradually opens out into a large, rolling field, leave the main track by bearing half-right along the edge of the woods, then across a swath of grass. Pass to the left of a horse jump and enter the woods. Go 130 yards, then bear right onto a wide path. Continue through the woods past another trail rising from the left. At a seven-way trail junction marked by a stone post showing the boundary between Topsfield and Ipswich, turn obliquely right and follow the main trail through the woods and back to your starting point.

# 6

# THE CRANE RESERVATION
## and other nearby sites

Located in Ipswich north of Boston, the Richard T. Crane, Jr. Memorial Reservation is one of Massachusetts' most spectacular landscapes. It includes Crane Beach, the dunes of Castle Neck, the estuarine salt marsh, and Castle Hill, where the Grand Allee leads half a mile from the Great House to the sea. **Map 8** on page 59 shows the reservation and outlines a walk of 9 miles (14.4 kilometers) through the dunes, up the beach, and across the hills.

The beach is open daily from 8 A.M. to sunset; the grounds at Castle Hill open at 9 A.M. An admission fee is charged per car. The amount changes seasonally. It is lowest in winter, higher from late spring to early fall, and highest on summer weekends. Dogs are allowed on the beach only from October through March; they are always prohibited elsewhere.

The Crane property is managed by The Trustees of Reservations. For information on fees and events, including concerts and **tours of the Great House**, call (978) 356-4351.

Two nearby properties of The Trustees of Reservations are **Greenwood Farm** and the **Stavros Reservation**. They provide good views toward Castle Hill and Castle Neck.

In Ipswich more than forty houses built before 1725 still stand. One is the Ipswich Historical Society's **Whipple House**. Across the street is the Federalist **Heard Museum**. Both houses are open to the public.

For automobile and walking directions to the Crane Reservation, please turn to page 56. Directions to Greenwood Farm, the Stavros Reservation, and the Whipple House and Heard Museum are on pages 60-61

---

IPSWICH WAS SETTLED by the English in 1633, when John Winthrop, Jr., the charismatic son of Governor John Winthrop, headed a group of thirteen men to establish a new town, at that time the most remote outpost of the Massachusetts Bay Colony. Only three years earlier some people who had attempted to settle the same site had been ordered by the General Court to remove themselves, on the grounds that they were too far away from Boston for collective defense. The younger Winthrop disposed of Indian claims in a manner regarded as entirely legitimate by the English: he bought a large tract for the new town, paying the Sagamore of Agawam £20 of wampum for a deed signed with his mark.

The peninsula of Castle Neck, now the Crane Reservation, was reserved by the settlers for cutting wood and grazing. "At a meeting holden the 5 day of January, 1634," the town records state, "ytt was ordered that the Neck of Land wheareuppon the great hill standeth, which is known by the name of Castle Hill, lyeinge on the other side of this River toward the Sea, shall remanye unto the common use of the Towne forever." Nonetheless, fearful of losing Winthrop, who was active at other settlements in Massachusetts and Connecticut and was much sought after, the townspeople gave him Castle Hill and the bordering salt meadow, "provided he lives in the Towne, and that the Towne may have what they shall need for the building of a Fort." For a period Winthrop did reside at Ipswich, where he was a magistrate and lieutenant-colonel of the Essex militia, but in 1646 he moved to New London and eventually became governor of Connecticut. At Ipswich he sold his land to Samuel Symonds, deputy governor of the Bay Colony. Castle Hill Farm, as the property became known, remained in Symonds' family until 1759, when it was sold to John Patch III, a farmer who had previously leased the land.

In 1909, Richard T. Crane, Jr. bought Castle Hill from the estate of a Patch descendant. A graduate of Yale with a degree in philosophy, Crane proved to be an able executive of the Crane Company, established by his father in 1855. By early in the twentieth century, the company was a major manufacturer of industrial valves, fittings, pumps, and engines. The younger Crane became president in 1914, two years after his father's death, and he expanded the company's line into elegant bathroom fixtures. For a period the Crane Company even made elevators, and it fabricated the cables for the Golden Gate Bridge.

Crane's business and principal residence were in Chicago. He later built a winter home on Jekyll Island, Georgia. For several years before buying Castle Neck, he and his family rented a summer house in fashionable Manchester-by-the-Sea while he scouted the North Shore for a place of his own. Eventually, Crane acquired nearly 3500 acres in Ipswich overlooking the ocean, beach, and marsh. He tore down several dozen summer cottages and hired the Olmsted Brothers (the sons of Fred erick Law Olmsted) to landscape his estate with terraced gardens, a Grand Allee, and statuary. Completed in 1911, the summer house was in the style of an Italian Renaissance villa with stucco exterior, tile roof, and dozens of rooms. There were separate bachelor quarters and a swimming pool set into the allee. The household consisted of Mr. and Mrs. Crane, their six-year-old son Cornelius (named for their close friend Cornelius Vanderbilt), two-year-old Florence, and the staff, including butler, housekeeper, personal maids, secretaries. tutor, nurse, and cook, plus a lower echelon of cleaning, serving, and scullery maids and washer-women, and also an estate superintendent, gatekeeper, chauffeurs, garden-ers, two full-time painters, boatmen, and other workers. Altogether, the house and grounds required a staff numbering about sixty people. Some were locals and others arrived and departed with the Cranes as they moved seasonally among their residences. In order for the huge household to run smoothly, meals were eaten at set times. For ordinary, informal dinners, male family members and guests wore blazers and white flannels; for formal occasions they wore white tie and tails. Amuse-ments included tennis, bathing in the sea or pool, motoring, picnics, clambakes on the beach, sailing, strolling about the gardens, bowling on the lawn, and golf at Mr. Crane's private course west of Castle Hill.

In 1924 the Italianate mansion was razed — Mrs. Crane had never liked it — and in its place a new residence, designed by famed Chicago architect David Adler, was built in the style of a Jacobean English Great House of the early seventeenth century. This is the house that stands today. Salvaged from an English manor, the paneling and ornate carving in the library were done by Grinling Gibbons, and other rooms too feature old paneling, mantels, parquet flooring, and antique decorative features. If you have never visited the Crane mansion, by all means take the tour noted in the introduction to this chapter.

Richard Crane died only three years after the Great House was com-pleted. For another eighteen years, his widow continued to spend summers at Ipswich, and then winters also to be near her daughter and grandchildren who lived west of Castle Hill on the Crane property at Labor-in-Vain Farm. In 1945 the Crane family gave a thousand acres, including most of the beach and dunes at Castle Neck, to The Trustees of Reservations, a private conservation trust that holds land for the use and enjoyment of the public, as discussed in Chapter 24. Upon her death in 1949, Mrs. Crane left The Trustees another 350 acres, including the Great House and most of Castle Hill, and in 1957 the Crane's daughter-in-law added 650 acres, including Hog Island.

≈        ≈        ≈        ≈

**AUTOMOBILE DIRECTIONS:** The **Crane Reservation** is located in Ipswich 28 miles north of Boston. (See •6 on **Map 1** on page 6, and also the corner panel of **Map 8** on page 59.) Two approaches are described below.

**To the Crane Reservation from Route 128:** Leave Route 128 at Exit 20A for Route 1A north. Follow Route 1A nearly 8 miles, then turn right onto Route 133 east toward Essex. After 1.7 miles, turn left onto Northgate Road and go 0.8 mile. At a T-intersection with Argilla Road, turn right and go 2.3 miles to the fee booth at the entrance for the Crane Beach parking lot.

**To the Crane Reservation from Interstate 95:** Leave I-95 at Exit 52 and follow Topsfield Road east 1.5 miles, at the end forking left past the large white Congregational Church of Topsfield. At a T-intersection with Route 97, turn left and go just 0.3 mile, then fork right onto Ipswich Road. Follow Ipswich Road 0.9 mile to and across **Route 1**, then continue another 5.6 miles to Ipswich itself. At an intersection with Route 1A (aka Route 133) in Ipswich, turn right toward Essex and go 0.4 mile. Just after the road curves right, turn left onto Argilla Road and follow it 4.1 miles to the fee booth at the entrance for the Crane Beach parking lot.

≈ ≈ ≈ ≈

**WALKING:** There are three main areas at the **Crane Reservation**:

**The beach** stretches 4.6 miles from the mouth of the Ipswich River in the northwest to Essex Bay in the southeast. Obviously, a round trip from one end to the other totals 9.2 miles. The distance from the parking lot to the northwestern tip and back is 3.6 miles. From the parking lot to the southeastern tip and back is 5.6 miles.

**Castle Hill** is topped by the Great House, from which the Grand Allee stretches to the bluff above the ocean. Several paths connect the beach with the house and allee. Visitors are welcome to walk around the grounds. The house itself is open for special events and also for tours on a regular basis. Call (978) 356-4351 or (978) 356-4355 for information.

**The dunes** of Castle Neck are like nothing else in the Boston region. For the preservation of the dunes, it is essential that you stay on the trails, which are marked with colored disks. The green trails are nearest the parking lot, the red and blue trails are midway down the peninsula, and the yellow trails are nearest the tip. The green trailhead is at the southern corner of the main parking lot — or that is, on the right as you face toward the ocean. There are also other places to enter and leave the dunes, as shown on the map.

Taking a walk through the dunes is definitely worthwhile. The trails pass from one secluded hollow to the next. Although slogging over sand hills can be hard work, the paths are for the most part fairly easy. They are infinitely superior in scope and variety to the very limited opportunities for dune walking at most seaside parks and reservations.

**Map 8** at right shows a 9-mile walk through the dunes, then along the beach and over Castle Hill.

**To get started,** locate the trailhead that enters the woods near the southern corner of the main parking lot. The first few dozen yards are sometimes flooded but can easily be detoured to the left.

At a T-intersection, turn right and follow the green-blazed trail past a series of numbered posts. Go about a mile and then, at another T-intersection, turn right and continue on a red-blazed trail that eventually leads to the back beach and tidal flats bordering the Castle Neck River. With the water on the right, follow the shore down and around the southeastern tip of the peninsula, then up the ocean beach and past the stairs and boardwalk that cross the dunes at the parking lot.

With the ocean on the right, continue north along the beach. Pass the bluff and boulders at Steep Hill, which like Castle Hill and every other hill in the vicinity, is a drumlin. At the narrow mouth of the Ipswich River, locate a trail issuing from the low dunes and follow it to a rutted road leading down the back edge of the dunes next to the salt marsh. At a T-intersection at the foot of Castle Hill, turn left. At the next intersection, turn right uphill. Continue more-or-less straight uphill past gravel roads that intersect from either side, then go straight across the Grand Allee and downhill past roads interesting from the right. Cross through low dunes and then turn right along the beach to reach the stairs and boardwalk at the parking lot.

MAP 8 — Crane Reservation and other nearby sites

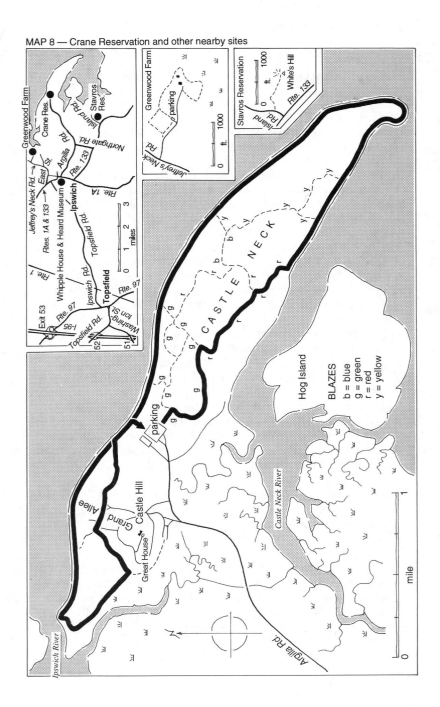

≈
≈      ≈      ≈      ≈
≈

**OTHER NEARBY SITES:**  On the way to or from the Crane Reservation, you may want to stop by some other places of interest that are described below.

**Greenwood Farm**, like the Crane Reservation, is a Trustees of Reservations property.  It provides a view southeast across the salt meadow and Ipswich River toward Castle Hill, site of the Crane mansion.  As shown on one of the small panels of **Map 8** on page 59, there is a 0.7-mile loop trail.

In the early years of the Massachusetts Bay Colony, the land at Greenwood Farm was part of a grant from the town of Ipswich to Robert Paine, whose son graduated from Harvard College in 1656 and served as jury foreman for the Salem witch trials in 1692.  Built about 1702, his saltbox house still stands to the northeast of the larger farmhouse erected early in the nineteenth century by Thomas Greenwood, a Paine descendant.  In 1916 Robert Dodge, a prominent Boston lawyer, purchased the property, which his family used as a country home.  Dodge, incidentally, was a partner of Bradley W. Palmer, whose country estate is featured in Chapter 5.

**To reach Greenwood Farm,** first locate the right-angle bend on Route 1A/133 in Ipswich, 0.3 mile south of the center of town.  This bend is opposite the Whipple House (discussed on page 61) and just north of the intersection with Argilla Road, which leads to and from the Crane Reservation.

At the bend in Route 1A/133, there is an intersection with County Road and Poplar Street.  Follow County Road 0.4 mile, then bear right onto East Street.  After another 0.4 mile, turn left onto Jeffrey's Neck Road and go 0.6 mile to the entrance on the right for Greenwood Farm.

**The Stavros Reservation** is yet another Trustees of Reservations Property.  It consists of White's Hill, from which there are views to the northeast across the salt marsh and Castle Neck River toward the Crane Reservation.  As indicated on the smallest panel of **Map 6** on page 59, a trail only 0.2 mile long leads to the top of the hill.  Like all of the hills within view, White's Hill is a drumlin, showing the hogback form molded by the last continental glacier.

**To reach the Stavros Reservation**, first locate the intersection of Route 1A and Route 133 about 0.8 mile south of Ipswich Center. (North of the intersection, Routes 1A and 133 are congruent through town; south of the intersection, they are separate.)

From the junction of Route 1A and Route 133, follow Route 133 east toward Essex. After 1.7 miles, you will pass Northgate Road, which provides access from the Crane Reservation and Argilla Road. Continue east on Route 133 for another 1.3 miles, then turn left onto Island Road and park at the trailhead by the side of the road.

**The Whipple House and Heard Museum** are properties of the Ipswich Historical Society. The two buildings are located on Route 1A/133, just 0.3 mile south of the center of town. Argilla Road, which leads to and from the Crane Reservation, intersects with Route 1A/133 within sight of the house and museum.

Constructed in stages starting in 1655, the Whipple House is an outstanding and ostentatious example (for its early period) of a well-to-do merchant's residence. Built about 1800, the Federal-style Heard Museum was the home of a West Indies trader whose son achieved great success and prominence in the China trade. The house and museum are open May through mid-October on Wednesday through Saturday from 10 A.M. to 4 P.M., and on Sunday from 1 to 4. The admission fee provides entrance to both places, which are located across the street from one another. For information, telephone (978) 356-2811 or (978) 356-2651.

**7**

## CAPE ANN
### including Halibut Point State Park, Dogtown Common, Ravenswood Park, and the Coolidge Reservation

Cape Ann is the large peninsula that projects into the Atlantic Ocean 30 miles northeast of Boston. The four sites discussed below are located close together in the vicinity of the cape, as indicated on the upper panel of **Map 9** on page 66.

The lower panel of Map 9 shows **Halibut Point State Park** at the northeastern tip of Cape Ann, where you can walk for about 2 miles (3.2 kilometers) around the Babson Farm Quarry and along the rocky headland pictured at left. Please use caution and control your children closely. In particular, stay back from the cliffs and surf and do not climb on the loose rubble from the quarry. The park is open daily from 8 A.M. to 8 P.M. during summer and for shorter hours during winter. An admission fee is charged from Memorial Day to Labor Day. Dogs must be leashed. The park is managed by the Massachusetts Department of Environmental Management in cooperation with The Trustees of Reservations, which owns part of the land. For the DOE, telephone (978) 546-2997. Directions start on page 65.

**Map 10** on page 71 shows **Dogtown Common**, where there are many miles of foot trails and cartways dating back to colonial times. Located on the highlands at the center of the cape, the common was the site of a village now indicated only by scattered cellar holes (if you can find them). Dotted with huge boulders and covered by woods and scrubby growth, the common is relished by some visitors for its atmosphere of desolation and neglect — and disliked by others for the same reason. Most of Dogtown Common is owned by the city of Gloucester and the rest by Rockport; telephone (978) 281-9781 and (978) 546-6786. For access by train or automobile, please turn to page 70. Walking directions start on page 72.

**Map 11** on page 77 outlines two walks at **Ravenswood Park**. The first is an easy 2 miles (3.2 kilometers) via carriage road, including a section of the Old Salem Road, abandoned in the eighteenth century. The pretzel-shaped second route is contrived to make a longer outing of 4 miles (6.4 kilometers). It follows footpaths across hills heaped with glacial boulders and twice crosses the Great Magnolia Swamp via boardwalk. The park is open daily from dawn to dusk. Dogs must be leashed. Ravenswood is managed by The Trustees of Reservations; telephone (978) 921-1944 or (978) 356-4351. Directions start on page 76.

**Map 12** on page 80 shows the **Coolidge Reservation**, where a trail leads to the Ocean Lawn. The round-trip distance is only 1.5 miles (2.4 kilometers), making the Coolidge Reservation not so much a walk as a vantage point. Although the reservation is open daily from 8 A.M. to sunset, the Ocean Lawn — far and away the main reason for going — is open only on Saturday, Sunday, and Monday. Dogs must be leashed and are not permitted at the Ocean Lawn. Like Ravenswood Park, Coolidge Point is a property of The Trustees of Reservations. Automobile and walking directions are on page 81.

---

## HALIBUT POINT STATE PARK

HALIBUT POINT — the first word is a corruption of "haul about" — is so-named because the headland was where sailing ships tacked or came about to round the northeastern tip of Cape Ann.

Starting in the late 1830s or early '40s, a local partnership opened the Babson Farm Quarry on the granite heights at Halibut Point. Now flooded by rain and seepage, the big hole was, of course, kept free of water during its nearly hundred years of active operation. Some quarries had pumps powered by oxen or windmills, but by the 1860s most used steam engines that ran continuously to keep the pits dry.

Steam replaced muscle-power in other aspects of quarrying as well. Generated at a single coal-fired plant just north of the Babson Farm pit, steam ran the huge mast-and-boom derricks that raised blocks of granite weighing as much as forty tons from the floor of the quarry to the rim. During the quarry's peak years early in the twentieth century, there were four derricks around the brink of the pit. From there the stone blocks were hauled, at first by oxen or horses and after 1910 by locomotive, to sheds where cutters sawed and chiseled and perhaps even polished the rock for a variety of uses, including building stone, curbing, paving blocks, bollards, and custom-made items. One arm of the quarry's rail-road ran westward less than a mile to a pier at Folly Cove, where stone products were transferred to ships.

In the early years of quarrying, rock was split from the quarry face and floor by drilling rows of holes by hand. The "drills" were not rotary bits but just chisels that the workers pounded with sledges. After drilling the holes, the quarrymen prised the rock apart by inserting two shims into each hole and then driving in a wedge between the shims. Using bigger drills and bigger hammers, the men sometimes bored deeper, larger holes for blasting with black powder. The invention of the steam-powered drill in the 1880s greatly increased productivity, making it possible to bore far deeper holes and to crack off huge blocks with dynamite. The drills resembled over-sized pneumatic hammers that were supplied with steam via hose from the generating plant.

After 1885, much of the output of the quarry at Halibut Point went to build the Sandy Bay Breakwater. This project was financed by the federal government in order to create a harbor of refuge at the tip of Cape Ann just south of the headland — or that is, to the right as you look at the ocean. The breakwater was to be a mile long, so as to create at 1600-acre anchorage. Because of lack of funding, work stopped on the Sandy Bay Breakwater in 1915, after about a third of it had been completed. Abandonment of the project marked the beginning of the end for granite quarrying at Halibut Point. The increased use of structural steel and concrete for buildings and bridges also contributed to the decline of the granite industry generally. In 1929 the Babson Farm Quarry closed, never to reopen. During the Depression of the 1930s, the entire Cape Ann granite industry collapsed.

In eastern Massachusetts, only a few locations, principally Chelmsford and Milford, still have large granite quarries supplying cut stone for curbing and custom projects. The Chelmsford quarry dates back to 1820; it was the source of stone for Quincy Market and the columns of the U.S. Treasury building in Washington, D.C. (as pictured on a ten dollar bill). The Milford quarry supplied the distinctive pink granite used at the Boston and New York public libraries. Perhaps no Massachusetts town is more closely identified with granite quarrying than Quincy, where the last pit closed in 1963.

≈ ≈ ≈ ≈

**AUTOMOBILE DIRECTIONS TO HALIBUT POINT STATE PARK:** Halibut Point is the extreme northern tip of Cape Ann. (See •7a on **Map 1** on page 6. For more detail, refer to **Map 9** on page 66.)

MAP 9 — Cape Ann (upper panel) and Halibut Point State Park (lower panel)

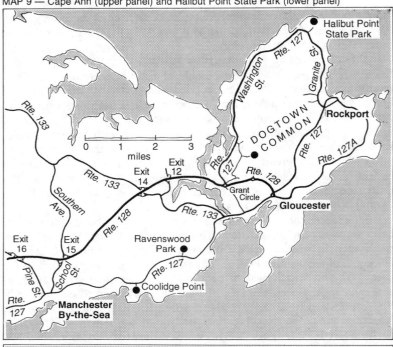

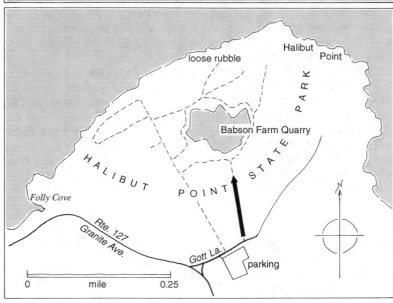

About 2 miles south of Halibut Point is the village of **Rockport**, which you may also want to visit.

**To Halibut Point State Park from Route 128:** Follow Route 128 north almost to its end. After passing Exit 12 and crossing the Annisquam River, continue to Grant Circle. Go three-quarters of the way around the rotary, then turn right onto Route 127 (Washington Street). Follow Route 127 north 6 miles, then turn left onto Gott Lane and go 0.1 mile to the parking lot on the right.

≈     ≈     ≈     ≈

**WALKING AT HALIBUT POINT:** As shown on the lower panel of **Map 9** at left, a trail leads from the parking lot, across Gott Lane, and down past the quarry to the shore at Halibut Point. Stay back from the edge of the quarry and use caution near the surf, where the rocks may be slippery. Also, don't go swimming here, even in calm weather. Just getting in and out of the water can be difficult, and people are sometimes badly cut or scraped on the barnacle-covered rocks.

≈
≈     ≈     ≈     ≈
≈

## DOGTOWN COMMON

CAPE ANN was first settled by the English in 1623, when the Dorchester Company established a fishing colony led by Roger Conant. The settlement's minister was the Reverend John Lyford, who had been banished from Plymouth Colony because he fostered dissension and spread slander — or as he asserted, because the Pilgrims opposed liberty of judgment and religion. At Cape Ann the men who stayed ashore cultivated a few fields and dried the catch of cod as it came in. In fall the salted fish were shipped back to England, while some men wintered over on the cape so that they could get an early start at fishing in the spring before the transport ships returned. After three years the enterprise was abandoned as unprofitable. The colonists at Cape Ann either went back to England or moved with Conant to a place called Naumkeag, where they founded Salem.

Cape Ann was settled again in 1631 under the auspices of the Plymouth Colony. The planters lived on small farms, where they grew crops, tended orchards, and raised cattle and sheep. And they fished — although at first fishing was not the dominant industry that it later became. A meetinghouse was established at Gloucester in 1642 at what is now Grant Circle on Route 128. Five years later the town was incorporated. The village center was sheltered from the wind and sea, yet adjacent to tidewater on the Annisquam River. It was near the narrow neck of land that linked the cape to the hinterland, and it was also close to Alewife Brook, which provided water power for a mill.

During the following century, the settlers established other villages at the cape's harbors as fishing and shipping became increasingly important. These places developed into Gloucester and Rockport. Some people, however, clustered in the new Commons Settlement or Upper Town, located on the highlands at the center of Cape Ann. Here the first houses, often just sod huts, were erected in about 1650 on the western edge of the commons. The farmers cultivated their own fields and used the public land for grazing livestock and cutting wood. By the third decade of the 1700s, most of the common land had been parceled out. Families occupied small walled-in farms and had separate lots for mowing, tillage, and woodcutting. By the middle of the century the Commons Settlement had over two hundred residents in about sixty houses. Most dwellings were single-story frame structures with a central chimney and a cellar. There was a school, a store, and a blacksmith forge, but no church. The site was convenient to Gloucester's original meetinghouse and mill and within an hour's walk of any of the harbors and coves where, in the latter 1700s, the residents of Cape Ann increasingly found employment as fishermen, mariners, and shipwrights.

By the time of the American Revolution, the Commons Settlement was losing population as subsistence farming on the meager soil became pointless in the burgeoning market economy based on fishing and trade. Also, a new road (now Washington Street) was opened northward along the shore of the Annisquam River, bypassing the Commons Settlement. As people moved away, they rented their houses to poor folk, including widows of men lost at sea or killed in the Revolutionary War. Some of these women earned a little money by gathering and selling herbs, concocting nostrums, and telling fortunes — and so gave rise to accounts of witches that have been elaborated by local writers and poets. By 1814 only six houses at the Commons Settlement were still occupied. Either literally or figuratively, the place went to the dogs and became known as Dogtown Common. In 1830 the final resident, Black Neil, formerly an itinerant hog butcher who had been living in the cellar of an abandoned dwelling, was taken to the town's poor farm. The last house was torn down in 1845.

Until the middle of the twentieth century, farmers pastured cattle and operated several piggeries on the highlands. Grazing and occasional fires kept the area as heath. Late in the nineteenth century, Mason A. Walton, the literary Hermit of Gloucester, described Dogtown Common as "a boulder-covered region of pasture-land, choked by huckleberry and blueberry bushes, with here and there large tangles of catbriar." Since then most of the area has grown up in woods and brush. Parts were re-acquired by Gloucester for reservoirs, watershed lands, and park, but much of the old common remained in private ownership. Concerned by prospects of development, the towns of Gloucester and Rockport, with help from the Essex County Greenbelt Association, undertook in 1984 to buy privately-held areas for conservation. For the most part this project has been carried out, financed in part by state Self-Help grants.

One man who took historical interest in Dogtown was Roger Ward Babson, a Gloucester native whose ancestors were born on Cape Ann for seven generations back, as he said in his book called *Cape Ann — A Tourist's Guide.* A few years after graduating from MIT in 1898, he founded the Business Statistics Organization. He published the very successful *Babson Reports* on business and finance, wrote many books on investing, and predicted the stock market crash of 1929. He founded Babson College in Wellesley and Webber College in Florida. Babson was the Prohibitionist party's presidential candidate in 1940. Some of his charity was focused on Gloucester, to which he contributed money for the local hospital. He also gave the city 1100 acres at Dogtown Common, some for Babson Reservoir and the rest to be kept forever as a public park. During the Great Depression, he provided relief to unemployed stone cutters by hiring them to carve mottoes, such as "HELP MOTHER," "NEVER TRY NEVER WIN," "BE ON TIME," and "INDUSTRY," on the large glacial boulders that litter the common. Some rocks bear numbers that are keyed to the text of Babson's guidebook. He said Dogtown provided an object lesson in the cyclical laws of history and economics by which some areas, families, businesses, and countries are in decline while others are ascendant. Another of Babson's unusual charities was the Gravity Research Foundation, which he established in 1949. The foundation has disbursed tens of thousands of dollars to colleges and universities in support of the sciences. It also sponsors annual awards for essays on gravitation. An admirer of Isaac Newton, Babson hoped that a shield or insulator could be invented to block gravity, reduce airplane accidents, and generate limitless clean energy by recycling water through a turbine. (That is, the water would fall under normal gravity, re-ascend through devices that blocked gravity, and then fall again and again — or so Babson speculated.) Yet another Babson charity is The Open Church Foundation, which he established after receiving spiritual comfort in an empty church that he found open on a weekday. Created in 1942, this foundation publishes and distributes evangelical literature and encourages churches to keep their doors unlocked, if possible. For more on Babson, you might enjoy visiting Babson College, where there is a small museum that includes Isaac Newton's actual study. After learning that Newton's house was going to be torn down, Babson's widow paid to have the room dismantled, transported to America, and reassembled at the college library.

≈    ≈    ≈    ≈

**TRAIN TO DOGTOWN COMMON:** From Boston's **North Station** (it is served by the MBTA's Green Line and Orange Line) take the commuter train to **Rockport**. At the Rockport station, turn left out the railroad parking lot and follow Route 127 (Railroad Avenue) 100 yards to the intersection with Summit Avenue. Turn left uphill and refer to page 73: "To start at Summit Avenue in Rockport." Or you can continue to Squam Road and follow it left up into the common.

**Rockport itself** is a popular tourist spot, best seen on a weekday, when the crowds are smaller. To reach the center of Rockport, turn right out the railroad parking lot and follow Route 127 (Railroad Avenue) downhill to a five-way intersection. Turn left onto Main Street and follow it downhill to the harbor area.

≈    ≈    ≈    ≈

**AUTOMOBILE DIRECTIONS TO DOGTOWN COMMON:** Dogtown Common is located at the center of Cape Ann in Gloucester and Rockport, 30 miles northeast of Boston. (See •7b on **Map 1** on page 6. For more detail, refer to the upper panel of **Map 9** on page 66, and also to **Map 10** at right.

**To Dogtown Common from Route 128:** Follow Route 128 north almost to its end. After passing Exit 12 and after crossing the Annisquam River, continue to Grant Circle. Go three-quarters of the way around the rotary, then turn right onto Route 127 (Washington Street) and right again *immediately* onto Poplar Street. After just 0.2 mile, turn left onto Cherry Street. Follow Cherry Street 0.7 mile, then turn right onto **Dogtown Road** and go 0.1 mile to a parking area on the right.

If there is no room to park, continue to the end of the road and try there. Another possibility is to go to a different entrance

MAP 10 — Dogtown Common

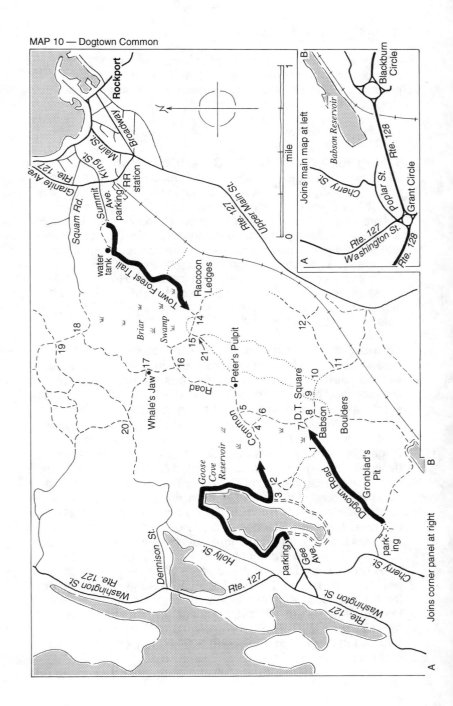

71

nearby, as follows: return to Cherry Street and go right 0.5 mile, then bear right on Gee Avenue. After 0.2 mile, park at the entrance to **Goose Cove Reservoir**, which in turn leads to Dogtown Common.

≈    ≈    ≈    ≈

**WALKING AT DOGTOWN COMMON:  Map 10** on page 71 shows the Dogtown trails. As indicated on the map, junctions are designated by numbers, but in reality some numbers are obscurely posted or even missing.

Three possible routes into Dogtown Common are discussed below, each starting at a different entrance. The major trails — actually, they are rocky roads — are interconnected by narrow footpaths. By referring to the map and the directions, you can easily plot a variety of loops through the area. However, because of lack of maintenance, some of the trails at Dogtown Common are becoming overgrown and may no longer be passable when you are there.

**To start at Dogtown Road,** enter the common via the left gate. Pass to the left of a cleared, level area and continue past a second gate. Follow the rough road past trail intersections that are identified by numbers posted on stakes or on trees — if the signs have survived vandals. These numbers are entirely separate from other numbers that you may notice inscribed on rocks by the edge of the trail. Carved at the instance of financier Roger Babson, the numbered rocks mark various Dogtown sites described by him in a guidebook called *Cape Ann — A Tourist's Guide*. For example, number 12 identifies the cellar of the long-vanished home of William Wilson, "associated in business with Nathaniel Babson (1784-1836), who operated a freighting business between Gloucester and Boston."

Follow old Dogtown Road three-quarters of a mile to junction 7, where a rock on the right is inscribed "D.T. Square." Continue uphill toward the right 160 yards on the main track, then bear right at junction 8. The plateau here is the site of many of the Babson Boulders, inscribed with various admonitions of a Horatio Alger nature. By circling left across the plateau from "STUDY" and "INDUSTRY," you can reach another trail that returns left to junction 8, passing "KEEP OUT OF DEBT" and other good advice.

From junction 9, a blazed trail leads through the woods to Briar

Swamp at junction 15. Apart from the blazes, this trail hardly exists, which provides a sort of game as you walk from one paint swatch to the next, passing near a heap of giant boulders along the way. The next trail to the south, originating at junction 10, also leads east to junction 15. This trail too consists chiefly of blazes, with almost no track on the ground.

At junction 7 on Dogtown Road, a narrow footpath leads through junction 6 to junctions 4 or 5 on Common Road.

**To start at Common Road,** pass through the gate off Gee Avenue, then go a few dozen yards and turn left at a T-intersection. Circle halfway around Goose Cove Reservoir, in the process passing three low earth dams. From the eastern side of the reservoir, turn left uphill onto Common Road, which is a rocky track. This road leads 1.5 miles to junction 14 at Briar Swamp, just beyond a low stone dike or dam. At junction 14, a narrow footpath — the Town Forest Trail — leads left to Summit Avenue in Rockport. The other trail at junction 14 continues to a heap of huge boulders called the Raccoon Ledges and then peters out in an area damaged by fire.

Another possibility is to turn off Common Road at junction 16. After crossing a small stream and a metal culvert, go 300 yards to a rock formation called The Whale's Jaw, which indeed resembled the gaping mouth of a whale until the lower jaw broke. By continuing past these rocks and eventually bearing right at junction 18, you can reach Squam Road in Rockport.

Yet another possibility is to turn off Common Road at junctions 2, 4, or 5 in order to follow narrow but well-worn footpaths to Dogtown Road, discussed above.

**To start at Summit Avenue in Rockport,** follow Summit uphill from the intersection with Route 127 just north of the railroad station. At the top of Summit Avenue, pass between stone gateposts and bear left. After passing a gate, go 40 yards, then turn left into the woods on Town Forest Trail opposite a huge water tank.

Follow the trail as it gradually becomes a rocky footpath. Bear right at a T-intersection and continue along the southern edge of Briar Swamp. Eventually, at junction 14, bear right toward a low stone dike or dam. (The trail just to the right of the dike leads to a boardwalk and then back to the main trail.)

By following the main track 1 mile, you can reach Goose Cove Reservoir via Common Road, which is discussed above.

≈
≈ ≈ ≈ ≈
≈

## RAVENSWOOD PARK

RAVENSWOOD PARK was created by the will of Samuel E. Sawyer, a prosperous Boston dry goods merchant who lived from 1815 to 1889. A native of Gloucester, he returned each summer to his family home east of the park near Freshwater Cove. He endowed the Sawyer Library in Gloucester and gave 300 acres of woods for the original section of Ravenswood. Sawyer's will also established a park endowment and a board of trustees that purchased another 200 acres before transferring Ravenswood to The Trustees of Reservations in 1993.

While walking at Ravenswood, you might notice a plaque to Mason Augustus Walton, the author of many articles and several books on natural history. Walton's observations on birds, plants, and woodland animals were gleaned over three decades during which he lived alone in a small but comfortably furnished cabin near the Old Salem Road at the north end of the park. For a colorful sobriquet, he adopted the name that others applied to him — the Hermit of Gloucester — although he regularly walked into town to eat and shop, pick up his mail, and read the newspapers at the Sawyer Library. A contributor to *Field and Stream*, he gained a wide following. He lectured throughout New England, was listed in *Who's Who*, and eventually became a local celebrity whose cabin was pictured on postcards. After Ravenswood became a park, the Hermit was allowed to continue there. He was written up in guidebooks as one of the attractions of the place. Sometimes as many as two hundred people stopped by on Sundays to sign his guest book and to talk.

Formerly a school teacher, farmer, and newspaper editor, Walton moved from Maine to Boston in 1880 to head up the delinquent accounts department of a pharmaceutical company. He was a widower whose wife of seven years, and also his infant, had died in childbirth. In 1884 Walton left Boston and moved to the Gloucester woods to save his life, as he was convinced. "I was in sore straits," he wrote. "Ill health had reduced my flesh until I resembled the living skeleton of a dime show. I realized that a few months more of city life would take me beyond the living stage . . . . I thought that I was fading away with consumption, but the doctors said my lungs were sound. I was advised to go into the woods and try life in a pine grove. As there was no money for the doctors in this advice, I looked upon it as kind and disinterested, but my mind ran in another direction."

At first Walton tried to arrange a voyage as passenger on a Gloucester fishing schooner, but no captain would have him, so he abandoned the idea of a sea cure and moved into a tent in the woods. Two weeks of outdoor life made him feel like a new man, he said. After four months he declared himself cured, but he never returned to his former way of life. Instead, he built a log cabin where he lived until a few days before his death in 1917 at age 79. He made a little money by selling garden flowers that he grew and wildflowers that he gathered. He mounted animals and birds and sold them. Occasionally he tutored children or worked in local businesses that manufactured items for the fishing industry. And he turned to journalizing and anecdotal nature writing in the first person, somewhat in the manner of Thoreau, whom he sometimes quoted, occasionally echoed, and clearly tried to emulate. He appears to have been contented with his life. In the introductory note to *A Hermit's Wild Friends*, published in 1903, Walton stated:

> During my eighteen years of hermit life, I claim to have discovered several new features in natural history, namely:
> That the cow-bunting watches over its young, assists the foster parents in providing food, and gradually assumes full care of the young bird, and takes it to the pasture to associate with its kind; that the white-footed mouse is dumb, and communicates with its species by drumming with its toes; that the wood-thrush conducts a singing-school for the purpose of teaching its young how to sing; that the chickadee can count; that the shad-bush on Cape Ann assumes a dwarf form, and grows in patches like the low-bush blueberry, fruiting when less than a foot in height; that the red squirrel owns a farm or fruit garden, and locates his male children on territory which he preempts for the purpose. I am aware that my claims will be vigorously assailed, but I have verified these discoveries by years of patient observation, and would say to my critics: "You would better investigate carefully before denying the probability of any one of these claims."

This last sentence was a riposte to an article in the March 1903 *Atlantic Monthly* assailing Walton, Ernest Thompson Seton, and other authors as "the new school of nature writers or natural history romancers that reads into birds and animals almost the entire human psychology."

≈     ≈     ≈     ≈

## AUTOMOBILE DIRECTIONS TO RAVENSWOOD PARK:
Ravenswood Park is located in Gloucester just west of the harbor. (See •7c on **Map 1** page 6. For more detail, refer to the upper panel of **Map 9** on page 66.)

MAP 11 — Ravenswood Park

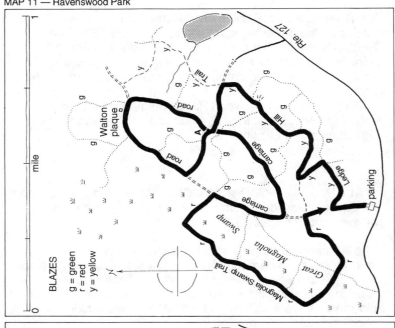

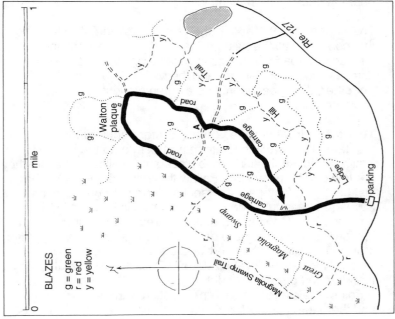

77

**To Ravenswood Park from Route 128:** Leave Route 128 near its northern end at Exit 14 for Route 133. Follow Route 133 east 2.9 miles to an intersection with Route 127 in front of Gloucester Harbor. Turn right and follow Route 127 south 1.9 miles to the entrance to Ravenswood Park on the right.

After visiting Ravenswood Park, you may want to continue south on Route 127 for 1.8 miles to the **Coolidge Reservation**, described at right.

≈     ≈     ≈     ≈

**WALKING AT RAVENSWOOD PARK: Map 11** on page 77 outlines two routes, one short and obvious, the other longer and more complicated.

The left panel of **Map 11** shows an easy 2-mile circuit via wide, smoothly-graded carriage roads. Assuming that you go clockwise, take care eventually to turn left at a T-intersection marked A on the map, and then — in 60 yards — continue straight past a dirt road intersecting from the left. At the next major junction, bear left back to the parking lot.

The right panel of **Map 11** shows a convoluted, 4-mile route that combines all the best trails at Ravenswood Park, including the carriage road, the Ledge Hill Trail (from which there is a view across Gloucester Harbor), and the Magnolia Swamp Trail. Together, these paths provide a complete look at the park's varied terrain.

**To start**, follow the wide gravel road for about 200 yards from the gate at the parking lot, then turn right onto the Ledge Hill Trail. (Supposedly, this trail is blazed with yellow disks, but they are few and far between.) Follow the trail 270 yards and then, just beyond a faint path intersecting from the right, turn left. Go 200 yards, then turn right. Pass other trails intersecting from right and left. Continue through an area densely strewn with boulders transported here by the last continental glacier. After crossing a hilltop with a view of Gloucester Harbor, descend gradually via the yellow-blazed trail. Pass above a small quarry, then turn left onto a wide dirt road.

Follow the dirt road to a T-intersection with the carriage road, and there turn right. After 50 yards, pass a carriage road intersecting from the right (and by which you will eventually arrive back at this junction). At a T-intersection, turn right and follow the carriage road clockwise around the circuit, bearing right shortly after passing the site of the cabin of Mason A. Walton, whose life here is discussed on pages 75-76.

When you arrive back at the intersection where you were before (marked A on the map), turn left, then continue past the dirt road intersecting from the left (and from which you came earlier). At the next intersection of carriage roads, turn sharply right and continue about a quarter of a mile to a junction with the red-blazed Magnolia Swamp Trail on the left. Follow this footpath downhill, across a boardwalk, and to the left along the edge of the swamp before again bearing left across another boardwalk. Pursue the red blazes across several knolls to a intersection with the carriage road, and there turn right back to the parking lot.

≈

≈      ≈      ≈      ≈

≈

## COOLIDGE RESERVATION

IN 1871 Thomas Jefferson Coolidge, a Boston financier active in textiles, banking, and railroads (he was associated with Henry Clay Frick in the Atchison, Topeka, and Santa Fe) bought the promontory in Manchester-by-the-Sea that has been known ever since as Coolidge Point. In addition to a large clapboard country home for his family, he built other houses for the use of relatives, and he sold several lots to friends and business associates. For nearly half a century until his death in 1920, Coolidge spent most summers in Manchester. He gave the money for the town's public library; he was an overseer of Harvard University; and in 1892 and '93 he was Minister to France, like his great-grandfather Thomas Jefferson.

In 1902 Coolidge's son, Thomas Jefferson Coolidge, Jr., built a house at Coolidge Point that was a monument to family wealth and pride. Designed by McKim, Mead and White in the classical revival style of Monticello, the brick and stone-trimmed house was one of the grandest Gold Coast mansions of its day. Known locally as the Marble Palace, it had a large central section flanked by two wings. Altogether it stretched 230 feet facing the sea. The Marble Palace was torn down in the late 1950s by the next Coolidge heir, but the site and size of the house are still indicated by an outline of stone slabs on the Ocean Lawn.

MAP 12 — Coolidge Point

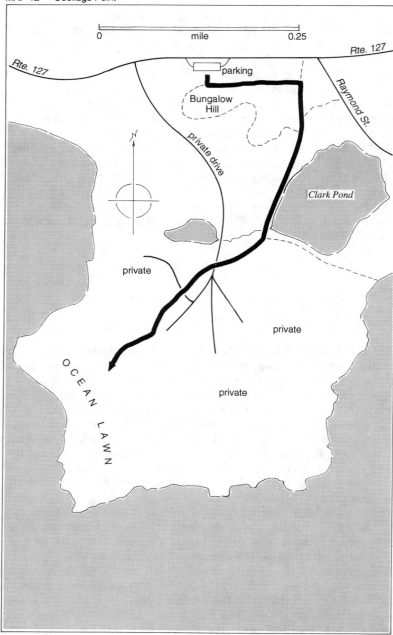

For a few days in August 1918, the Marble Palace was turned over to President Woodrow Wilson and his entourage. There was the usual story — it exists in several versions on the North Shore, each with a different visiting dignitary as its subject. Supposedly the president was shadowed and almost arrested by the local police as a suspicious character during his rambles around the neighborhood.

In 1990 and '91, the Coolidge family donated their 42-acre property at Coolidge Point to The Trustees of Reservations. Another 16 acres were given by the Essex County Greenbelt Association, to which the Coolidges had donated the land a decade earlier. Within the reservation, however, are private residences on the parcels sold by Thomas Jefferson Coolidge to friends a century earlier. As a courtesy to the owners of these houses, please stay on the trails as you walk to and from the Ocean Lawn.

≈　　　≈　　　≈　　　≈

**AUTOMOBILE DIRECTIONS TO THE COOLIDGE RESERVATION:** The reservation is located in Manchester by-the-Sea near the boundary with Gloucester. (See •7d on **Map 1** on page 6. For more detail, refer to the upper panel of **Map 9** on page 66.)

**To the Coolidge Reservation from Route 128:** Leave Route 128 near its northern end at Exit 16 for Pine Street. At the bottom of the ramp, turn left and follow Pine Street 1.6 miles to an intersection with Route 127 in Manchester by-the-Sea. Turn left and follow Route 127 north for 2.9 miles to the entrance to the Coolidge Reservation on the right.

After visiting the Coolidge Reservation, you may want to continue north on Route 127 for 1.8 miles to **Ravenswood Park**, described starting on page 75.

≈　　　≈　　　≈　　　≈

**WALKING AT THE COOLIDGE RESERVATION:** Go to Coolidge Point on Saturday, Sunday, or Monday, when the Ocean Lawn section of the reservation is open.

The main trail is shown on **Map 12** at left. The path leads by the pond and out past the manager's house and garage to the Ocean Lawn, formerly the site of the Coolidge mansion. The round-trip distance is about 1.5 miles. A side trail leads to Magnolia Harbor, where the beach is private.

81

# 8

# LYNN WOODS RESERVATION
# SAUGUS IRON WORKS

Located north of Boston, **Lynn Woods Reservation** is a municipal park similar in size and character to the large wilderness reservations of the Metropolitan District Commission. It is, in fact, the nation's second largest municipal park, after Fairmount Park in Philadelphia. As shown on **Map 13** on pages 86-87, about 10 miles of fire roads and 30 miles of foot trails explore the park's rugged, rocky hills and hollows. Trail junctions are clearly identified and keyed to the map, so you can wander at large but always know where you are.

Lynn Woods is open daily from sunrise to sunset. The area is managed jointly by the City of Lynn's Department of Public Works, Park Commission, and Water & Sewer Commission. It is patrolled by the Lynn Woods Rangers; telephone (781) 477-7123. For access by train or automobile, please turn to page 85. Walking directions are on page 89.

Before or after a visit to the Lynn Woods, you may want to see the nearby **Saugus Iron Works National Historic Site**, where the blast furnace, forge, and rolling and slitting mill that operated here in the 1640s have been reconstructed. The site is open daily, except Thanksgiving, Christmas, and New Year's Day, from 9 A.M. to 5 P.M. April through October — and until 4 P.M. the rest of the year. It is managed by the National Park Service; telephone (781) 233-0050. Directions to the iron works are on page 89.

---

BIG BOULDERS, sometimes perched precariously atop hills or bare ledges, are a common occurrence throughout New England, but they are especially numerous at the Lynn Woods. The rocks were plucked from their original locations by the ponderous ice sheet that four times advanced across New England during the last million years, retreating most recently about twelve thousand years ago. Dislodged from their parent ledges, the boulders were dragged along the surface of the ground beneath the ice. Sometimes bigger than a house and weighing thousands of tons, the largest rocks were rarely transported more than a mile or two. Smaller ones may have been carried hundreds of miles before coming to rest as the ice melted and left them strewn over the landscape or buried in glacial till. Big and small, the boulders invariably lie to the south or southeast of their place of origin, indicating that the continental ice sheet advanced from the north. Transported far enough, the rocks may be composed of material unlike anything in their vicinity, and so they are called *erratics*. For example, boulders of red jasper are found in Kentucky, six hundred miles from the nearest bedrock ledge of this type north of Lake Superior.

Usually glacial boulders are found in areas of granite or other hard bedrock where the outcrops were more easily split apart than ground down by the ice. The ledges and hills from which the rocks were taken have a characteristic shape: a smooth and gradual northwestern slope (or *stoss*) and a more abrupt and craggy southeastern slope (or *lee*). When the ice sheet rode up the stoss slope and over the top, it scoured the surface, yet failed to remove much bedrock by abrasion. But as the ice pushed down the lee slope, it tugged at the ledges and outcrops and broke off large blocks along the cracks that all rock formations have. After the rocks were plucked out and drawn away, their rough edges were smoothed by grinding as the ice sheet dragged the boulders for a distance before dropping them here and there, sometimes in freakish positions. The plucking action on lee slopes has in some instances lowered the surface by as much as 100 feet, compared to a maximum of 10 or 15 feet on the stoss slopes and hilltops. As you walk at the Lynn Woods and other rocky areas near Boston, you can judge for yourself whether the ledges and hills show stoss and lee asymmetry.


IT MAY SEEM a matter of course that a city or town can acquire and develop public parks. However, when the Boston parks movement got underway in the early 1870s, there was some doubt about whether the acquisition of parkland via eminent domain and public debt was a valid exercise of municipal power. To resolve the issue, the Massachusetts legislature passed the Park Act in May 1875, authorizing Boston and several adjacent towns to establish park commissions and to take land within their municipal boundaries. One object of the law was to promote cooperation among the city and its neighbors, but apart from Boston, only Brookline made use of the legislation in order to join the city in developing the Fenway. Towns that did not border Boston fell outside the terms of the law.

Although a regional approach to parks remained elusive, the Massachusetts legislature went on to authorize local parks throughout the state. In 1882 the Public Domain Act was passed, enabling any town or city to set up a park commission and to acquire land within its borders. And even before that, the state enacted a special law just for the city of Lynn, authorizing a seven-man board — the Trustees of the Free Public Forest — to acquire the Lynn Woods by gifts and purchases. The city raised $35,000, which was matched by donations from citizens. By 1890 Lynn had assembled nearly 1700 acres surrounding the municipal reservoirs. Most of this area had been the town's common land before it was divided into private holdings early in the eighteenth century. Good for little except timber and pasture, the boulder-strewn highlands were still mostly unoccupied when they re-entered the public domain nearly two centuries later. The "City of Shoes" went on to develop a system of carriage roads that now provide good walking and ski touring throughout the park. But it is the many foot trails — for example, the Undercliff Path bordering Tomlin's Swamp and the trails in the vicinity of Mount Gilead, Burrill Hill, Balanced Boulder, Weetamoo Cliff, and Bow Ridge — that best show the area's rugged terrain.

One curiosity at Lynn Woods is a sloping, hundred-foot tunnel at Dungeon Rock. The shaft was dug by spiritualist Hiram Marble and his son Edwin during the 1850s and '60s in the belief, so they said, that they would find buried pirate treasure. To finance the excavation, the Marbles issued bonds and invited tourists to view the tunnel. For people who bring their own flashlights and assume entirely to themselves all risk of injury, the tunnel is open May through October from 11 A.M. to 4 P.M.

≈     ≈     ≈     ≈

**PUBLIC TRANSIT:** From Boston's **North Station** (it is served by the MBTA's Green Line and Orange Line) take the commuter train to **Lynn**, then exit from the station for Central Square. Board Bus 436 and go about 3 miles. Get off at the intersection with Great Woods Road, immediately after passing St. Mary's Cemetery on the left. Follow Great Woods Road straight 0.2 mile to the entrance for the Lynn Woods.

≈     ≈     ≈     ≈

**AUTOMOBILE DIRECTIONS: The Lynn Woods Reservation** is located in the towns of Lynn and Saugus 10 miles north of Boston. (See •8 on **Map 1** on page 6, and also the corner panel of **Map 13** on page 87.) Two approaches —

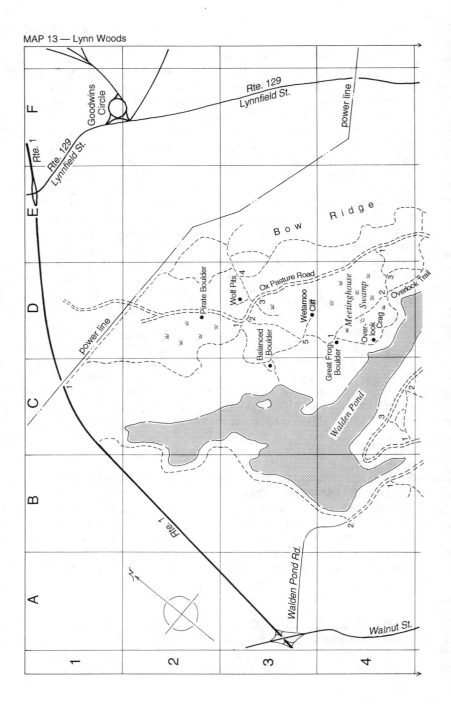

MAP 13 — Lynn Woods

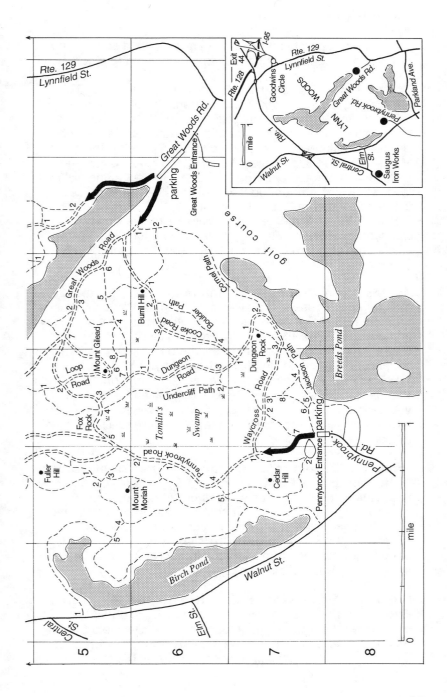

they lead to separate entrances — are described below. There are also directions to get from each entrance to the other.

**To the Lynn Woods from Boston via Route 1:** This approach goes to the reservation's Pennybrook Entrance.

Follow Route 1 north as it splits off from Boston's Central Artery and passes through Charlestown and across the Tobin Bridge. Continue north past the exits for Chelsea, Revere, Malden, Route 99, and eventually past the giant cactus and cattle at the Hilltop Steak House. Leave Route 1 at the exit for **Walnut Street** *eastbound* toward Lynn and Saugus (i.e., immediately before Route 129 west).

Follow Walnut Street east 2 miles to an intersection with Pennybrook Road at a traffic light, and there turn left. Follow Pennybrook Road 0.3 mile to the entrance for Lynn Woods Reservation, where there is a parking lot.

**To the Lynn Woods from Interstate 95 (Route 128):** This approach goes to the reservation's Great Woods Entrance.

Leave I-95 at Exit 44 for Route 1 south toward Boston, then immediately follow the signs for **Route 129** east toward Lynn. (From the northbound lanes of I-95, there is a separate Exit 44B connecting directly to Route 129 toward Lynn.)

Follow Route 129 east for 2.7 miles, then turn right onto Great Woods Road where Route 129 rises slightly and bends left. (If you pass St. Mary's Cemetery on the right, you have gone too far.) Follow Great Woods Road straight 0.2 mile to a large parking lot.

**From the Pennybrook Entrance to the Great Woods Entrance:** Follow Pennybrook Road 0.3 mile out of the reservation, then turn left onto Walnut Street. After just 0.4 mile, turn left uphill onto Parkland Avenue. Go 1.4 miles, then turn 90 degrees left at a T-intersection. Stay left on Route 129 (Lynnfield Street) and follow it 0.7 mile. When Route 129 bends right downhill, turn left onto Great Woods Road and go straight 0.2 mile to a large parking lot.

**From the Great Woods Entrance to the Pennybrook Entrance:** Follow Great Woods Road 0.2 mile out of the reservation, then turn right onto Route 129 (Lynnfield Street). After 0.7 mile, turn right onto Parkland Avenue. Go 1.4 miles, then turn right onto Walnut Street and follow it 0.4 mile.

Turn right at a traffic light onto Pennybrook Road and go 0.3 mile to a parking lot.

≈        ≈        ≈        ≈

**WALKING: Map 13** on pages 86-87 shows the carriage roads and foot trails at the **Lynn Woods Reservation**. Major intersections are identified by signs. There is also an excellent coordinate system of letters and numbers that are posted on trees and keyed to the map. For example, an intersection might be posted B7-1. The initial combination of a letter and number indicates a grid square, and the final number after the hyphen identifies a particular intersection within that square. Thus, B7-1 designates the intersection of Pennybrook Road and Waycross Road. In addition, white blazes mark footpaths that lead to park entrances — but with the map you can do better by referring to the specific intersection numbers. Finally, blue blazes designate secondary foot trails.

Although Lynn Woods is a great place to wander without any preconceived route, there are a few spots that you may want to seek out, including Balanced Boulder in grid square C3 and Dungeon Rock just west of intersection D7-1. Burrill Hill in square D6 is the highest hill in the reservation, but nearby Mount Gilead in square C5 has better views. Both hills have towers that are closed because they are in poor condition (although the tower at Burrill Hill may be restored). For a note on Dungeon Rock, see page 85.

≈
≈        ≈        ≈        ≈
≈

## SAUGUS IRON WORKS

**AUTOMOBILE DIRECTIONS to the SAUGUS IRON WORKS NATIONAL HISTORICAL SITE:**

**To the Iron Works from Route 1:** From Route 1 about 2 miles south of Exit 44 off Interstate 95 (Route 128), take Walnut Street east toward Lynn and Saugus. Go 0.4 mile to a traffic light with Central Avenue, and there turn right. Follow Central Avenue 1.2 miles (it zig-zags toward the end), then turn left into the parking lot for the Saugus Iron Works.

# 9

# BREAKHEART RESERVATION

Located north of Boston in Saugus and Wakefield, the Breakheart Reservation was formerly the private hunting and fishing preserve of two wealthy attorneys from Lynn. Acquired by the Metropolitan District Commission in 1934, the 700-acre reservation consists of large ponds that are surrounded by wooded hills and abrupt granite knobs. Two walks, one easy and the other more strenuous, are described below.

**Map 14** on page 95 outlines a walk of 4.5 miles (7.2 kilometers). The route follows narrow, paved roads constructed by the Civilian Conservation Corps during the Great Depression of the 1930s. The roads are closed to cars, except for an occasional park shuttle serving the swimming beach during summer. Directions start on page 94.

**Map 15** on page 96 shows a circuit of 4 miles (6.4 kilometers). The route follows blazed foot trails up and down over the rocky hills. Directions start on page 97.

The Breakheart Reservation is open daily from dawn to dusk. Dogs must be leashed. The reservation is managed by the Metropolitan District Commission; telephone (781) 233-0834.

For automobile directions to the Breakheart Reservation, please turn to page 93.

---

IN WHAT SORT OF SETTING would you expect to find a beech tree? Sycamore? Pitch pine? Elm? Field guides contain this sort of information, but far more fun is simply to see for yourself. Every outing is an opportunity to practice the visual habit of relating different species of trees to the settings where they typically grow.

Some species are so tolerant in their moisture, soil, and sunlight requirements that they are very broadly distributed. Examples are red, black, and white oak and the several species of hickory (shagbark, mockernut, pignut, and bitternut). These are the main forest trees in southern New England. Sometimes called sprout hardwoods, they often occur with two, three, or even four trunks, indicating that they grew from suckers emerging from the stumps or roots of older trees that were cut down or burned. Also common in upland areas are black (or sweet) birch, sugar maple, and white ash. As conditions get wetter, red maple (another of the sprout hardwoods), striped maple, yellow birch, and occasionally American basswood and slippery elm join the mix. Somewhat drier conditions are good for red pine and chestnut oak, pin oak, post oak, and scarlet oak. All these species can occupy both the canopy and the understory in different combinations or associations.

Some small trees, including redbud, dogwood, sassafras, and American mountain-ash, rarely escape the understory. Allegheny serviceberry (or shadbush) occurs in forest borders, where its five-petaled flowers are conspicuous.

Like oak and hickory, white pine is abundant in southern New England, scattered throughout the forest. Sometimes it naturally forms pure stands in areas of sandy loam, or it may be planted for timber or watershed protection. Sun-loving and fast-growing, pines also occur in stands where farm fields have been abandoned and colonized by pine seedlings. Pine forests, however, are not self-sustaining; the canopy of full-grown trees blocks light from the shade-intolerant pine seedlings. Instead, it is hardwood saplings such as maple, birch, beech, and some oaks — and perhaps also hemlock — that establish themselves in the understory, then make a spurt of growth in the sun when the mature pines die or are cut or blown down.

Formerly, the dominance of oaks, hickories, and pine in southern New England was shared by American chestnut, but early in the twentieth century all mature American chestnut trees were killed by chestnut blight, a fungus that affects the bark. The disease continues to kill chestnut saplings as they sprout from old root systems, but only after the new growth reaches a height of ten or twenty feet and an inch or two in diameter. Clusters of sickly chestnut suckers are a common sight.

Some species are especially opportunistic. Eastern redcedar and gray birch are among the first trees, along with white pine, chokecherry, and staghorn sumac, to grow in abandoned fields. White (or paper) birch, yellow birch, quaking aspen, and pin cherry quickly reseed burned areas. Unusual for a conifer, pitch pine sometimes sprouts back from its base after fire.

Some trees find a niche in extreme conditions. Pitch pine, redcedar, scrub (or bear) oak, and gray birch are among the few species that can tolerate the dry, meager soil of rocky hilltops. So can dwarf oak, which is really just a shrub. Pitch pine, scrub oak, and dwarf oak, together with huckleberry and blueberry, are also common species in the sandy, sterile barrens of southeastern Massachusetts and Cape Cod.

Excessively wet conditions favor certain species of trees. Tamarack (or American larch), black spruce, and Atlantic white-cedar grow in bogs and saturated soils. White-cedar also occurs in coastal swamps. Other swamp trees of southern New England are red maple, American elm, swamp white oak, sour-gum, tupelo, and black ash, although all grow in drier settings also.

Moist floodplains support many species of trees, including American sycamore, silver maple, green ash, black willow, holly, and American hornbeam (or ironwood, which has a fluted, muscular-looking trunk and smooth gray bark). From a hilltop or highway in winter, you can sometimes trace a nearby watercourse simply by the broad swath of white-branched sycamores occupying the floodplain. Others species, including black willow, witch-hazel, boxelder, and smooth alder (usually a shrub with little cones), typically occupy the banks of streams and lakes. Cool, shady ravines and moist, north-facing slopes provide a suitable environment for hemlock, often in pure stands with no understory. Beech trees, which have a very shallow root system, also favor areas where there is ample surface moisture.

Acting over long periods of time, the tendency of each species to thrive in certain settings and to fail, or at least lag, in others gives rise to more or less stable associations of trees. The associations blend into one another where the terrain changes gradually, but show sharp demarcations where conditions change abruptly. However, even as the forest organizes itself along broadly predictable lines, it is often visited with reversals. At any time hurricanes, ice storms, insect infestations, blights, floods, fires, and other such events can undo many decades of maturation and provide the opportunity, here and there, for a new mix of trees and shrubs to establish themselves. These then begin again the process of natural succession that leads eventually to stable plant associations adapted to local conditions and the prevailing climate.

≈　　　≈　　　≈　　　≈

**AUTOMOBILE DIRECTIONS: The Breakheart Reservation** is located 9 miles north of Boston in Saugus and Wakefield. (See •9 on **Map 1** on page 6, and also the corner panels of **Maps 14 and 15** on pages 95 and 96.) Two approaches are described below.

**To the Breakheart Reservation from Boston via Route 1:** Follow Route 1 north as it splits off from Boston's

Central Artery and passes through Charlestown and across the Tobin Bridge. Continue north past the exits for Chelsea, Revere, Malden, Route 99, and eventually past the giant cactus and cattle at the Hilltop Steak House. Leave Route 1 at the exit for the Lynn Fells Parkway toward Melrose and Stoneham. The long exit ramp leads to a T-intersection. Turn left and go only 0.1 mile, then turn right onto Forest Street at the entrance to the Breakheart Reservation. Follow Forest Street 0.3 mile, then park by the loop at the end of the street.

**To the Breakheart Reservation from Interstate 95 (Route 128):** Leave I-95 at Exit 44 for Route 1 south toward Boston. Follow Route 1 about 2.7 miles, then take the exit for the Lynn Fells Parkway toward Melrose and Stoneham. After just 0.3 mile, turn right onto Forest Street at the entrance to the Breakheart Reservation. Follow Forest Street 0.3 mile, then park by the loop at the end of the street.

≈     ≈     ≈     ≈

**WALKING:** Two different routes at the **Breakheart Reservation** are described below. The first is much easier than the second.

**Map 14** at right shows a route that follows **narrow, paved roads** that are closed to motor vehicles (except for an occasional park shuttle serving the swimming beach during summer). Arranged in a double loop, the roads are an easy walkway through deep woods and around rocky hills. The total distance is 4.5 miles.

**To start** in the manner suggested by the map, enter the woods between the large fieldstone gateposts to the right of the maintenance garage. Follow the paved road gradually downhill. As you approach Pearce Lake, pass a road intersecting from the right. Continue nearly a mile and then, at an intersection of paved roads, turn right and go another mile to a park gate. Without exiting through the gate, turn right and continue along the paved road. Eventually, turn right at a T-intersection. For the second time, follow the road past the beach at Pearce Lake. At each intersection, continue straight to return to the parking area where you started.

MAP 14 — Breakheart Reservation: circuit of paved roads

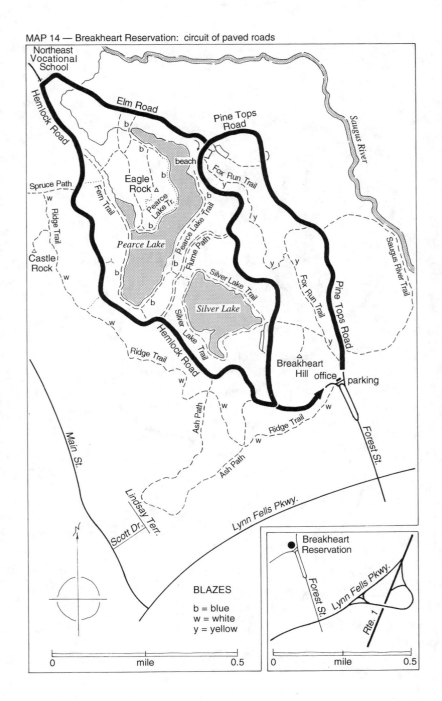

Northeast Vocational School

Hemlock Road

Elm Road

Pine Tops Road

Saugus River

Spruce Path

beach

Fox Run Trail

Eagle Rock

Fern Trail

Pearce Lake Tr.

Ridge Trail

Castle Rock

Pearce Lake

Pearce Lake Trail

Flume Path

Silver Lake Trail

Silver Lake

Fox Run Trail

Pine Tops Road

Saugus River Trail

Hemlock Road

Silver Lake Trail

Ridge Trail

Breakheart Hill

office

parking

Ash Path

Ridge Trail

Ash Path

Forest St.

Main St.

Lindsay Terr.

Scott Dr.

Lynn Fells Pkwy.

N

BLAZES

b = blue
w = white
y = yellow

0        mile        0.5

Breakheart Reservation

Forest St.

Lynn Fells Pkwy.

Rte. 1

0        mile        0.5

95

MAP 15 — Breakheart Reservation: circuit of foot trails

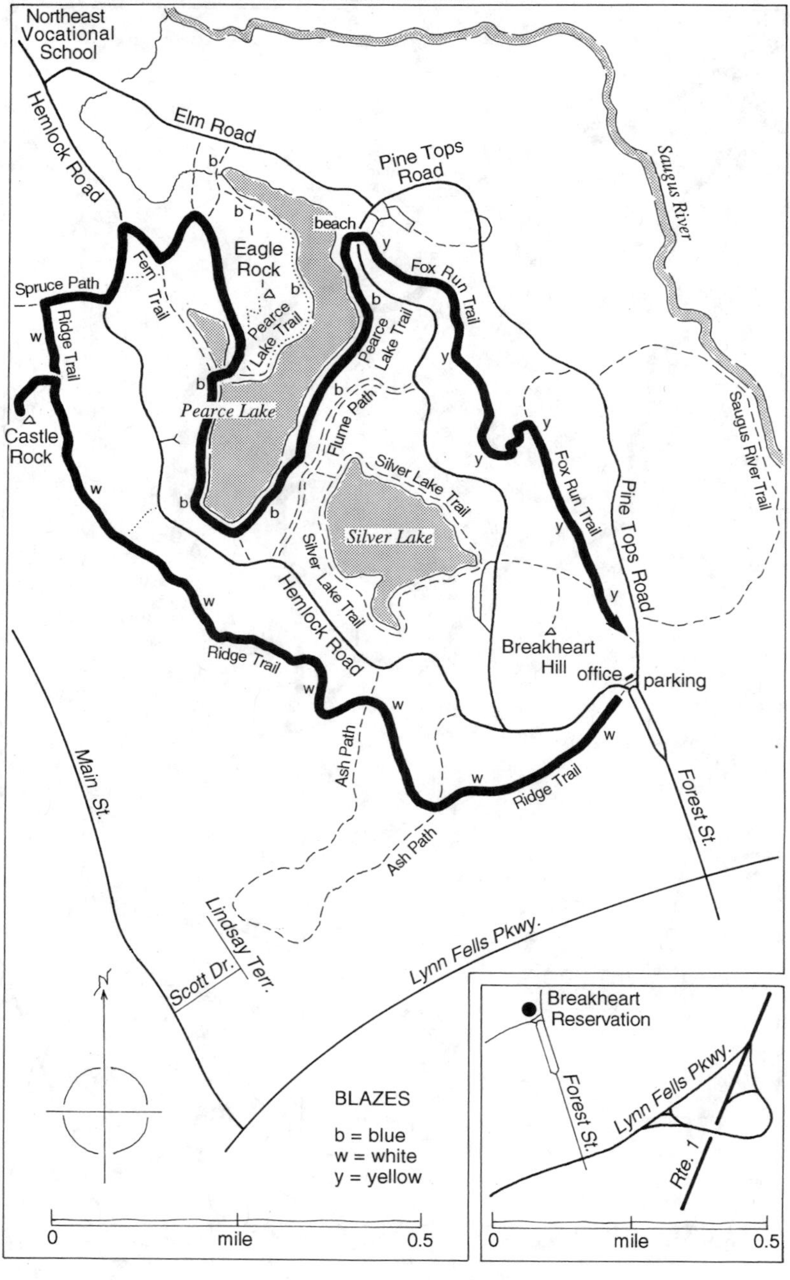

Northeast Vocational School

Hemlock Road

Elm Road

Pine Tops Road

Saugus River

b

Eagle Rock

b

b

beach

y

Fox Run Trail

Spruce Path

Fern Trail

Pearce Lake Trail

Pearce Lake Trail

b

w

Ridge Trail

b

Pearce Lake

y

Flume Path

b

Saugus River Trail

Castle Rock

w

b

Silver Lake Trail

y

Silver Lake

Fox Run Trail

y

w

Ridge Trail

Hemlock Road

Silver Lake Trail

y

Pine Tops Road

w

Breakheart Hill

office

parking

Ash Path

w

w

w

Ridge Trail

w

Forest St.

Main St.

Ash Path

Lindsay Terr.

Scott Dr.

Lynn Fells Pkwy.

N

BLAZES

b = blue
w = white
y = yellow

Breakheart Reservation

Forest St.

Lynn Fells Pkwy.

Rte. 1

0                    mile                    0.5

0                    mile                    0.5

96

**Map 15** at left shows a rugged 4-mile circuit that strings together a series of blazed **foot trails**.

**To start**, locate the trailhead for the white-blazed Ridge Trail to the left of Hemlock Road (which in turn is to the left of the office/maintenance building).  The Ridge Trail leads across rocky terrain from one hilltop to the next, in the process crossing the Ash Path twice.  Toward the end, the Ridge Trail passes Castle Hill, where a short spur trail leads to the top.  Eventually, when the Ridge Trail reaches a T-intersection with the Spruce Path, turn right and continue to the paved Hemlock Road.

Follow Hemlock Road left downhill 210 yards to the Fern Trail on the right at a gap in the guardrail.  Turn right onto the Fern Trail and follow it straight through the woods for 110 yards, then turn left across a tiny bridge.  Go another 110 yards, then bear right onto a wide path.  Ignoring small trails that intersect from the left, follow the wide path through the woods.  After a pond-like appendage of Pearce Lake appears on the right, follow the blue-blazed Pearce Lake Trail half-right to a small bridge.  Cross the bridge, then turn left to continue counter-clockwise around Pearce Lake on the blue-blazed trail, which eventually leads to the swimming beach.  Although the route is not always clear, you cannot go wrong if you keep the water toward the left.

From the swimming beach, cross the road to the entrance of a parking area, and there pick up the yellow-blazed Fox Run Trail leading steeply uphill to the right.  Follow the yellow blazes up and down over rocky hills.  Eventually, after passing immediately below a large, leaning outcrop, descend to the right for 30 yards, then bear left for 60 yards to an intersection with the Saugus River Trail.  Turn right to continue on the yellow-blazed Fox Run Trail, which leads to the reservation entrance where you started.

# 10

# MIDDLESEX FELLS RESERVATION

There are dozens of miles of trails at the huge Middlesex Fells Reservation just 8 miles north of Boston. Because the reservation is split by Interstate 93, its eastern and western halves are best treated separately, with different automobile directions, hiking routes, and maps.

The lower panel of **Map 16** on page 103 shows the **Rock Circuit Trail** in the eastern Fells. Although it is only 4 miles long (6.4 kilometers), you should allow two or three hours for this strenuous outing, which links a series of rocky knobs. Directions to the eastern Fells (including public transit) start on page 102.

**Map 17** on page 109 shows the **Skyline Trail** in the western Fells. It is 7 miles long (11.2 kilometers). The route crosses rocky hills that occasionally provide distant views. Directions to the western Fells (including public transit) start on page 107.

Finally, **Map 18** on page 110 shows the **Reservoir Trail** in the western Fells. At 5.2 miles long (8.3 kilometers), it is the easiest of the three routes outlined in this chapter. Directions are on page 111.

The Middlesex Fells Reservation is open daily from 8 A.M. to dusk. It is managed by the Metropolitan District Commission; telephone (781) 662-5230.

---

## EASTERN MIDDLESEX FELLS

IN THE FIRST YEARS of the Massachusetts Bay Colony, the Middlesex Fells were known simply as the Rocks or Charlestown End. "An uncouth wilderness full of timber," was the way one explorer described the area in 1629, the year after Charlestown was founded. Like all the early towns, Charlestown encompassed an area far larger than now, including the Fells and even land northward to present-day Reading and westward to Arlington. In his diary entry for February 7, 1632,

Governor John Winthrop recorded a day's reconnaissance at the Fells. Referring to himself in the third person, he wrote:

The Governor, Mr. Norwell, Mr. Eliot and others, went over Mistic River at Medford; and, going North and East among the rocks about two or three miles, they came to a very great Pond, having in the midst an island of about one acre, and very thick with trees of pine and beech; and the pond had divers small rocks standing up here and there in it, which they therefore called Spot Pond. They went all about it upon the ice. From thence (towards the Northwest about half a mile) they came to the top of a very high rock beneath which (towards the North) lies a goodly plain, part open land and part woody from whence there is a fair prospect, but it being then close and rainy, they could see but a small distance. This place they called Cheese Rock, because when they went to eat, they had only cheese (the Governor's man forgetting, for haste, to put up some bread).

From the Charlestown hinterland, oaks and other hardwoods and also white pines "more than a gun shot high" provided the settlers with timbers for buildings and for ships. Logs were hauled from the Fells by ox team down the rough roads to the banks of the Mystic River, where the *Blessing of the Bay*, the first oceangoing vessel built at the nascent Medford shipyards, was launched in 1631.

Wood was also the only fuel. Householders resorted to the forests for cordwood with which to heat their homes and to cook. They cut the trees into sled lengths (eight to twelve feet) and hauled them during winter to their sheds in town. Logs were reduced to charcoal for use in early iron smelters east of the Fells, and in time wood fueled the world-famous rum distilleries in Medford and the kilns of the important brick industry.

At first the settlers reserved the Fells as common land subject to cutting regulations enacted as early as 1639 and reaffirmed periodically by new legislation as Charlestown was divided into smaller towns. For example, in 1689 the Malden town meeting voted "that no young trees under a foot round are to be felled for firewood under a penalty of paying five shillings for every such tree." At the same time, the common land was used for grazing, as was usual in the early towns. Marked by brands or by various ways of slashing and cropping the ears, herds of cattle and swine roamed the woods and browsed from the undergrowth until deep snow came. To clear the Fells of predators, a bounty of ten shilling for every wolf and two shillings for every fox was offered in 1635. Bears were taken in the area as late as 1735.

Eventually, the common land was apportioned to individual settlers, as was done in all the towns of the Bay Colony. People moved into the Fells and established farms. Some areas were parceled out as private woodlots. In 1694 Malden voted that "ye common shall be divided: bottom and top, its land and wood." By then the area east of Spot Pond was already the site of several farms, and there were scattered households elsewhere among the hills. In 1706 James Barrett owned a sawmill on Spot Pond Brook. Haywardsville, an industrial village, was built along this stream where it descends the Fells' eastern slope.

During the eighteenth and nineteenth centuries, farming and timbering continued. Today there are still stone walls running through the Fells, delineating old fields and woodlots. Stands of Atlantic white-cedar were cut for shingles and fence posts, and groves of white birch went to make pegs for fastening on the soles of boots and shoes. Quarries for granite were established. From the 1830s through the 1870s, quarrymen excavated a pit for dark building stone and gravel northwest of Pine Hill; some of this gravel was used for paths in the new Boston Public Garden and the adjacent Boston Common. In 1881 F.W. Morandi sunk a mine shaft a half-mile south of the present-day Sheepfold parking area and extracted minuscule quantities of gold and silver. As at many New England ponds, companies cut blocks of ice from Spot and Wright's ponds for use in icebox refrigerators.

By the middle of the nineteenth century, the Fells were called the Five Mile Woods, although many parts had been cut repeatedly or cleared for fields and pasture. The "uncouth wilderness" had become a picturesque location for outings and even residential development. In the 1840s speculators subdivided the shore of Spot Pond into expensive waterfront lots. Wealthy families built summer homes or even year-round residences, of which the only one remaining is John Botume's stone house in the Italianate style characterized by a shallow, projecting hip roof, large jig-work brackets under the eaves, and tall windows. Now on the National Register of Historic Places, it is used as the park headquarters.

The Fells were also eyed by public authorities as a good source of water. In 1870 Spot Pond was designated the water supply for Malden, Medford, and Melrose, and later that decade the town of Winchester dammed the valleys in the western Fells to create three reservoirs. In 1898 the Metropolitan Water and Sewerage Board (now the Massachusetts Water Resources Authority) incorporated Spot Pond into its far-flung system. There are other, smaller reservoirs in the Fells atop Bear Hill and Cairn Hill, to which water from as far as Quabbin Reservoir in central Massachusetts is pumped, and from which it is distributed by gravity to some of the forty-six towns and cities served by the system.

As the pace of development accelerated in the Boston region during the second half of the nineteenth century, the movement to set aside the rugged highlands in Medford, Malden, Winchester, Stoneham, and

Melrose for a big public park got underway and slowly gained momentum. Among the first to advocate the idea was Elizur Wright, an actuary, professor of mathematics, and champion of legislative reforms that required life-insurance companies to maintain adequate reserves and to pay back cash for lapsed policies. To promote conservation of the area, Wright bought property near Pine Hill, atop which Wright's Tower, paid for by his descendants, was built by workers of the Civilian Conservation Corps during the Great Depression. Wright worked successfully for passage of the Public Domain Act by the Massachusetts legislature in 1882. This law authorized municipalities to establish public parks and forests, thus in some ways re-creating the commons of two centuries earlier. The evocative name "Middlesex Fells" — the word "fells" means an elevated, wild moor — was coined as part of the conservation effort. It was first used in 1879 in an article for the *Boston Herald* urging acquisition of the area for a huge park. With support from local public domain clubs, The Trustees of Reservations, the Appalachian Mountain Club, and other groups, the state legislature created the Metropolitan Parks Commission (now the Metropolitan District Commission) in 1893. During the next few years, the parks commission bought thousands of acres of rocky hills and hollows traversed by the walks described in this chapter.

≈        ≈        ≈        ≈

**PUBLIC TRANSIT TO THE EASTERN FELLS:** From **Malden Station** on the MBTA's Orange Line, take Bus 99. Rather than worrying about where to get off, I suggest you ride all the way to the end of the line at the Boston Regional Medical Center. Stay on the bus while it reloads and starts back toward Malden, then get off at the John W. Flynn Memorial Rink, which is the first stop. After your walk, catch the bus at the same place.

≈        ≈        ≈        ≈

**AUTOMOBILE DIRECTIONS TO THE EASTERN FELLS:** This area is located mostly in Medford and Melrose. (See •10a on **Map 1** on page 6, and also the upper panel of **Map 16** at right.)

**To the eastern Fells from Interstate 93:** Leave I-93 at Exit 33 for Route 28 and the Fellsway West. At the top of the ramp there is a large traffic circle that spans the highway. Follow the signs for Route 28 North. Go just 0.5 mile, then turn right

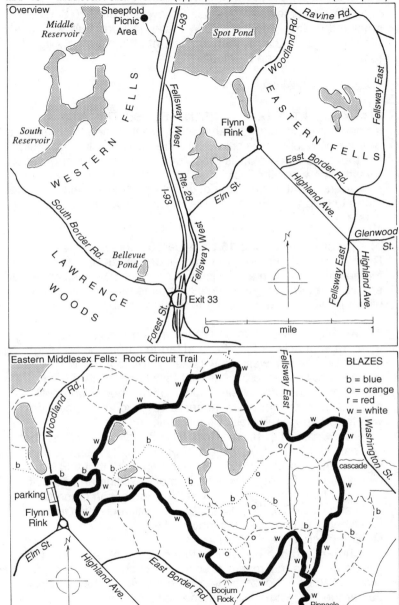

MAP 16 — Middlesex Fells: overview (upper panel) and Rock Circuit Trail (lower panel)

**Overview**

Middle Reservoir

Sheepfold Picnic Area

Spot Pond

I-93

Woodland Rd.

Ravine Rd.

W E S T E R N   F E L L S

E A S T E R N   F E L L S

Fellsway West

Rte. 28

Flynn Rink

South Reservoir

Fellsway East

East Border Rd.

Highland Ave.

Elm St.

I-93

Glenwood St.

South Border Rd.

Bellevue Pond

Fellsway West

Fellsway East

Highland Ave.

L A W R E N C E

W O O D S

Forest St.

Exit 33

N

0    mile    1

**Eastern Middlesex Fells: Rock Circuit Trail**

BLAZES

b = blue
o = orange
r = red
w = white

Woodland Rd.

Fellsway East

Washington St.

cascade

parking

Flynn Rink

Elm St.

Highland Ave.

East Border Rd.

Boojum Rock

Pinnacle Rock

N

0    mile    0.5

103

onto Elm Street toward Melrose. Follow Elm Street 0.6 mile to a small rotary, then turn left onto Woodland Road. Follow Woodland Road just 0.3 mile, then turn left into the large parking lot for the John W. Flynn Memorial Rink.

≈      ≈      ≈      ≈

**WALKING AT THE EASTERN FELLS:** This area is among the most rugged in the Boston region, and accordingly a preliminary caution is in order. If you're up for a billy-goat walk, the trail described below is great fun, but don't go during wet or icy weather, when the rocks may be slippery. If you fall and injure yourself badly, you cannot count on someone else coming along to help you. For a less demanding excursion, go to the western Fells.

The lower panel of **Map 16** on page 103 shows the 4-mile **Rock Circuit Trail**. Marked with white blazes, this strenuous footpath is almost a practical joke — or at any rate, a stunt — that entails clambering from one rocky knob to the next, many of which provide good views of the Boston basin.

**To start,** go to the north end of the parking lot at the John W. Flynn Memorial Rink (i.e., the end farthest from the building), then follow the sidewalk a few dozen yards to a row of wooden posts. With caution, cross the motorway and follow a blue-blazed path (the Cross Fells Trail) into the woods and uphill along a fire road for several hundred yards to an intersection with the white-blazed Rock Circuit Trail.

As shown on Map 16, the Rock Circuit Trail forms a loop that you can, of course, follow in either direction. I recommend going counterclockwise, or that is, to the right, so that you start (while you are fresh) with the trail's more exciting and difficult half. But first, take a good look at the intersection of the Cross Fells and Rock Circuit trails, so that you will recognize this junction when you complete the loop and want to return to your starting place at the Flynn Rink.

In the Fells' broken terrain, verbal directions cannot usefully supplement the trail markers, so just follow the white blazes closely. When in doubt, bear in mind that the trail strings together the biggest rocks. In some sections, particularly on the trail's southern arc, blazes are infrequent, so that following the path becomes a game of sorts. After crossing a road (the Fellsway East), there is a spur trail leading to Pinnacle Rock, an immense solitary mass near a tower with transmission dishes. And at the easternmost edge of the Fells, the trail follows the rim of cliffs overlooking the Melrose Valley, before circling back across the Fellsway East and through the highlands. If you get lost or get tired, you can always use the system of fire roads that are also shown on the map.

≈

≈    ≈    ≈    ≈

≈

## WESTERN MIDDLESEX FELLS

IT CAME WITH A RUMBLING NOISE, or low murmur like unto remote thunder. As the noise approached nearer, the earth began to shake and came at length with that violence as caused platters and dishes, and such like things as stood upon shelves, to clatter and fall down; yea, persons were afraid of the houses themselves, so powerful is the mighty hand of the Lord as to make both the earth and sea to shake, and the mountains to tremble before Him when He pleases; and who can stay His hand?

So wrote William Bradford, leader of the Pilgrims and governor of the Plymouth Colony, when he described an earthquake that struck eastern Massachusetts in 1638. A worse quake — one that toppled many chimneys and masonry gables in Boston — occurred in 1755. Such accounts are one way to recall the fact that seismic tremors are by no means rare events in eastern Massachusetts. In fact, Boston ranks in the middle range for risk of damage from earthquakes. Apart from descriptions of past quakes, another good way to imagine the earthly convulsions that have shaken the Boston region is to take a walk in the Middlesex Fells, where the consequences of ancient volcanic activity and ongoing movements in the earth's crust are readily apparent in the landscape.

The oldest rocks in the Fells originated more than a billion years ago as marine sediments scoured from land. Carried by wind and by rivers to the ocean, or eroded from the shore by waves, the sediments were deposited in a shallow sea. As the sediments accumulated, they were compacted by their own weight into sedimentary rock. Between 500 and 200 million years ago, the sedimentary strata were bowed and lifted above sea level, then folded like an accordion — all as a part of the same process that produced the Appalachian Mountains. In the heat and pressure, the sedimentary strata changed into metasedimentary rocks, or that is, metamorphic rocks of sedimentary origin.

Intermixed with the metasedimentary rocks are igneous masses. Originating more than 600 million years ago, the igneous rocks are the remains of magma that intruded into the sedimentary strata, in some places flowing out over them. The Lynn Volcanics (as the dramatic rocks in the southeastern Fells are called) have a fine-grained texture. The small crystals indicate that the magma cooled quickly at or near the surface. In contrast, the Dedham Granodiorites (as the rocks in the northwestern and southwestern Fells are called) have crystals ranging from medium to coarse, indicating that the magma cooled slowly beneath the earth's surface. These rocks include light-colored granite, dark-colored diorite, and a combination of the two — as the name *granodiorite* is supposed to indicate.

Crossing the Fells are so-called *dikes* indicating where, between 225 and 190 million years ago, magma rose through cracks in the older material and cooled quickly into dark, fine-grained rock of varied composition. Dikes are visually distinct from the rock that sandwiches them on either side. They can range from a few inches in width to many feet, and they may be as much as half a mile long. In the Fells, the dikes generally run east and west. Some have been quarried for building stone and gravel. One dike is conspicuously apparent in the wall of the highway cut where Interstate 93 first enters the Fells from the south. Another dike, not as hard as the rock through which it intruded, has deteriorated and now forms the valley where Spot Pond Brook drains eastward out of Spot Pond.

One striking feature of the Fells is the steep bluff that runs along the southern border of the highlands, where the land toward Boston has sheared and dropped little by little. A good vantage point from which to appreciate this process is Wright's Tower at Pine Hill, located on the Skyline Trail just west of Bellevue Pond. From the tower, the Boston basin stretches south fifteen miles to the Blue Hills, visible on the horizon to the right of the downtown skyscrapers. From the coast the lowland extends west twelve miles to Prospect Hill in Waltham. The smaller hills that rise in places from the basin floor are mostly masses of clay and gravel deposited relatively recently by the last continental glacier. The basin's sunken profile is partly the result of erosion of the softer metasedimentary rocks (principally slate) that compose the basin's floor. But the lowland has also dropped considerably in a series of block faults. The poor bearing strength of the slate has caused pieces of the basin floor to settle over the eons. The area of settlement includes not only metropolitan Boston but also Massachusetts Bay. Each slight drop produces earth tremors, which have continued to present times. The abrupt slope at the foot of the observation tower is one of the fault scarps, which can be seen stretching east toward the ocean and curving west and south through Arlington Heights, Belmont Hill, and Waltham before bending east through the Blue Hills to close the giant ring of bluffs circling the Boston basin on all landward sides.

≈      ≈      ≈      ≈

**PUBLIC TRANSIT TO THE WESTERN FELLS:** From **Wellington Station** on the MBTA's Orange Line, take Bus 100. Rather than worrying about where to get off, I suggest you ride all the way to the end of the line at the intersection of Elm Street and the Fellsway next to Interstate 93. Stay on the bus while it waits briefly before starting back toward Wellington, then get off at South Border Road, which is the first stop. After your walk, catch the bus at the same place.

To join the walk shown on **Map 17** on page 109, follow South Border Road a quarter-mile to the Fells entrance on the right at Bellevue Pond and Wright's Tower. Follow the dirt Quarry Road to the right of the pond. About a hundred yards beyond a stone parapet at the far end of the pond, turn right uphill on the white-blazed **Skyline Trail**. But first, take a good look at this spot so that you will know it when you eventually complete the circuit.

≈      ≈      ≈      ≈

**AUTOMOBILE DIRECTIONS TO THE WESTERN FELLS:** This area is located mostly in Winchester, Stoneham, and Medford. (See •10b on **Map 1** on page 6, and also the upper panel of **Map 16** on page 103.)

**To the western Fells from Interstate 93:** Leave I-93 at Exit 33 for Route 28 and the Fellsway West. At the top of the ramp there is a large traffic circle that spans the highway. Follow the signs for Route 28 North. Go 1.5 miles and then, after passing under the highway, turn left into the Sheepfold Picnic Area. Follow the entrance road uphill to the parking lot.

If the lots at the Sheepfold Picnic Area are full, you can try parking at Bellevue Pond at the southern end of the Fells. To do so, return to the traffic circle atop the highway, and from there follow the sign for South Border Road and Winchester. Go 0.2 mile to a parking lot on the right. If it too is full or if it is closed, there are usually spaces along the side of the road beyond the parking lot. Using **Map 17** on page 109, you can easily pick up the white-blazed **Skyline Trail** as it passes nearby.

≈ · ≈ ≈ ≈

**WALKING AT THE WESTERN FELLS:** There is such a labyrinth of trails at the Middlesex Fells that the best approach is to follow one of the blazed routes, such as those described below. The blazes will also steer you clear of areas which, although they are shown on the maps, are off limits to visitors because they border the Winchester reservoirs or are privately owned. For each walk, there are directions that will help you to get started, but in the Fells' wooded, broken terrain, verbal descriptions cannot usefully augment the guidance provided by the blazes and the maps. If you lose track of the blazes, retrace your steps until you again pick up your trail and eventually complete whichever loop you are following.

**Map 17** at right shows the 7-mile **Skyline Trail**. This strenuous footpath is marked with white blazes that lead up and down — and up and down again and again and again — across the rocky hills and hollows that make the Fells such a fascinating area. A few of the higher hills provide distant views. In particular, the stone tower at Pine Hill overlooks the Boston basin to the south. At the northern end of the Fells, a spur trail leads to another tower at Bear Hill.

**To start** on the Skyline Trail, go to the sign board at the end of the main parking lot at the Sheepfold Picnic Area. Follow a worn track across the meadow. After crossing a paved soapbox derby track, join the white-blazed Skyline Trail as it enters the woods half-left, in the angle created by the intersection of two wider paths. Continue on the white-blazed path through the woods to a ledge overlooking Winchester's North Reservoir.

This should at least get you underway. Only once does the trail emerge from the woods to pass around the tip of North Reservoir on a residential street. Note that occasionally the white-blazed Skyline Trail is congruent with the shorter and easier Reservoir Trail, marked with orange blazes and shown on **Map 18** on page 110 — and to which you can switch if you get tired. Eventually, at the southern edge of the Fells, the Skyline Trail passes Wright's Tower, where there are good views over the Boston basin, as discussed on page 106.

At the very end of the Skyline Trail, you will descend to a T-intersection in front of a chainlink fence, where you should bear right to return to the Sheepfold Picnic Area.

MAP 17 — Western Middlesex Fells: Skyline Trail

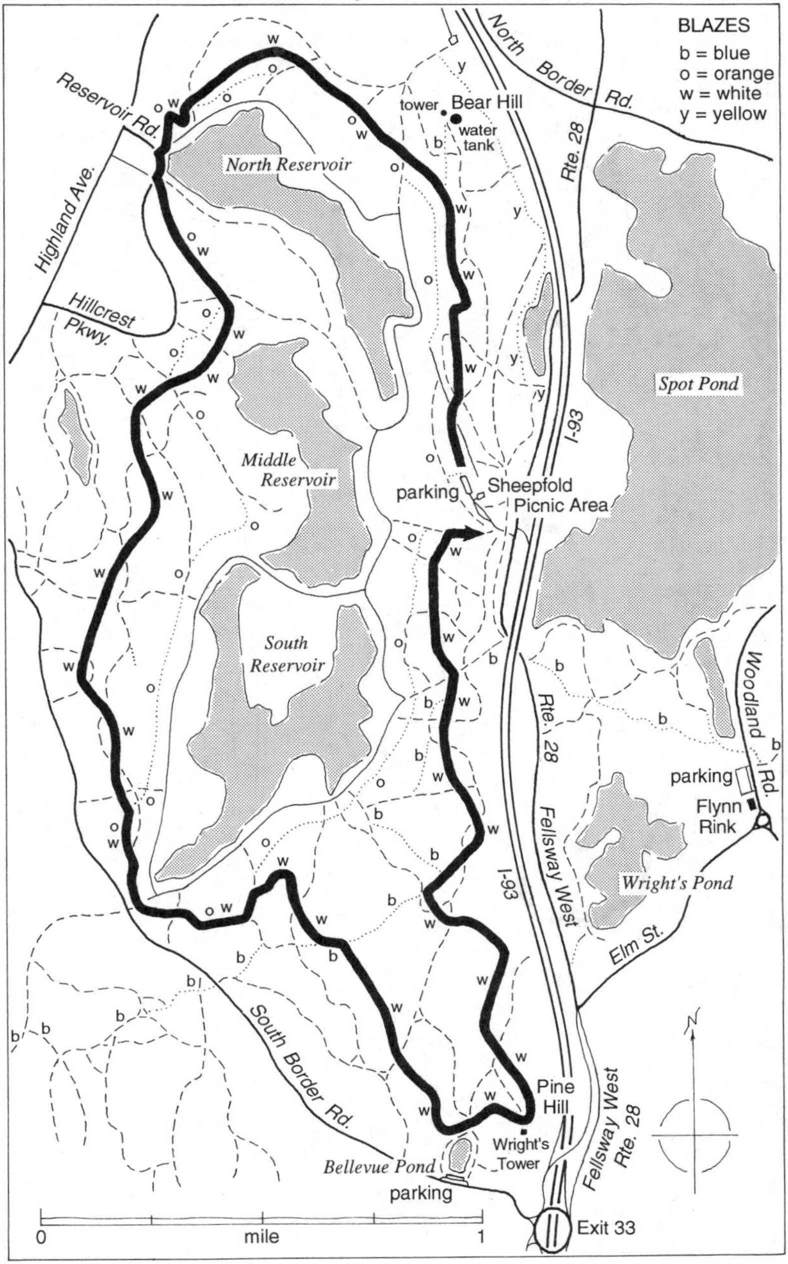

BLAZES

b = blue
o = orange
w = white
y = yellow

North Border Rd.

Reservoir Rd.

w
o
w
o
tower
Bear Hill
water tank
b

Highland Ave.

North Reservoir

o
w

Hillcrest Pkwy.

o
w
w
w
o

Rte. 28

Spot Pond

Middle Reservoir

o

y
w
w
w
o
w

parking
Sheepfold Picnic Area
w

I-93

South Reservoir

w
o
w
o
w
o

o
w
b
w
b
o
w
b
w

Woodland Rd.

parking
Flynn Rink

b
o
w
b

Wright's Pond

o w
w
b
b
b
w
w

Rte. 28

Fellsway West

Elm St.

b
b
b
b

South Border Rd.

w
w
w
w
w

I-93

N

Pine Hill

w
w
w

Wright's Tower

Bellevue Pond
parking

Fellsway West
Rte. 28

Exit 33

0        mile        1

109

MAP 18 — Western Middlesex Fells:  Reservoir Trail

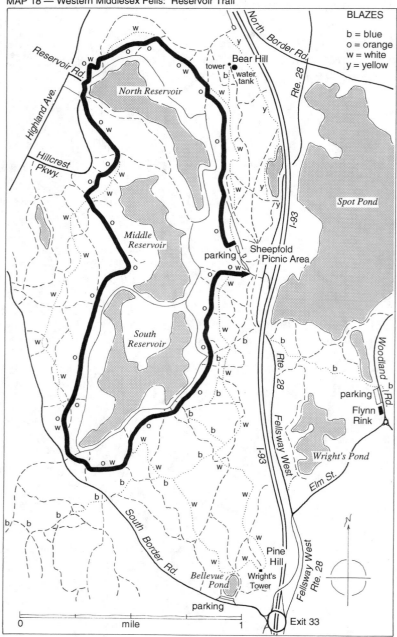

**Map 18** at left shows the 5.2-mile **Reservoir Trail**. Marked with orange blazes, it alternates between easy fire roads and more rugged footpaths. (The Reservoir Trail's oblong orange blazes should not be confused with the orange square mountain-bike blazes, displaying a bicycle emblem.)

**To start** on the Reservoir Trail, go to the sign board at the end of the main parking lot at the Sheepfold Picnic Area. Walk toward the left directly downhill across the grass. Pick-up the orange-blazed path a dozen yards into the woods and follow it right. Continue along the edge of the woods, then bear left on a paved soapbox derby track. At the track's end, bear left to follow the orange-blazed foot trail through the woods and around the loop. Only once does the trail emerge from the woods to pass around the tip of North Reservoir on a residential street.

Note that occasionally the orange-blazed Reservoir Trail is congruent with the longer and more difficult Skyline Trail, marked with white blazes and shown on **Map 17** on page 109.

At the end of the Reservoir Trail, follow the orange blazes counterclockwise around a chainlink enclosure and back to the Sheepfold meadow where you started.

# 11

# MINUTEMAN BIKEWAY

Ten miles long (16 kilometers), the paved Minuteman Bikeway runs through Arlington, Lexington, and Bedford northwest of Boston. The route is shown on **Maps 19 and 20** on pages 120-121. Another 1.5 miles of hike-bike path, called the Linear Park or Seven Hills Park, joins the eastern end of the Minuteman Bikeway and continues through Cambridge into Somerville. Eventually, the trail may extend all the way to Boston. And from the other end of the bikeway in Bedford, a rough, muddy path continues west along the old railbed for 4 miles to Concord Center, but this section is not recommended. Much better is a path — the Narrow-Gauge Rail-Trail — that runs north 3 miles from Bedford to the boundary with Billerica. Paved with hard-packed stone dust, it may some day go all the way to Billerica Center.

The Minuteman Bikeway is open from 5 A.M. to 9 P.M. year-round. Dogs must be leashed to avoid accidents with cyclists. In turn, cyclists should ride single file and yield as necessary.

The main place of interest along the bikeway is Lexington Center, site of the Battle of Lexington on April 19, 1775. The **Lexington Visitor Center** is open daily from 9 A. M. to 5 P. M., or until 4 in the winter; telephone (781) 862-1450. Next door is the colonial **Buckman Tavern**, shown on page 117. It is open for tours from early March through early December. The hours vary with the seasons. An admission fee is charged. For information, telephone (781) 862-5598.

For directions via public transit to the Minuteman Bikeway, please turn to page 118. Automobile directions to the eastern trailhead at Arlington start on page 119. Directions to the western trailhead at Bedford are on page 122.

---

DESPITE ITS NAME, the Minuteman Bikeway has only a tangential link with the events of April 19, 1775. Running along a railroad bed built three-quarters of a century after the outbreak of the Revolution, the trail at one point passes Lexington Green, where colonial militia first opposed the British march to Concord — and where later in the day the British rallied during their retreat to Charlestown. The trail also goes through Arlington Center, which saw fierce fighting. But for the most part, the bikeway does not recall the revolutionary period. Instead, it cuts a scenic cross-section through the suburbs, showing their patchwork pattern of old and new neighborhoods, ponds, woods and wetlands. For the real revolutionary Battle Road, you should drive along Massachusetts Avenue and visit Minute Man National Historical Park in Lincoln and Concord, as discussed in Chapter 12.

ON SEPTEMBER 23, 1844, citizens of present-day Arlington (then called West Cambridge) met to explore the feasibility of a railroad from their town east to Cambridge proper, where a junction could be made with the recently-built Fitchburg Railroad into Boston. With support from Lexington, proponents of the plan obtained a charter from the state legislature. Construction went quickly, and in September 1846 passenger and freight service began on the 6.6-mile Lexington and West Cambridge Railroad. Although the line was owned by local investors, it was operated by the Fitchburg Railroad under a ten-year lease that was not renewed. Disappointed with the small return on their investment, the railroad's backers bought engines and rolling stock and hired their own managers to run the line as a civic enterprise. But after another ten years — with the company's balance sheet in the red and just $110 in the cash account — the investors sold their stock to a more experienced partnership.

In 1870 the Boston and Lowell Railroad bought the line and, five years later, extended the right-of-way through Bedford to Concord. For a period the line made money transporting materials for construction of the Massachusetts State Penitentiary. Other improvements included a branch built on the abandoned right-of-way of the narrow-gauge Billerica and Bedford Railroad. (At Billerica there was a connection with the Boston and Lowell's main line.) Eight trains daily ran through Arlington, Lexington, and Bedford to Concord. A promotional booklet called *Summer Saunterings by the B&L* boasted, "There are few railroads in the country of equal length which pass so many grandly historic localities," including Arlington (population 4100), Lexington (2460), Bedford (931), and Concord (3922). The last stop, perhaps in more senses than one, was Prison Station. No doubt more agreeable accommodations were found at Bedford Springs, "with its fine summer hotel and beautiful surroundings."

In 1887 the Boston & Lowell was absorbed into the Boston & Maine, which also acquired the Fitchburg Railroad in 1900. At the turn of the century, thirty-eight trains per day ran through Arlington, bringing in bulk supplies like coal and lumber and taking out farm products and a surprising variety of manufactured goods, including tools, oval picture frames, and piano casings. Trains carried ice cut from Spy Pond, flour from local mills, and fresh vegetables from market gardens that operated year-round in greenhouses. For passengers on the Lexington Branch, as the line was called, there were commuter trains with names like the Minuteman, the Patriot, and the Paul Revere.

In the late 1920s, however, the Boston & Maine began to eliminate trains as automobile ownership and trucking increased. Passenger service west of Bedford was terminated on the Lexington Branch. Old industries closed and were not replaced by businesses that used the railroad. Gasoline rationing during World War II provided a temporary stimulus for the Lexington Branch, but afterwards business fell off again. The decline in ridership led to deteriorating equipment, increased fares, and further loss of passengers. Stops were eliminated and stations torn down. By the mid-1960s, passenger service on the Lexington Branch consisted of one self-propelled diesel car into Boston in the morning and back out again in the late afternoon — and even that was made possible only by a subsidy from the MBTA, which eventually bought all the Boston & Maine lines in eastern Massachusetts. Finally, after a severe snowstorm early in 1977, the bankrupt Boston & Maine, which was still running the railroads for the MBTA, removed the passenger coach from the Lexington Branch and never brought it back. Freight trains ran until 1980, when the right-of-way was severed so that part of it could be used for extension of the MBTA's Red Line to Alewife. For the railroad west of Alewife, local planners advocated its conversion to a commuter bikeway. The MBTA approved the proposal, subject to its power to reclaim the right-of-way for commuter rail use if necessary in the future. The bikeway project was finally allowed to go ahead when the Interstate Commerce Commission declared the line to be abandoned. Funded by $2 million from the Commonwealth of Massachusetts, construction of the bikeway began in 1991 and was completed two years later.

THERE ARE SEVERAL points of interest along the trail. East of Arlington Center is **Spy Pond**, where at the beginning of the twentieth century, visitors arrived by train to stay at the resort-style Spy Pond Hotel. In the early years of the railroad, when an icebox was literally just that, the Boston Ice Company cut the pond's frozen surface into slabs the size of mattresses. Men with pikes and horses shod with cleated shoes pulled the blocks from the water and hauled them ashore. Bordering the pond were rows of huge icehouses where the company stored the slabs before shipping them by railroad into Charlestown. For decades during the middle of the nineteenth century, ice was even a major export from New England. Packed tightly in straw for insulation, the blocks were shipped throughout the southern states and even as far as South America and India. Under a series of companies, the ice houses at Spy Pond continued to be used well into the twentieth century, storing locally-cut ice or, during mild winters, ice from New Hampshire. Across the tracks from the pond was a factory for making ice tools. The last of the ice houses burned in the 1930s and the waterfront land was converted to park use.

At **Arlington Center** there is the restored **Jefferson Cutter House**, built in 1830 and moved here in 1989. It is now a museum for local artists, including Arlington sculptor Cyrus Dallin. The Cutter House is open daily from noon to four o'clock. That Arlington Center was still a village when the railroad was built can be surmised from the fact the line runs at grade through the major intersection in the middle of town. Even as recently as the mid-1940s, East Arlington near Alewife was the site of fields and greenhouses used for market gardening.

At the time of the Revolution, Arlington was called Menotomy. During the British retreat on April 19, 1775, the heaviest fighting occurred at the western approaches to the village late in the afternoon. By then the British had been reinforced. The number of minutemen had also swelled as companies continued to arrive from outlying towns. Over 5,000 troops fought, and each side lost more men at Menotomy than at any other place along the Battle Road.

In Lexington the bikeway is bordered for a period by the **Great Meadows** (different from the Great Meadows in Concord discussed in Chapter 14). Peat was dug here until the town of Arlington bought the area in 1873 and set the meadows aside as a watershed for the town reservoir. The meadows now are a local conservation area where there is a complex network of trails. For Arlington residents, the bikeway provides convenient access to their town's conservation land in Lexington.

In **Lexington Center** the trail passes through the covered train shed of the old depot, built in 1873. Nearby is the **Lexington Visitor Center**, where a diorama shows the Battle of Lexington. The staff at the visitor center can tell you about other sites, including the adjacent **Buckman Tavern** — well worth touring — and the more distant **Hancock-Clarke House** and **Munroe Tavern**. Across Bedford

Street from the Buckman Tavern is **Lexington Common**, also called the **Battle Green**, where the militiamen mustered, and where eight of them died or received fatal wounds in the confrontation that marked the beginning of open war between the British and provincial forces.

Finally, at **Bedford Station** there is a substantial depot including old warehouses. Bedford Depot Park has a Budd Company diesel commuter coach of the kind that last operated on the line. Formerly, the railroad continued to Concord, and another branch ran northward to Billerica. This latter line occupied the abandoned right-of-way of the Billerica and Bedford Railroad, which in the late 1870s was the nation's first narrow-gauge common carrier. (Now the roadbed has been converted to the Narrow-Gauge Rail-Trail, extending three miles to the boundary with Billerica.) Of course, trains could not transfer to or from the Billerica line until it was acquired by the Boston & Lowell, which installed standard gauge tracks in 1885.

$$\approx \qquad \approx \qquad \approx \qquad \approx$$

**PUBLIC TRANSIT:** There are two possibilities. One is to take the MBTA's Red Line to **Davis Square** in Somerville and from there follow the Linear Park west to the Minuteman Bikeway at Alewife Station. The other is to take the Red Line directly to **Alewife Station** and begin there. The directions below will get you started at each place.

**To start at Davis Square**, locate the Linear Park trailhead behind the MBTA station next to the Somerville Theater. The trailhead is marked by tall pylons, one of which is topped by a clock and sign saying *Seven Hills Park*. Follow the path west, in the process crossing Massachusetts Avenue and bearing right halfway around a playing field. After passing under Route 2, circle counter-clockwise halfway around the huge Alewife Station. Join the Minuteman Bikeway at a gate representing a waving flag. Pass massive stones carved with Alewives and follow the bikeway west.

**To start at Alewife Station**, bear half-right after exiting through the turnstiles. Follow a long ramp and a short flight of stairs straight to the street. Turn right across the entrance to the Passenger Drop Off/Pick Up. With the building on the right, follow the sidewalk to the corner, and from there continue straight across the street. Join the Minuteman Bikeway at a gate representing a waving flag. Pass massive stones carved with Alewives and follow the bikeway west.

≈     ≈     ≈     ≈

**AUTOMOBILE DIRECTIONS TO THE EASTERN TRAILHEAD:** The eastern end of the Minuteman Bikeway is near the Arlington-Cambridge boundary behind the MBTA's Alewife Station. (See •11a on **Map 1** on page 6, and also panel #3 of **Maps 19 and 20** on pages 120-121.)

*For a small fee,* you can park all day in the **Alewife Station garage.** After parking, descend to ground level, then locate the entrance to the Passenger Drop Off/Pick Up. With the building on the right, follow the sidewalk to the corner. With caution, cross the street and join the bikeway, marked by a gate representing a waving flag and — soon after that — by massive stone blocks carved with alewives.

*To park free of charge* (but only for two hours), use the lot at **Thorndike Field**.

Several approaches to Alewife Station and Thorndike Field are described below.

**To Alewife Station or Thorndike Field from Boston:** Follow Storrow Drive west along the Charles River toward Newton and Arlington. After passing Harvard University, take the exit for **Route 2** toward Arlington. In quick succession, cross the Eliot Bridge, then bear right, then left for Route 2 westbound (the Fresh Pond and Alewife Brook parkways). Go 2 miles to **Alewife Station** on the left.

For **Thorndike Field**, continue on Route 2 *past* Alewife Station, then bear left to follow Route 2 west for 0.5 mile. Leave Route 2 at Exit 60 for Lake Street and East Arlington. At the bottom of the ramp, turn right and go 0.5 mile to Margaret Street, which is also marked with a sign for Thorndike Field. (If you cross the bikeway, you have gone too far.) Turn right onto Margaret Street and follow it to the entrance for Thorndike Field on the left at the end of the street.

**To Alewife Station or Thorndike Field from Massachusetts Avenue:** Massachusetts Avenue and Route 16 (Alewife Brook Parkway) intersect at the boundary between Arlington and Cambridge. Follow Route 16 west 0.4 mile to its juncture with Route 2.

For **Alewife Station**, continue straight west on Route 16 for just 0.2 mile, then turn right into the station entrance.

MAP 19 — Minuteman Bikeway

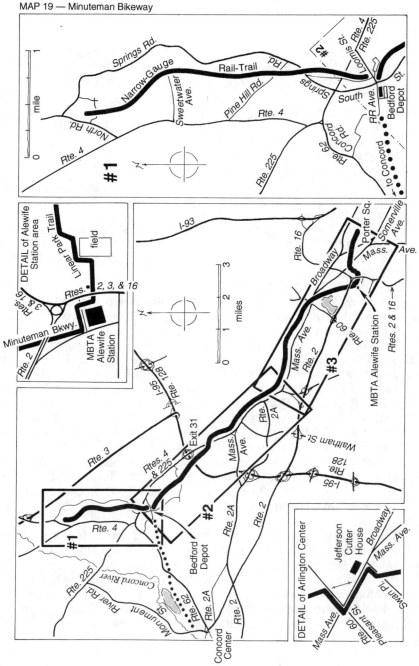

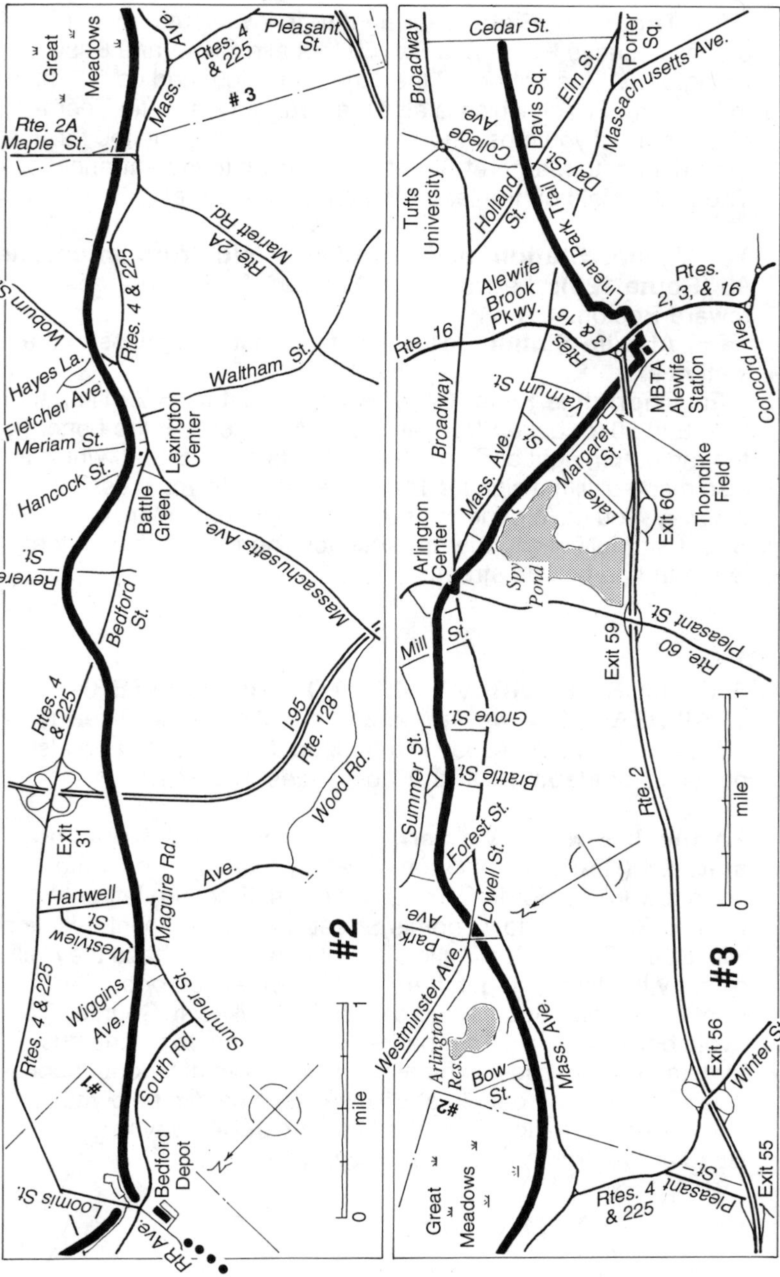

MAP 20 — Minuteman Bikeway

**#2**

**#3**

121

For **Thorndike Field**, bear right to follow Route 2 west for 0.5 mile. Leave Route 2 at Exit 60 for Lake Street and East Arlington. At the bottom of the ramp, turn right and go 0.5 mile to Margaret Street, which is also marked with a sign for Thorndike Field. (If you cross the bikeway, you have gone too far.) Turn right onto Margaret Street and follow it to the entrance for Thorndike Field on the left at the end of the street.

**To Alewife Station or Thorndike Field from Interstate 95 (Route 128):** Leave I-95 at Exit 29A for Route 2 east toward Boston.

For **Alewife Station**, follow Route 2 east for 6 miles to the station exit.

For **Thorndike Field**, follow Route 2 east for 5.7 miles, then take Exit 60 for Lake Street and East Arlington. At the bottom of the ramp, turn right and go 0.5 mile to Margaret Street, which is also marked with a sign for Thorndike Field. (If you cross the bikeway, you have gone too far.) Turn right onto Margaret Street and follow it to the entrance for Thorndike Field on the left at the end of the street.

≈  ≈  ≈  ≈

**AUTOMOBILE DIRECTIONS TO THE WESTERN TRAILHEAD:** The western end of the Minuteman Bikeway is located in Bedford. (See •11b on **Map 1** on page 6, and also panel #2 of **Maps 19 and 20** on pages 120-121.)

**To the bikeway's western end at Bedford from Interstate 95 (Route 128):** Leave I-95 at Exit 31B for Route 4 north toward Bedford. Go nearly 2 miles, then turn left onto Loomis Street. Follow Loomis Street 0.4 mile to an intersection with South Road. Parking lots are planned — perhaps they will exist by the time you get there — with entrances *opposite* the front of Bikeway Source and also *behind* Bikeway Source. To avoid being towed, do not park in spots reserved for the customers of businesses in the area. If you have any doubt about where to park, the people at Bikeway Source can help you.

The western trailhead for the Minuteman Bikeway is at South Road across from the front of Bikeway Source.

≈  ≈  ≈  ≈

**WALKING and BICYCLING:** The several panels of **Maps 19 and 20** on pages 120-121 show the 10-mile **Minuteman Bikeway** and also the extensions at each end. Panel #1 is farthest to the northwest, and panels #2 and #3 show segments that are progressively farther southeast, with overlap between each panel.

Once you are on the trail, the route is obvious. The paved path, signs, and bicycle-seat bollards show the way. The only possible difficulty is at Arlington Center, shown in the small corner panel of Map 19. The trend of the path as you arrive at Arlington Center will point to where you should resume after crossing several major streets at nearby traffic lights.

There are also **mileposts**. These indicate the distance traveled from each end. Thus, the numbers inscribed on opposite sides differ from each other. The numbers are carved in Roman numerals, with the V (for five) inexplicably upside down and the other symbols tilted sideways. Incidentally, when these mileposts were installed, the measurements were made from the Alewife end of the trail. Consequently, milepost 1 out of Bedford (incised on the reverse side of milepost 10 out of Alewife) occurs after only a few dozen yards.

From the Bedford end of the trail, a rough and muddy track follows the old railbed west 4 miles to Concord (as shown by the dotted line on Map 19). To reach this extension, simply follow Railroad Avenue for a few hundred yards, then continue straight where the road curves right. Another option is to switch to the **Narrow-Gauge Rail-Trail** north toward Billerica (shown on panel #1 of Map 19). The path does not yet extend all the way to Billerica Center. The trailhead is located on Loomis Street 125 yards north of the intersection with South Road and Railroad Avenue at Bedford Depot. The first few hundred yards are paved with asphalt; the rest is paved with hard-packed stone grit.

Finally, you may want to continue east from Alewife Station to Davis Square via the **Linear Park** (shown at the right end of panel #3 of Map 20). To do so, locate a sloping slab of concrete near the glassed-in escalator at Alewife. Go under Route 2 and past a smaller subway kiosk. Follow the path away from the station, to the left halfway around a playing field, and on to Davis Square. From the other side of Davis Square, the path continues for 0.6 mile to Cedar Street. In the future it may be run farther toward Boston.

# 12

# MINUTE MAN NATIONAL HISTORICAL PARK

**Map 21** on page 143 shows the Battle Road and Trail, stretching 8 miles (12.8 kilometers) from Lexington to Concord northwest of Boston. The purpose of the park is to preserve and re-create the setting of the opening conflict of the American Revolution. The route consists of several sections of the old road that have been restored more-or-less to their appearance in 1775, plus a hike-bike path that detours around other sections where the Battle Road is occupied by present-day Route 2A. From Meriam's Corner westward through Concord Center to the North Bridge, the route is simply a sidewalk bordering local roads.

The park is open from early morning until sunset year-round. Dogs must be kept on a short leash to avoid accidents with cyclists. In turn, cyclists should ride single file and yield as necessary.

The **Minute Man Visitor Center** is open daily from 9 A.M. to 5 P.M. mid-April through October, and from 9 to 4 the rest of the year. In addition, there are other important sites administered by the Park Service, including the **Captain William Smith House**, the **Hartwell Tavern** (shown at left), the **Wayside** (home of a militia leader and later of the Alcotts and Hawthornes), and the **North Bridge Visitor Center**. For schedules and other information, call the National Park Service at (978) 369-6993, extension 22.

Also worth seeing along the way are several other houses and museums, each managed by its own organization. The **Orchard House** was yet another home of the Alcotts; telephone (978) 369-4118. The **Concord Museum** has richly-furnished period rooms; telephone (978) 369-9609. Across the street from the Concord Museum is the **Ralph Waldo Emerson House**; telephone (978) 369-2236. Next to the North Bridge is the **Old Manse**, home of the Reverend William Emerson, Concord's patriot minister; telephone (978) 369-3909. All of these places are worth seeing, although you cannot possibly visit every site in a single day. Call beforehand for information on schedules and entrance fees.

For directions on getting to the park via public transit or automobile, please turn to page 141. Walking directions start page 142.

---

IN RESPONSE to the Boston Tea Party, which the British government saw as a direct challenge to its authority in Massachusetts, Parliament passed the Boston Port Bill and other coercive measures early in 1774. Called by Americans the Intolerable Acts, the legislation closed the port of Boston, annulled the colonial charter, and prohibited most town meetings throughout Massachusetts. The Intolerable Acts also established new courts more friendly to the Royal government and transferred political cases to England for trial. These and other provisions potentially affected all the colonies, which responded by convening the First Continental Congress. Not surprisingly, the reaction in Massachusetts was stronger still. Leading Whigs (they were the party in opposition to the conservative Tories) established local Committees of Correspondence to organize resistance throughout the province and to concert with like-minded groups in other colonies. In Massachusetts jurors refused to serve in the new courts, and the judges who presided were threatened and harassed. The ban against town meetings was ignored more often than not or circumvented by legalisms, such as claiming that meetings were a continuation of prior assemblies that had only temporarily adjourned. Also, the Whigs convened *county* meetings, where they proclaimed that the new British laws were a tyrannical abrogation of the colonists' ancestral rights of self-government. The Suffolk Resolves and similar resolutions adopted by other counties urged the people of Massachusetts to set up their own provincial government and to arm for its defense.

Meanwhile, in the summer of 1774, Thomas Gage, the commander in chief of British forces in North America, was appointed governor of Massachusetts, with instructions to reduce the province to obedience and peace. He had only himself to blame for this unhappy assignment; the Intolerable Acts were based on his own recommendations. One of his first strokes, designed to avoid bloodshed by disarming the colonists, occurred on September 1. In a sudden, successful sortie, British troops quartered in Boston seized New England's largest stock of gunpowder, stored in the Provincial Powderhouse that still stands today at Powderhouse Square, Somerville. Thousands of militiamen, some from as far as Connecticut, mustered in response to the British incursion, but the New Englanders were too late. The next day, a mob in Cambridge compelled prominent Tories to resign their government positions or to forswear enforcing the Intolerable Acts. At least two Tories were chased into Boston, never to return to their homes.

Also on September 1, General Gage issued an announcement for the Great and General Court (that is, the provincial legislature) to assemble on October 5. This was to be a routine session, except that it would be held in Salem as a slight to Boston. But because trouble was brewing, Gage canceled the assembly a week beforehand. The delegates met anyway and elected John Hancock to preside in Gage's place. Then they voted "to resolve themselves into a Provincial Congress" at a meeting to be held October 11 in Concord. When it convened, the Congress took over the government of Massachusetts. The delegates appointed a new treasurer to collect taxes, pointedly gave the governor's councilors ten days to resign (most already had), and established an executive Committee of Safety and a Committee of Supplies to oversee defense against British raids. The urgency of acquiring and protecting gunpowder and other military supplies became more acute when word reached Massachusetts that a ministerial Order in Council had been issued in London, prohibiting the export of munitions to the colonies.

As the provincial government prepared to defend the hinterland, General Gage concentrated his forces in Boston. There Paul Revere — silversmith, Whig activist, courier, and indefatigable joiner of Patriot associations — helped organize a group to watch British troops and to alert the countryside if they mounted an expedition. In December Revere rode to Portsmouth, New Hampshire to warn the local Committee of Correspondence that the British were planning to seize the powder and cannon at Fort William and Mary overlooking the harbor. In response militiamen overawed the fort's token garrison and removed about a hundred barrels of gunpowder, sixteen cannon, and sixty muskets.

Another incident, very different from what happened later at Lexington and Concord, occurred on Sunday, February 26, 1775. The British thwarted American snoops by seizing three of them, then quickly sailed to Marblehead to confiscate naval guns that were being converted to fieldpieces at Salem. Surprised on their Sabbath, the unarmed townsfolk nonetheless delayed the British, who were led by Lieutenant Colonel Alexander Leslie. Unwilling to order his troops to fire, and aware also that militiamen were mustering, Leslie compromised by agreeing to a token march in and out of Salem. Heaped with ridicule, the troops returned to their transport after a fruitless expedition and humiliating confrontation.

Tension increased with the approach of the campaigning season in the spring of 1775. Gage adhered to his intention of seizing provincial munitions — if he could get at them. Not altogether successfully disguised, two British officers scouted the road to Worcester but concluded that the goal was so far that surprise was impossible. In March the same two men went to Concord, which they found to be an armed camp where large quantities of munitions were kept. While dining at the home of a Tory named Daniel Bliss, the officers and their host received a threatening message and so all three men abruptly left town. On the way to Boston, Bliss showed the spies the best route to Concord through Lexington, Menotomy (as present-day Arlington was called then), and Cambridge.

Gage also received reports about Concord from other Loyalists, one of whom sent a detailed inventory of munitions and a building-by-building account of where they were stored. On the basis of these various reports, Gage selected Concord as the target for his next mission. In early April he ordered Lieutenant Colonel Francis Smith, a mature and prudent though perhaps unenergetic officer, to march "with the utmost expedition and secrecy to Concord, where you will seize and destroy all the Artillery, Ammunition, Provisions, Tents, Small Arms, and all Military stores whatever."

The colonists too prepared for action. The Provincial Congress collected stocks of arms and powder and directed all men between the ages of sixteen and fifty to enlist in their local militia. Older men formed a reserve. To help purge the militia of Tory influence, the men elected their officers. The Congress further recommended that all Massachusetts towns organize at least one quarter of their militia into special companies of minutemen prepared to respond "at the shortest notice" to a system of alarms and express riders. Much the same thing had been done before during times of danger. In town meetings, the people voted to tax themselves to purchase ammunition and equipment, including muskets for those who had none. In a few towns Whigs of large means donated funds. Some individuals were equipped with bayonets and cartridge boxes, and some companies had fifers, drummers, and standard bearers. The men drilled two, three, and even four times a week, and also practiced marksmanship and volleying. They agreed on places for mustering and signals of alarm, including bells, repeated gunshots, and bonfires. Also, riders were designated to carry the alarm from town to town. Among both Whigs and their opponents, many men observed that large preparations on both sides made bloodshed inevitable.

In Boston General Gage could not hope to keep secret the fact that his troops were preparing for the field. Indeed, to condition the men and to accustom the populace to a pattern of false alarms, he sent regiments out on short marches west of the city. After learning that British officers had been ordered to scout the road through Cambridge, Menotomy, and Lexington, the few Whig leaders who still remained in Boston, including

Dr. Joseph Warren, guessed that the regulars would strike at Concord on Sunday, April 9. On Saturday Warren sent Paul Revere to carry a warning to the Provincial Congress, which was then sitting in Concord. Although no raid occurred the next day, the Whig leaders were convinced that an expedition was imminent. Parliament had recently declared Massachusetts to be in a "state of rebellion," and the province had learned that the king and his cabinet had ordered General Gage to arrest the insurrection's key men. Even though Gage took no steps to seize Whig leaders, the possibility existed that they were targets of the expected sortie. The Provincial Congress adjourned for three weeks, its members left town, and the people of Concord started moving munitions to scattered sites in the countryside and to other communities.

A week later Revere rode out to Lexington to warn John Hancock and Samuel Adams, who were staying at the home of the Reverend Jonas Clarke, that eleven elite regiments of light infantry and grenadiers had been relieved of all duties, probably in preparation for some special use. As he returned to Boston, Revere met with confederates in Cambridge and Charlestown to work out a plan for lantern signals from the steeple of Old North Church. This fall-back method of communication was necessary in case the regulars suddenly marched from Boston in the middle of the night, when British guards could block Whig couriers attempting to leave via the city's two exits. (At that time, of course, Boston was nearly isolated on a peninsula joined to Roxbury by a narrow neck; there was also a ferry crossing to Charlestown.)

On Tuesday, April 18, General Gage put his plan into effect. In the morning groups of British officers and sergeants, all on horseback, left Boston and took up positions on various roads to the west. Some were seen near Lexington, riding slowly with no apparent purpose. Their job was to prevent any alarm from reaching Concord, but their presence was itself taken as a warning. That evening, eight militiamen were posted at the Clarke parsonage to protect Hancock and Adams, and thirty men gathered nearby at the Buckman Tavern. At nine o'clock two of them set out to watch the movements of the redcoat officers, and another was dispatched to alert Concord. All three men were seized on the road by a British patrol.

At about the same time, the grenadiers and light infantrymen in Boston were awakened by their sergeants one by one. In silence they dressed and marched in small parties to a beach at the foot of the Common. From there longboats manned by sailors carried the troops across the Back Bay to Cambridge in two trips. There were about 840 soldiers, 74 of them officers. The men waded ashore and struggled through a marsh. When they reached a farm road, they waited more than an hour for the boats to bring over ammunition and a day's rations, plus horses for the officers. After food and 36 cartridges were distributed to each infantryman, the column started marching toward Concord at about two o'clock in the morning. They passed through what is now Union Square in Somerville and eventually joined the "great road" (Massachusetts Avenue) near present-day Porter Square.

Even before the regulars embarked, Dr. Warren had learned with certainty that the British mission was planned for that night. From Paul Revere and other sources, many reports arrived describing snatches of overheard conversations, loose talk among sailors on shore, soldiers dressed for battle, and movements among the longboats. There is evidence that Dr. Warren also received explicit confirmation of the expedition from a secret source close to General Gage, possibly even the commander-in-chief's American wife.

Between 9 and 10 o'clock that night, Warren instructed William Dawes and Paul Revere to carry written messages to Lexington and Concord. Dawes was a tanner whom the British guards often saw on the road. He managed to slip out of Boston via Roxbury. Revere, meanwhile, left from the North End. After telling accomplices at the Old North Church to hang two lanterns as a signal that the British were setting out by water, he had two men row him across to Charlestown. There other collaborators supplied Revere with a horse. Having seen the lantern signal, they had already dispatched a rider to Cambridge and Lexington, but he never got through. Another rider (his identity is not known) headed north. By two o'clock in the morning, he was twenty-five miles from Boston in Tewksbury, where he reported directly to the commander of the local militia that he had warned all the towns between there and Charlestown. Revere himself had to detour through Medford to avoid a British patrol. Although he was off his planned route, he took the time to stop at the house of Captain Isaac Hall, the town's militia commander. Hall immediately implemented the planned system of alarms. He also sent Dr. Martin Herrick riding to the northeast. Herrick went as far as Lynnfield, setting in motion yet other riders along the way. Revere continued through Menotomy, where he started riders toward the north. Between 11 P.M. on the 18th and 10 A.M. on the 19th, virtually all the towns to the north and northwest of Boston received the alarm and mustered their militia, which then marched toward Lexington and Concord.

Revere himself reached the Clarke parsonage in Lexington at about midnight. Immediately the alarm was sounded. Between one and two hours later, men equipped with muskets and provisions began to assemble on the common. Not long after Revere arrived, Dawes appeared also, but he had spoken to no one along the way, with the result that towns to the south were alerted only later. Even Lexington let down its guard after a scout who had been sent eastward reported that no British troops were on the road from Cambridge or Charlestown. The militia commander, Captain John Parker, dismissed his men but ordered them to stay nearby within call of the drum. Many of them went to the Buckman Tavern adjacent to the common.

After resting and refreshing themselves in Lexington, Revere and Dawes continued toward Concord. On the road they were overtaken by Dr. Samuel Prescott. He had been courting his fiancee in Lexington and was now on his way home. Finding that he was a "high son of liberty," Revere and Dawes explained their mission, in which Prescott joined. As a precaution against being thwarted by British patrols, the three men stopped briefly at every house along the road, urging the residents to help spread the warning. But as they passed though Lincoln, Revere and his companions were accosted by four British soldiers, who ordered them at gunpoint into a pasture where several prisoners, including the three Lexington men taken earlier, were already held by other troopers. Dawes wheeled around and eventually made it back to Lexington. Prescott spurred his horse, jumped a wall, and shook off his pursuers by riding through the woods and along obscure lanes and paths known to him. After returning to the main road farther west, he continued to Concord, warning residents along the way and recruiting messengers to carry the alarm to the south. In Concord Center Prescott rousted someone to ring the town bell at about the same time that Colonel Smith's column of British troops, still back in Cambridge, began its march. Prescott also reported to Concord's militia leaders and the minister, William Emerson, grandfather of Ralph Waldo Emerson. From Concord Prescott spread the alarm to Acton, while his brother rode to Sudbury and Framingham. An unknown horseman went from Sudbury to Natick and Dover, while other riders carried the word east to Needham, Dedham, Watertown, Milton, Brookline, Dorchester, and even Roxbury at the gate to Boston.

As for Paul Revere, he failed to get away from the British patrol. But he so rattled his captors by telling them spiritedly about the British expedition, the alarms, the militia, and the urgency of warning their own troops to turn back that they eventually decided to do just that. After hearing gunfire and bells, they released their prisoners, cut the bridles and cinches of the provincials' mounts, took Revere's horse, and rode off to the east. Revere walked back to Lexington, where he found Hancock and Adams still at the Clarke parsonage. After escorting the two men northward out of town, Revere returned to Lexington just as another scout — the second of two sent out by the militia's Captain Parker— arrived with word that the British column was only a mile away. Again Lexington's men mustered in response to drumming, the firing of alarm guns, and the clangor of the meetinghouse bell. Meanwhile, Revere helped Hancock's clerk remove a heavy trunk of confidential documents from the Buckman Tavern. As the two men carried the trunk across the common in the dawn light, the British vanguard came into sight.

Colonel Smith and his soldiers had long since become aware that the countryside was fully forewarned. As they entered Menotomy at three o'clock in the morning, the troops heard gunfire. Shortly afterward they encountered the patrol that had captured and released Paul Revere. As if to emphasize the news that the militia were mustering, bells and more gunfire sounded in the distance from all sides. Colonel Smith dispatched a messenger to General Gage, saying that surprise had been lost and suggesting that reinforcements were needed. At about the same time, a gentleman heading toward Boston in a small carriage told the British vanguard that 600 armed men were assembled in Lexington. He was followed by a wagon driver carrying cordwood to Boston, who spoke of 1000 militiamen. As dawn approached the regulars saw numerous figures with guns hurrying in the dim light across fields on either side of the road, moving faster than the column itself toward their common goal. Soldiers at the head of the column thought that someone fired at them. The British troops were ordered to load. With increasing apprehension, anger, and excitement, they pressed on. To the redcoats, it looked as though finally they were going to teach the scurrilous New England rabble a lesson.

At dawn the British vanguard, led by Major John Pitcairn, rounded a curve in the road and saw two long ranks of militiamen, one behind the other, falling into line on Lexington Common. There were only about 75 provincials. The regulars headed straight for them at quick march. Seeing that his men were greatly outnumbered, and mindful of a directive from the Provincial Congress "to act solely on the defensive so long as it can be justified on the principles of reason and self-preservation and no longer," Lexington's Captain Parker told his men, "Let the troops pass by." And he added, "Don't molest them, without they being first."

But the British officers did not choose to go by. To do so would have left these armed men on their flank. Instead, the first two companies of redcoats forked right toward Bedford, passed the Buckman Tavern, then swung left across the common and stopped. As they formed a line facing the militia, the regulars roared their traditional battle cry. Other British companies stopped slightly to the rear. Some officers on horseback approached the militia at a canter, shouting things like "Lay down your arms, you damned rebels," and "Ye villains, ye rebels, disperse, damn you disperse," and "Throw down your arms and you shall come to no harm," as witnesses afterward recalled. One British officer said that he heard Major Pitcairn call out, "Soldiers, don't fire, keep your ranks, form and surround them." Lexington's Captain Parker testified that "I immediately ordered our militia to disperse and not to fire." Some of his men began to move away in confusion, but others who had not heard the order stayed.

Suddenly there was a shot, or possibly several shots, audible by many men on both sides. The sound came from neither the ranks of militiamen nor the regulars, most witnesses agreed. The British said that rebels to one side behind a wall or a hedge or the corner of a house fired first, while some Americans swore they clearly saw a British officer on horseback discharge his pistol at them. Several witnesses said they saw and heard a British officer order his troops to fire. In any case, the regulars began shooting, first irregularly, then in a roaring volley that was repeated as the soldiers quickly reloaded and fired again. A few militiamen fell, some fired back, most scattered, and spectators fled. A British officer recounted that "our men without any orders rushed in upon them, fired, and put 'em to flight." Smoke obscured Lexington Common as the regulars pursued militiamen or fired in different directions.

During the confusion, Colonel Smith arrived at the scene with the main body of British troops. He ordered a drummer to beat "to arms" (that is, cease fire). Slowly the officers restored order, "putting a stop," as Smith later said, "to all further slaughter of those deluded people." Smith then assembled his officers and told them for the first time that Concord was their objective. Many were dismayed and urged him to turn back in view of what had just happened. But Smith marched his column off to the west, after first allowing the troops to fire a victory salute and to shout three cheers. Behind them the British left eight militiamen dead or dying and seven wounded, all but one of them from Lexington. In nearby Woburn Sam Adams had heard the shooting. According to tradition, he told John Hancock, "It is a fine day."

Smith's force left Lexington at about 7 o'clock in the morning and reached Concord without opposition two hours later. Some of the young minutemen who had mustered there proposed to stop the British east of town. But as the long red column came into sight, the sun glistening on muskets and bayonets, even the local hotheads agreed to retreat westward across the Concord River and to wait there for more men to arrive. In the center of town, the regulars immediately set about searching for munitions. They found and destroyed three cannon, burned some gun carriages and other miscellaneous items, threw kegs of musket balls into the millpond (most were retrieved the next day), and also heaved a supply of flour into the water. But for the most part, the large stores of supplies that were the object of the raid had vanished.

While most of his men scoured the town, Colonel Smith posted troops at the North and South bridges on the far side of the Concord and Sudbury rivers. Four companies marched more than a mile beyond the

North Bridge to search the house and mill of Colonel James Barrett, commander of the Middlesex militia. Two other companies of regulars occupied high ground along the route, and a single company guarded the North Bridge itself.

While the British were at the Barrett property, about 400 militiamen, emboldened by their increase in numbers, approached Concord's mustering ground atop a hill overlooking the North Bridge. A company of redcoats retreated before them, keeping a few hundred yards away. Looking across the river, the Americans could see smoke rising from Concord Center. Lieutenant Joseph Hosmer, a young man who was among the more vociferous Whigs, asked Colonel Barrett, "Will you let them burn the town down?" Other officers announced that they and their men were prepared to go. After telling the troops to load and to fire only if the British fired first, Barrett ordered the men to advance in double file, their arms at their sides. As the Americans came on, the British fell back across the bridge and started to tear up its planking. Major John Buttrick, commander of the Middlesex minutemen (they were mostly younger than Barrett's militia), shouted to the regulars to leave the bridge alone. Buttrick was on his own land, within sight of his house. He had told his men that if they would follow him, he favored driving the British away.

To their astonishment, the regulars saw men, most of them in the clothes of farmers, advancing "with the greatest regularity" and "in a very military manner," as some soldiers later said. The British commander at the bridge ordered his men to form for street fighting, or that is, into closely-packed ranks to concentrate their fire across the bridge and down the causeway. But as some troops retreated across the bridge, they collided with those already on the other side. Then one solider fired without orders, followed by others in a ragged volley. Two Americans were killed instantly and four wounded.

The New Englanders advanced to within fifty yards of the British before Major Buttrick shouted, "Fire, fellow soldiers, for God's sake, fire!" In the first round of shooting, the Americans wounded four of eight British officers, distinguishable because their red coats were newer and therefore less faded than the uniforms of the troops. Three infantrymen were killed and five wounded. As the firing continued, the regulars crowded backwards, then turned and fled toward Concord. An ensign wrote, "The weight of their fire was such that we was obliged to give way, then run with the greatest precipitance."

Confusion overcame the Americans as well. One later said that "after the fire every one appeared to be his own commander." Some men advanced and others retreated. A few men walked away and returned home, having had enough of fighting. Eventually, the officers restored order. Colonel Barrett decided to withdraw the militia to the mustering ground and to position the minutemen under Major Buttrick on a hill just east of the bridge, where they blocked British reinforcements that marched from the town but did not attack. Later the American forces allowed the redcoats who had been to Barrett's house to return across the bridge without opposition.

By 11:30 A.M. all of the British troops had returned to Concord Center. For half an hour regiments marched from place to place, sometimes advancing, then withdrawing. At noon the entire column, including carriages commandeered for the wounded, headed east toward Boston. Already the Americans had starting moving cross-country around the town, hoping to cut the British off, but Colonel Smith deployed flankers on both sides of the road to keep the Massachusetts men at a distance.

At Meriam's Corner a mile east of town, the flankers were drawn in to cross a bridge over a small stream. Militia and minutemen from several towns to the north, including distant Tewksbury, were waiting. Some stood openly in a field. Others took cover behind the Meriam farm buildings and farmyard walls. As the British passed, one of the colonials fired. The regulars turned and volleyed, and the American fired in return. No provincials were hit, but by the time the British column marched out of range, several regulars had been shot, some fatally. One Concord minuteman recalled (probably with exaggeration) that "a great many lay dead and the road was bloody."

Similar engagements occurred repeatedly along the narrow road, which mostly was bordered by fields and rocky pastures, but in some places dipped through ravines and passed below wooded bluffs and hills. By early afternoon, the number of American troops in the vicinity exceeded the British and continued to climb. Arriving from the surrounding towns or skirting through fields to get ahead of the regulars, companies of militia and minutemen took up sheltered positions behind walls and ditches and among woods overlooking the road. These tactics were not the spontaneous work of swarming individuals, each fighting on his own, but rather the action of organized military units directed by their officers. Occasionally, whole regiments numbering several hundred men operated together. Most of the time, the colonials were pushed back by British flankers, but at some places they stood their ground and forced the regulars to pass through their fire.

As the British marched rapidly toward Boston, fighting occurred in turn at Brooks Hill and then at the Brooks Tavern. At a bend in the road farther east, 200 militiamen from the Woburn regiment occupied a rise covered with thick woods, and more fighters filled the forest opposite them. A militiaman from Reading recalled that "the enemy was now completely between two fires, renewed and briskly kept up. They ordered out a flank guard on the left to dislodge the Americans from their posts behind large trees, but they only became a better mark to be shot at." The British fought through, only to be attacked again at the next bend five hundred yards farther on. This stretch of road became known as the Bloody Angle, where the regulars had eight men killed and more than twenty wounded.

East of the Bloody Angle, Colonel Smith again deployed flankers to keep the Americans away from his column, but his vanguard was ambushed anyway near the Hartwell farm by militiamen who in turn were attacked from behind by flanking parties. Successive skirmishes occurred at other houses passed by the regulars, who occasionally took casualties from Americans firing at long range. Another bloody engagement was fought at Parker's Revenge, where Captain Parker of Lexington posted his militia company on a rocky, wooded hillock north of the road. Some of these men had been hit earlier in the day. Parker gave the order to fire only after the British were very close, and among those wounded was Colonel Smith himself. The regulars charged, taking and dealing casualties, and pushed the Americans away from the road. But after marching less than a mile, the column was attacked again at Fiske Hill on the south.

By now the British soldiers were running out of ammunition. Many of the men, including officers, had been wounded, and the entire column was exhausted. Some fell out and waited to be captured. Men in the vanguard began to run forward, leaving the others behind. One officer later recalled the desperate situation:

> When we arrived within a mile of Lexington, our ammunition began to fail, and the light companies were so fatigued with flanking that they were scarce able to act, and a great number of wounded scarce able to get forward, made a great confusion; Col. Smith (our commanding officer) had received a wound through his leg, a number of officers were also wounded. . . . [W]e began to run rather than retreat in order. The whole behaved with amazing bravery but little order. We attempted to stop the men and form them two deep, but to no purpose, the confusion increased rather than lessened.

Nonetheless, under threats of death from their officers, the soldiers began to form up under heavy fire as the column approached Lexington Common. Then the vanguard unexpectedly cheered. Arrayed in a line of battle on a rise just east of the town's center was a full brigade of British reinforcements. Colonel Smith's column passed to safety as fire from two six-pounder field guns scattered American pursuers.

Commanded by Brigadier the Right Honorable Hugh Earl Percy, son of the Duke of Northumberland (one of the richest men in England), the British reinforcements at Lexington had been sent out that morning after

General Gage had received a message from Colonel Smith that the colonials were mustering. At about two o'clock in the afternoon, Percy reached Lexington as the sound of battle to the west grew louder. He had already learned from a wounded British officer, who had somehow gotten through in a carriage, that Smith's force was retreating, and so Percy deployed his troops to receive them and to stop the militia and minutemen who dogged their flanks and rear. Percy kept the Americans at a distance by posting a screen of skirmishers and by burning three houses that provided cover for snipers. For a period the fighting died down as both sides reorganized. Percy was amazed to learn that "the rebels were in great numbers, the whole country having collected for twenty miles around." Concerned that his cannon had just 24 balls each, his soldiers only 36 cartridges apiece, and Smith's men almost none, he sent an officer back to Boston for more reinforcements and ammunition, but this man arrived there too late to do the British any good. On his own initiative, General Gage had already sent an ammunition wagon to catch up with Percy, but its guards were waylaid on the road and the wagon captured.

Percy resumed the march toward Boston at three o'clock in the afternoon. Altogether he had between 1800 and 1900 men. He deployed very strong flanking parties which, he said, were "absolutely necessary, as there was not a stone wall, though before in appearance evacuated, from whence the rebels did not fire upon us." So as not to tire his men, and to allow his flankers to keep abreast of his main column, he decided to march slowly. At the front, where he expected little resistance, he put a small vanguard, and at the rear — from which he expected most of the attacks to come — he placed a much larger force, plus his artillery.

On the American side, Brigadier General William Heath of the Massachusetts militia took command during the lull at Lexington. He believed that fighting in open order, advancing and withdrawing as necessary, avoiding close action, and taking advantage of every element of the irregular terrain was the best way for New Englanders to counter the tight formations and concentrated firepower of the British. One American described Heath's deployment of troops as "*dispersed* tho' *adhering*." Lord Percy, the target for these tactics, afterward described the battle this way: "We retired for 15 miles under an incessant fire, which like a moving circle surrounded and followed us wherever we went."

This "moving circle" was maintained with some difficulty. When he arrived at Lexington, General Heath helped rally the troops who had been scattered by Percy's field guns. After sorting out units that had mingled together, Heath directed some regimental commanders to attack the British flanks as soon as the column started toward Boston. He sent couriers to units marching from outlying towns, directing them to the east to intercept the British line of retreat. Other regiments pressed the regulars from behind, so that their rear guard was forced to walk backward, taking casualties that eventually exceeded ten percent. Although the Americans marched to battle in large formations that sometimes reached regimental strength, they attacked in much smaller companies. One British officer recalled that the Massachusetts men were "much scattered, and not above fifty of them to be seen in any one place." Percy himself wrote,

"During the whole affair, the rebels attacked us in a very scattered, irregular manner, but with perseverance and resolution, nor did they ever dare to form into any regular body. Indeed they knew too well what was proper, to do so. Whoever looks upon them as an irregular mob, will find himself very much mistaken. They have men amongst them who know very well what they are about, having been employed as rangers against the Indians and Canadians, and this country being much covered with wood, and hilly, is very advantageous for their method of fighting.

By the time the British column entered Menotomy, both flanks as well as the rear were under fire, and eventually their vanguard also was attacked. Some of those who sniped at the lead troops were mounted militiamen who rode ahead of the column, occasionally dismounted to aim carefully and shoot, then again trotted forward to a new position. One British officer said,

Numbers of them were mounted, and when they had fastened their horses at some little distance from the road, they crept down near enough to have a shot; as soon as the column had passed, they mounted again, and rode round until they got ahead of the column, and found some convenient place from whence they might fire again. These fellows were generally good marksmen, and many of them used long guns made for duck-shooting.

As the British entered the village of Menotomy, they caught and killed some militia units and local householders who ambushed the regulars at close range. Fighting raged from house to house as the British passed through. One officer wrote, "We were now obliged to force almost every house in the road, for the rebels had taken possession of them and galled us exceedingly, but they suffered for their temerity, for all that were found in the houses were put to death." Both sides suffered their worst casualties of the day. In Menotomy the British lost at least 40 killed and 80 wounded, the Americans 25 dead and 9 wounded. Some regulars, maddened with fighting and intoxicated with liquor that they found in houses and taverns, killed their prisoners in revenge for all that had occurred, including the hatcheting (or scalping, as rumor had it) of a wounded British soldier at Concord that morning. Many regulars joined in looting Menotomy before their officers regained control and got their troops through the town.

In Cambridge the fighting continued as fresh regiments of militia arrived, sometimes attacking the British in close formation before adopting the safer tactics of dispersal. British flankers fought to keep the colonials far from the road, but the regulars were running low on ammunition. In contrast, each new American unit had ample supplies. Some militia companies were even resupplied in the field by horseman with saddlebags full of bullets.

Earlier in the afternoon, General Heath had ordered part of the Watertown militia to remove the planking from the bridge over the Charles River near Harvard College. This was the route from Roxbury that Percy had taken earlier in the day, and by which the colonials thought he would return. But instead Percy directed his column toward Charlestown and in so doing escaped the colonials' circle of fire. Later Percy said that he chose the Charlestown road for three reasons: "Lest the rebels should have taken up the bridge at Cambridge (which I find was actually the case), and also as the country was more open and the road shorter." Arriving from the North Shore, some militia companies were in a position to attack the British from hills in present-day Somerville, but these forces were either repelled by cannon fire or held back by their officers. Still pursued by the Americans, the regulars reached Charlestown at about seven o'clock in the evening, and gradually the fighting died down in the dusk. General Heath decided that it would futile to assault the British on the Charlestown hills where they could be supported by the big guns of *H.M.S. Somerset* anchored nearby. As a precaution against counter-attack during the night, Heath withdrew most of the militia a few miles to Cambridge. Meanwhile, longboats ferried the British — first the wounded and then the rest of the exhausted column — across to Boston in the dark, returning with fresh troops to hold Charlestown.

In the days following the battle, the militia dead were gathered up and taken to their towns for burial, and the wounded cared for until they either died or returned home. Some of the British dead were interred in the graveyards of the towns along the route of battle, but most were buried where they fell. Altogether 49 Americans were killed or died of wounds. About 40 men were reported wounded, but probably many more wounds went unreported. The British suffered about 70 dead, 180 wounded, and 25 missing. One in every six redcoats who fought that day was a casualty.

News of the battle was carried by express riders that reached eastern Connecticut the next day, New York on the 23rd, and Philadelphia on the 24th.    Printers published broadsides that directed hot indignation toward the British, sang the praises of the provincial troops and the worthy dead, and gave gratitude to God for a glorious victory in defense of liberty.  In Massachusetts the Committee of Safety circulated a letter to all the towns, proposing to raise and feed an army of 8000 men for the siege of Boston.    In response yet more thousands of militiamen poured in, not just from Massachusetts but also from New Hampshire, Connecticut, and Rhode Island.    The letter spoke of the "barbarous murders committed on our innocent brethren, on Wednesday, the 19th instant" and described the need to "defend our wives and children from the butchering hands of the inhuman soldiery, who, incensed at the obstacles they met in their bloody progress, and enraged at being repulsed from the field of slaughter, will, without the least doubt, take the first opportunity in their power to ravage this devoted country with fire and sword." Within days the Committee of Safety collected sworn depositions from eyewitnesses, including British prisoners (some on their death beds) regarding the question of who had fired the first shots at Lexington and Concord.    These accounts were combined with a report steeply slanted against the British.  The colonials' extensive military preparations went unmentioned.  The fact that the American casualties at Lexington were armed militiamen was downplayed by describing them as a "small party of the inhabitants  .  .  .  some with and some without firearms." Similarly, the 400 militiamen who advanced on the British at Concord became "inhabitants . . . collected at the bridge."   This story and the supporting depositions were sent secretly to London and published by the newspapers there two weeks before General Gage's own report crossed the Atlantic.  Without much effect, Gage published his version of events in Massachusetts, showing "that the people of this Province were the first aggressors, and that the conduct of the leaders here is the cause of all the misfortunes that have happened, or shall arise."

Reacting to the events in Massachusetts, other colonies too mobilized their militias, and the Continental Congress started organizing for the common defense.  On June 15 Congress appointed George Washington to take command of the forces besieging Boston, where the New Englanders had long since stopped all food and supplies from entering the city.  "In the course of two days," one British officer wrote, "from a plentiful town, we were reduced to the disagreeable necessity of living on salt provisions, and were fairly blocked up in Boston."   The siege continued for nearly a year before the British were forced to evacuate the city by ship.  In the meantime, the nation debated whether reconciliation with England on American terms was possible.  The fighting at Lexington and Concord, the subsequent Battle of Bunker Hill, and the ongoing siege of  Boston persuaded most New Englanders that America must become independent, and eventually the same conclusion prevailed in the rest of the colonies and in Congress.

≈     ≈     ≈     ≈

**PUBLIC TRANSIT:** The western end of Minute Man National Historical Park is in Concord, which is served by commuter train from **North Station** in Boston and from **Porter Square** in Cambridge. (North Station can be reached via the MBTA's Green or Orange Line, and Porter Square is on the Red Line.)

From the train station in Concord, follow Sudbury Road toward the center of town. Join Main Street and continue to Monument Square. Turn left to the end of the rectangular "square," then bear right to follow Monument Street 0.5 mile. Just beyond the Old Manse, a broad walkway leads left across the Concord River to the **North Bridge Visitor Center**, shown at the left end of **Map 21** on page 143.

≈     ≈     ≈     ≈

**AUTOMOBILE DIRECTIONS:** The main visitor center for **Minute Man National Historical Park** is located on the boundary between Lexington and Lincoln 14 miles northwest of Boston. (See •12 on **Map 1** on page 6, and also **Map 21** on page 143.) Several approaches are described below.

**To Minute Man National Historical Park from Boston:** The fastest route is to take the **Massachusetts Turnpike** (Interstate 90) west to Exit 15 for Interstate 95 northbound. Fork right immediately after the tollbooths, then bear left for I-95 north and follow the directions that start at the top of page 142: "To Minute Man National Historical Park from Interstate 95 (Route 128)."

Another approach is to follow **Storrow Drive** west along the Charles River toward Newton and Arlington. After passing Harvard University, take the exit for **Route 2** toward Arlington. In quick succession, cross the Eliot Bridge, then bear right, then left for Route 2 westbound. Go 2.1 miles on Route 2 (the Fresh Pond and Alewife Brook Parkways). After passing the MBTA's Alewife Station, bear left to continue west on Route 2 for 6 miles to Exit 52B for Interstate 95 northbound. Once you are on I-95, follow the directions in the next section: "To Minute Man National Historical Park from Interstate 95 (Route 128)."

**To Minute Man National Historical Park from Interstate 95 (Route 128):** Leave I-95 at Exit 30B for Route 2A west toward Concord. Go 0.9 mile, then turn right into the entrance for the **Minute Man Visitor Center.** A path runs several hundred yards from the parking lot's right side to the visitor center building, where a movie and exhibits describe the grievances and hostile preparations that led to the eruption of fighting on April 19, 1775.

**To Minute Man National Historical Park from Interstate 495:** Leave I-495 at Exit 29A for Route 2 east toward Boston. Go 7 miles to the traffic circle at the Massachusetts penitentiary. From the rotary, continue east on Route 2 for 4.5 miles. At the intersection where Route 2 veers right toward Boston, continue straight on Route 2A for 2.5 miles to the entrance on the left for the **Minute Man Visitor Center.** A path runs several hundred yards from the parking lot's right side to the visitor center building, where a movie and exhibits describe the grievances and hostile preparations that led to the eruption of fighting on April 19, 1775.

≈　　　≈　　　≈　　　≈

**WALKING and BICYCLING:** The bold line on **Map 21** at right shows the 8-mile **Battle Road and Trail** at Minute Man National Historical Park. There is no automobile traffic on the restored sections of the Battle Road, but there are a half-dozen road crossings, including one at Hanscom Drive that the National Park Service declares to be closed until an underpass is built. Call (978) 369-6993, extension 22 for information.

**To get started on the Battle Road and Trail,** follow a path from the end of the parking lot at the **Minute Man Visitor Center.** Go 50 yards, then turn left onto the Battle Road itself, heading west toward Concord. Walking in this direction, you are in the role of a British soldier on the way to destroy the military supplies amassed at Concord under the authority of the Massachusetts Provincial Congress, which was the *de facto* government established in opposition to the British regime and army in Boston.

As you draw near Route 2A, turn right to continue on the hike-bike trail past the **Paul Revere capture site**, where Revere, William Dawes, and Samuel Prescott, all on their way to Con-

MAP 21 — Minute Man National Historical Park

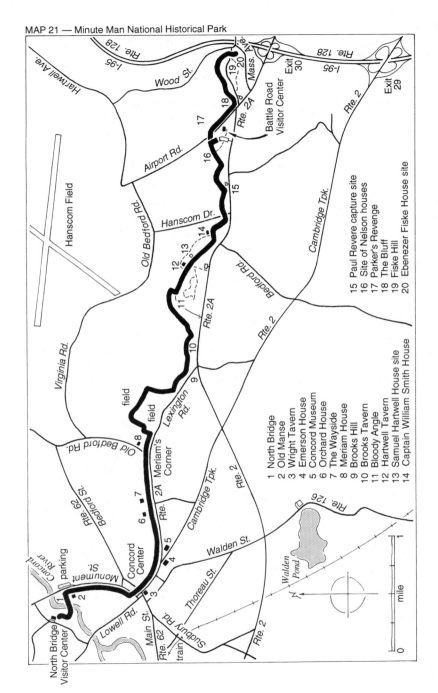

1  North Bridge
2  Old Manse
3  Wright Tavern
4  Emerson House
5  Concord Museum
6  Orchard House
7  The Wayside
8  Meriam House
9  Brooks Hill
10  Brooks Tavern
11  Bloody Angle
12  Hartwell Tavern
13  Samuel Hartwell House site
14  Captain William Smith House

15  Paul Revere capture site
16  Site of Nelson houses
17  Parker's Revenge
18  The Bluff
19  Fiske Hill
20  Ebenezer Fiske House site

cord, were surprised in the early hours of April 19 by a British patrol. Revere was detained for an hour or more, Dawes was forced back toward Lexington, but Prescott eluded the British and carried the alarm to Concord.

After passing the **house of Captain William Smith** of the Lincoln Minute Men, bear right to join the next section of the actual Battle Road, which leads west past the **Hartwell Tavern**. This building is typical of stopping places where travelers and local residents discussed the news and issues of the day.

At the **Bloody Angle**, the Battle Road bends left, but you should turn right to follow the hike-bike trail, which at one point passes around a large field that gives some idea of the open farm landscape at the time of the Revolution. Once the British retreat from Concord got underway, militiamen ran eastward across these fields to get ahead of the English and to prepare an ambush at the Bloody Angle, where eight British soldiers were killed.

Eventually, the trail ends at the Meriam House near the intersection of Lexington Road and Old Bedford Road. Called **Meriam's Corner**, this is where the retreating British column had to draw in its flankers to cross a small bridge just to the east, thus allowing the militiamen to get close enough to make the first of many attacks against the regulars as they marched back toward Boston.

With caution, cross Old Bedford Road and follow the sidewalk along Lexington Road, which should be on your left. Continue all the way into Concord Center, in the process passing the **Wayside** (one of Nathaniel Hawthorne's homes), the **Orchard House** (home of the Alcotts), the **Concord Museum**, and — on the far side of the museum — the **Emerson House**, all of which are open to the public.

At Concord Center, continue straight past Monument Square. At a T-intersection with Monument Street, cross to a sidewalk on the far side of the road. Turn right and follow the sidewalk half a mile to the **Old Manse**. Belonging to the Emerson family, this house is where Nathaniel and Sophia Hawthorne lived for several years following their marriage. Just beyond the Old Manse, a broad walkway leads across the Concord River to the **North Bridge Visitor Center**. It was here that Concord militiamen, fearing that the British were burning the town, attacked three companies guarding the bridge. This action, and the running battle that followed as the regulars retreated to Boston, marked the beginning of open war between the American colonies and Great Britain.

Even after the colonists lay siege to Boston and after the Continental Congress appointed George Washington to lead a regular army against the British, many people during the next year hoped and worked for a rapprochement based on English recognition of American rights. However, the British Parliament and people backed King George III's determination to crush the rebellion by a combination of economic and military measures. In response a majority of Congress voted in July 1776 for independence as the only acceptable way forward.

After you return along the Battle Road and Trail, you may want to continue past the Minute Man Visitor Center to the park's eastern end at **Fiske Hill**, where British flankers fought at close quarters with American ambushers overlooking the road. From here the fighting continued on to Lexington, where the British were reinforced, and then through Menotomy (present-day Arlington) and Cambridge before the regulars crossed Charlestown Neck and reached safety at Bunker Hill.

# 13

# WALDEN POND
# ADAMS WOODS
# FAIRHAVEN TRAIL

The route shown on **Map 23** on pages 158-159 has two parts.
A circuit of 2 miles (3.2 kilometers) around **Walden Pond** is a
tribute to Henry David Thoreau. Linked to this loop is a figure-
eight of 3.8 miles (6 kilometers) through **Adams Woods to
Fairhaven Bay**. As pleasant as Walden is, the area to the
southwest toward Fairhaven is still more attractive, and because of
its greater seclusion, it better preserves the spirit of Thoreau.

There is a good way and a bad way to see Walden Pond. The
good way is to go off-peak — for example, early in the morning or
in poor weather. The bad way is to go on a fine weekend afternoon when hundreds of other people have the same idea. You
may not even be able to park. It is of course ironic that worldwide
regard for Thoreau, who came to Walden Pond in search of solitude, regularly results in throngs of people circling the pond to
pay their respects.

For a longer outing you may prefer to park in the town of Lincoln
and walk to Walden Pond from there. Start at the Lincoln train
station and follow the route shown on **Map 22** on page 155. This
approach is described on page 156. Round-trip, it adds about 4
miles to the route shown on Map 23.

Walden Pond State Reservation is open daily starting at 7 A.M.
The closing time changes with the seasons and corresponds
approximately with dusk. There is an admission fee during
summer when the bathhouse and swimming beach are open.
Dogs are prohibited, even if leashed. During winter the pondside
trail is often coated with ice. The reservation is administered by
the Massachusetts Department of Environmental Management;
telephone (978) 369-3254.

Adams Woods and the land bordering Fairhaven Bay are open
from sunrise to sunset and are managed by the Lincoln Conservation Commission and the Concord Land Conservation Trust.

For directions to Walden Pond via public transit, please turn to
page 154. Automobile directions to Walden start on page 156.

For directions to Lincoln (if that approach interests you), turn to page 179 in Chapter 15. Walking directions start on page 157.

---

HENRY DAVID THOREAU lived from 1817 to 1862. After studying at Harvard, he spent four unsatisfying years as a schoolmaster, then left teaching for a life of austerity and extreme individualism. He earned what little money he needed by surveying and working as a handyman. At times he was the live-in caretaker at the house of Ralph Waldo Emerson, and for a period he helped edit Emerson's transcendentalist magazine, *The Dial*. Thoreau read much and wrote steadily — essays, poetry, and a multi-volume journal, from which he culled and rewrote bits to make *Walden*. In part the book is an account, full of closely observed details and evocative descriptions, of the first year of his twenty-six month stay in a tiny cabin that he built overlooking Walden Pond on land belonging to Emerson. It is also a manifesto of sorts: a call for simplicity in life and (what is the other side of the same coin) a trenchant, droll, and sometimes crabbed critique of materialism and self-imposed drudgery. And finally *Walden* is transcendentalist scripture, describing Thoreau's growing sense of affirmation in solitude and nature.

Thoreau began to build his cabin in March, 1845. He describes how "I borrowed an axe and went down to the woods by Walden Pond, nearest to where I intended to build my house, and began to cut down some tall arrowy white pines, still in their youth, for timber."

It was a pleasant hillside where I worked, covered with pine woods, through which I looked out on the pond, and a small open field in the woods where pines and hickories were springing up. The ice in the pond was not yet dissolved, though there were some open spaces, and it was all dark colored and saturated with water. There were some slight flurries of snow during the days that I worked there, but for the most part when I came out onto the railroad, on my way home, its yellow sand heap stretched away gleaming in the hazy atmosphere, and the rails shone in the spring sun, and I heard the lark and pewee and other birds already come to commence another year with us. They were pleasant spring days, in which the winter of man's discontent was thawing as well as the earth, and the life that had lain torpid began to stretch itself.

After hewing timbers, Thoreau framed the house and then, with the help of friends, erected it. He sheathed it with boards from an old shanty he had bought and torn down, reusing even the nails.

Thoreau started living at Walden on Independence Day. At first he cooked outside. Eventually, before winter, he applied shingles to the cabin's exterior, plastered the interior, and built a chimney at one end opposite the door. The house was ten feet wide by fifteen feet long, with a window on each side. Today a replica stands near the entrance to the reservation's parking lot, and the site of the real cabin is clearly marked near the pondside trail. All told, Thoreau's house cost $28 — or slightly less, he pointed out, than the annual rent for his room at Harvard. He claimed that by living simply, six weeks of work were enough to meet all of the expenses necessary to sustain himself for a year.

In one of his most famous passages, Thoreau describes the purpose of his experiment:

> I went to the woods because I wished to live deliberately, to front only the essential facts of life, and see if I could not learn what it had to teach, and not, when I came to die, discover that I had not lived. I did not wish to live what was not life, living is so dear; nor did I wish to practice resignation, unless it was quite necessary. I wanted to live deep and suck out all the marrow of life, to live so sturdily and Spartan-like as to put to rout all that was not life, to cut a broad swath and shave close, to drive life into a corner, and reduce it to its lowest terms, and, if it proved to be mean, why then to get the whole and genuine meanness of it, and publish its meanness to the world; or if it were sublime, to know it by experience, and be able to give a true account of it in my next excursion.

Thoreau's daily routine started at dawn. "Every morning was a cheerful invitation to make my life of equal simplicity, and I may say innocence, with Nature herself. I have been as sincere a worshiper of Aurora as the Greeks. I got up early and bathed in the pond; that was a religious exercise, and one of the best things which I did. They say that characters were engraven on the bathing tub of King Tching-thang to this effect: 'Renew thyself completely each day; do it again, and again, and forever again.' I can understand that."

Much of each day was spent in activity that took on the quality of loose meditation. Thoreau describes how, even when he was working in his bean field, he was given to thought, memory, observation, and listening. And there were times when he did no work at all:

> I love a broad margin to my life. Sometimes, in a summer morning, having taken my accustomed bath, I sat in my sunny doorway from sunrise till noon, rapt in a revery, amidst the pines and hickories and sumacs, in undisturbed solitude and stillness, while the birds sang around or flitted noiseless through the house, until by the sun falling in at my west

window, or the noise of some traveler's wagon on the distant highway, I was reminded of the lapse of time. I grew in those seasons like corn in the night, and they were far better than any work of the hands would have been. They were not time subtracted from my life, but so much over and above my usual allowance. I realized what the Orientals mean by contemplation and the forsaking of works. For the most part, I minded not how the hours went. The day advanced as if to light some work of mine; it was morning, and lo, now it is evening, and nothing memorable is accomplished. . . . This was sheer idleness to my fellow-townsmen, no doubt; but if the birds and flowers had tried me by their standard, I should not have been found wanting.

Thoreau regularly spent hours each day walking, sometimes to other ponds or to Fairhaven Bay or the Concord River, which together he termed his Lake District. His characterization of himself as an "inspector of snowstorms" capsulizes his attitude of wonder at the world. "I frequently tramped eight or ten miles through the deepest snow to keep an appointment with a beech tree, or a yellow birch, or an old acquaintance among the pines." In his essay "Walking," published in 1862, Thoreau says:

I have met but one or two persons in the course of my life who understood the art of Walking, that is, of taking walks — who had a genius, so to speak, for *sauntering*. . . .

[I]f their own assertions are to be received, most of my townsmen would fain walk sometimes, as I do, but they cannot. No wealth can buy the requisite leisure, freedom, and independence which are the capital in this profession. It comes only by the grace of God. It requires a direct dispensation from Heaven to become a walker. You must be born into the family of Walkers. *Ambulator nascitur, non fit.* Some of my townsmen, it is true, can remember and have described to me some walks which they took ten years ago, in which they were so blessed as to lose themselves for half an hour in the woods; but I know very well that they have confined themselves to the highway ever since, whatever pretensions they may make to belong to this select class. No doubt they were elevated for a moment as by the reminiscence of a previous state of existence, when even they were foresters and outlaws. . . .

I think that I cannot preserve my health and spirits, unless I spend four hours a day at least — and it is commonly more than that — sauntering through the woods and over the hills and fields, absolutely free from all worldly engagements. You may safely say, A penny for your thoughts, or a thousand pounds. When sometimes I am reminded that the mechanics and shopkeepers stay in their shops not only all the forenoon, but all the afternoon too, sitting with crossed legs, so many of them — as if the legs were made to sit upon, and not to stand or walk upon — I think that they deserve some credit for not having all committed suicide long ago.

Reading was another big part of Thoreau's life at Walden Pond, although not during his first summer and fall, when he was cultivating his bean field and finishing his house. But afterwards he read Homer and other ancient Greek literature, and also Far Eastern texts. "My residence was more favorable, not only to thought, but to serious reading, than a university; and though I was beyond the range of the ordinary circulating library, I had more than ever come within the influence of those books which circulate round the world, whose sentences were first written on bark, and are now merely copied from time to time onto linen paper." He describes bathing his intellect in the "stupendous and cosmogonal philosophy of the Bhagvat Geeta, since whose composition years of the gods have elapsed, and in comparison with which our modern world and its literature seem puny and trivial." He mentions also the European and English classics, and early on a few "shallow books of travel" on which he was ashamed to waste his time. Somewhat obnoxiously, he scorned those who eagerly consumed the literary cotton-candy of the day. He cites a book called *Little Reading*, "which I thought referred to a town of that name which I had not been to." He continues:

[A]s for the sacred Scriptures, or Bibles of mankind, who in this town can tell me even their titles? Most men do not know that any nation but the Hebrews have had a scripture. A man, any man, will go considerably out of his way to pick up a silver dollar; but there are golden words, which the wisest men of antiquity have uttered, and whose worth the wise of every succeeding age have assured us of; and yet . . . our reading, our conversation and thinking, are all on a very low level, worthy only of pygmies and manikins.

As a writer Thoreau eventually achieved fame commensurate with the standard of literature that he favored — though not during his lifetime. By the end of his first year at Walden Pond, he finished *A Week on the Concord and Merrimack Rivers*, but it did not appear until 1849, the same year as *Civil Disobedience*. *The Maine Woods* came out in 1848. And by the time Thoreau left Walden Pond and returned to Concord, he had completed the first draft of *Walden*. The book went through at least one more draft before its publication in 1854. The essays "Walking," "Life Without Principle," and "Cape Cod" appeared shortly after Thoreau's death in 1862. As his reputation soared, his complete writings, running to twenty volumes, were published in 1906.

Three chapters of Walden are called "Solitude," "Visitors," and "The Village," and each in a way qualifies the others. Despite living alone in the woods, Thoreau was no hermit, nor was he far from the center of Concord or nearby roads. Every day or two, he strolled into the town "to hear the gossip which is incessantly going on there, circulating either from mouth to mouth, or from newspaper to newspaper, and which, taken in homeopathic doses, was really as refreshing in its way as the rustle of leaves and the peeping of frogs." At his Walden house, Thoreau frequently received visits from acquaintances and even curious strangers. "If one guest came he sometimes partook of my frugal meal, and it was no interruption to conversation to be stirring a hasty-pudding, or watching the rising and maturing of a loaf of bread in the ashes, in the meanwhile." Still, it was solitude that Thoreau chiefly sought and valued:

> I experienced sometimes that the most sweet and tender, the most innocent and encouraging society may be found in any natural object, even for the poor misanthrope and melancholy man. There can be no very black melancholy to him who lives in the midst of Nature and has his senses still. . . .
>
> Some of my pleasantest hours were during the long rainstorms in the spring or fall, which confined me to the house for the afternoon as well as the forenoon, soothed by their ceaseless roar and pelting; when an early twilight ushered in a long evening in which many thoughts had time to take root and unfold themselves.

Thoreau ended his stay at Walden Pond on September 7th, 1847. He felt little need to justify his departure. "I left the woods for as good a reason as I went there. Perhaps it seemed to me that I had several more lives to live, and could not spare any more time for that one." With one book finished and another of a very original quality well underway — and with a sense too that he had vindicated his chosen way of life despite the tut-tutting of society — Thoreau had something to crow about. He concluded:

> I learned this, at least, by my experiment; that if one advances confidently in the direction of his dreams, and endeavors to live the life which he has imagined, he will meet with a success unexpected in common hours. He will put some things behind, will pass an invisible boundary: new, universal and more liberal laws will begin to establish themselves around and within him; or the old laws be expanded, and interpreted in his favor in a more liberal sense, and he will live with the license of a higher order of beings. In proportion as he simplifies his life, the laws of the universe will appear less complex, and solitude will not be solitude, nor poverty poverty, nor weakness weakness. If you have built castles in the air, your work need not be lost; that is where they should be. Now put the foundations under them.

≈        ≈        ≈        ≈

AS FOR WALDEN POND ITSELF, like many ponds in New England, it occupies a so-called kettlehole dating back ten or twelve thousand years to the recession of the last continental glacier. As the southern margin of the ice sheet melted and more and more ground was revealed, there remained for a period isolated fragments of stagnant ice ranging greatly in size and often covering many acres, particularly in the valleys, where the ice melted last. Some of these ice remnants became buried — or half-buried — in sand and gravel carried by the meltwater that poured off the receding glacier. Gradually the isolated fragments also melted, leaving abrupt depressions. Some are no bigger than house-size craters (or State-House size craters); others are much larger. Those that filled with groundwater became ponds. Kettle ponds tend to be deep with steep banks, indicating that a thick block or disk of ice that formerly bolstered the surrounding land has simply melted away, allowing the sandy soil to slump into its natural angle of repose.

Walden Pond fits this profile. Its greatest depth is slightly more than a hundred feet. Thoreau himself made a thorough survey with compass, chain, and sounding line while the pond was frozen. He then pointed out that "the deepest ponds are not so deep in proportion to their area as most suppose, and, if drained, would not leave very remarkable valleys. They are not like cups between the hills; for this one, which is so unusually deep for its area, appears in a vertical section through its center not deeper than a shallow plate."

Southwest of Walden Pond is Fairhaven Bay. This is the last vestige of glacial Lake Sudbury, which once filled the Sudbury Valley and stretched eight miles to the site of Framingham. The reason the water was so much higher than the present-day river is that the outlet to the north was blocked, at least in part, by the glacier. Only after the Merrimack Valley became clear of ice did Lake Sudbury drain down to its present level. Farther downstream, there was also a Lake Concord occupying much of the present-day town.

≈        ≈        ≈        ≈

**PUBLIC TRANSIT:** Walden Pond is located in Concord but touches the boundary with Lincoln. Although the railroad station at **Concord** is slightly closer, the 2.7-mile walk from **Lincoln Station** through woods and fields to Walden Pond is much more attractive and is really a bonus. The route is shown on **Map 22** at right and is described below.

To reach Lincoln, take the commuter train from **North Station** in Boston or from **Porter Square** in Cambridge. (North Station can be reached via the MBTA's Green or Orange Line, and Porter Square is on the Red Line.)

MAP 22 — Route from Lincoln Station to Walden Pond

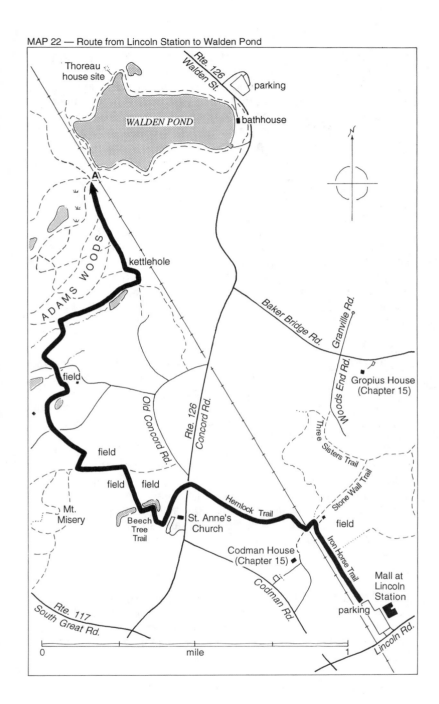

**After getting off the train at Lincoln** (or after arriving by car, if you choose this approach to Walden), descend from the station platform to the commuter parking lot, which is located behind a larger parking lot that serves the mall. The trailhead is at the back end of the commuter lot next to the railroad.

With the railroad on the left, follow a gravel road called the Iron Horse Trail, which leads past a small ball field. Continue through the woods and past a large field. At the end of the road, veer left into the woods, then left again onto the Stone Wall Trail. Cross a bridge over the railroad, then immediately turn right onto the Hemlock Trail. Follow the main path through the woods and then straight through scrubby growth to Concord Road.

With caution, cross Concord Road and continue downhill into the woods. Bear right next to a parking lot. Enter a weedy field and immediately turn right. Follow the Beech Tree Trail along two sides of the field, then turn right onto a causeway between two marshy ponds. Continue straight across a field. As you come abreast of the corner of a wooded lot on the right, turn left and follow the path across the field toward the distant woods.

Just before entering the woods, turn right along the edge of the field. Go 150 yards, then turn left into the trees on a trail leading to Adams Woods. This trail crosses private property but is open to the public courtesy of the landowners. Follow the path through the woods, across a gravel drive, and then down-hill through very tall pines. Eventually, turn left along the end of a grassy field, then re-enter the woods. Cross a small stream and a paved drive. Continue to a T-intersection, and there turn right. Follow the side of a ravine, with the slope rising on the left. After passing a pond, bear left at a trail intersection and continue uphill past a large kettlehole. At the top of the slope, bear right and continue past trails intersecting from the left. Eventually, at a five-way trail junction that is marked A on the map, turn right and go 30 yards to the railroad. With caution, cross the railroad and descend to Walden Pond.

≈          ≈          ≈          ≈

**AUTOMOBILE DIRECTIONS: Walden Pond** is located in Concord 16 miles northwest of Boston. (See •13 on **Map 1** on page 6, and also the corner panel of **Map 23** on page 158.) The best access is from the Route 2 bypass that swings to the west around Concord Center. Three approaches are described below.

**To Walden Pond from Boston:** The fastest route is to take the **Massachusetts Turnpike** (Interstate 90) west to Exit 15 for Interstate 95 northbound. Fork right immediately after the tollbooths, then bear left for I-95 north and follow the directions in the next section: "To Walden Pond from Interstate 95 (Route 128)."

Another approach is to follow **Storrow Drive** west along the Charles River toward Newton and Arlington. After passing Harvard University, take the exit for **Route 2** toward Arlington. In quick succession, cross the Eliot Bridge, then bear right, then left for Route 2 westbound. Go 2.1 miles on Route 2 (the Fresh Pond and Alewife Brook Parkways). After passing the MBTA's Alewife Station, bear left to continue west on Route 2 nearly 11 miles, then turn left onto Route 126 southbound and go 0.3 mile to the entrance for Walden Pond State Reservation on the left.

**To Walden Pond from Interstate 95 (Route 128):** Leave I-95 at Exit 29B for Route 2 west. Follow Route 2 for 4.6 miles, then turn left at a traffic light onto Route 126 southbound and go 0.3 mile to the entrance for Walden Pond State Reservation on the left.

**To Walden Pond from Interstate 495:** Leave I-495 at Exit 29A for Route 2 east toward Boston. Go 7 miles to the traffic circle at the Massachusetts penitentiary. From the rotary, continue east on Route 2 for 3.4 miles. At a traffic light turn right onto Route 126 southbound and go 0.3 mile to the entrance for Walden Pond State Reservation on the left.

≈    ≈    ≈    ≈

**WALKING:** As shown on **Map 23** on pages 158-159, the excursion described below has two distinct sections — a 2-mile circuit around **Walden Pond** and a 3.8-mile figure-eight that leads through the **Adams Woods to Fairhaven Bay.** The two sections are separated by a railroad, which can be crossed at the point indicated on the map. Obviously, there are ways to shorten this walk by cutting off all or part of the outing southwest of the railroad — but why would you want to do that? As attractive as Walden Pond is (and it has been much improved in recent years by restoration around the shore), the Adams Woods are better still.

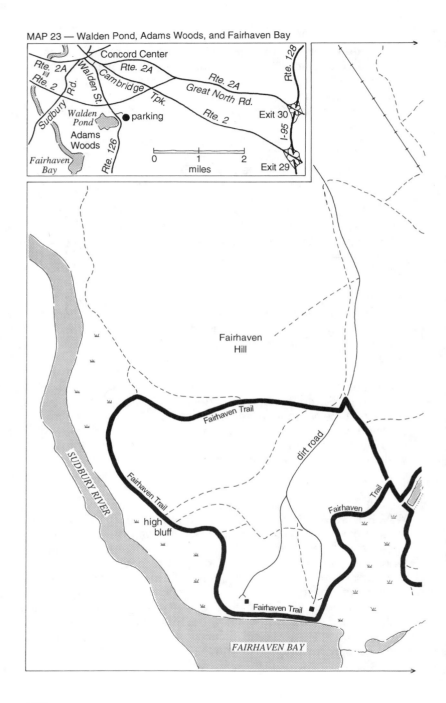

MAP 23 — Walden Pond, Adams Woods, and Fairhaven Bay

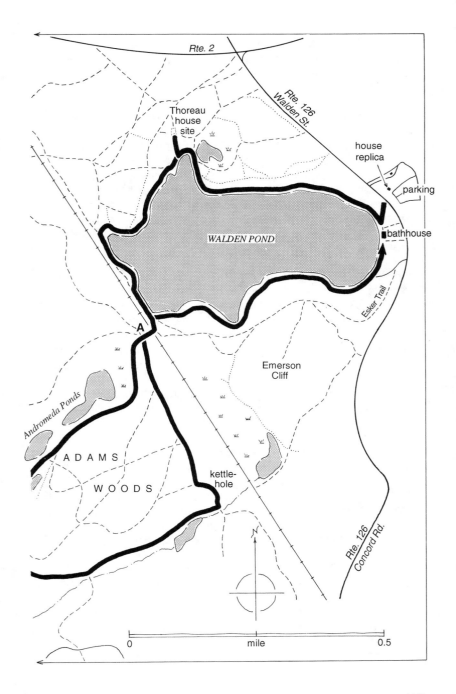

Rte. 2

Rte. 126
Walden St.

Thoreau
house
site

house
replica

parking

WALDEN POND

bathhouse

Esker Trail

A

Emerson
Cliff

Andromeda Ponds

A D A M S

W O O D S

kettle-
hole

Rte. 126
Concord Rd.

N

0                              mile                              0.5

159

**To get started** from the parking lot at Walden Pond, cross Route 126 and descend to the shore. With the water on the left, follow the path counter-clockwise around the pond. **The site of Thoreau's cabin** is about a third of the way around the pond, just after a cove. There is a sign at the trail indicating the cabin site, which is located somewhat back from the water's edge.

From the site of Thoreau's cabin, continue counter-clockwise around Walden Pond. Pass a cove at the end of the pond opposite the swimming beach. At the next cove, the trail follows the water's edge along the foot of a railroad embankment topped by a chainlink fence. At the end of the embankment, where the shoreline curves left, climb straight away from the waterside trail to the top of the embankment. With caution, cross the railroad and re-enter the woods.

**Southwest of the railroad** and about 30 yards into **Adams Woods**, there is an intersection of several trails that is marked A on Map 23. From this trail junction, go straight away from the railroad in order to descend toward a marshy pond, the first of the **Andromeda Ponds**, as they were called by Thoreau. At two intersections, fork right to follow a ridge past ponds on the right, then another pond on the left. At a T-intersection, turn right. Go 75 yards, then turn left downhill on the Fairhaven Trail.

**The Fairhaven Trail** is blazed with the white disks of the Concord Land Conservation Trust. With the slope rising on the right and a swamp on the left, follow the trail toward Fairhaven Bay. Within sight of a residential garage, fork left downhill. Pass below a house, then around to the right below the house and along the shore of Fairhaven Bay. Pass a boathouse and then, in 200 yards, another house. Continue as the trail turns inland and gradually rises along the slope to the top of the bluff. With the **Sudbury River** on the left, continue around a big bend. After the path curves inland at a swampy cove, fork right uphill. Follow the blazed trail past horse jumps and gradually up a shallow ravine. Continue as straight as possible past trails intersecting from either side. Eventually, after passing some posts blocking automobile access to the path, join a well-graded dirt road that serves the two houses that you passed earlier.

Follow the road left 50 yards, then turn right onto another path marked by more posts. Go 90 yards to a trail intersection. If you want to return to Walden Pond by the shortest route, turn left, but for the route shown on Map 23, continue straight 240 yards to the intersection where you first followed the Fairhaven Trail. Continue straight 75 yards to a junction at one of the Andromeda Ponds. Continue past the end of the pond, then bear right. Pass a trail intersecting from the left, then bear left in front of a trail blocked by a fence. Pass a trail intersecting from the right. (It leads to **Mt. Misery**; see Chapter 15.) With the slope rising on the left, follow the side of a ravine. After passing a pond, bear left at a trail intersection and continue uphill past a large kettlehole. At the top of the slope, bear right and continue past trails intersecting from the left in order to return to the five-way trail junction marked A just southwest of the railroad.

With caution, cross back over the railroad to the waterside trail at Walden Pond. With the water on the left, complete the circuit around the pond.

# GREAT MEADOWS

Great Meadows National Wildlife Refuge is mainly a place for bird watching as you slowly amble around the loop trails that are shown on **Map 25** on page 170.

The upper panel of Map 25 shows the **Dike Trail in Concord**, overlooking large marshy pools. The circuit is 2 miles (3.2 kilometers.) This is one of the best inland birding areas in Massachusetts.

The lower panel of Map 25 shows the **Weir Hill Trail in Sudbury**, where a wooded drumlin rises steeply from the floodplain. The loop is 1 mile (1.6 kilometers).

The trails at Great Meadows are open from half an hour before sunrise to half an hour after sunset. Dogs must be leashed. During most of the year, the **visitor center at Weir Hill** is open daily from 8 A.M. to 4 P.M.; during winter it is closed weekends and holidays. The refuge is managed by the U.S. Fish and Wildlife Service; telephone (978) 443-4661.

For directions to Great Meadows via public transit, please turn to page 167. Automobile directions to the Dike Trail in Concord start on page 168. To drive from Concord to Sudbury's Weir Hill, refer to page 171 and to the lower panel of **Map 24** on page 169.

---

GREAT MEADOWS is named for the grassy floodplain from which the Concord River recedes — or used to recede — each summer. In *A Week on the Concord and Merrimack Rivers*, which chronicles a trip taken in 1839, Thoreau says that *Musketaquid*, the Indian name for the Concord River, means Grass-ground or Meadow River. He continues:

> To an extinct race it was grass-ground, where they hunted and fished; and it is still perennial grass-ground to Concord farmers, who own the Great Meadows, and get the hay from year to year. . . . For a long time, they made the most of the driest season to get their hay, working sometimes till nine o'clock at night, sedulously paring with their scythes in the twilight round the hummocks left by the ice; but now it is not worth the getting

when they can come at it, and they look sadly round to their woodlots and uplands as a last resource.

The change that made the meadows worthless for hay was the building of a milldam in Billerica early in the nineteenth century. The dam flooded the meadows upstream to Wayland, as still seen today. Thoreau relates:

> Its farmers tell me that thousands of acres are flooded now, since the dams have been erected, where they remember to have seen the white honeysuckle or clover growing once, and they could go dry with shoes only in summer. Now there is nothing but bluejoint and sedge and cut-grass, standing in water all year round.

Transformed from grasslands into marsh, the meadows became prime waterfowl habitat, attracting hunters from throughout the region. Thoreau describes how, if his readers were to visit the river, "You shall see men you never heard of before, whose names you don't know, going away down through the meadows with long ducking guns, with watertight boots wading through the fowl-meadow grass, on bleak, wintry, distant shores, with guns at half-cock; and they shall see teal — bluewinged, green-winged — sheldrakes, whistlers, black ducks, ospreys, and many other wild and noble sights before night, such as they who sit in parlors never dream of."

In 1928, Samuel Hoar, a hunter, purchased part of the meadows in Concord. He built dikes through the marshland to impound the water and enhance still further the area's attractiveness for waterfowl. In 1944 Hoar gave 250 acres — the area at the present-day Dike Trail — to the U.S. Fish and Wildlife Service. Expanding on Hoar's gift, the government started buying more land in the 1960s to create what is now the 30,000-acre Great Meadows National Wildlife Refuge flanking the Sudbury and Concord Rivers for twelve miles.

AS IN THOREAU'S DAY, the Great Meadows are still one of the better places near Boston to see a variety of waterfowl. But identifying them is another matter, even if you have binoculars or a telescope. Far more than is the case with birds of field and forest, it is hard to get close, and lighting conditions on the water can be difficult. Problems of distance, haze, twilight, back-lighting, glare, and even molting often combine to render the colored, close-up pictures in field guides almost irrelevant. So what follows is a brief discussion of several key factors (in addition to plumage) that help to identify waterfowl.

The distinction between dabblers and divers is basic to identifying ducks, and is in turn closely allied to habitat preference. Mallards, black ducks, pintails, gadwalls, widgeons, shovelers, wood ducks, and several varieties of teal feed by dabbling at food that is floating on the surface of the water, or by upending their bodies in order to reach with their heads down to the bottom while their tails point in the air. Not surprisingly, dabblers prefer shallow marshes, ponds, and streams. Most of these so-called marsh ducks can be seen at Great Meadows, and some are present year-round. In contrast, redheads, canvasbacks, ring-necked ducks, scaup, goldeneyes, buffleheads, ruddy ducks, and mergansers feed or escape from danger by diving, often to considerable depths. They are typically found on larger, deeper lakes, rivers, and bays, and are seen at Great Meadows only during spring and fall migrations and in rare sightings during winter. Harlequin ducks, eiders, scoters, and oldsquaws also feed by diving but do not come inland as far as the Great Meadows. They are sea ducks and, with red-breasted mergansers, are seen along New England's coast in winter. To complicate matters, however, most surface-feeders occasionally dive. And you should keep in mind that there are some strong divers that are not classified as waterfowl, including loons, grebes, and cormorants, all of which are seen at the Great Meadows. Coots, which both dabble and dive, are also present.

The distinction between surface-feeding ducks and diving ducks is reflected in a few physical adaptations. Since diving requires more propulsive force than does dabbling or tilting, divers typically have bigger feet than surface-feeders, and their legs are located nearer their tails. These adaptations make them strong swimmers but awkward on land. In contrast, the smaller feet of surface-feeders enables them to walk and run well on land. Consequently, ducks seen feeding in fields are almost certainly surface-feeders (often mallards, pintails, or widgeons).

One conspicuous difference between surface-feeding ducks and diving ducks has to do with the way that they take flight. Surface-feeders take off nearly vertically, seeming to jump from the water. Divers, however, are heavier in relation to their size, and in consequence they only become airborne by first pattering along the surface for a considerable distance, like a seaplane gaining speed and taking off. An exception, however, is the bufflehead, a diver that jumps from the water like a surface-feeding duck.

In his booklet for bird watchers and hunters called *Ducks at a Distance*, naturalist Bob Hines outlines a checklist of identification traits to which observers can refer at different ranges. Even when ducks are far away, their flocking patterns on the water or in the air can be observed. For example, some species, such as pintails, widgeons, canvas-backs, redheads, scaup, and eiders gather in large rafts on the water during winter. When in flight, a few species (such as black ducks, mallards, pintails, and ring-necked ducks) are characterized by loose, random formations, while other species (such as gadwalls, widgeons, shovelers, teal, and scaup) usually fly in tight bunches. Mergansers and eiders fly in Indian file, low over the water, while canvasbacks and scoters fly in wavy lines and irregular V's, shifting back and forth between the two.

As with flight, idiosyncrasies of swimming distinguish certain birds. The ruddy duck, which cannot walk on land, often swims with its tail cocked vertically. Coots pump their heads back and forth while swimming. Common loons and cormorants float very low in the water, so that often it is difficult to see more than their heads and necks, with occasional glimpses of the top of their backs.

At mid-range it is sometimes possible, even in poor light conditions, to identify waterfowl simply by their silhouettes. For instance, unlike other ducks, pintails and oldsquaws have long needle-pointed tails; in addition, pintails have long, slender necks. Some profiles show highly distinctive features, like the disproportionately large, spatulated bills of shovelers or the swept-back crests of wood ducks and some mergansers. Also, wood ducks have large heads and short necks, and mergansers have long, narrow bills.

Plumage is basic to identification, but only if you have time to examine the birds in good light either up close or through binoculars or a telescope. But even then plumage can be confusing due to the fact that nearly all ducks lose their body feathers twice each year. When drakes shed their bright plumage after mating and enter what is called eclipse, they resemble the comparatively drab females of the species for a few weeks before assuming a motley, messy look as they return to breeding plumage. After the summer molt, shovelers and blue-winged teal may remain in eclipse even into winter.

As outlined by Roger Tory Peterson in his *A Field Guide to the Birds*, when ducks are flying, bold patterns of light and dark on either surface of the flapping wings may be conspicuous. For example, the contrasting pattern of a very dark body with flashing white wing linings helps to identify the black duck. In flight, the widgeon has a white belly and large white patches on each *fore*wing. The gadwall too has a white belly, but white patches are on the *rear* edge of the wing. And so on. Peterson's field guide includes a particularly good collection of black-and-white drawings showing how ducks appear in flight.

Even in pre-dawn darkness and other abysmal light conditions, some accomplished birders and hunters can identify waterfowl solely by their calls, although those of us who prefer to remain in bed may be tempted to dismiss such claims as just so much quackery. For what it is worth, I merely note here that different field guides employ an amazing variety of terms to describe duck calls, including *croak, peep, growl, grunt, twitter, purr, meow, moan, wheeze, squeak,* and *squeal.* Some authors are even given to mimicry. Hines, for example, has a rich vocabulary that starts with the basic *kwek-kwek* and goes on to *kack-kack, kaow, woh-woh, took-took, hoo-w-ett, cr-r-ek, squak, speer-speer,* and *kow-kow-kow-kow.* Clearly, however, something is lost in translation. For instance, while Hines hears oldsquaws, which are among the most vocal of ducks, say *caloo-caloo,* Peterson hears *ow-owdle-ow* and *owl-omelet.* This babble of duck talk raises the issue of what the various species are perceived to say once they migrate northward into French-speaking Quebec province and southward into Mexico. (For a relevant discussion, see Noel Perrin's suggestively-titled "Old MacBerlitz Had a Farm," which appeared in the *New Yorker* for January 27, 1962.)

Finally, for one of the ultimate niceties in the truly enjoyable pastime of bird watching and bird identification, some authorities say that a few ducks (particularly goldeneyes, also called whistlers) can be identified just by the singing, swishing, or rushing sounds made by their wings.

≈    ≈    ≈    ≈

**PUBLIC TRANSIT:** As described below, Concord is served by commuter train. Even so, getting from the train station at the center of town out to Great Meadows entails walking 2 miles — and, of course, another 2 miles back. But after all, walking is what this book is all about and Concord is an attractive town.

To reach Concord, take the commuter train from **North Station** in Boston or from **Porter Square** in Cambridge. (North Station can be reached via the MBTA's Green or Orange Line, and Porter Square is on the Red Line.)

The upper panel of **Map 24** on page 169 shows, by the dotted line, the route from the train station in Concord to Great Meadows. Directions are as follows: from the station, follow Sudbury Road toward the center of town. Join Main Street and go to Monument Square, then continue on Bedford Street (Route 62 east). After 1.4 miles, turn left onto Monsen Road and follow it to Great Meadows.

Incidentally, stretching for half a mile along Bedford Street is Sleepy Hollow Cemetery, where you may want to locate the graves of Thoreau, Hawthorne, Emerson, and Alcott on Author's Ridge. Some other places worth visiting in Concord are also shown on Map 24.

≈    ≈    ≈    ≈

### AUTOMOBILE DIRECTIONS TO GREAT MEADOWS
**(Concord Unit):** This section of the wildlife refuge is located in Concord 18 miles northwest of Boston. (See •14a on **Map 1** on page 6, and also **Map 24** at right.) Several approaches are described below.

**To Great Meadows (Concord Unit) from Boston:** The fastest route is to take the **Massachusetts Turnpike** (Interstate 90) west to Exit 15 for Interstate 95 northbound. Fork right immediately after the tollbooths, then bear left for I-95 north and follow the directions in the next section: "To Great Meadows (Concord Unit) from Interstate 95 (Route 128)."
   Another approach is to follow **Storrow Drive** west along the Charles River toward Newton and Arlington. After passing Harvard University, take the exit for **Route 2** toward Arlington. In quick succession, cross the Eliot Bridge, then bear right, then left for Route 2 westbound. Go 2.1 miles on Route 2 (the Fresh Pond and Alewife Brook Parkways). After passing the MBTA's Alewife Station, bear left to continue west on Route 2 nearly 10 miles to an intersection where Route 2 bends left. Leave Route 2 here and continue straight 1.6 miles into Concord Center. At Monument Square, turn right onto Route 62 east (Bedford Street). After 1.4 miles, turn left onto Monsen Road. Go just 0.3 mile, then turn left into Great Meadows National Wildlife Refuge. Follow the entrance road 0.2 mile to the parking lot.

**To Great Meadows (Concord Unit) from Interstate 95 (Route 128):** Leave I-95 at Exit 29B for Route 2 west toward Concord. Go 3.5 miles and then — where Route 2 bends left at an intersection — continue straight 1.6 miles into Concord Center. At Monument Square, turn right onto Route 62 east (Bedford Street). After 1.4 miles, turn left onto Monsen Road. Go just 0.3 mile, then turn left into Great Meadows National Wildlife Refuge. Continue 0.2 mile to the parking lot.

**To Great Meadows (Concord Unit) from Interstate 495:** Leave I-495 at Exit 29A for Route 2 east toward Boston. Go 7 miles to the traffic circle at the Massachusetts penitentiary. From the rotary, continue on Route 2 east another 1.4 miles, then turn left onto Route 62 eastbound and go 1.5 miles through Concord Center to a T-intersection at Monument Square. Bear left then immediately turn right to continue on Route 62 east (Bedford Street). After 1.4 miles, turn left onto

MAP 24 — Great Meadows

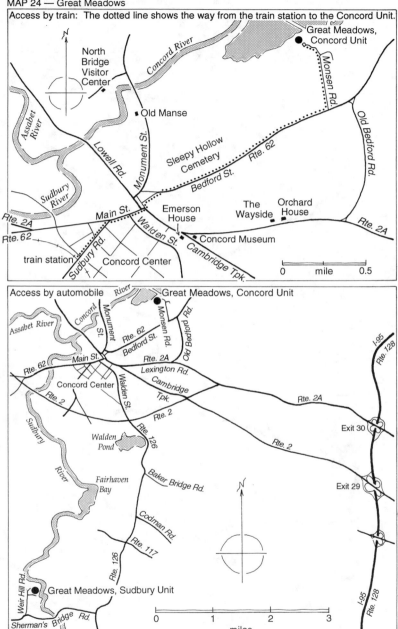

Access by train: The dotted line shows the way from the train station to the Concord Unit.

Access by automobile

MAP 25 — Great Meadows: Concord Unit (upper panel) and Sudbury Unit (lower panel)

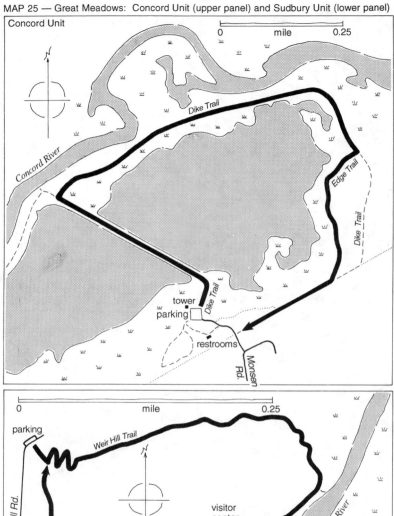

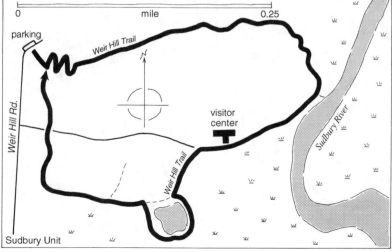

Monsen Road. Go just 0.3 mile, then turn left into Great Meadows National Wildlife Refuge. Follow the entrance road 0.2 mile to the parking lot.

≈    ≈    ≈    ≈

**WALKING:** The upper panel of **Map 25** at left shows the **Concord Unit of Great Meadows National Wildlife Refuge**. The main trail is a 2-mile loop from which a few minor paths branch off.

From the parking lot, head out across the Dike Trail, then continue clockwise around the circuit.

≈
≈    ≈    ≈    ≈
≈

**AUTOMOBILE DIRECTIONS from the Concord Unit of Great Meadows to the Sudbury Unit:** Weir Hill in Sudbury is south of Concord. (See •14b on **Map 1** on page 6, and also the lower panel of **Map 24** on page 169.)

From Great Meadows in Concord, return toward the center of town via Bedford Street. As you approach Concord Center, you must fork right onto Court Lane. At the next intersection, turn left to continue on Route 62 west, then left again at Monument Square, then right onto Main Street. After just one block, turn left onto Walden Street, which becomes Route 126 south-bound. Go 5 miles. (In the process you will cross Route 2, pass Walden Pond, cross Route 117, and enter Wayland.) At the end of the 5 miles, turn right onto Sherman's Bridge Road. Go 1.3 miles across the Sudbury River, then turn right onto Weir Hill Road and follow it 0.4 mile to the parking lot at the end of the road — or, if it is open, you can turn into the entrance for the visitor center after just 0.3 mile.

≈    ≈    ≈    ≈

**WALKING:** The lower panel of **Map 25** at left shows the mile-long Weir Hill Loop Trail at the **Sudbury Unit of Great Meadows National Wildlife Refuge**. From the parking lot at the end of Weir Hill Road, cross the street and follow the trail uphill to the circuit shown on the map. Or, if it is open, you can start at the visitor center.

# 15

# LINCOLN

Located northwest of Boston, the town of Lincoln has about seventy miles of trails that are open to the public (residents and non-residents alike) from dawn to dusk.

**Map 26** on page 181 shows a walk of 6 miles (9.6 kilometers). The route leads through woods and meadows to **Mount Misery** and the **Sudbury River**. The return leg and the spur at the end lead take in two historic houses.

The **Codman House**, shown on page 177, is a magnificent federal-style mansion. It is open June 1 through October 15, Wednesday through Sunday. Tours start each hour from 11 A.M. to 4 P.M. There is an admission fee to the house; the grounds are open free of charge. The house is owned by the Society for the Preservation of New England Antiquities (SPNEA). For information, telephone (781) 259-8843.

Providing a piquant contrast with the Codman House is the 1938 **Walter Gropius House**, designed by the architect as his home. Despite its modern style, it too is a SPNEA property. Gropius was founder of the Bauhaus in Germany, which he left to teach at Harvard's Graduate School of Design. From June to mid-October, the Gropius House follows the same schedule as the Codman House. During the rest of the year, it is open every weekend with tours each hour from 11 A.M. to 4 P.M. Again, there is an admission fee. For information, telephone (781) 259-8098.

For directions to Lincoln via public transit, please turn to page 178. Automobile directions start on page 179, and walking directions begin on page 180.

---

LIKE MOST NEW ENGLAND TOWNS, Lincoln was carved out of other, older towns. In the Massachusetts Bay Colony the first step toward the creation of a town occurred when a group of sponsors and settlers petitioned the General Court (that is, the legislature) to establish a provisional settlement called a plantation. After going through the form of obtaining land title from the Indians, the General Court appointed a committee of proprietors to arrange for distribution of house lots and fields among the settlers. When the plantation was well established, it was raised by the General Court to the status of a town, which required sending a representative to the Court. Each town was also required to support a local minister, for the Congregational Church was the social, political, and educational as well as spiritual center of the settlement.

The early towns encompassed huge areas. The original grant to the town of Dedham, for example, contained nearly two hundred square miles. In the mid-1600s, Cambridge included territory as far to the northwest as present-day Bedford and Billerica. Even nowadays, the towns of Plymouth and Middleborough to the south of Boston have 98 and 70 square miles, respectively. Such large areas guaranteed to the original settlement an adequate mix of plowland, pasture, timberland, water, and waterpower. In a system reminiscent of feudal England, each family's need for different types of land was met by allotting it several tracts, although ownership was outright rather than by tenancy. The house lots (typically ten or fifteen acres each) were at the town center, and nearby around the edge, in separate parcels, were each man's field, pasture, and woodlot, totaling several hundred acres per household. In the usual course of development, however, the first few decades of a town's existence saw a series of divisions by which the common land farther and farther from the town center was distributed to individuals. Often the original settlers raised capital by selling their initial holdings to newcomers and then moving onto larger tracts in the hinterland. The result was the dispersal of the settlement from the village lots to the outlying districts, despite laws requiring all dwellings to be within a certain distance of the meetinghouse in order to promote attendance, mutual aid, and defense. As the settlers spread out through the countryside, complaints about the long trip to church were met by granting winter privileges of nonattendance. Later, as the outlying population increased, new parishes were established and ultimately became independent towns. This did not take place without opposition from the mother towns, which resisted the loss of tax revenue.

Lincoln followed this familiar pattern. Long known as Niptown among the surrounding towns from which parts were bitten off, Lincoln was pieced together from the remote areas — the farms, as such outlying districts were called — of Concord on the west and of Lexington and Weston on the east. These last two towns had previously been the farms of Cambridge and Watertown. Complaining that they were "under great difficulties and inconveniences by reason of their distance from their respective places of worship," the residents of Lincoln first petitioned to create an independent town in 1734 so that they could establish their own local church. Their plea was finally granted by the General Court in 1754.

Although Lincoln became a town, it never developed a strong commercial center, as did nearby Lexington and Concord. Even after arrival of the railroad in the early 1840s, and even as wealthy merchants and professionals from the city established country estates at the end of the nineteenth century and beginning of the next, Lincoln remained largely agricultural in character. Its farmers prospered through dairying, raising livestock, and growing produce, fruit, and hay for the Boston market. Some newcomers became gentlemen farmers. Despite suburbanization that started in the 1930s and accelerated after World War II, Lincoln still retains its rural tone today. Just how this has been achieved is the subject of the next section.

SKEPTICS MAY SAY that the preservation of Lincoln's rural appearance simply reflects its wealth, but the fact is that Lincoln has accomplished far more in regard to land conservation than many other towns with similar economic profiles. By using a variety of techniques that are applicable to any municipality, Lincoln has become a model showing how towns can accommodate growth while yet preserving historic landscapes and rural countryside.

One agency that is active in preserving open space in Lincoln is the town's Conservation Commission. In 1957 the Massachusetts legislature passed an act enabling towns to create a municipal agency for the protection of land and water resources. Each commission was encouraged to prepare a plan for conservation and outdoor recreation based on a survey of the town's natural assets and needs. By preparing such plans, towns became eligible to receive funds from the state's Self-Help Program for the purchase and preservation of undeveloped land. Over the years, these state grants have often been accompanied by still larger sums from the federal Land and Water Conservation Fund. Lincoln's Conservation Commission was one of the first in the state, and it now manages nearly 1700 acres, much of it purchased with state and federal aid. But it has been the residents' willingness to tax themselves, expressed time and again at town meeting, that has provided the essential local funding, which cumulatively has averaged about 50 percent of purchase costs. The town's single largest acquisition was 227 acres at Mount Misery, which is one of the areas featured in the walk outlined at the end of this chapter. Lincoln purchased Mount Misery in 1969 for approximately $1.8 million, of which a quarter came from the state and half from the federal government. Some of the town's acquisitions, such as Adams Woods described in Chapter 13, have been assisted also by major fund-raising drives and by charitable gifts from the landowners themselves.

One way to stretch conservation dollars is to purchase not the entire fee interest in land but rather just the development rights (if the seller is willing). In 1989 one Lincoln landowner — a descendant of one of the town's original settlers in the 1640s — sold the town the development rights to his farm field for less than half the full market value of the land. Under such arrangements, the continuation of farming is not only permissible but is also made economically feasible because burdensome property taxes are reduced to reflect the loss of development potential. At the same time the owner gets some cash. In towns that are striving to preserve traditional landscapes, the purchase of development rights may be appropriate whenever the owner wants to retain his land as it is, and yet at the same time is sorely tempted to sell because of high taxes and big offers from developers.

Municipal conservation commissions help to preserve natural areas in other ways as well. Under the Wetlands Protection Act of 1972, conservation commissions were given responsibility to review all development plans in order to prevent, or at least to constrain, the filling of swamps and marshes. Lincoln's Conservation Commission led an effort to map more than 1300 acres of wetlands in the town and to oversee adoption of a municipal law restricting their development. Headed by a local geologist, volunteers spent thousands of hours walking the edges of the town's wetlands to accurately determine their boundaries. Although wetlands conservation does not provide for public access, it is nonetheless relevant to the overall process of steering development to appropriate and predictable places.

Innovative zoning has been another municipal tool for preserving open space. Just south of Mount Misery is Farrar Pond Village, Lincoln's first development in an Open Space Residential District formulated by the Planning Board and approved by town meeting in 1972. Under this zoning provision, houses and condominiums were clustered on the upland at a distance from the pond, while the shore was preserved as a buffer and trail corridor managed by the Farrar Pond Conservation Trust.

There is also a town-wide land trust. The private, nonprofit Lincoln Land Conservation Trust was established in 1957 "for the purpose of maintaining the rural character of the community by holding land in trust for the benefit of the inhabitants of Lincoln." Although it is supported only by membership dues and charitable gifts of land and money, the Trust has acquired nearly 400 acres. In some cases where land was offered for development, the trust acted quickly to purchase the property with funds donated principally by neighboring owners seeking

to preserve their surroundings. In addition to acquiring land, the Trust has linked distant parts of town with trails marked by colored disks. The Trust even publishes *A Guide to Conservation Land in Lincoln*, a 149-page pocketbook. These trails are open to all, whether they live in Lincoln or not. Please stick to the blazed paths, and if you see any litter, please pick it up. The straightforwardness with which Lincoln has opened and publicized its conservation land compares favorably with many other towns.

Yet another conservation organization at Lincoln is the Rural Land Foundation, a national pioneer of a technique called limited development. Established in 1965, this nonprofit foundation is run by a board of trustees that is elected by the general membership of the Lincoln Land Conservation Trust. On several occasions the Rural Land Foundation has bought a tract and then subdivided some of it in order to finance preservation of the rest. The Foundation's first project was Wheeler Farm at the southeast Corner of Route 2 and Bedford Road. Using pledge guarantees of $10,000 each from thirty Lincoln residents as collateral for a loan, the Foundation bought 109 acres, created a 55-acre subdivision of eleven lots, and transferred the remaining 54 acres to the Lincoln Land Conservation Trust. Another project was the Mall at Lincoln Station, where the walk described in this chapter starts. The mall and the adjacent 125-units of low- and moderate-income housing occupy 17 acres that were leased by the Foundation to the developer, who pays a yearly ground rent plus a share of the profits over a certain amount. Fifty-five adjacent acres that were part of the original parcel were set aside permanently for conservation and recreation. A portion of this tract is a hay meadow maintained by Codman Community Farms, an organization that administers garden plots and grazes livestock on municipal conservation land. Other tracts are cultivated by kids from the suburbs and Boston who, under the auspices of the Food Project, annually donate tons of vegetables to food banks. Some municipal fields are leased to organic-food co-ops and commercial farmers.

$$\approx \qquad \approx \qquad \approx \qquad \approx$$

**PUBLIC TRANSIT:** Lincoln is served by commuter train from **North Station** in Boston and from **Porter Square** in Cambridge. (North Station can be reached via the MBTA's Green or Orange Line, and Porter Square is on the Red Line.)

After getting off the train at Lincoln, descend from the station platform to the commuter parking lot, which is located behind a larger parking lot that serves the mall. The trailhead is at the back end of the commuter lot next to the railroad.

≈     ≈     ≈     ≈

**AUTOMOBILE DIRECTIONS:  Lincoln** is located 13 miles northwest of Boston just outside Interstate 95.  (See •15 on **Map 1** on page 6, and also the corner panel of **Map 26** on page 181.) Several approaches are described below.

**To Lincoln from Boston:** The fastest route is to take the **Massachusetts Turnpike** (Interstate 90) west to Exit 15 for Interstate 95 northbound. Fork right immediately after the toll-booths, then bear left for I-95 north and follow the directions in the next section: "To Lincoln from Interstate 95 (Route 128)."

Another approach is to follow **Storrow Drive** west along the Charles River toward Newton and Arlington. After passing Harvard University, take the exit for **Route 2** toward Arlington. In quick succession, cross the Eliot Bridge, then bear right, then left for Route 2 westbound. Go 2.1 miles on Route 2 (the Fresh Pond and Alewife Brook Parkways). After passing the MBTA's Alewife Station, bear left to continue west on Route 2 for 8.6 miles to Bedford Road toward Lincoln. (The exit is a jug handle on the right, just after the traffic light.) Follow Bedford Road 1.1 miles. At an intersection with Trapelo Road, continue straight on Lincoln Road 1.4 miles and then — just before a railroad crossing — turn right into the entrance for the Mall at Lincoln Station. Follow the left edge of the mall's parking lot to the commuter parking lot at the rear. Although a sign says "no un-authorized or unregistered vehicles," this lot is an approved place for trail users to park.

**To Lincoln from Interstate 95 (Route 128):** Leave I-95 at Exit 28B for Trapelo Road west toward Lincoln. Go 2.6 miles, then turn left onto Lincoln Road. Follow Lincoln Road 1.4 miles and then — just before a railroad crossing — turn right into the entrance for the Mall at Lincoln Station. Follow the left edge of the mall's parking lot to the commuter parking lot at the rear. Although a sign says "no unauthorized or unregistered vehi-cles," this lot is an approved place for trail users to park.

**To Lincoln from Interstate 495:** Leave I-495 at Exit 29A for Route 2 east toward Boston. Go 7 miles to the traffic circle at the Massachusetts penitentiary. From the rotary, continue east on Route 2 for 5.7 miles, then turn right onto Bedford Road toward Lincoln. Follow Bedford Road 1.1 miles. At an intersection with Trapelo Road, continue straight on Lincoln Road 1.4 miles and then — just before a railroad crossing — turn right into the entrance for the Mall at Lincoln Station. Follow the left edge of the mall's parking lot to the commuter parking lot at the rear. Although a sign says "no unauthorized or unregistered vehicles," this lot is an approved place for trail users to park.

≈        ≈        ≈        ≈

**WALKING:  Lincoln** has an town-wide system of foot trails and bridle paths altogether totaling about 70 miles. Located mostly on land owned by the municipal Lincoln Conservation Commission and the private Lincoln Land Conservation Trust, these trails are open to the public. The route that is described below is merely one of many that are possible in Lincoln. For more information you may want to buy a map of town trails, sold at the Town Offices on Lincoln Road. The Lincoln Land Conservation Trust publishes *A Guide to Conservation Land in Lincoln,* sold at the Old Town Hall Exchange across from the town offices.

**Map 26** at right shows a 6-mile walk through woods and fields to **Mount Misery** and the **Sudbury River**, then back past the eighteenth-century **Codman House**. The spur at the end leads 1.5 miles round-trip to the **Gropius House**, epitomizing the International Style of the 1930s. The Codman House and the Gropius House are open to the public per the schedules noted in the introduction on page 173. By all means take the time to tour one or both houses.

**To get started** from the commuter parking lot at Lincoln Station, go to the back of the lot near the railroad. With the railroad on the left, follow a gravel road called the Iron Horse Trail, which leads past a small ball field. Continue through the woods and past a large meadow. At the end of the road, veer left into the woods, then left again onto the Stone Wall Trail. Cross a bridge over the railroad, then immediately turn right onto the Hemlock Trail. Follow the main path through the woods and then straight through scrubby growth to Concord Road.

  With caution, cross Concord Road and continue downhill into the woods. Bear right next to a parking lot. Enter a weedy field and immediately turn right. Follow the Beech Tree Trail as it bends left, then right in order to cross a causeway between two

MAP 26 — Lincoln

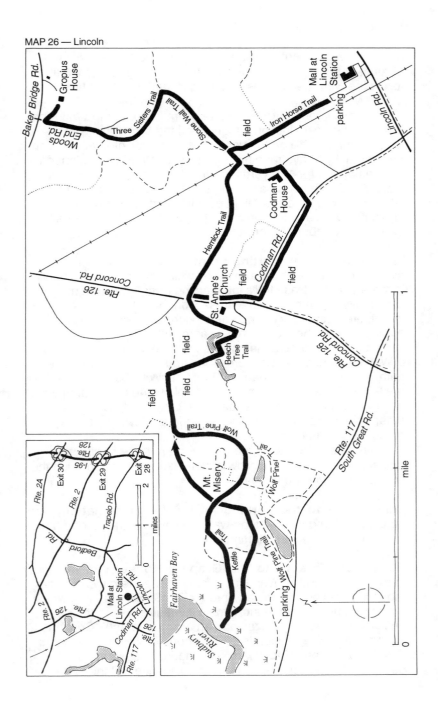

marshy ponds. Continue straight across a field. As you come abreast of the corner of a wooded lot on the right, turn left and follow the worn track across the field toward the distant woods at Mount Misery.

Enter the woods and immediately turn left onto the Wolf Pine Trail. At the next junction, fork right off the Wolf Pine Trail, keeping a rocky hill on the right. At a four-way intersection, continue straight. At yet another four-way junction, go straight on the Kettle Trail for 120 yards, then fork left to stay on the Kettle Trail. (The path soon passes a large kettlehole on the left.) Continue more or less straight past trails intersecting from left and right. With a marsh on the right, go all the way to the trail's end at the Sudbury River.

**To return to your starting point,** follow the trail straight away from the river, past the trail by which you came, and uphill into the woods. Pass trails intersecting from left and right. Eventually, at an oblique T-intersection, bear left. At subsequent intersections, continue as straight as possible. After emerging from the woods, return across the fields by the way you came. Bear left at the parking lot to return to Concord Road.

With caution, cross Concord Road and turn right on a paved path. Cross Codman Road and turn left. With Codman Road on the left and a large field on the right, follow the paved path about a third of a mile to the entrance to the Codman House on the other side of the road. Follow the Codman driveway to the mansion and garden.

To complete your walk, go to the greenhouse behind the mansion and from there follow a trail past a cottage, through the woods, and over the railroad.

**To go back to the parking lot by the train station,** turn right through a gap in a stone wall to follow the gravel road (the Iron Horse Trail) to the starting point.

**To follow the spur to the Gropius House,** continue straight on the Stone Wall Trail after crossing the railroad. After the stone wall ends, turn left onto the Three Sisters Trail, which gradually curves right. Ignore trails intersecting from the left (including one where blazes and an arrow lead left). Continue to a paved driveway that leads left to Woods End Road. With caution, follow Woods End Road. The modern house at #5 was design by Marcel Brauer as his own residence. At the intersection of Woods Road and Baker Bridge Road is the Gropius House on the right at the top of a meadow, through which you can walk to reach the house. The garage at the entrance to the driveway off Baker Bridge Road has been converted into a waiting room for people who want to tour the house.

After visiting the Gropius House, return by the way you came. About 20 yards before the railroad, turn left through a gap in a stone wall to follow the gravel road (the Iron Horse Trail) to the starting point at the commuter parking lot at Lincoln Station.

# 16

# MOUNT AUBURN CEMETERY

Located on the Cambridge-Watertown boundary, Mount Auburn is America's first and most famous garden cemetery. It is also a magnificent arboretum, containing trees and shrubs from temperate climates around the world. The calendar of bloom starts in March and continues through the summer and into fall — although spring, of course, is the peak season.

The landscape at Mount Auburn at is a labyrinth of swales and ridges connected by miles of winding drives outlined on **Map 27** on page 192. Several ponds occupy the hollows, and much of Boston is visible from the Washington Tower at the center of the cemetery. The funerary monuments are fascinating and sometimes fantastical, ranging from modest, weatherworn tablets to allegorical statuary, family mausoleums, and even a massive granite sphinx that commemorates the Union's Civil War dead. There are graves and memorials of many noteworthy people, and much of the sculpture and architecture is of historic interest. Neither depressing nor spooky, the cemetery is a highly enjoyable place to wander for an hour or the better part of a day.

Mount Auburn Cemetery is open daily from 8 A.M. to 5 P.M. During daylight saving time, the gates stay open to 7 P.M. Visitors are welcome, but please keep in mind that this is an active cemetery, not a park. Dogs, bicycling, roller-skating, jogging, and picnicking are prohibited. For information on audio tape tours, lectures, and other programs, telephone (617) 547-7105.

For directions to Mount Auburn via public transit or automobile, please turn to page 190.

---

WELL BEFORE THE FOUNDING of Mount Auburn Cemetery, Boston was outgrowing its graveyards. Between 1790 and 1825, the city's population tripled, and of course the number of people dying each year also soared. During the colonial period, the common practice was to inter the urban dead in crowded burial grounds next to churches or in vaults within the churches themselves, but by the early nineteenth century the cramped graveyards and crypts were thought to be a menace to public health, possibly (it was feared) polluting wells or exuding noxious gases.

Urban burial was deplored for its insecurity as well. Final resting places were not at all final. Space was so limited that bones were often dug up to make way for the more recently dead.

Also contributing to the movement for burial reform were changing attitudes toward death. By the beginning of the nineteenth century, the liberal wing of the Congregational church had become Unitarian. Its leaders preached a "softened" theology of universal salvation and toleration that accommodated a wide range of thinking and speculation about the afterlife. For Unitarians leaning toward pantheism, death was a melding of the individual with the natural world. This was the theme of William Cullen Bryant's poem *Thanatopsis* (meaning "meditation on death"), published in 1817 and well received in Boston. At the same time, an elegiac sensibility of pastoral melancholy was popularized by the English school of eighteenth-century graveyard poets.

Tangential to burial reform was the desire, shared by many Americans, to commemorate the new nation's heroes and history by developing public monuments like those in Europe. Accordingly, numerous publicly supported memorials were erected in the second and third decades of the nineteenth century. Baltimore, for example, undertook to build a monument to Washington in 1815 — the first of many throughout the country. In 1820 the bicentennial of the Pilgrims' landing was solemnized by a monument at Plymouth, where Daniel Webster delivered an address saying that such memorials were an appropriate way to cultivate a sense of national history and to inspire future generations. The Bunker Hill Monument was begun in 1825. In much the same spirit, families — or wealthy and distinguished families, at any rate — sought a place where they could memorialize themselves and honor their ancestors by erecting family tombs.

These several currents gave rise to proposals for large rural cemeteries as an alternative to crowded urban graveyards. Proponents pointed to the example of classical Greece and Rome, where burial grounds were outside the city walls. While not the first to suggest the idea, one energetic advocate was Dr. Jacob Bigelow, a physician and amateur botanist who in 1825 convened a meeting of prominent Bostonians to explore the possibility of establishing a new cemetery in a country setting near the city. Although the proposal was well received, it languished because of the lack of an appropriate and affordable site. In 1830, however, Bigelow suggested to George Brimmer, a friend who owned Mount

Auburn, that his property be used to create a rural burial ground, if enough subscribers could be found to buy the land. Brimmer had purchased the site only a few years before with the aim of developing it as a country estate. He had already started planting ornamental trees and had laid out several avenues, but he enthusiastically backed the cemetery proposal and agreed to sell his land at no profit to himself.

In order to dispel prejudice against the creation of a new cemetery, Bigelow next enlisted the aid of the recently established Massachusetts Horticultural Society, for which he was the corresponding secretary. This organization wanted to found a botanical garden for research in all branches of horticulture, but it had no money, and so it agreed to a combined garden and cemetery as a way to pay for land through the sale of burial lots. In its first report, the cemetery committee identified several objectives. First and foremost, burial places would be permanent: the dead would be able to "repose undisturbed through countless ages." Attractive and appropriate landscaping would soothe the bereaved and encourage visits to the "bower-sequestered monument of a much loved friend." The patronage of distinguished families and individuals would be sought so that the monuments could keep fresh the example of great men. Indeed, the souls of the deceased themselves would "commune with those who come to do honor to their names." And finally, the cemetery would provide "a place of healthful, refreshing, and agreeable resort." With these goals in mind, the Horticultural Society agreed to buy the land as soon as a hundred burial lots were spoken for, as occurred after just two months. Accordingly, in 1831 the Massachusetts legislature expanded the scope of the Horticultural Society to include the running of a cemetery. Mount Auburn thus became the first garden cemetery in America, setting the pattern for what has since become the usual form of burial ground throughout the nation. In another innovation for America, Mount Auburn adopted a nonsectarian policy modeled on the cemetery of Pere Lachaise outside Paris, which since 1804 had been used for burial of persons of different faiths.

Mount Auburn Cemetery was an unqualified success from the beginning. Within a few years the proprietors saw that the whole property would be wanted as a burial ground, and that there would be no room for experimental nurseries. Arrangements were made within the Horticultural Society to let the cemetery go its own way as an independent corporation. In 1835 the Horticultural Society conveyed the Brimmer tract and other adjoining land to the new cemetery corporation in return for receiving annually one quarter of the very substantial income from the sale of lots in the original section. Ten years later the Society built its first Horticultural Hall, paid for largely by Mount Auburn Cemetery.

The cemetery developed steadily, becoming the region's most distinguished place of burial. In a manner novel for a cemetery, Mount Auburn was a fashionable carriage drive where visitors could view the many memorials and the attractive landscaping. Patrons bought family lots and erected family tombs, often inscribed with the genealogy of prior generations buried elsewhere. Some monuments, such as the statues of Universalist clergyman Hosea Ballou and mathematician and astronomer Nathaniel Bowditch (author of *The New American Practical Navigator*), were major artistic commissions paid for by grateful followers and admirers. A few cenotaphs were erected by individuals and by groups to honor men not buried-at Mount Auburn. For example, the wealthy bibliophile Thomas Dowse built a monument to Benjamin Franklin in the 1850s. The castellated tower at Mount Auburn was built in 1852 as a memorial to George Washington — and also to add a touch of the picturesque in the tradition of eighteenth century English landscaping that the proprietors of Mount Auburn sought to emulate. Landscape work included recontouring large areas to reduce the height of hills, fill marshy areas, and turn large ponds into the smaller "lakes" seen today. Gradually, the rural cemetery of the early years, located in a natural forest, was transformed into a garden cemetery dominated by monuments and specimen trees, thinned and trimmed high to improve views. In addition to native trees, there were (and are) numerous exotic species from Europe and northern Asia.

During its 170-year history, Mount Auburn Cemetery has gone through several phases, some of which are apparent in the monuments and landscaping. At first the preferred style for memorials was classical, as was the case at Pere Lachaise and other contemporary European cemeteries. A few tombs are based on specific Greek and Roman examples. Common features include classical pediments, urns, and single columns, sometimes expressively "broken" or draped with stone shrouds. Egyptian motifs, principally obelisks, were also deemed appropriate. After all, the Egyptian style had palpable funerary associations and overtones of permanence. Early in the nineteenth century, a widespread interest in things Egyptian was sparked by illustrated books prepared by French archeologists who had accompanied Napoleon's army to Egypt in 1798. The cemetery gate (designed by Jacob Bigelow and built in 1842) was modeled on examples from Dendera and Karnac, or so Bigelow said. There are also several family crypts in the Egyptian manner, with massive walls, flat pilasters, and distinctive lintels. In the middle of the nineteenth century, the Gothic Revival affected funerary monuments as it did architecture generally. The cemetery has numerous gothic crypts and little gothic tabernacles. Built in the late 1840s, the Bigelow Chapel (it is shown on page 184) is in the gothic style, somewhat simplified because of the difficulty of working in granite. As the Victorian period progressed, funerary motifs became more sentimental, including sheaves of cut grain, angels, lambs, watchful dogs, and figures of women representing Hope, Faith, Charity (each has its distinctive insignia) or the abstract idea of Grief.  At the same time, some patrons commissioned tombs in the showy French style of the Second Empire.  The Romanesque Revival, signaled by construction of Boston's Trinity Church during the 1870s, is also apparent in some monuments.  By the early twentieth century, Celtic crosses were regarded as a tasteful alternative to Victorian sentimentality and ostentation, per the example of art critic John Ruskin, champion of anonymous medieval craftsmanship and ethnically appropriate architecture.  Of Scottish descent, Ruskin died in 1900, and for his grave at Coniston churchyard in England he specified a Celtic cross.  Dating tombs by their style, however, is problematic because different designs and motifs were used repeatedly over long periods, and many monuments are an eclectic compilation.

One nineteenth-century fashion has been purposefully curtailed and even eradicated in part. During the cemetery's early decades it was common for families to enclose their plots with fences of cast or wrought iron.  Later, in the 1860s, granite curbing was used to demarcate the lots.  To reduce clutter, the cemetery encouraged gradual removal of these features over a period of half a century beginning in the 1870s.  As the cemetery opened new sections, new rules were introduced in keeping with the Landscape Lawn style developed at Spring Grove Cemetery in Cincinnati.  At the southern end of Mount Auburn, for example, the rules limit lots to one major monument, without fences or curbs.  Subsidiary grave markers are permitted only if they don't exceed thirty inches in height.  This trend in part reflected the cemetery corporation's growing responsibility for upkeep.  During the first few decades, individual lots were maintained by each family, while the rest of the cemetery was left in relatively wild woods and rough meadow.  But as families moved away or died out, neglect of private lots became increasingly common.  Sometimes the management was forced to condemn and take out deteriorated features such as rusting fences.  At first merely an option, perpetual care was included in the price of lots after 1876.  As remedial action, the cemetery repurchased unused portions of old lots in exchange for perpetual care of the used parts.  By the end of the nineteenth century, when the Victorian Gardenesque style prevailed, the cemetery company was maintaining nearly the entire grounds to the standard of an urban park, including ornamental flower beds planted with annuals.

Since the early twentieth century, the trend in monuments and landscaping has been increasingly toward simplicity, both as a matter of taste and economy.  Near Willow Pond, for example, monuments are required to be flush to the ground in order to reduce what designer Laurence Caldwell called the "hodge podge of objects and the monotonous view of tombstones." One throwback, however, is the Governor Winthrop Lot. Laid out in 1944 and featuring slate stones in a compact setting, it aims to duplicate the atmosphere of an old colonial burying ground. Reflecting the popularity of newly renovated Colonial Williamsburg, the Winthrop Lot was an ironic switch for a cemetery that had been created a century earlier in reaction against such graveyards. More recently, as space has become limited, the cemetery has turned to structural innovations, including the Auburn Court Crypts near Auburn Lake, developed in 1973 as a sort of mortuary condominium.

Meanwhile, in the older sections of the cemetery, the artificiality of the Victorian Gardenesque style has been replaced by more naturalistic plantings of flowering trees and shrubs, including masses of rhododendrons, azaleas, mountain laurel, dogwood, lilacs, and crabs, as well as evergreens for year-round interest. This trend was initiated in the 1930s. Recent landscaping includes a makeover, in the early 1990s, of the banks of Willow Pond, showing the popularity of ornamental grasses and ground covers, combined with trees and shrubs that provide winter berries for birds. There are also weeping varieties of willow, beech, and cherry — long deemed appropriately funereal and picturesque.

≈　　　≈　　　≈　　　≈

**PUBLIC TRANSIT:** From the MBTA's **Harvard Station** on the Red Line, take Trolley-Bus 71 or 73 (Watertown or Waverley). The ride to Mount Auburn takes less than five minutes. Soon after the bus crosses Fresh Pond Parkway, the cemetery comes into sight on the left. Get off at the intersection with Brattle Street or Aberdeen Avenue on the right, near the cemetery's large stone gate.

≈　　　≈　　　≈　　　≈

**AUTOMOBILE DIRECTIONS:** Mount Auburn Cemetery is located on the boundary between Cambridge and Watertown, 7 miles west of Boston. (See •16 on **Map 1** on page 6, and also the lower panel of **Map 27** on page 192.) Four approaches are described below.

**To Mount Auburn Cemetery from Boston:** Follow Storrow Drive west along the Charles River toward Newton and Arlington. After passing Harvard University, take the exit for Routes 2 and 3 toward Arlington. Cross the Eliot Bridge, then immediately bear right, then left for Routes 2 and 3. Quickly, move to the left lanes in order to turn left toward Route 16 and Watertown. Go 0.4 mile, then turn left into Mount Auburn Cemetery. Parking is permitted only on cemetery roads that have no green line down the center.

**To Mount Auburn Cemetery from Harvard Square:** Follow Brattle Street 1.4 miles to its end at the intersection with Mount Auburn Street, then turn left into the cemetery. Parking is permitted only on cemetery roads that have no green line down the center.

**To Mount Auburn Cemetery from Route 16:** In Cambridge and Watertown, Route 16 is simply a succession of local roads and parkways, so you must follow the signs closely.

   **From the intersection of Route 16 and Massachusetts Avenue** on the boundary between Arlington and Cambridge, follow Route 16 west 2.1 miles, in the process turning right at Huron Avenue and left onto Aberdeen Avenue. At a T-intersection with Mount Auburn Street, turn left *off Route 16,* then immediately turn right into Mount Auburn Cemetery. Parking is permitted only on cemetery roads that have no green line down the center.

   **From Watertown Square at the Charles River**, follow Route 16 east 2 miles. At the intersection where Route 16 turns left onto Aberdeen Avenue, continue straight a few hundred feet to the cemetery entrance on the right. Parking is permitted only on cemetery roads that have no green line down the center.

**To Mount Auburn Cemetery from the Massachusetts Turnpike (Route 90):** Leave the turnpike at Exit 18 for Cambridge. After paying the toll, fork right for Cambridge, then move to the far left lane as you merge onto River Street. In less than a hundred yards (and immediately before the bridge over the Charles River), turn left toward Newton and Arlington via Soldiers Field Road, which is the extension of Storrow Drive *away from Boston.* Go 1.1 miles, then exit to the right for Routes 2 and 3 toward Arlington. Cross the Eliot Bridge, then immediately bear right, then left for Routes 2 and 3. Quickly, move to the left lanes in order to turn left toward Route 16 and Watertown. Go 0.4 mile, then turn left into Mount Auburn Cemetery. Parking is permitted only on cemetery roads that have no green line down the center.

MAP 27 — Mount Auburn Cemetery

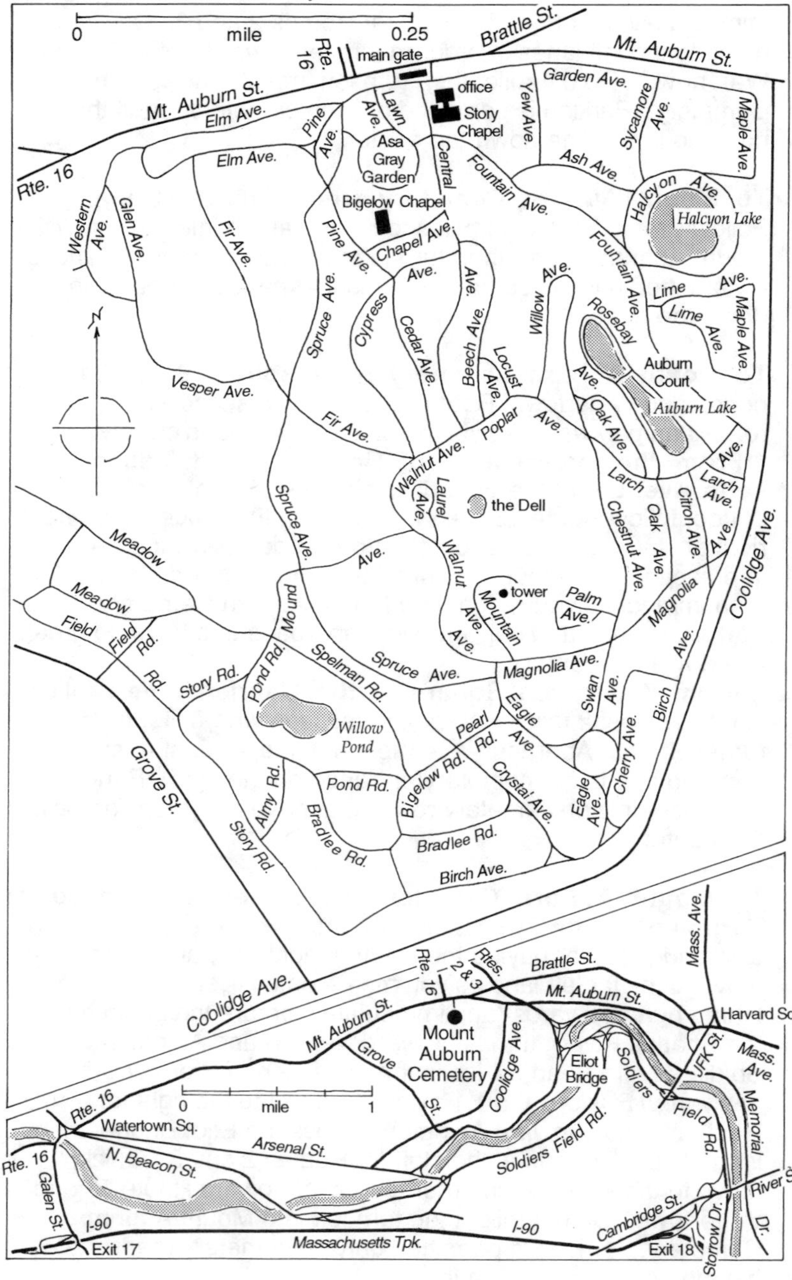

≈      ≈      ≈      ≈

**WALKING:  Map 27** at left shows the roads at **Mount Auburn Cemetery**.  A more detailed map pinpointing note-worthy memorials and the graves of prominent people is avail-able for a small charge at the cemetery gate or at the nearby office.  There is also a map showing the names and locations of over fifty "big trees," many of them state or New England champions.

The best way to see the cemetery is just to wander at large, enjoying the memorials and landscaping.  But if you want a few pointers, start by heading toward Halcyon Lake at the northeast corner of the cemetery (i.e., left as you enter through the front gate), then work your way southwest to Auburn Lake, the Dell, the Washington Tower at Mountain Avenue, and Willow Pond. Other highlights are the Asa Gray Garden and the Bigelow Chapel.

# 17

# ARNOLD ARBORETUM
# FRANKLIN PARK
# THE EMERALD NECKLACE
# SOUTHWEST CORRIDOR PARK

The Arnold Arboretum and Franklin Park are, of course, two of the major "gems" on Boston's string of parks, boulevards, and parkways known as the Emerald Necklace. And joining the Emerald Necklace at Forest Hills is the new Southwest Corridor Park, with its upper end at Back Bay Station. The system of interconnected parks makes possible a variety of outings, as described below.

**Map 28** on page 202 shows the **Arnold Arboretum**, a beautiful landscape of grassy hills planted with just about every variety of tree or shrub that can be made to grow in Boston's climate. You can walk here happily for an hour or the better part of a day. The winding road, which is closed to cars, makes an easy promenade. From one end to the other, the road is about 3 miles long (4.8 kilometers). There are also many smaller paths, as well as the opportunity to wander freely over the hills. The arboretum is open without charge from sunrise to sunset. Dogs must be leashed. The arboretum is administered by Harvard University but is owned and policed by Boston. For information call the Hunnewell Visitor Center at (617) 524-1718. Directions to the arboretum via public transit are on page 201. Automobile directions start on page 203.

**Map 29** on page 208 outlines a walk of 3 miles (4.8 kilometers) around **Franklin Park**. Directions are on pages 206-209.

**Map 30** on page 215 shows a walk of 7 miles (11.2 kilometers) from one end of the **Emerald Necklace** to the other — or that is, from Franklin Park, past the Arnold Arboretum and through the Back Bay Fens to the Public Garden and Boston Common. Add more miles for exploring places along the way. Directions start on page 213.

Finally, the dotted line on Map 30 shows the **Southwest Corridor Park**. This linear park is 4 miles long (6.4 kilometers). A variation on the tour of the Emerald Necklace is to walk from

Franklin Park to Dartmouth Street at Commonwealth Avenue, then return to Forest Hills via the Southwest Corridor Park, as described on page 217.

---

## ARNOLD ARBORETUM

THE ARNOLD ARBORETUM is one of the great botanical gardens of the world. Established in 1872 from the bequest of James Arnold (an amateur horticulturist), it contains about four thousand different kinds of trees, ornamental shrubs, and vines from around the world. Although the groupings are naturalistic in appearance, the plants are in fact arranged along the arboretum's winding road in a scientifically accepted botanical sequence of plant families based on morphological similarities. The road and grounds were laid out by Charles Sprague Sargent, the arboretum's first director, in collaboration with Frederick Law Olmsted, principal designer of Boston's park system. Different kinds of plants are in bloom from early April through September — or even into winter if you count the inconspicuous blossoms of native witch-hazel. Each specimen is labeled with its common and scientific names and country of origin. The arboretum is thus the perfect place to learn both native and foreign trees, or just to go for a walk in a beautiful setting. Best of all is to do both at the same time, identifying species and varieties as you follow the curving drive and wander up and down the grassy hillsides.

Learning to identify trees is not difficult. Every walk, bicycle ride, or automobile trip is an opportunity for practice. Notice the overall forms and branching habits of the trees, and also the distinctive qualities of their twigs, buds, bark, leaves, flowers, and fruits or seeds. These factors are the key identification features that distinguish one species from another. Finally, when using a field guide, check the maps or descriptions that delineate the geographic range within which a tentatively identified tree or shrub is likely to be found.

Some trees, of course, have very distinctive and reliable forms. Familiar evergreens like balsam fir and Eastern redcedar have a conical shape, like a dunce cap, although in dense stands the redcedar tapers very little and assumes the columnar form of the Italian cypress, which it somewhat resembles. The deciduous littleleaf linden, imported from Europe and used as a street tree, is also more or less conical in shape, but with wider-spreading lower branches than the evergreens mentioned above. The American elm displays a spreading form like a head of broccoli. A full-bodied egg-shape is characteristic of sugar maple and beech, although both will develop long, branchless trunks in crowded woods, as do most forest trees competing for light. The vertically exaggerated cigar shape of Lombardy poplar — a form called fastigiate — and the pendulous, trailing quality of weeping willow are unmistakable. (Both Lombardy poplar and weeping willow have been introduced to North America from abroad.)

Branching habit is an important clue to some trees. White pine, for example, has markedly horizontal branches with a slight upward tilt at the tips, like a hand turned with its palm up. Norway spruce (another imported species) is a very tall evergreen — sometimes reminding me of a pagoda — with long, evenly-spaced, festoon-like branches. The slender lower branches of pin oak slant downward, while those of white oak and red oak are often massive and horizontal, especially on mature trees growing in the open. The lower branches of the horse chestnut (yet another European import) also droop but then curl up at the tips in chunky twigs. American elm branches spread up and out like the mouth of a trumpet. The trunk of the mature honeylocust diverges into large branches somewhat in the manner of an elm. Even the reviled *ailanthus* or tree of heaven, which in many East Coast cities springs up in dense groves of spindly, spiky saplings wherever earth has been disturbed, eventually develops a spreading form somewhat like an elm or honeylocust.

A good botanist or forester can identify trees by their twigs alone — or that is, by the end portion of the branch that constitutes the newest growth. During winter the shape, color, size, position, and sheathing of buds are important. For instance, beech buds are long and pointed, tan, and sheathed with overlapping scales like shingles. Sycamore and magnolia buds are wrapped in a single scale. The twigs of horse chestnut are tipped with big, sticky, brown buds, while those of silver maple, and to a lesser extent red maple, end with large clusters of red buds. Some oaks, such as white oak, have hairless terminal buds, while other species, such as black oak, have hairy end buds.

Aside from buds, other characteristics of twigs are the size, shape, and position of leaf scars marking where the leaf stems were attached. The scars can be circular, polygonal, crescent, or even heart-shaped, and they also show different numbers of bundle scars or vascular dots. One fundamental factor is the distinction between *opposite* and *alternate* scars. The location of leaf scars in opposite pairs along the twigs (as with maples) distinguishes a wide variety of trees and shrubs from those with leaf scars arranged alternately, first on one side and then on the other (as with oaks).

Yet other twig characteristics are color, thorns, odor, hair, and pith.

For example, most maple twigs are reddish brown, but the twigs of striped maple and mountain maple are greenish. Thorns and spines are significant because relatively few trees have them, notably honeylocust, black locust, Hercules club, prickly ash, buckthorn bumelia, devil's walking stick, Osage-orange, American plum, some crabapples, and the many varieties of hawthorn. *Ailanthus* twigs, which show huge heart-shaped leaf scars, have a rank odor when broken open, and the twigs of black birch (also called sweet birch) have a strong wintergreen odor. Most oaks have hairless twigs, although some species such as blackjack oak are distinctly hairy. As for pith, it can be chambered, solid, spongy, or of different colors, depending on the species. Oak and hickory are common forest species in the Boston region, but only the pith of white oak in cross section forms a star. All of these distinguishing features can best be appreciated simply by examining the twigs of different species.

Bark is not always a reliable clue for identifying trees, as the color and texture of bark change with age or from trunk to branches to twigs. Often the distinctive character of bark is seen only in the trunks of large, mature trees. Bark can be smooth, furrowed, scaly, plated, shaggy, fibrous, crisscrossed, or papery. Some trees, of course, may be clearly identified by their bark. The names *shagbark hickory* and *paper birch* speak for themselves. Striped maple has longitudinal, whitish stripes in the smooth green bark of the younger trees. The crisscrossed ridges of white ash, the light blotches on sycamores, and the smooth gray skin of beech are equally distinctive. Birches and some cherries are characterized by horizontal lenticels like random dashes.

Most people notice leaves, particularly their shape. The leaves of the gray birch are triangular; ginkgo, fan-shaped; catalpa, heart-shaped; sweetgum, star-shaped; beech, elliptical (or actually pointed at each end); and black willow narrower still and thus *lanceolate*. Notice also the leaf margin or edge. Is it smooth like rhododendron, wavy like water oak, serrated like basswood, or deeply lobed like most maples? And how many lobes are there? Tulip trees, for example, have easily recognized four-lobed leaves shown at right; maples have three- or five-lobed leaves. Also, are the lobe tips rounded like white oak or pointed like red oak? Or maybe, as with sassafras and red mulberry, the same tree has leaves that are shaped differently, the most distinctive being those with a single asymmetrical lobe creating a leaf outline like a mitten. In some trees, such as the large-leaf magnolia with its tobacco-like foliage, the sheer size of the leaves is significant. Sycamores have leaves resembling sugar maples or red maples, but usually bigger and coarser.

Some leaves such as those of the Japanese maple, horse chestnut, and Ohio buckeye are *palmately* compound, meaning that they are actually

composed of leaflets radiating from the end of the stem. In the fall the whole compound leaf may drop off the tree as a unit, or the leaflets may fall off individually, and then finally the stem. Other leaves, such as ash, hickory, and sumac, are *pinnately* compound, being composed of leaflets arranged in opposite pairs along a central stalk. With pinnately compound leaves growing from the top of a branchless trunk, the saplings of *ailanthus* resemble little palm trees. Still other leaves are *bipinnately* compound, somewhat like a fern. The leaflets grow from stalks that, in turn, spread from a central stalk. Honeylocust, Kentucky coffeetree, and the ornamental imported silktree are examples.

Although the needles of evergreens are not as varied as the leaves of deciduous plants, there are still several major points to look for, such as the number of needles grouped together. White pine has fascicles of five; pitch pine, loblolly pine, and sometimes shortleaf pine have fascicles of three; and jack pine, red pine, Virginia pine, Austrian pine, and sometimes shortleaf pine have fascicles of two. Needles of spruce, hemlock, and fir grow singly, but are joined to the twig in distinctive ways. Spruce needles grow from little woody pegs, hemlock needles from smaller bumps, and fir needles directly from the twig, leaving a rounded pit when pulled off. Spruce needles tend to be four-sided, hemlock flat, and fir somewhere in-between. The needles of larch (also called tamarack) grow in dense clusters and all drop off in winter. The needles of bald cypress also drop off — hence its name.

Flowers are a spectacular, though short-lived, feature of some trees and shrubs. Three variables are color, form, and (less reliably) time of bloom. Shadbush (also called Allegheny serviceberry), with small, white, five-petaled flowers, is among the first of our native trees to bloom, usually in mid- or late April. As members of the rose family, cherries, peaches, plums, pears, apples, and hawthorns all have flowers with five petals (usually pink or white) in loose, white clusters, typically blooming from late April through late May. Redbud, with red-purple clusters, blooms in early or mid-May. The blossoms of flowering dogwood, which also appear in early or mid-May, consist of four white, petal-like bracts, each with a brown notch at the tip, while the flowers of alternate-leaf dogwood consist of loose, white clusters. These are a few of our native species commonly thought of as flowering trees, but the blossoms of other native species are equally distinctive, such as the small but numerous flowers of red maples, appearing with forsythia early in April, or the tuliplike flowers and durable husks of tulip trees, appearing in mid-June. Unlike most trees, witch-hazel — which produces small, yellow, scraggly flowers — blooms in fall or winter.

Finally, the seeds or fruit of a tree are a conspicuous element in summer and fall, sometimes lasting into winter and spring. Even if a tree is bare, the fruits and seeds (or for that matter, the leaves) can often be found littered on the ground around the trunk.  Nobody who sees a tree with acorns could fail to know that it is an oak, although some varieties, such as willow oak and shingle oak (also known as northern laurel oak) are deceptive.  Distinctive nuts are also produced by beech trees, horse chestnuts, hickories, and walnuts.  Some seeds, like ash and maple, have wings; such winged seeds are termed *samaras*.  Others, such as honeylocust, Kentucky coffeetree, and redbud, come in pods like beans and in fact are members of the same general legume family.  The seeds of birches and alders hang in catkins that in some species develop into conelike strobiles.  Sweetgum and sycamore form prickle-balls (as do the shells of horse chestnut and buckeye).  Eastern cottonwood and quaking aspen produce seeds that are wind-borne by cottonlike tufts.  And, of course, brightly colored berries and fruits are produced by many species, such as crabapples, dogwood, holly, hawthorn, and hackberry.  The female ginkgo has pale pink, globular, and remarkably foul-smelling fruit.  Among needle evergreens, spruce and pine cones hang from the twigs, while fir cones stand upright like stubby candles, and the small hemlock cones grow from the twig tips.

In conclusion, the trick to tree identification is to consider, either simultaneously or in rapid succession, a wide variety of features of which the ones discussed here — form and branching habit, twigs, buds, bark, leaves, flowers, and fruits or seeds — are the most obvious.  Don't get hung up pondering any single ambiguous or inconclusive feature; move on to consider other clues.

≈      ≈      ≈      ≈

**PUBLIC TRANSIT TO THE ARNOLD ARBORETUM:**
The arboretum is located south of Back Bay and Jamaica Plain in Boston.  The MBTA's Orange Line to **Forest Hills** or the Green Line to **Arborway** provide access.  If you arrive via the Green Line, the first thing to do is to go into the adjacent pavilion at Forest Hills Station, even if only to come right back out again per the following directions.

Signs for the Arnold Arboretum will direct you out of the Forest Hills Station at the north end of the pavilion.  Turn left and follow the sidewalk parallel with the long Monsignor Casey Bridge.  With caution, cross Washington Street and continue with the bridge on the right.  At the end of the bridge where the parapet stops, turn left through the arboretum's Forest Hills Gate.  The automobile gate here is usually closed, but the adjacent pedestrian gate is open sunrise to sunset.

MAP 28 — Arnold Arboretum

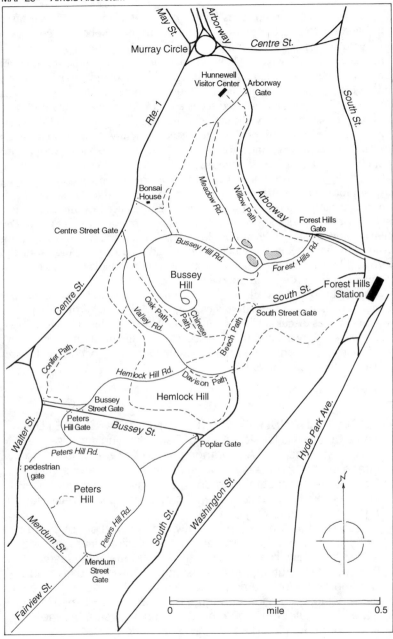

≈     ≈     ≈     ≈

**AUTOMOBILE DIRECTIONS TO THE ARNOLD AR-BORETUM:** The arboretum is located in Boston south of Back Bay and Jamaica Pond and east of Brookline. (See •17 on **Map 1** on page 6 and also **Map 30** of the Emerald Necklace on page 215.) Street parking is permitted at the arboretum's several gates shown on **Map 28** at left. There is no parking within the arboretum. Three approaches are described below to the Arborway Gate, where the Hunnewell Visitor Center is located.

**To the Arnold Arboretum from Storrow Drive in Boston:** Leave Storrow Drive at the exit for the Fenway and Route 1 south. Go 0.3 mile and then — in quick succession — fork right for the Riverway and left for Park Drive. Continue 0.9 mile, with the Victory Gardens and the Back Bay Fens on the left. After crossing Brookline Avenue, get into the second lane from the left, then bear somewhat left onto the Riverway toward Dedham. Continue 2.9 miles as the Riverway leads to the Jamaicaway, and the Jamaicaway to the Arborway. At Murray Circle, pass half-way around the rotary (i.e., *do not* bear right toward Dedham and Providence). Continue just 0.1 mile to the arboretum's Arborway Gate.

**To the Arnold Arboretum from Interstate 95 (Route 128) west of Boston:** Leave I-95 at Exit 20A for Route 9 east (Boylston Street). Follow Route 9 for 6.2 miles, then turn right for the Jamaicaway toward Dedham. Go 1.8 miles on the Jamaicaway and the Arborway. At Murray Circle, pass half-way around the rotary (i.e., *do not* bear right toward Dedham and Providence). Continue just 0.1 mile to the arboretum's Arborway Gate.

**To the Arnold Arboretum from Interstate 93 south of Boston:** Skirting the Blue Hills, this segment of I-93 (old Route 128) runs east-west between the junctions with Interstate 95 and Route 3.

Leave I-93 at Exit 2B for Route 138 north (Blue Hill Avenue). After 4.3 miles, join Route 28 and continue north. (The road is still called Blue Hill Avenue.) Go 1.3 miles on Route 28, then turn left at a traffic light onto Morton Street — also called Route 203 west. This intersection occurs after Woolson Street and Landor Road intersect from the right.

Follow Morton Street west 1.4 miles to a traffic circle. Go halfway around the rotary, then continue another 1.4 miles across a viaduct and along the Arborway, which has a median strip down the middle. To reach the arboretum entrance, circle completely around the next rotary and return just 0.1 mile to the Arborway Gate.

≈ ≈ ≈ ≈

**WALKING AT THE ARNOLD ARBORETUM:** Map 28 on page 202 shows the roads and paths at the arboretum, which is a spectacular place to wander while enjoying the landscaping and the views from the hilltops. Notice that the arboretum includes a large section — one that is well worth seeing — south of Bussey Street.

≈
≈ ≈ ≈ ≈
≈

## FRANKLIN PARK

WHY DOES BOSTON'S LARGEST PARK commemorate Benjamin Franklin, whose life and work are so closely identified with Philadelphia and the Commonwealth of Pennsylvania?

When Franklin died in 1790, a codicil to his will included a bequest to the city of Boston, where he had been born in 1706. The amount slightly exceeded £1000, with which Franklin devised a testamentary lesson demonstrating the power of compound interest. He directed that the earnings from the bequest were to accumulate for a hundred years. He calculated that by the end of this period the fund should have multiplied 130-fold if invested at five percent compounded annually. After the fund's first century, £100,000 were "to be used for public works which may be judged of most general utility to the inhabitants, such as fortifications, bridges, aqueducts, public buildings, baths, pavement, or whatever may make living in the town more convenient to its people and render it more agreeable to strangers resorting thither for health or temporary residence." The balance of the fund, which Franklin figured would be about £31,000, was then to accumulate earnings for *another* hundred years before final disbursement, 25 percent to Boston and 75 percent to Massachusetts.

Ninety years after Franklin's death, the Boston Park Commission adopted the plan prepared by Frederick Law Olmsted for improvement of what was tentatively called West Roxbury Park. To pay for the land, the city decided to use the soon-to-be-due first disbursement from the Benjamin Franklin Fund. Accordingly, the proposed West Roxbury Park was renamed Franklin Park "in honor of the testator who so generously endowed his native town." The money, however, was not forthcoming. Instead, it was tied up in a lawsuit brought by Franklin's heirs, who complained of irregularities in the administration of the fund. By the time the first disbursement became available in 1905 — it amounted then to more than $400,000 — Franklin Park had been completed using funds from a special bond issue. So instead of going to the park, the first payment of the Franklin Fund was paired with a matching gift from Andrew Carnegie to establish the Franklin Institute of Boston, a vocational school located on Berkeley Street in the South End. When the second and final disbursement became due, the city's share of $1.2 million was used to augment the school's scholarship program, and the state's share of approximately $4 million was added to the school's endowment. As for Franklin Park, the name was retained despite the use of Franklin's bequest for an entirely different purpose.

In broad outline, Olmsted's design for Franklin Park has survived intact to the present day, although many specific features that affect the tone have been torn down, altered, or added. Olmsted divided the park into two conceptually distinct parts. The northeastern third is the so-called *Ante-Park* (as in anteroom). It includes the main entrance off Blue Hill Avenue, the Playstead athletic fields, and Franklin Park Zoo, all of which attract large crowds. A long, formal allee called the Greeting was never built, but the expansion of the zoo into this area has given it a highly developed quality. In contrast, the southwestern two-thirds of Franklin Park comprise a *Country Park* for the quiet enjoyment of natural scenery. This area includes the Wilderness, Scarboro Hill, Scarboro Pond (not an original feature), and the golf course (an anomalous modification of the valley meadow specified by Olmsted). Referring to the farmscape that existed when the land was acquired for park use in the early 1880s, Olmsted said, "Relieved of a few . . . houses, causeways and fences, [and] left with an unbroken surface of turf and secluded by woods on the hillsides, this [area] would at once supply a singularly complete and perfect though limited example of a type of scenery which is perhaps the most soothing in its influence on mankind of any presented by nature." In fact, Olmsted intended the Country Park to be far more pastoral than it is today. He even specified that the grass was to cropped by sheep rather than be uniformly mowed. Unfortunately, this ostensibly rural area has been marred by the transfer of seventeen acres in 1954 for construction of Lemuel Shattuck Hospital, which now looms over the park. Circuit Drive, formerly a carriage road, was opened to automobiles in 1924, bringing streams of city traffic through the Country Park. The southern part of Circuit Drive from the golf house to Scarboro Pond is now closed to cars, raising the question of whether the rest of the loop can be closed as well in order to restore some country quality to the Country Park.

≈ ≈ ≈ ≈

**PUBLIC TRANSIT TO FRANKLIN PARK:** The park is located in Boston south of Back Bay and Jamaica Plain and east of the Arnold Arboretum. The MBTA's Orange Line to **Forest Hills** or the Green Line to **Arborway** provide access. If you arrive via the Green Line, the first thing to do is to go into the adjacent pavilion at Forest Hills Station, even if only to come right back out again per the following directions.

Signs for Franklin Park will direct you out of the Forest Hills Station on the east side of the pavilion. Cross Hyde Park Avenue. With the long Monsignor Casey Bridge on the left, follow the Arborway, which here is just a small street that passes the West Roxbury Courthouse. Continue to a traffic circle. With caution, go counter-clockwise two-thirds of the way around the rotary and then continue toward Franklin Park on a broad walkway. Turn right just beyond Shattuck Hospital, where there is a sign for the Boston Park Department Maintenance Yard. For the walk outlined on **Map 29** and discussed starting on page 209, cross the entrance drive a few dozen yards from the intersection and bear left onto a paved path opposite Shattuck Hospital.

≈ ≈ ≈ ≈

**AUTOMOBILE DIRECTIONS TO FRANKLIN PARK:** Franklin Park is located in Boston east of the Arnold Arboretum and south of Jamaica Plain and Roxbury. (See **Map 30** of the Emerald Necklace on page 215.) Numerous signs provide directions to the Franklin Park Zoo, but for walkers a better place to park is near Shattuck Hospital. Three approaches are described below.

**To Franklin Park from Storrow Drive in Boston**: Leave Storrow Drive at the exit for the Fenway and Route 1 south. Go 0.3 mile and then — in quick succession — fork right for the Riverway and left for Park Drive. Continue 0.9 mile, with the

Victory Gardens and the Back Bay Fens on the left. After crossing Brookline Avenue, get into the second lane from the left, then bear somewhat left onto the Riverway toward Dedham. Continue 2.9 miles as the Riverway leads to the Jamaicaway, and the Jamaicaway to the Arborway. At Murray Circle, pass half-way around the rotary (i.e., *do not* bear right toward Dedham and Providence). Continue on the Arborway for 1.1 miles, in the process passing the Arnold Arboretum and crossing the long bridge at Forest Hills. Go three-quarters of the way around another traffic circle and continue into Franklin Park. After just 0.3 mile, turn right at an intersection that is marked by a sign for the Boston Park Department Maintenance Yard. Park your car on the side of the street by a low stone wall opposite Shattuck Hospital.

**To Franklin Park from Interstate 95 (Route 128) west of Boston:** Leave I-95 at Exit 20A for Route 9 east (Boylston Street). Follow Route 9 for 6.2 miles, then turn right for the Jamaicaway toward Dedham. Go 1.8 miles on the Jamaicaway and the Arborway. At Murray Circle, pass half-way around the rotary (i.e., *do not* bear right toward Dedham and Providence). Continue on the Arborway for 1.1 miles, in the process passing the Arnold Arboretum and crossing the long bridge at Forest Hills. Go three-quarters of the way around another traffic circle and continue into Franklin Park. After just 0.3 mile, turn right at an intersection that is marked by a sign for the Boston Park Department Maintenance Yard. Park your car on the side of the street by a low stone wall opposite Shattuck Hospital.

**To Franklin Park from Interstate 93 south of Boston:** Skirting the Blue Hills, this segment of I-93 (old Route 128) runs east-west between the junctions with Interstate 95 and Route 3.

Leave I-93 at Exit 2B for Route 138 north (Blue Hill Avenue). After 4.3 miles, join Route 28 and continue north. (The road is still called Blue Hill Avenue.) Go 1.3 miles on Route 28, then turn left at a traffic light onto Morton Street — also called Route 203 west. This intersection occurs after Woolson Street and Landor Road intersect from the right.

Follow Morton Street west 1.4 miles to a traffic circle, then bear right into Franklin Park. After just 0.3 mile, turn right at an intersection that is marked by a sign for the Boston Park Department Maintenance Yard. Park your car on the side of the street by a low stone wall opposite Shattuck Hospital.

MAP 29 — Franklin Park

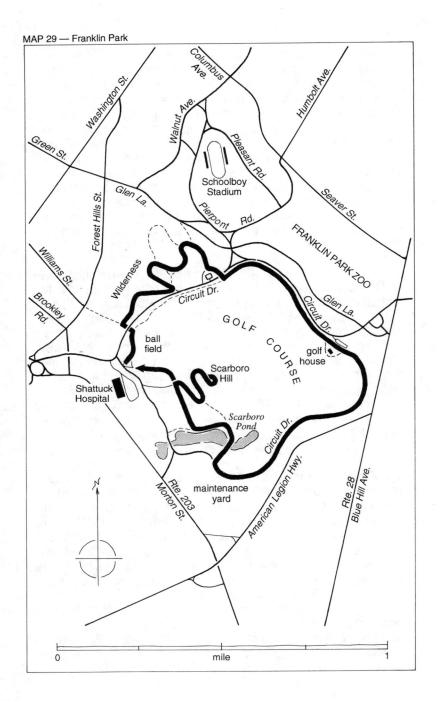

0  mile  1

≈     ≈     ≈     ≈

**WALKING AT FRANKLIN PARK:  Map 29** at left shows a 3-mile loop around the park on Circuit Drive, including a brief digression through the Wilderness and a spur to the top of Scarboro Hill.  Directions are as follows:

**To get started from the vicinity of Shattuck Hospital,** leave the tall hospital building to the rear and follow the paved path clockwise around the circuit.  At a pedestrian underpass opposite a ball field, turn left under Circuit Drive.  Go 40 yards, then bear right up a series of stone steps leading to the Wilderness.  After descending gradually back to Circuit Drive, turn left up a wide path that curves along the top of a plateau.  At a T-intersection overlooking a parking lot and the golf course in the distance, bear left and continue to Circuit Drive.  With caution, cross Circuit Drive toward the golf course, then bear left along the roadside path.

Follow the walkway next to Circuit Drive.  At the golf clubhouse, pass straight through the parking lot and continue on a section of Circuit Drive that is closed to motor vehicles.  Eventually, descend toward Scarboro Pond and across a masonry bridge, then bear left along the water's edge.  At an intersection opposite the middle of the pond, turn right in order to head slightly uphill between two knolls.  Partway through the woods, there is a crossroads with an asphalt drive that is closed to cars.  Turn right to follow the road to the top of Scarboro Hill, where there are some plaques discussing the history of Franklin Park.  From the hilltop, return to the four-way intersection and bear right to continue clockwise around the circuit and back to the starting point near Shattuck Hospital.

≈

≈     ≈     ≈     ≈

≈

## THE EMERALD NECKLACE

THE EMERALD NECKLACE includes the Boston Common, Public Garden, Back Bay Fens, Olmsted Park, Jamaica Pond, Arnold Arboretum, and Franklin Park, all strung together by a series of boulevards and parkways, as shown on Map 30 on page 215.  The Common dates back to 1634, at the outset of the Puritan settlement, but the adjacent

Public Garden was not laid out until 1859 on land that had been reclaimed from the Back Bay tidal flats two decades earlier. (Now, of course, the Charles River is no longer tidal because the basin is perpetually flooded by the dam at the river's mouth.)

In 1857 Boston embarked on a thirty-year project to fill in the rest of the Back Bay. The filling proceeded from east to west, and the construction of buildings followed just one step behind as the area immediately became Boston's most fashionable residential district. Choicest of its new streets was Commonwealth Avenue, 240 feet wide. At the west end of the new Back Bay district there remained a broad salt marsh at the mouth of the Muddy River, which flowed into the Charles and drained parts of Brookline and Roxbury.

Meanwhile, New York City was developing Central Park, for which the land was acquired in 1856. Two years later Frederick Law Olmsted and Calvert Vaux won the competition for the project's design. Their work was in the naturalistic, pastoral style of eighteenth-century English landscape gardening, characterized by winding carriage roads, ever-changing views of meadow and water, and irregular but artful grouping of trees. Olmsted and Vaux went on to design New York's Prospect Park, the university campus at Berkeley in California, South Park in Chicago, and other projects. After 1872 Olmsted worked by himself out of his New York residence.

Following New York's lead, Boston created the Public Garden, but proposals for a larger park system were repeatedly rejected at the polls. Not until 1875 did Boston establish a three-man Park Commission to develop public grounds throughout the city, which had recently expanded its area several-fold by annexing Roxbury, Dorchester, Brighton, Charlestown, and West Roxbury. After inviting and considering numerous suggestions, the commission published a plan for a string of major parks and parkways. There were also to be smaller neighborhood parks and playgrounds in almost every section of the city. The outline more or less resembles what eventually was built, although the plan was elaborated and in some places greatly altered during its implementation over the next twenty years.

The first project was a park to occupy the salt marsh and mud flats at the mouth of the Muddy River — or that is, what is now the Back Bay Fens. The city appropriated just $450,000 for the acquisition of not less than 100 acres. To stretch the money as far as possible, the Park Commission bought "land" along the main tidal channel where the flats were underwater most of the time. Then in 1878, after a design competition that produced no satisfactory proposals, the Park Commission contracted with Frederick Law Olmsted to develop a plan for the Fens

and (at his insistence) to oversee its construction as designed. Already the commissioners had consulted with Olmsted from time to time for help in evaluating potential park sites. So skillful and comprehensive was Olmsted's work at the Fens that he went on to design and oversee all the other parks and parkways in the proposed system. Because of the volume of work, which continued for the rest of his professional life, Olmsted moved from New York to Brookline, where he opened an office and took on partners and apprentices. His home and office on Warren Street off Route 9 are now a national historic site that is open to the public. For information, telephone (617) 566-1689.

Olmsted's basic idea for the Back Bay Fens was to preserve the tidal salt marsh on a reduced scale as something refreshingly different from what ordinarily occurs in the middle of a city. He said that such an area "will be found to be, in the artistic sense of the word, natural, and possibly to suggest a modest poetic sentiment more grateful to town-weary minds than an elaborate and elegant garden-like work would have yielded." (So much for the Public Garden, designed by architect George F. Meacham!) Although the Fens were completely reconfigured by dredging and filling, the wiggly watercourse is reminiscent of streams that meander through natural salt marshes. Olmsted replanted large areas with marsh grass and put trees along the edges of the park to screen out the neighboring houses that were developed on reclaimed land. The design, however, was rendered obsolete by construction of the Charles River Dam in 1910, which permanently flooded the salt marsh. Tall, dense stands of freshwater reeds displaced the short marsh grass, so that Muddy River is often no longer visible. The city added more fill along low lying banks, which in places were regraded for playing fields or given over to monuments and gardens. Although still pleasant, the result is a somewhat muddled and decidedly unnatural hodgepodge of features.

From the Back Bay Fens, Olmsted next directed his attention farther up Muddy River. The original plan had been for a straight mall to lead from the Fens to Jamaica Pond, but Olmsted suggested instead that the park follow both banks of the river. By means of dredging, filling, damming, regrading, and relocation of the stream itself, he turned the minor watercourse into a chain of ponds, glens, groves, and rolling, open fields. Although it looks natural or at least naturalesque, the entire landscape was remade to Olmsted's specifications as far upstream as Leverett Pond above Huntington Avenue. Still farther upstream, the kettlehole at Wards Pond was incorporated unchanged into the plan. Few alterations were made at Jamaica Pond, where land was so expensive that only a narrow strip around the shore was purchased for park use. Beyond Jamaica Pond, the curving linearity of the river was continued via the

Arborway, which leads past the Arnold Arboretum to Franklin Park. There is scarcely a right angle in the whole scheme, which has an organic quality like a vine with pumpkins.

As originally conceived and built, the roads that border and connect the parks — starting with the Fenway and continuing via the Riverway and Jamaicaway to the Arborway — were scenic carriage roads. Unfortunately, the chain of parkways has become a major traffic artery, "improved" in some places by the addition of elevated viaducts that have obliterated Olmsted's work. If you want to minimize the noise and sight of traffic, take the walk described below early on a weekend morning.

≈      ≈      ≈      ≈

**THE EMERALD NECKLACE — Walking from Franklin Park to the Boston Common via the Arnold Arboretum, Jamaica Pond, Olmsted Park, the Back Bay Fens, Commonwealth Avenue, and the Public Garden:** How does Boston's nineteenth-century park system fare 120 years after its creation? To find out, wear your most resilient shoes and spend a day touring the city's famous Emerald Necklace.

Outlined on **Map 30** on page 215 and described below, this excursion is 7 miles long, not counting additional rambles at places passed along the way. Add 3 miles for a circuit around **Franklin Park** and another few miles for wandering at the **Arnold Arboretum**. And finally, add 4 miles if you decide to make a circuit by returning from downtown to Franklin Park via the **Southwest Corridor Park**, as described on page 217 and indicated by the dotted line on Map 30.

For the one-way trip shown by the bold line, you presumably will use **public transit** at one end or the other — or both. As discussed on page 206, the MBTA's Orange Line and also the Green Line provide access to Franklin Park. At the upper end of the Boston Common is the Park Street Station on the Red Line.

For **automobile directions** to Franklin Park, see pages 206-207.

**Start your trek** at the western corner of Franklin Park, where Circuit Drive passes Shattuck Hospital. After exploring Franklin Park, leave Shattuck Hospital behind on the left . Follow the park road west 0.3 mile to a traffic circle. With caution, pass clockwise two-thirds of the way around the rotary and then — at the end of a brick parapet — get onto the sidewalk of a long

213

bridge. Follow the bridge high above the Forest Hills Station on the left. At the other end of the bridge, turn left across an exit ramp and enter the Arnold Arboretum at the Forest Hills Gate.

The **Arnold Arboretum** is shown on **Map 28** on page 202. After exploring the arboretum, exit through the Arborway Gate near the Hunnewell Visitor Center and turn left. With caution, circle clockwise halfway around Murray Circle and continue toward Boston with the Arborway on the right. Like the other Emerald Necklace "ways," — e.g., the Jamaicaway, the Riverway, and the Fenway — the Arborway was conceived as a scenic and recreational carriage road but has since become a major automobile artery.

Follow the Arborway straight to Jamaica Pond and circle clockwise around the shore on a footpath. At the far end of the pond, turn left off the shore path. Cross Perkins Street and continue on a paved path, which soon curves right to follow a small stream called Muddy Creek. Continue with the stream and a series of ponds on the right. At intervals the water runs underground for substantial distances, and at times the path is merely a dirt or cinder track. Use caution crossing major streets such as Huntington Avenue and Brookline Avenue, where you may have to detour to the nearest light. After each crossing continue with Muddy Creek and the linear park on the right.

Eventually, bear right to pass the colossal beige brick Landmark Center (as the old Sears building is now called). Cross Brookline Avenue for the second time and continue until the water again appears on the right. Follow the riverside path through the Back Bay Fens and past pedestrian bridges leading to the **Isabella Stuart Gardner Museum** and the **Boston Museum of Fine Arts**. Take a few minutes to view the Victory Gardens, which are rental plots that originated during World War II. The arrangement proved so popular that it has continued ever since.

At the northern end of the Back Bay Fens, cross the Massachusetts Turnpike, then turn right onto Commonwealth Avenue. During the last third of the nineteenth century, Back Bay was developed as Boston's most fashionable residential district after the tidal flats that give the area its name were filled. At the eastern end of Commonwealth Avenue, continue through the Public Garden, then across Charles Street and through the Boston Common. At the Common's upper-right corner, near the white spire of the Park Street Congregational Church, is the MBTA's Park Street Station.

MAP 30 — Emerald Necklace (bold line) and Southwest Corridor Park (dotted line)

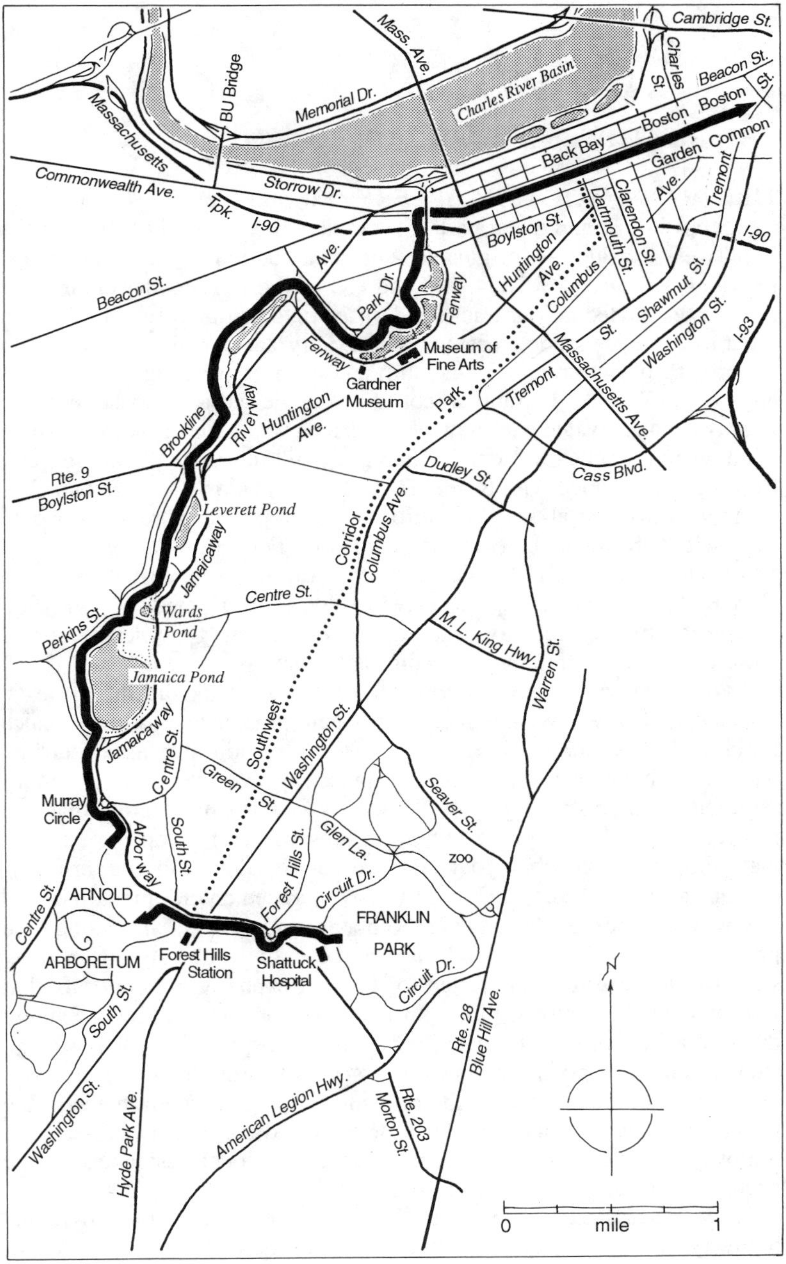

215

≈

≈      ≈      ≈      ≈

≈

## THE SOUTHWEST CORRIDOR PARK

THE TRANSPORTATION ARTERY that now combines a railroad, rapid transit line, and linear park — and that is known altogether as the Southwest Corridor — originated with construction of the Boston and Providence Railroad in 1834.  At the end of the nineteenth century, the line was expanded to four tracks and raised onto a granite embankment in order to eliminate grade crossings in Roxbury and Jamaica Plain.  With the growth of automobile ownership and the interstate highway system after World War II, the railroad corridor was viewed as a possible right-of-way for an elevated expressway.  This idea was given detailed form in 1963 when the state developed a plan to extend Interstate 95 into the city from the interchange with Route 128 at Fowl Meadow (see Chapter 21).  Running beside or above the railroad, the proposed expressway would link with an inner beltway through the Fenway, Cambridge, and Somerville.  The MBTA's Orange Line was to be relocated from the elevated tracks at Washington Street to the highway median.  In 1966 demolition for the highway began in Boston, entailing the destruction of more than five hundred buildings during the next seven years.

As preparations for the highway got underway, so too did the protests. The anti-highway movement began in Cambridge and spread to Jamaica Plain and Roxbury, where most of the demolition was occurring. Assuming that construction of the expressway was inevitable, Roxbury residents at first strove just to lessen its impact by urging that the project be built below grade.  Other groups wanted to stop the expressway altogether, and this goal emerged as the chief rallying cry.  A demonstration at the State House in 1969 included environmentalists and highway opponents from neighborhoods and towns all along the proposed route as far south as Milton and Canton — and also from other suburbs where residents objected to different expressway proposals that were part of the regional plan.  In response, Governor Francis Sargent declared a highway moratorium while the transportation plan was re-studied, although construction of Interstate 93 through Somerville was allowed to continue.  In 1972 the re-evaluation process culminated in the governor's cancellation of the Inner Beltway and the Southwest Corridor highway, coupled with retention, as urged by local residents, of the proposal to relocate the Orange Line.

In 1975 Massachusetts became the first state to trade unused federal highway monies for funding approved by the new Urban Mass Transit

Administration. The UMTA funds were used for drastic revision of the Southwest Corridor project. During the next few years, the state and city worked in consultation with neighborhood groups to iron out the details of a plan that put the railroad and mass transit lines into a trench bordered by a linear park. In 1978 Massachusetts received a huge UMTA grant for construction of the project, which continued for nearly a decade as the railroad embankment was torn out and the train and transit lines were sunk below grade. At one point an $81 million shortfall threatened to eliminate important features, but eventually the project was completed in accordance with the plan. The new railroad and transit lines started operating in 1987, and two years later the Southwest Corridor Park was dedicated.

≈      ≈      ≈      ≈

**THE SOUTHWEST CORRIDOR PARK — Walking from Commonwealth Avenue to Forest Hills Station:** Leave Commonwealth Avenue in order to follow Dartmouth Street across Newbury and Boylston and past the Boston Public Library at Copley Square. After passing the intersection with Stuart Street, turn right into the linear Southwest Corridor Park, which starts opposite the Back Bay train station. Follow the park through Boston's South End, to the left around Carter Field, and along the Orange Line all the way to the Forest Hills Station.

# 18

# BOSTON HARBOR ISLANDS

The harbor islands are shown on **Map 31** on page 227. An outing to the islands combines a scenic boat ride with the opportunity to explore old fortifications and to roam over egg-shaped, glacial hills and along beaches of shells and shingle. Each of the islands is discussed in turn below. Of course, the larger ones provide more scope for walking, but all are worth visiting. For detailed maps, see pages 228-231.

**Georges, Lovells, and Peddocks islands** are managed by the Metropolitan District Commission; telephone (617) 727-5290. **Gallops, Bumpkin, and Grape islands** are administered by the Massachusetts Department of Environmental Management; telephone (781) 740-1605, extension 201 or 205. Spring through fall, there is **boat service** to and among these six islands, as discussed on page 226. Dogs are prohibited. Camping is permitted on some of the islands; see page 234. For directions to the boat terminals via public transit and automobile, please refer to pages 232-234.

Finally, **Thompson Island**, which is one of the bigger, more varied islands, is in a category by itself, with its own boat, mainland landing, fare, and schedule, as discussed on page 235. The island is owned and managed by the Thompson Island Outward Bound Education Center; telephone (617) 328-3900.

---

**GEORGES ISLAND**, which is shown in the upper-right panel of **Map 32** on page 228, is the hub of the system of ferries and water taxis serving the harbor islands. It is also the site of massive Fort Warren.

At the outbreak of the American Revolution, the harbor islands were used chiefly for growing crops and grazing livestock. Only Castle Island, now attached to the mainland in South Boston, was strongly fortified. Some of the harbor islands were a source of provisions for the besieged British until they evacuated Boston in March of 1776.

The first fortifications on Georges Island were earthworks constructed in the summer of 1778 by French sailors and marines sent to aid the colonists. Their commander, the Comte d'Estaing, had planned to attack Newport, but his fleet was damaged by a storm and put in at Boston for repairs. The French placed batteries on Georges Island and on Hull at the tip of Nantasket peninsula to protect their ships from British cruisers lurking in Massachusetts Bay.

In 1820 Georges Island was surveyed in preparation for a far larger fort named for revolutionary leader Joseph Warren, who died at the Battle of Bunker Hill. Dominating the entrance to Boston, Quincy, and Hingham bays, the island was considered to be the key to the area's maritime defense. Lieutenant Colonel Sylvanus Thayer, known as the "Father of West Point" because of his reorganization of the academy into an effective military institution, designed a bastioned, pentagonal fort and later supervised its construction. Work began on the sea wall in 1825 and on the fort itself eight years later. The fort includes casemate chambers where cannon could fire through small embrasures similar to the gunports on a man-of-war, but with the obvious advantage that the fort is made of granite and cannot sink. Cast at the U.S. Arsenal in Watertown, big Rodman guns that could fire 15-inch projectiles three miles were eventually mounted atop the walls on swivel carriages. Two sides of the fort have a supplementary exterior wall mantled with earth. This cover face was intended to absorb fire from siege guns that might be emplaced on the Brewsters or nearby Lovells and Gallops islands, if those outposts were seized by enemy ships. During the Civil War, just such as assault was made successfully by Union forces against Savannah's Fort Pulaski, where the attacking Federals used rifled cannon and quickly reduced the fort's masonry walls to rubble.

Fort Warren was a huge project. The fortifications occupy most of the island's thirty acres. The inside perimeter of the walls is nearly a mile. Each block of granite was cut and faced by hand to fit its position — a process that took from one to two days. In 1836 the fort's intended strength was upwards of 300 guns manned by a siege garrison of 1,500 troops. There were also large vaulted chambers for prisoners-of-war. By 1840 the fort's armament was projected at 336 pieces, including cannons, carronades, howitzers, and mortars. As of 1851 the cost of the fort exceeded the original estimate by nearly 60 percent, and no doubt the final overrun was substantially more. Although most construction was finished by the outbreak of the Civil War, when Fort Warren was garrisoned for the first time, some work continued until 1869. Eventually, about a hundred guns were mounted.

During the war, Fort Warren served initially as a training camp for Union recruits and then as a prison for as many as 2400 Confederate soldiers. More than 150 civilian supporters of the South were also held on the island. Suspects were arrested on unsubstantiated charges and confined without trial, for President Lincoln had suspended the writ of habeas corpus during the national crisis.

The fort was unprepared for the droves of prisoners that arrived. Boston newspapers undertook a campaign to raise donations of food, beds, and other supplies, partly on the grounds that considerate treatment of the Confederate soldiers would promote corresponding compassion toward Union prisoners in the South. The generosity shown to the prisoners at Fort Warren in time became a political issue. Public officials who had supported the relief program were accused of being too lenient toward the enemy. Boston's Mayor Joseph Wightman, unsuccessfully running for reelection in 1862, rhetorically complained that he found himself "charged with humanity." As the war continued, gifts were prohibited, partly in reaction to conditions at some prison camps in the beleaguered Confederacy. In particular, at Andersonville in Georgia, tens of thousands of Union troops were confined in conditions so bad that over twelve thousand died.

Among the notable prisoners at Fort Warren were, for a few weeks, James Murray and John Slidell, Confederate commissioners seized on their way to England and France to seek diplomatic recognition and military assistance for the South. They were aboard the British mail packet *Trent* when the ship was stopped on the high seas by a Union warship and the two men removed. In England the act aroused a storm of indignation, and Britain appeared to be on the verge of declaring war against the Union. The release of Mason and Slidell was demanded in a letter with a seven-day deadline for reply. Three days after the note was presented, Secretary of State Seward disavowed the seizure and promised to release the two envoys, which was soon done.

Several distinguished Confederate prisoners arrived at Fort Warren toward the end of the war. Alexander Hamilton Stephens, the Vice President of the Confederacy, John Reagan, the Postmaster General, and other Confederate officials and generals were detained for months after the fighting stopped. Although Stephens was at first put in solitary confinement in a damp chamber, eventually he and the other notables were given comfortable quarters and were allowed to wander freely about the fort. As was customary, prisoners with money could use their own funds to buy supplementary food and liquor from the Boston sutler who supplied provisions to the fort's garrison. Even some Confederate troops pooled their resources to purchase cheese, sausage, crackers, and other staples.

At the end of the nineteenth century, the old armaments at Fort Warren were replaced by two 12-inch and five 10-inch "disappearing rifles" mounted in concrete revetments. These guns had carriages that swung down behind the walls while the artillery was loaded. Several 4-inch and

221

3-inch guns were also installed. During World War I the fort was the Harbor Defense Headquarters, but during World War II its guns were scrapped in favor of 16-inch rifles with a range of thirty-one miles installed at Nahant and Hull. Nonetheless, Georges Island was part of the harbor's mine defense system. In 1946 the fort was mothballed, but a few years later it was reactivated. Eventually, the island was transferred from the Navy to the General Services Administration, which in 1958 sold it to the Metropolitan District Commission for park use.

**GALLOPS ISLAND**, shown in the bottom panel of **Map 32** on page 228, is a short ride by water taxi from Georges Island. Like most of the harbor islands, sixteen-acre Gallops was farmed in colonial times, and even well into the nineteenth century. In the mid-1700s, John Gallop, a Boston harbor pilot, had a summer home there. In the 1830s, the island became the site of a summer inn established by the widow of a farmer named Newcombe. Operated later by the Snow family, the inn was known especially for its clam chowder.

During the Civil War, Gallops Island became a military camp where Union troops trained and where at war's end they returned from the South prior to discharge. The camp had more than twenty wooden barracks. After the war, the City of Boston used the site as a quarantine hospital where tens of thousands of immigrants were examined each year. Those thought to have contagious diseases, or to have been exposed to contagious diseases, were isolated for weeks or even months before being allowed to enter the country or, as occasionally happened, returned to Europe. Some died on the island and were buried there. In 1916 the facility was taken over by the federal government, which continued to run the hospital until 1937.

During World War II, the United States Maritime Service Radio Training School was located on Gallops Island. Staffed by nearly three hundred people, the school had several dozen buildings (some of them left over from the quarantine hospital). More than five thousand Merchant Marine radio operators were trained, and also smaller numbers of machinists and cooks. The parade ground is still evident, and also the concrete foundation of the school's recreation hall. After the war, a few of the structures were moved to the mainland and the rest torn down. Used as a dump for several years, Gallops Island became part of the Boston Harbor Islands State Park in 1973.

**LOVELLS ISLAND**, shown on **Map 33** on page 229, is the next stop after Georges and Gallops on the water-taxi circuit. Named for William Lovell, one of the first settlers of Dorchester in the 1630s, the

island in 1900 became the site of Fort Standish. Massive concrete emplacements for guns were built, scattered around the island so that damage to one position would not affect the others. Most of these works still stand. Particularly impressive is Battery Morris-Burbeck, consisting of four huge revetments facing northeast at the middle of the island, where 10-inch disappearing rifles were formerly sited. Atop the hill just to the rear is Battery Strong Vincent, where there were four 3-inch guns. At the island's southeastern end, flat concrete circles at Battery Whipple show where two 6-inch guns were mounted in the open. The smaller emplacements nearby were Battery Williams for three 3-inch guns. And at the island's northwestern end are the remains of Battery Terrill, formerly having three 6-inch disappearing rifles.

Apart from the fortifications, the main appeal of Lovells is the stony beach, which provides a pleasant walk around the island. There are unobstructed views west toward Boston and east toward the Brewsters.


**PEDDOCKS ISLAND**, shown in the upper panel of **Map 34** on page 230, is reached from either Georges Island or Hewitts Cove in Hingham. Because of its size (more than 130 acres), its long shoreline (4.5 miles), and its varied topography (five separate hills joined by low saddles and strands), Peddocks Island offers more scope for exploration than any of the other harbor islands.

Peddocks' two eastern hills (together called East Head) are the site of Fort Andrews, built at the end of the nineteenth century in response to the recent war with Spain. Although America was never seriously threatened during the short conflict, the nation was made conscious that its coastal defenses were outmoded. New fortifications were built also at Lovells and Georges islands and at other American ports. Fort Andrew's armaments included two 8-inch mortars and three batteries for 6-, 5-, and 3-inch rapid fire guns. During World War II, more than a thousand Italian prisoners of war were housed at East Head. Many of the fort's structures still stand, including barracks, officers' quarters, guardhouse, quartermaster storehouse, gymnasium, hospital, and other facilities. Because some of these buildings are dilapidated, do not enter any that are not clearly open to the public. Near the dock is the fort's chapel.

Peddocks' middle hill (or Middle Head) is occupied by summer cottages. Like all the island's trails, the paths at Middle Head are open to the public.

The island's western end (West Head) is a wooded wildlife sanctuary with a salt marsh, brackish pond, and rookery of black-crowned night herons. Nearby is a long spit projecting southward to Prince Head, which provides good views back toward the rest of the island. (Take care to avoid the abundant poison ivy.)

**BUMPKIN ISLAND**, shown in the lower panel of **Map 34** on page 230, is located in Hingham Bay and is reached from either Georges Island or Hewitts Cove. It is small (thirty-five acres) and covered with scrubby growth, chiefly sumacs, aspens, and redcedars.

In 1681 Samuel Ward bequeathed Bumpkin Island to Harvard College, which for more than two centuries leased the island to tenant farmers who grew hay, fruits, and vegetables. (The island's name is a corruption of *pumpkin*.) In 1900 Albert Burrage, a Boston philanthropist, acquired a 500-year lease to the island and built a large brick hospital for children with severe physical disabilities. When the United States entered World War I, Burrage transferred his lease to the federal government, which used the hospital as the administration building for a naval training station. Fifty-six temporary wooden structures were erected. As many as 1800 people at a time lived on the island, and altogether the training station graduated nearly 15,000 seamen. After the war the camp was dismantled, but the hospital did not reopen until 1940. Five years later it burned down. Remnants of the hospital, training station, and an old stone farmhouse are located on the island, which became part of the Boston Harbor Islands State Park in 1973.

**GRAPE ISLAND**, shown in the upper panel of **Map 35** on page 231, is similar to Bumpkin Island, only somewhat larger (fifty acres). It is located just a mile from the ferry terminal at Hewitts Cove in Hingham but is also accessible from Georges Island. Formerly Grape Island was joined to the mainland during low tide, but at the end of the nineteenth century a channel was dredged across the narrows to improve navigation in and out of Weymouth Back River.

At the time of the American Revolution, the island was owned and farmed by Elisha Leavitt, a Tory who lived in Hingham. On May 21, 1775, about a month after the battles at Lexington and Concord, three British ships from Boston anchored off Grape Island and dispatched troops to remove from Leavitt's barn about eighty tons of hay for the army's horses and livestock in the besieged city. Two thousand colonial militiamen assembled on the mainland opposite the island. Gunfire was exchanged and the British were driven off after taking about three tons of hay. The Grape Island Alarm, as the incident is called, concluded when the militia burned Leavitt's barn and the remaining hay.

The island continued to be farmed until the middle of the twentieth century. For a long period it was owned by the Bradley family of Hingham, proprietors of a fertilizer factory in Weymouth. At Grape Island the Bradleys grazed horses and grew hay for use at their polo grounds on the mainland. Grape Island became part of the Boston Harbor Islands State Park in 1973.

**THOMPSON ISLAND** is shown in the lower panel of **Map 35** on page 231. Located close to South Boston, the island has its own ferry, as detailed on page 235. Its large size (157 acres) and varied terrain make it one of the best islands for walking.

Even before the Puritan Migration, Thompson Island was the site of a trading post established in 1626 by David Thompson of the Plymouth Colony. Thompson died in 1628, and six years later the island was acquired by the new town of Dorchester, which leased it to farmers. In 1833 the Boston Asylum and Farm School for Indigent Boys was established on the island. The school's purpose was to educate and reform boys who "are exposed to extraordinary temptations, and are in danger of becoming vicious and dangerous or useless members of society." This mission cannot have been helped when twenty-three boys drowned in 1841 while on an outing intended as a reward for good behavior. Another eight boys were lost in 1892 when the school's sloop capsized in a squall.

In 1907 the vocational program was expanded and the institution became the Farm and Trades School. When a full high-school curriculum was introduced in 1955, the name was changed to Thompson Academy. Then in 1975 the Thompson Island Education Center was established to hold conferences and symposiums catering to the region's business community, partly as a way to pay for a variety of youth programs. In 1988 the Center merged with Outward Bound. Now the Thompson Island Outward Bound Education Center runs retreats, rope courses, and other challenging excursions for adults and children. The aim is to foster teamwork, self-confidence, and environmental awareness. One program for kids is a two-week voyage in open boats. The Center also sponsors the Willauer School, which is a private middle school with an outward bound slant.

≈      ≈      ≈      ≈

**BOATS TO THE ISLANDS:** From the three mainland terminals described below, Boston Harbor Cruises operates ferries to Georges Island. (See **Map 31** at right.) Telephone (617) 227-4321 for information on fares and schedules. The initial fare includes shuttle service among the islands and back to the mainland at day's end. In rough weather, the boats may not go, so call beforehand. Other inquiries should be directed to the Harbor Islands Field Office at (617) 727-5290.

≈      ≈      ≈      ≈

MAP 31 — Boston Harbor Islands

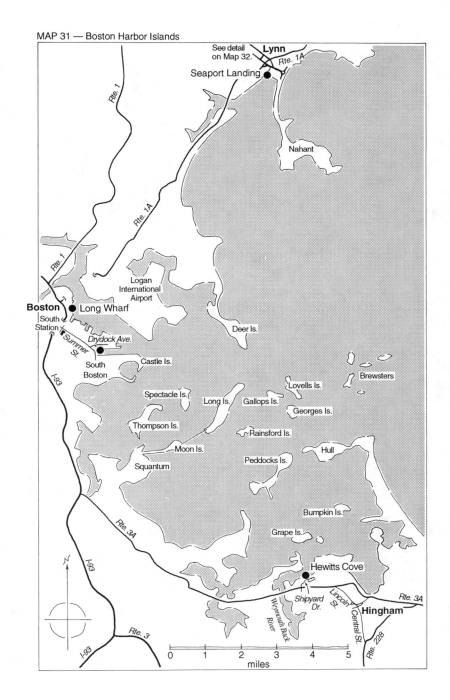

227

MAP 32 — Seaport Landing (Lynn) and Georges and Gallops Islands

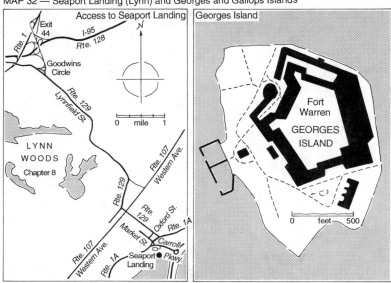

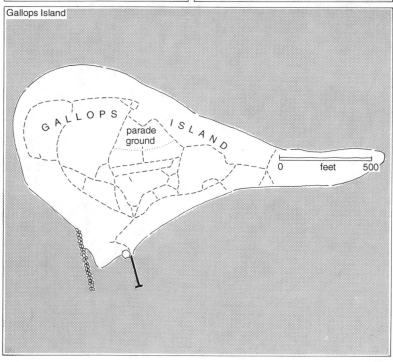

MAP 33 — Lovells Island

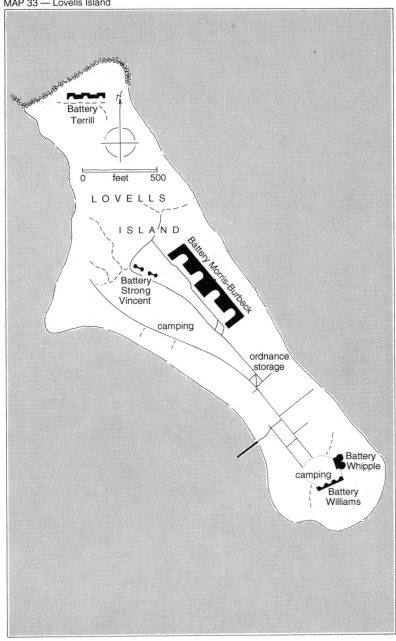

MAP 34 — Peddocks Island (upper panel) and Bumpkin Island (lower panel)

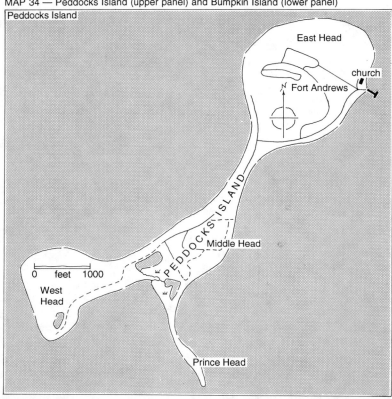

Peddocks Island

East Head

church

N Fort Andrews

PEDDOCKS ISLAND

Middle Head

0 feet 1000

West
Head

Prince Head

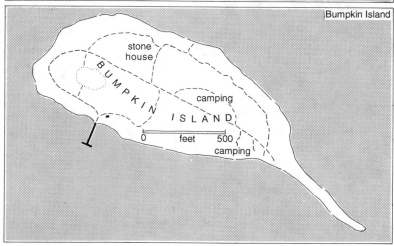

Bumpkin Island

stone
house

BUMPKIN ISLAND

camping

0 feet 500

camping

MAP 35 — Grape Island (upper panel) and Thompson Island (lower panel)

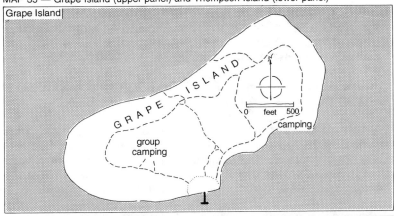

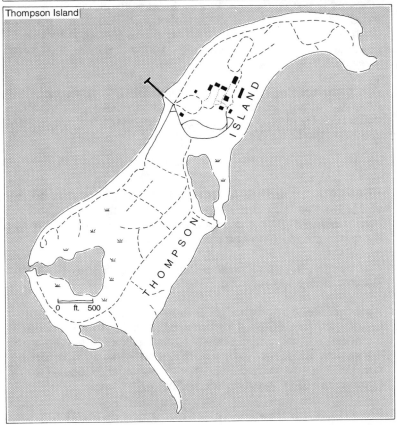

**LONG WHARF IN BOSTON:** The wharf is located at the end of State Street next to the New England Aquarium. This is the chief mainland terminal, from which boats to the harbor islands run daily spring through fall.

**Public transit to Long Wharf:** The wharf is located within sight of the MBTA's **Aquarium Station** on the Blue Line.

**Automobile directions to Long Wharf:** Interstate 93 (the Central Artery) passes close to Long Wharf, which is located at the foot of State Street next to the New England Aquarium. Two approaches are described below. Parking is available at nearby garages and lots, including those for Quincy Market.

*Approaching from the north on Interstate 93,* take the exit for the Callahan Tunnel — although, of course, you do not want to go through the tunnel itself. Instead, follow the signs for the aquarium and the Long Wharf Ferry Terminal serving the Boston Harbor Islands.

*Approaching from the south on Interstate 93,* take the exit for Atlantic Avenue. Follow the signs for Atlantic Avenue and the aquarium. By turning right at State Street, you will arrive directly in front of the Long Wharf Ferry Terminal.

≈    ≈    ≈    ≈

**SEAPORT LANDING MARINA IN LYNN:** Located north of Boston, this ferry terminal provides limited service to the harbor islands. On summer weekends, there is one boat daily, leaving in the morning and returning at the end of the afternoon.

The upper-left panel of **Map 32** on page 228 shows roads leading to Seaport Landing.

**Automobile directions to Seaport Landing:** Seaport Landing fronts on Carroll Parkway, which links Route 1A (the Lynnway) with the traffic rotary at Nahant Neck. The entrance to the landing is accessible only from Carroll Parkway's *eastbound lanes* and occurs immediately after a pedestrian bridge. Two approaches to Lynn are described below.

*From Route 1* just south of Exit 44 off Interstate 95 (Route 128), follow Route 129 east into Lynn for 5.2 miles. This route entails a number of sharp turns. For example, after 4.3 miles Route 129 turns left at Lynn Plaza onto Washington Street, so follow the route signs closely.

As you enter downtown Lynn, cross Essex, Liberty, and Andrew streets, then turn right at a traffic light onto Oxford Street. Go one block, then turn left onto Market Street and follow it to the second traffic light. Turn left onto Carroll Parkway. Go just 0.1 mile, then turn right into Seaport Landing and Lynn Heritage State Park immediately after a pedestrian bridge. Turn right again into the parking lot.

*Route 1A* is another approach, passing close to Seaport Landing in Lynn.

Coming from the north, follow Route 1A through downtown Lynn. After passing straight through an intersection with Washington Street and Nathan Place, turn left onto Market Street. At the next traffic light, turn left onto Carroll Parkway. Go just 0.1 mile, then turn right into Seaport Landing and Lynn Heritage State Park immediately after a pedestrian bridge. Turn right again into the parking lot.

Coming from the south on Route 1A, watch for the intersection with Carroll Parkway, which is marked by signs indicating that 1A turns inland toward downtown Lynn and Salem. Don't turn left; instead, go straight just 0.1 mile, then turn right into Seaport Landing and Lynn Heritage State Park. Turn right again into the parking lot.

≈    ≈    ≈    ≈

**HEWITTS COVE IN HINGHAM:** Located south of Boston, this ferry terminal is reached from Route 3A just east of the bridge over the Weymouth Back River. Boats to the harbor islands run daily during summer but only on weekends during spring and fall. On the way to and from Georges Island, the Hingham boat usually stops by at Grape, Bumpkin, and Peddocks islands.

**Public transit to Hewitts Cove:** Originating at the MBTA's **Quincy Center Station** on the Red Line, Bus 220 follows Route 3A southeast past Hewitts Cove. Tell the driver you want to get off at the intersection with William B. Terry Drive, across from the Hingham Shipyard. With caution, cross Route 3A and follow Shipyard Drive 0.3 mile to the Harbor Islands and Commuter Boat Terminal.

**Automobile directions to Hewitts Cove:** The nearest major expressway is **Route 3** south of the juncture with **Interstate 93** in Quincy.

Leave Route 3 at Exit 14 for Route 228. Follow Route 228 north toward Nantasket 4.6 miles. When Route 228 turns sharply right, go straight on Central Street for 1 mile to Hingham Center. Pass through the business district, then fork right onto Lincoln Street past a seated statue of Abraham Lincoln. Follow Lincoln Street 0.8 mile to Route 3A, then continue north on 3A for 1 mile to the entrance to Hewitts Cove on the right. The entrance occurs at a traffic light and is marked by a sign for commuter boats to Boston. Follow this road (Shipyard Drive) 0.3 mile to the Harbor Islands and Commuter Boat Terminal on the left. Free parking is available in the large lot across the street.

≈      ≈      ≈      ≈

**TOURING THE HARBOR ISLANDS:** The first ferry from each of the mainland terminals leaves at 10 A.M. After visiting an island, you can get to another via the free water taxi that makes regular rounds. Be sure to pick up a current schedule so that you will know how the water taxi works and when boats return to the mainland. In a full day, you can easily visit two or even three islands.

There is no fresh water on any of the islands, so bring your own bottled water or soft drink. You can also buy beverages and snacks on some of the boats and at Georges Island.

For your first trip, plan to spend ample time at Georges Island, site of Fort Warren, where you can walk the ramparts and tour the casemate chambers and living quarters. There are also fortifications on Lovells and Peddocks. The latter is the largest island and provides the most scope for exploration.

≈      ≈      ≈      ≈

**CAMPING:** Lovells, Peddocks, Bumpkin, and Grape islands have campsites. Permits are required. For information and a permit to Lovells and Peddocks, telephone the Metropolitan District Commission at (617) 727-5290. For information and a permit to Bumpkin and Grape, telephone the Massachusetts Department of the Environment at (781) 740-1605, extension 201 or 205.

≈        ≈        ≈        ≈

**THOMPSON ISLAND:**  As noted in the introduction to this chapter, Thompson Island is in a category by itself.  The island and its ferry are operated by the Thompson Island Outward Bound Education Center.  The boat leaves the mainland from a landing in the seaport district near South Boston.  Public access to the island is permitted each Saturday from early June through late September.  During this period, call (617) 328-3900 for information on the current ferry schedule and fare.  There is no water taxi service from Thompson Island to the other islands, but Thompson is big enough to be worth a full day.  The lower panel of **Map 35** on page 231 shows the island's roads and trails.

**Public Transit to the Thompson Island boat:**  Take the MBTA's Red Line to **South Station**.  From there, walk 1 mile east on Summer Street to Drydock Avenue, which leads left into Marine Industrial Park.

After entering Marine Industrial Park, turn right at the first opportunity.  The boat to Thompson Island operates from the bulkhead straight ahead, in the angle formed by the Summer Street bridge.

**Automobile directions to the Thompson Island boat from Interstate 93 (the Central Artery):**  Leave I-93 at the exit for South Station in Boston.  From the station, follow Summer Street east 1 mile, then turn left onto Drydock Avenue, which enters Marine Industrial Park.  Turn right at the first opportunity.  The boat to Thompson Island operates from the bulkhead straight ahead, in the angle formed by the Summer Street bridge.

After locating the boat landing, the next thing to do is to find a legitimate spot to park.  The best place is probably the five-story public garage with red stairs, located at the diagonally opposite corner of the block at the intersection of Drydock Avenue and Design Center Place.

# 19

# WORLD'S END
# WHITNEY AND THAYER WOODS
# WOMPATUCK STATE PARK

The three sites discussed here are located close together in Hingham, Cohasset, and Scituate southeast of Boston.

**Map 36** on page 241 shows **World's End**, where there are 4 miles (6.4 kilometers) of tree-lined carriage roads and a few more miles of foot trails. For scenery and sauntering, the hillside meadows are unsurpassed in the Boston region. The reservation is open daily from 10 A.M. to 5 P.M. during summer and from 11 to 4 during winter. An admission fee is charged. Dogs must be leashed. World's End is managed by The Trustees of Reservations; telephone (781) 821-2977 for information. Directions start on page 240.

**Map 37** on page 243 shows the **Whitney and Thayer Woods**, where there are 12 miles of attractive cartways and foot trails through varied terrain. The route outlined on the map is 4 miles long (6.4 kilometers). Like World's End, the site is a property of The Trustees of Reservations. It is open free of charge every day from dawn to dusk. Directions start on page 242.

**Map 38** on page 247 outlines a route of 5 miles (8 kilometers) at **Wompatuck State Park**, which is open daily from sunrise to sunset. Wompatuck State Park is administered by the Massachusetts Department of Environmental Management; telephone (781) 749-7160. Automobile and walking directions are on page 246.

---

## WORLD'S END RESERVATION

WORLD'S END is a promontory of large, egg-shaped hills extending into Hingham Bay behind the still larger peninsula of Hull. From the hilltops, Boston is silhouetted on the horizon to the northwest. Also visible are the harbor islands, which show the same smooth, elongated form as the massive mounds of World's End, and were in fact molded by the same geologic process. Such streamlined hills are called *drumlins* and are the work of continental glaciers.

When the last great ice sheet advanced across New England starting about seventy thousand years ago, it picked up earth, boulders, and rock fragments and carried or smeared this material forward. Sometimes the debris gathered into cohesive masses beneath the moving ice. This usually happened in areas underlain by bedrock that is relatively soft — such as the abundant slate of the Boston basin — and so was ground into sticky clay. Gradually the ice flowed over these masses, adding still more earth and rock to them, and molding them into their oval, streamlined shape. The eroded western shore of World's End provides a cutaway view of the jumble of cobbles and clay that form these giant mounds.

Hills deposited in this manner occur throughout New England both singly and in swarms, as clusters of drumlins are called. If you take many of the walks featured in this book, you will see drumlins again and again. Boston itself has many drumlins, all elongated on a north-westerly axis, indicating the angle from which the ice sheet advanced. Beacon Hill, Bunker Hill, and the hills at the Arnold Arboretum are drumlins, as are the harbor islands, isolated by a rise in sea level that accompanied the melting of the massive ice sheet. Formerly, World's End itself was two islands until they were linked to each other and to the mainland by causeways.


LIKE THE HARBOR ISLANDS, World's End was stripped of timber in the early years of English settlement. Thereafter, the area was used for crops, hay, and pasture by generations of farmers who owned pieces of the peninsula but lived elsewhere. Then in 1855 John R. Brewer, a wealthy Boston businessman, started to buy land here for a country estate and farm. On Cushing's Neck just south of the present-day reservation, Brewer built a four-story frame house, near which he clustered a dozen or more other structures, including barns, greenhouses, a stable, a house for his farm superintendent, and apartments for some of his farm hands. Eventually Brewer and his children acquired all of World's End. After experimenting unsuccessfully with Ayrshire cattle and sheep, the family raised Jersey cattle that won many prizes at agricultural fairs in Hingham and Boston.

In the late 1880s Brewer hired Frederick Law Olmsted, the designer of much of Boston's park system, including the Fenway and Franklin Park, to lay out a subdivision at World's End as a financial contingency. Brewer may have seen the possibility of developing summer or even

year-round residences within walking distance of the Plymouth-to-Boston railroad. Olmsted's plan called for 163 house lots fronting on gracefully looping, tree-lined roads that wound around the hills. There were also to be two boat landings and a bridge to Nantasket Beach. Brewer proceeded to construct most of the roads and to plant trees very much as Olmsted specified, but fortunately the project never progressed beyond the landscaping. Although Olmsted's plan at World's End was for a subdivision, the resulting landscape is today a successful treatment in the pastoral style: no structures, no recreational facilities, no cars, and no gardens or manicured lawns. To make a brief comparison, this was the look that Olmsted wanted for the inner sanctum at Franklin Park — what he called the "Country Park" — but where now the carriage roads are busy motorways and the meadow is a golf course.

Farming continued at World's End until the death of Brewer's last surviving child in 1936. During the next few years, nearly all the structures, including the old mansion, were torn down. In the 1940s and '50s, Brewer's granddaughter, Helen Brewer Walker, subdivided the land bordering Martin's Lane but declined developers' offers for World's End, where she continued to employ a small crew of men to maintain the peninsula's old carriage roads, drainageways, trees, and meadows. Eventually, after an extraordinary campaign that raised a half-million dollars by public subscription, primarily in Hingham and neighboring towns, The Trustees of Reservations was able to buy World's End in 1967. For a discussion of this organization, which is Massachusetts' preeminent land conservation trust, see Chapter 24.

≈      ≈      ≈      ≈

## AUTOMOBILE DIRECTIONS TO WORLD'S END:
Located 12 miles southeast of Boston, World's End projects into Hingham Bay behind the much larger peninsula of Hull. (See •19a on **Map 1** on page 6, and also the corner panel of **Map 36** at right.)

**To World's End from the juncture of Route 3 and Interstate 93 in Quincy:** Follow Route 3 south toward Cape Cod for nearly 8 miles, then leave Route 3 at Exit 14 for Route 228. Follow Route 228 north toward Nantasket for 6.5 miles to **Route 3A**. Turn left onto Route 3A and follow it north 0.5 mile to an intersection with Summer Street. Turn right onto Summer Street and go 0.3 mile to a traffic light. Continue straight across the intersection and follow Martin's Lane 0.7 mile to the reservation's entrance at the end of the road. After passing through the gate, bear right to park.

240

MAP 36 — World's End

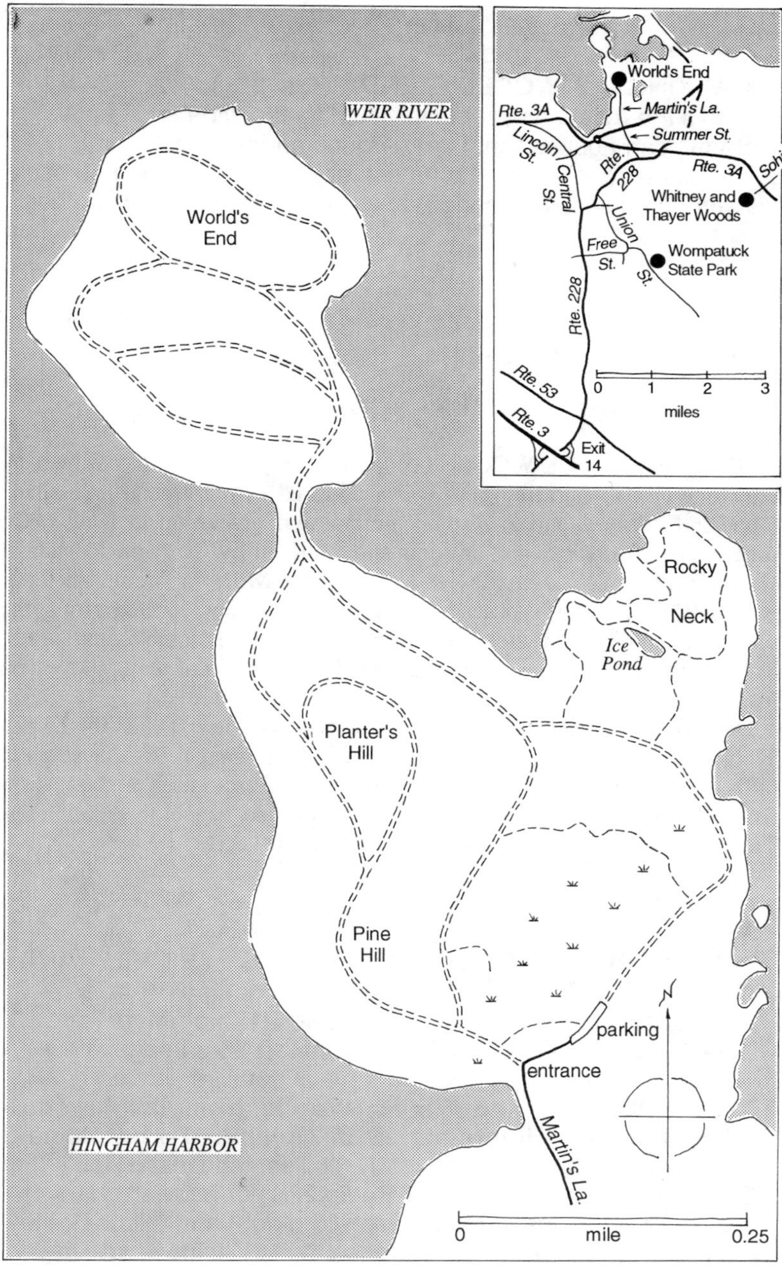

WEIR RIVER

World's End

Rocky

Neck

Ice
Pond

Planter's
Hill

Pine
Hill

parking

entrance

Martin's La.

HINGHAM HARBOR

N

0                    mile                    0.25

World's End

Rte. 3A

Lincoln St.

Central St.

Martin's La.

Summer St.

Rte. 3A

Sohier St.

Rte. 228

Whitney and
Thayer Woods

Free St.

Union St.

Wompatuck
State Park

Rte. 228

Rte. 53

Rte. 3

Exit
14

0        1        2        3

miles

241

≈　　　≈　　　≈　　　≈

**WALKING AT WORLD'S END: Map 36** on page 241 shows the reservation's trails, including the wide and gently graded carriageways that wind around and over the main hills. The distance to the northernmost loop at World's End and back is about 3 miles. Exploring Rocky Neck adds perhaps another mile.

≈

≈　　　≈　　　≈　　　≈

≈

## WHITNEY AND THAYER WOODS

THESE BEAUTIFUL WOODS occupy former pastures still outlined by old stone walls. Farming here was abandoned in the second half of the nineteenth century, and since then the land has grown up in hardwoods, pine, and hemlock with an understory of holly and rhododendron. Particularly attractive in May and June is the Millikin Memorial Path, profusely planted with azaleas and rhododendrons and located along the southern boundary of the reservation next to Wompatuck State Park. The Millikin Memorial Path is included as part of the walk shown on Map 37 at right.

Named for two families that long held property here, the Whitney and Thayer Woods have been pieced together from many gifts, principally 640 acres in 1933 from the Whitney Woods Association and 28 acres from Mrs. Ezra Thayer in 1943. There have also been some purchases. The reservation presently includes more than 800 acres.

≈　　　≈　　　≈　　　≈

**AUTOMOBILE DIRECTIONS TO THE WHITNEY AND THAYER WOODS:** The reservation is located 16 miles southeast of Boston in Cohasset. (See •19b on **Map 1** on page 6, and also the corner panel of **Map 36** on page 241.)

**To the Whitney and Thayer Woods from the juncture of Route 3 and Interstate 93 in Quincy:** Follow Route 3 south toward Cape Cod for nearly 8 miles, then leave Route 3 at Exit 14 for Route 228. Follow Route 228 north toward Nantasket for 6.5 miles to **Route 3A**. Turn right and follow Route 3A south for 2 miles to the entrance to the Whitney and Thayer Woods on the right, opposite Sohier Street.

MAP 37 — Whitney and Thayer Woods

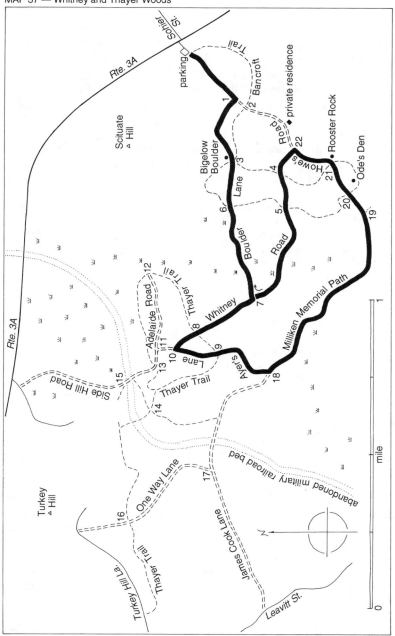

≈        ≈        ≈        ≈

## WALKING AT THE WHITNEY AND THAYER WOODS:
The bold line on **Map 37** on page 243 shows a 4-mile excursion that follows the reservation's most attractive trails. The entire route is via unpaved woods roads — or what The Trustees of Reservations calls cartways. There are also foot trails, indicated by dashed lines, and an abandoned railroad bed that served the military depot at what is now Wompatuck State Park.

If you want a longer walk, you can hike to **Turkey Hill** at the reservation's northwest corner, then back again. Turkey Hill is a drumlin, and has the same form as the hills at World's End. Scituate Hill — yet another drumlin — is visible to the east from the top of Turkey Hill. Other evidence of glaciation includes huge erratics, such as Rooster Rock and Ode's Den.

Whatever route you take while at Whitney and Thayer Woods, navigation is made easy by the numbers posted on trees at trail intersections and shown also on the map.

≈

≈        ≈        ≈        ≈

≈

## WOMPATUCK STATE PARK

IN THE FALL OF 1941, the federal government, using its power of eminent domain, suddenly bought five square miles of rocky hills and swamps in the backwoods of Cohasset and two neighboring towns. During the following year, contractors built a depot for the assembly and storage of naval munitions of all kinds. Overall capacity was about twenty million pounds of high explosives, including bombs, depth charges, mines, rockets, detonators, fuses, black powder, TNT, and ammunition of every size, ranging from bullets to 16-inch gun shells weighing 2800 pounds each for the largest battleships. Called the Cohasset Annex, the new facility was linked by military railroad to the older and much smaller U.S. Naval Depot on the Weymouth Back River in Hingham. The Hingham depot, in turn, was joined by rail to deepwater slips at Hewitts Cove, not far to the north.

The background for development of the Cohassett Annex was the increasing possibility of war with Germany. Hitler's *Wehrmacht* had quickly overrun Poland in September 1939 and had conquered Denmark, Norway, the Low Countries, and France the following spring. In September 1940 Congress for the first time in our history authorized peacetime conscription. That same month President Franklin D.

Roosevelt transferred fifty old destroyers to Great Britain in exchange for 99-year leases on naval and air bases in the Caribbean, Newfoundland, and Bermuda. To save England from collapse, Congress voted Lend-Lease aid early in 1941, providing ships, munitions, food, machinery, and other supplies. In April the United States occupied Greenland and started patrolling the North Atlantic sea lanes.

As war loomed, the Department of the Navy determined in the spring of 1941 that the existing munitions depot at Hingham could not adequately support increased naval operations in the North Atlantic. After conducting a survey of undeveloped areas where the depot could expand, the Navy selected the Cohassett site in June. The place was far enough from existing communities to provide safety, and big enough so that the magazines, or storage bunkers, could be separated from one another by large distances in order to prevent a chain reaction if one were to blow up. By the time the land for the annex was acquired late in October and construction started in November, the United States was engaged in a *de facto* naval war with Germany. After an American destroyer and a German submarine fought on September 4, the President ordered the navy to "shoot on sight" any U-boat encountered, and the Germans responded in kind. Seven American merchant vessels and one destroyer, the *Reuben James*, were sunk before Hitler declared war in December.

During World War II, the Hingham and Cohasset depots together supplied most of the ammunition for naval forces in the North Atlantic. The Cohasset facility included more than a hundred concrete, earth-covered magazines. (Nearly all have since been torn out.) For trains there were twenty sidings within slit trenches for the storage of up to 135 freight cars. The trenches were "barricaded," or that is, banked with sloping concrete walls to direct accidental explosions skyward. (The train trenches still exist, but have been filled nearly to the top to prevent accidents.) An elaborate system of roads provided access to magazines not reachable by rail. Trucks carried high explosives back and forth between the magazines and a transfer depot by the railroad. (Today, some of the trails follow the roads and also the railroad bed.) Originally, the transfer depot had no protecting barricades, but after there was an explosion at a similar facility at Hastings, Nebraska in September 1944, earthen and concrete embankments were added. Other structures were a building for assembling mines and, of course, military barracks.

At the end of the war, production at the Hingham and Cohasset depots stopped immediately. The flow of munitions was reversed as ships were decommissioned and their explosives were stored away. Total employment fell from a wartime high of 2378 to as low as 50 until the depots were reactivated in 1950 for use during the Korean War. Afterwards, many thousands of pounds of explosives were burned or detonated at the

Cohasset Annex. In 1961 the Navy announced that the annex was no longer needed, and six years later the federal government gave most of the site to Massachusetts for a state park that opened in 1969. Nearly all of the remaining land, after being used for different military activities, was purchased by Massachusetts in 1986 and added to Wompatuck State Park.

≈     ≈     ≈     ≈

## AUTOMOBILE DIRECTIONS TO WOMPATUCK STATE PARK: The park is located 17 miles southeast of Boston, mostly in Hingham and Cohasset. (See •19c on **Map 1** on page 6, and also the corner panel of **Map 36** on page 241.)

**To Wompatuck State Park from the juncture of Route 3 and Interstate 93 in Quincy:** Follow Route 3 south toward Cape Cod for nearly 8 miles, then leave Route 3 at Exit 14 for Route 228. Follow Route 228 north toward Nantasket for 3.8 miles to an intersection with Free Street. Turn right onto Free Street and go 0.9 mile, then turn right onto Union Street. After entering the park, go 0.2 mile to the main bike path parking lot on the left, opposite the visitor center.

≈     ≈     ≈     ≈

**WALKING AT WOMPATUCK STATE PARK: Map 38** at right shows an easy 5-mile route through the park's eastern half, where there is an extensive system of paved paths. The route described below is blazed with blue markers bearing a bicycle emblem. Obviously, the route can be lengthened, if you want, by exploring other trails that are also shown.

**Start** at the parking lot across Union Street from the visitor center. Enter the woods on the narrow, paved hike-bike path, just to the right of a wider road that also leads into the woods. At the first intersection, turn right, then turn left after a few dozen yards. Go to a T-intersection and turn right. Eventually, within sight of a gate at Union Street, turn left to continue uphill on the paved hike-bike path. Merge with a trail intersecting from the right-rear. At the next intersection — it is marked A on the map — continue straight, then bear right at subsequent junctions. When you close the circuit by again reaching junction A, turn left and continue to the parking lot by the way you came.

MAP 38 — Wompatuck State Park

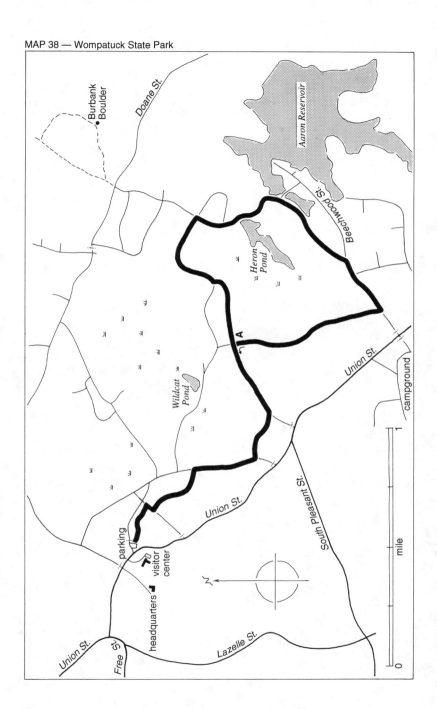

# 20

# NORRIS  RESERVATION

Located in Norwell southeast of Boston, the Norris Reservation offers a pleasant circuit through the woods, as outlined on **Map 39** on page 252.  The route is just 2 miles (3.2 kilometers).  The main attraction, however, is the adjacent salt marsh along the **North River**, familiar to many motorists on Route 3 as the only break in the visual monotony between Braintree and Cape Cod.  The photograph at left, in fact, was taken from the Route 3 bridge.  The marsh is accessible from the Norris Reservation, so that if you want, you can leave the circuit trail and walk freely over the salt meadow.

The reservation is open from dawn to dusk.  It is managed by The Trustees of Reservations; telephone (781) 821-2977.  For automobile and walking directions, please turn to page 253.

---

TIDAL RIVERS are a typical setting for salt marsh formation. Sediments that have been eroded from throughout the watershed are carried downstream, where they finally settle out in the slackening current of the estuary as the river nears the sea.  Also, silt and sand eroded by waves striking the coast are carried upstream into the estuary because of the fact that inflowing tides have a greater velocity than ebbing tides.  (After all, the tide is a sort of ponderous, global wave, more abrupt at its forward than its trailing edge.)  The result is that the tide tends to carry more material into the estuaries than it takes away.

As the sediments accumulate, they form mud flats that are exposed at low tide and that gradually are colonized by marsh grasses.  The dense, grassy carpet slows and filters the muddy tidewater that twice daily inundates the marsh, thus further contributing to the deposition of sediments.  Thick layers of peaty mud develop, bound in a matrix of partially decomposed roots and leaves of marsh grasses.

As long as the marsh is flooded by the tide, upward growth of the surface continues because of the ongoing processes of sedimentation and peat formation. But as the marsh builds vertically toward the high water level, less material is washed onto the surface and upward growth slows. The limit is about a foot above average high water. At that level only storm tides or the highest tides of the year during spring and fall cover the marsh, so that there is no longer enough deposition to raise the level of the marsh appreciably. To some extent, the accumulation of dead and decaying salt grass builds up the surface. But at the same time, the underlying peat is continually decomposing and compacting under its own weight, which causes the surface of the marsh to settle back toward the level of the yearly high tides. The marsh is thus in equilibrium among the processes of deposition, plant growth, compaction, and decay, which altogether produce a remarkably level surface, as flat as the silt-bearing floodwater itself.

There are, however, some differences in elevation, which are reflected in different varieties of plant life. *Spartina patens* (commonly called saltmeadow cordgrass or saltmarsh hay) dominates the high marsh that is flooded only during the year's greatest tides or storm surges. This grass is fairly short, dense, and soft-textured in appearance, but actually rather coarse to the touch. It lies nearly flat on the ground except for its characteristic cowlicks. Also occupying the high marsh is the short and rigid *Distichlis spicata* (salt grass). The far taller *Spartina alterniflora* (seven or eight feet high and commonly called saltmarsh cordgrass) occupies lower areas and channel banks that are inundated during every high tide.

Salt marshes are extraordinarily productive. Their shallow sunlit waters permit photosynthesis to take place at a very rapid rate. Great quantities of algae and animal microorganisms are produced. Algae are even able to grow during the winter. According to John and Mildred Teal, authors of *Life and Death of the Salt Marsh*, the grasses and algae capture up to 6 percent of the solar energy falling on the marsh during the year, compared to 2 percent for a corn field at its peak. The algae in turn consume only 10 percent of their energy intake, passing 90 percent along to the myriad of animals that feed on them. An acre of salt marsh yields about ten tons of organic material yearly, compared to fifteen tons for wheat fields (including stems and leaves) and four tons for the very best hay fields.

Coastal marshes are prime feeding and breeding grounds not only for migratory waterfowl but also for fish. Worms, shrimp, shellfish, and baitfish thrive on the algae and rotting vegetation. In turn, the young of larger fishes find food and protection in these rich nurseries. According to the Teals, two-thirds of the value of the commercial harvest of fish and shellfish caught on the East Coast comes from species that spend at least part of their life cycle in coastal and estuarine marshes. Such areas are about ten times as productive of fish as the coastal waters of the continental shelf, and about one hundred times more productive than the open ocean. Because of their importance, salt marshes have been protected from unregulated dredging or filling by the Massachusetts Wetlands Protection Act and also the Coastal Wetlands Restriction Act.

TURNING TO THE HISTORY of the North River, English settlement here was underway before 1628 as people moved up the coast from the Plymouth Colony. In the early 1630s Puritans began to arrive, both from the vicinity of Boston and directly from England. The town of Scituate (encompassing also present-day Norwell, Hanover, and parts of Marshfield and Rockland) was incorporated in 1636. By the end of the seventeenth century, the river had at least a dozen shipyards, plus other landings and fishing stations, located where twists and turns brought the channel close to the upland that borders the marsh. Some of these shipyards were as far upstream as Plymouth road (now Route 53), eighteen miles from the river's mouth. Over the course of two and a half centuries, more than a thousand vessels were built, including barks, brigantines, and schooners. After the ships were launched, men with poles and ropes guided them downstream on the ebb tide. Sometimes the larger vessels had to be winched over shoals with lines and anchors, or floated high by smaller boats lashed to the sides. Probably the most famous ship from the North River was the 220-ton *Columbia*, built in 1773. Its name was given to the Columbia River, which Captain Robert Gray explored during a voyage around the world. Launched in 1812, the 500-ton *Mount Vernon* was the biggest vessel ever built on the river, and the last was the *Helen M. Foster*, launched in 1871 at Norwell, which had split off from Scituate in 1849. Many of the ships were made for the coastal and West Indies trade and for cod-fishing on the Grand Banks. And there were also numerous small, undocumented craft built here, including flat-bottomed gundalows that were sailed or poled up and down the river, carrying farm products and supplies or just moving tons of hay from the salt marsh to local barns for fodder.

Like nearly all rivers as they approach the sea, the North River meanders across the salt marsh from one edge of the adjacent upland to the other. "There is one reach," says an 1831 account, "which has long been called the 'no gains' from the circumstance, that, after flowing from side to side, and almost turning backward several times, it has in fact flowed several miles, and gained but a few rods in its direct progress to the sea."

Feeding into the North River are tributaries that powered various mills. In 1690 John Bryant built a sawmill on Second Herring Brook at what is now the Norris Reservation. Bryant soon afterwards added a gristmill, and from then until 1927 a succession of mills occupied the

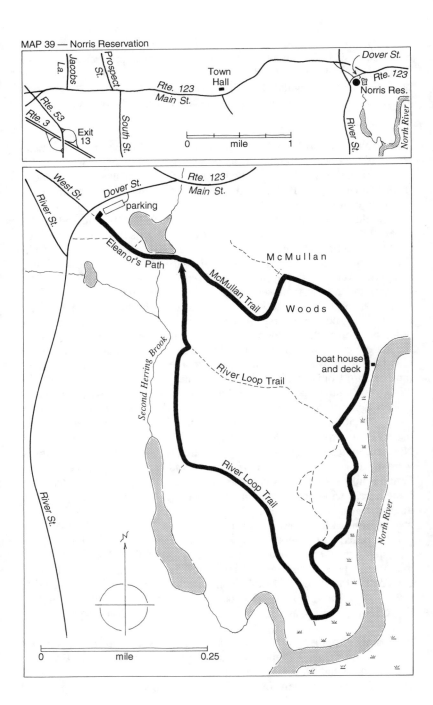

MAP 39 — Norris Reservation

site. Today there is still a millpond and dam. One of the old millstones lies near the main trail 150 yards beyond the dam. In 1829 Second Herring Brook had two gristmills, a sawmill, and a shingle mill. As for the rest of the reservation, much of it was at one time cleared for fields and pasture, as is evident from stone walls that now run through the woods.

The Norris Reservation takes its name from Albert Norris, who started buying land here in the 1920s, and whose wife Eleanor gave the property to The Trustees of Reservations in 1970. The reservation has since been expanded by the gift of more land from the McMullan family.

≈      ≈      ≈      ≈

**AUTOMOBILE DIRECTIONS:   The Norris Reservation** is located in the town of Norwell, 20 miles southeast of Boston. (See •20 on **Map 1** on page 6, and also the upper panel of **Map 39** at left.)

**To the Norris Reservation from the juncture of Route 3 and Interstate 93 in Quincy:** Follow Route 3 south toward Cape Cod for 10.5 miles, then leave Route 3 at Exit 13 for Routes 53 and 123. Follow Route 53 north 0.4 mile, then turn right onto Route 123 eastbound. Go 3.3 miles and then, after passing through the old village center, turn sharply right onto Dover Street. Continue just 0.1 mile to the parking lot for the Norris Reservation on the left.

≈      ≈      ≈      ≈

**WALKING:** The lower panel of **Map 39** at left shows a 2-mile loop around the **Norris Reservation**.

**To start,** follow the trail into the woods. Immediately after passing an old millpond, continue straight as another path branches off to the right. After reaching the North River, continue with the water on your left. (Incidentally, as you face the river, downstream is to the left, although sometimes you will see the incoming tide flowing upstream to the right.)

As you continue along the trail, bear left at three successive trail junctions. From a vantage point overlooking the marsh and river at the southern end of the reservation, continue around the circuit on the main path, bearing left at a T-intersection and left again past the millpond and back to the parking lot.

# 21

## BLUE HILLS RESERVATION
### including Fowl Meadow and Ponkapoag Pond

Stretching from Quincy to Canton south of Boston, the Blue Hills Reservation is huge: about 11 square miles with more than 125 miles of trails. The granite hills mimic on a smaller scale the form and substance of New Hampshire's White Mountains. From their rocky summits, hikers can see over much of metropolitan Boston. West of the hills is Fowl Meadow, and to the south is Ponkapoag Pond, also part of the reservation.

Because the Blue Hills Reservation is so large, several different walks are described below, each with its own map and its own automobile directions to the different trailheads. For an overview of the entire reservation, see **Map 40** on page 259. The rest of the maps in this chapter outline specific routes, as described below. For longer outings, these routes can be combined, or you can use the maps to devise your own excursion. The maps overlap at the edges, providing linkage from one to another. Note that the Skyline Trail, blazed with blue markers, extends east-west along the entire range of hills.

**Map 41** on pages 260-261 shows a walk in the Blue Hills' **eastern section**. The route is 7.5 miles long (12 kilometers). It alternates between easy paths through the woods and more strenuous sections across the hilltops. Directions to the eastern Blue Hills via public transit and automobile start on page 258; the hike itself is described starting on page 262.

**Map 42** on pages 266-267 outlines a strenuous walk of 6.5 miles (10.4 kilometers) in the Blue Hills' **western section**. Highlights are Great Blue Hill and Buck Hill, both of which provide broad views. For people who want a shorter, easier outing, **Map 43** on pages 268-269 shows two routes, each 3 miles long (4.8 kilometers). Automobile directions to the western Blue Hills start on page 265, and hiking directions start on page 270.

At the foot of Great Blue Hill is the small but excellent **Trailside Museum** (really half zoo) devoted to the natural history of the Blue Hills Region. It is open daily except Monday from 10 A.M. to 5

P.M. It is also open Monday holidays. There is a small admission fee. For information, telephone (617) 333-0690.

**Map 44** on page 274 shows **Fowl Meadow**, where the trail follows a dike through the marsh and low, wet woods bordering the Neponset River, with Great Blue Hill a backdrop to the east. The round-trip is 3.8 miles long (6 kilometers). Directions to Fowl Meadow are on page 275.

Finally, **Map 45** on pages 278-279 shows a circuit of 5 miles (8 kilometers) around **Ponkapoag Pond**, including a spur via boardwalk through a quaking bog. Automobile directions start on page 277, and walking directions start on page 281.

The Blue Hills Reservation is open from dawn to dusk. It is managed by the Metropolitan District Commission; telephone (617) 698-1802.

---

## EASTERN BLUE HILLS

THE BLUE HILLS RESERVATION was among the first areas acquired for public recreation after establishment of the Metropolitan Parks Commission more than a hundred years ago. Municipal parks and woodland reservations were then a relatively new idea. As urban centers spread, the nation's largest cities felt pressured to do what they had never done before: preserve extensive open spaces for public use. Spurred by the success of New York's Central Park, created in 1856, Boston purchased the land for the Fenway in 1877, and in the following two decades developed Franklin Park, Jamaica Pond, the Charlesbank near the present-day Science Museum, and other parks and parkways throughout the city.

There was no framework or precedent, however, for Boston and the surrounding towns to cooperate on a regional basis to preserve land for public recreation. The best beaches and the largest and most picturesque tracts of open land were available at relatively low prices in the outlying municipalities. But these towns — most could not yet be called suburbs — saw no reason to bear the expense of buying parks within their borders that would benefit the city-dwellers as much or more than themselves. Frequently the areas most suited to park development, such as river banks and rocky highlands, served as municipal boundaries, so that each town was reluctant to secure land on its side of the line without corresponding action by its neighbor. (One rare example of cooperation

256

was the improvement to Muddy River made by Brookline and Boston in accordance with the plan of Frederick Law Olmsted.) Also, many towns simply could not muster the necessary funds for park development, nor was the expense warranted by their small populations. Boston had money, but it balked nonetheless. Why should it alone pay for parks far outside the city, even were the courts to uphold legislation authorizing it to do so?

A regional park authority was seen as a way to cut through this impasse. Foremost among the advocates of the regional approach were Charles Eliot, a landscape architect with the firm of Frederick Law Olmsted, and Sylvester Baxter, a journalist who had written a book entitled *Greater Boston: A Study for a Federalized Metropolis Comprising the City of Boston and the Surrounding Cities and Towns.* In 1891 Eliot proposed, and Baxter helped promote, creation of a privately-funded and privately-managed organization called The Trustees of Reservations to hold land throughout Massachusetts for public use. The following year the state government established a temporary Metropolitan Parks Commission to prepare a plan for publicly-funded regional parks. The commissioners engaged Eliot as landscape architect and Baxter as secretary to draft a proposal for submission to the next session the legislature. The report suggested acquisition of beaches and several large sites and the construction of connecting parkways. In keeping with the nascent conservation movement, most of the proposed parks were to be kept as natural areas, such as were fast disappearing near the big city. The proposed *reservations* — the word expressed a setting-aside of natural places — were seen as an antidote to enervating town life and as a sort of natural restorative for physical and mental health.

With broad support from the public, the local governments, and various conservation and hiking groups, the Massachusetts legislature in 1893 permanently established the Metropolitan Parks Commission, which then continued to employ Eliot as chief planner. The Commission was empowered to buy land within Boston and thirty-six surrounding cities and towns, using eminent domain where necessary. The state provided a low-interest loan, which was repaid by assessing the municipalities. The first apportionment required Boston to pay 50 percent. The current apportionment is based on a complicated formula that has reduced Boston's share as the growth of its population, land values, and industries have lagged the suburbs.

In the first ten years, the Commission acquired 80 percent of the present metropolitan parks system, including the beaches at Nahant, Revere, Winthrop, Quincy, and Nantasket. The Middlesex Fells and the Blue Hills were also purchased, with no hindrance from the fact that each of these reservations includes parts of five separate towns. In 1919 the

Commission merged with the Metropolitan Water and Sewerage Board to form the Metropolitan District Commission (from which, in turn, the Massachusetts Water Resources Authority split off in 1984). Presently the Metropolitan District Commission, or MDC, administers parkland, historic sites, and recreational facilities — including skating rinks, swimming pools, and athletic fields — spread among fifty-three municipalities in the Boston region. Although it is no longer involved in water treatment and delivery, the MDC also owns extensive reservoir lands in central Massachusetts.

≈     ≈     ≈     ≈

**PUBLIC TRANSIT TO THE EASTERN BLUE HILLS:**
There are several alternatives, as described below.

If you don't want to bother with making a connection with the local bus, take the MBTA's Red Line to **Quincy Adams Station**. From there, the trailhead at the Blue Hills is a 1.5-mile walk, as follows: after passing through the turnstiles, turn right out of the station toward Burgin Parkway. Cross the street at the traffic light, then turn left and follow the sidewalk to the next light. Turn right onto Centre Street and follow it 0.9 mile to Town Hill Street. Turn left one short block to West Street, then follow West Street 0.6 mile to the ice rink and trailhead at the end of the street.

If, however, you want to ride all the way to the trailhead, there is bus service from the **Quincy Center Station** on the Red Line. Board Bus 238. Tell the driver you want to get off at the MDC ice rink where West and Willard streets join.

If you miss Bus 238, take Bus 215 from the Quincy Center Station to Boyd Square (a small park on the left with a statue in the center) at the intersection of Common and Copeland streets. With the park on your left, walk one block uphill on Common Street to West Street, then follow West Street to the right 0.6 mile to the ice rink and trailhead at the end of the street.

≈     ≈     ≈     ≈

**AUTOMOBILE DIRECTIONS TO THE EASTERN BLUE HILLS:** This area is located mostly in Quincy, 9 miles south of downtown Boston. (See •21a on **Map 1** on page 6, and also **Map 40** at right.) Two approaches are described below.

MAP 40 — Overview of Blue Hills Reservation

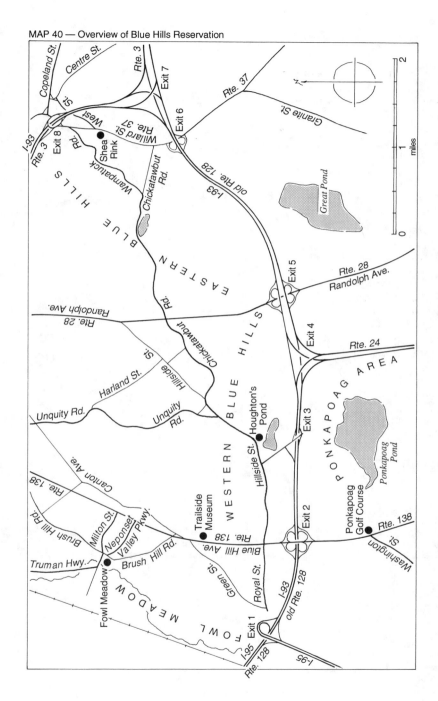

MAP 41 — Eastern Blue Hills

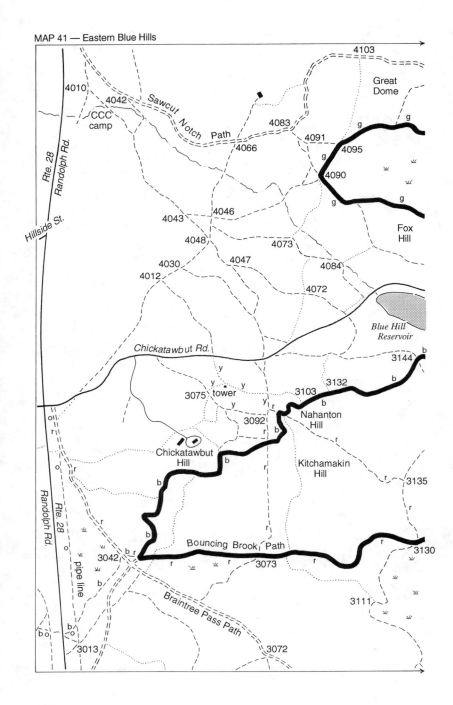

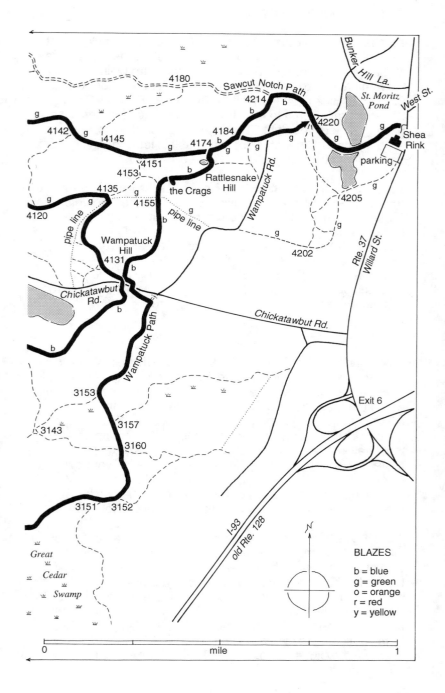

261

**To the eastern Blue Hills from Boston**: Take Interstate 93 south (the Southeast Expressway). Leave the expressway at Exit 8 for the Furnace Brook Parkway toward Quincy. Follow the ramp and road straight 0.4 mile, then fork right for Willard Street and Blue Hills, then left for Braintree. Follow Willard Street 0.4 mile south to the MDC's indoor Shea Memorial Ice Skating Rink on the right. There is a large parking area just beyond the rink. Although signs say that this lot is for rink patrons only, hikers may also park here.

**To the eastern Blue Hills from Interstate 93 south of Boston:** Skirting the Blue Hills, this segment of I-93 (old Route 128) runs east-west between the junctions with Interstate 95 and Route 3.

Leave I-93 at Exit 6 for Route 37 north toward West Quincy and Willard Street. Go 0.9 mile to the MDC's indoor Shea Memorial Ice Skating Rink on the left. There is a large parking area just before the rink. Although signs say that this lot is for rink patrons only, hikers may also park here.

≈        ≈        ≈        ≈

**WALKING IN THE EASTERN BLUE HILLS:** A route totaling 7.5 miles is outlined on **Map 41** on pages 260-261. The rationale for this route is threefold: to cross the hilltops from which there are good views, to alternate difficult and easy going, and to follow, most of the time, blazed trails for simplicity of navigation. There are also four-digit numbers that are posted at most trail intersections and that are shown on the map. You may prefer to use the map and the numbers to devise your own route.

Please note that the route described below *is not* the St. Moritz Nature Trail with its trailhead at the parking lot.

**To get started** from the large parking lot on the south side of the Shea Memorial Ice Skating Rink, walk around to the other side of the building, where there is a smaller parking area and the St. Moritz livery stable. From there, a gravel bridle path marked with green blazes descends into the woods. Follow the trail past a softball field, across a causeway at St. Moritz Pond, and uphill straight through a trail junction to Wampatuck Road. With caution, cross the road and continue 60 yards past a gate to where the blue-blazed Skyline Trail (a narrow footpath) heads off to the left.

From here to Chickatawbut Road, simply follow the blue blazes — except for a short side excursion at the Crags, where a trail leads left a few dozen yards for good views from the summit. At Chickatawbut Road, the route shown on Map 41 leaves the blue-blazed Skyline Trail in order to follow an easy and pleasant fire road. (Later, on the return leg, you will follow the Sky Line Trail from the west back to this same point.) To reach the fire road, follow the shoulder of Chickatawbut Road left for 50 yards. With caution, cross the road and enter the woods on a path which, although obscure at first, soon becomes clear, running parallel with Chickatawbut Road toward the left. Go 150 yards, then turn right onto a fire road. For nearly 2 miles, follow the main trend of the fire road, referring if necessary to the numbers posted at trail intersections and shown also on the map. After the first mile, you will reach an intersection where red blazes lead both right and straight ahead. Follow the red-blazed fire road more or less straight to an intersection with the blue-blazed Skyline Trail.

Turn sharply right onto the blue-blazed Skyline Trail and follow it east, back toward your starting point. For the next 2 miles, trace the blue blazes up and down over Chickatawbut Hill, Kitchamakin Hill, and Nahanton Hill, before descending to Chickatawbut Road.

With caution, cross Chickatawbut Road and follow a wide path downhill to the left. At a fork in the path (junction 4131) bear right downhill. Eventually, reach an intersection with the green-blazed St. Moritz Loop. Turn left onto the green-blazed trail and for 2 miles follow it in a gradual clockwise circuit through the woods. After crossing Wampatuck Road, descend to an intersection with the trail that you followed at the outset. Bear right to return past St. Moritz Pond to your starting point at Shea Rink.

≈
≈ ≈ ≈ ≈
≈

## WESTERN BLUE HILLS

THE BLUE HILLS show the round, swelling form characteristic of granite masses. The most westerly and highest summit is Great Blue Hill, a nearly perfect dome 635 feet high. These hills originated when huge volumes of molten rock welled up from the interior of the earth but solidified before reaching the surface. The coarse grains in the granite indicate that it cooled slowly, enabling the constituent minerals to sort themselves out as they crystallized. The rate of cooling was slow because the magma was insulated under thick layers of slate and sedimentary rocks. These materials have been eroded away to reveal the igneous intrusions below — although in some places within the Blue Hills Reservation, the pre-existing strata can still be seen. There have also been seismic adjustments. Together the range of hills forms a giant fault block that has settled at the eastern end more than in the west.

At the top of Great Blue Hill is the stone Eliot Tower, which provides panoramic views. Named for Charles Eliot, a leading advocate for creation of the Metropolitan Parks System and its first professional planner, the tower also serves as a memorial to its builders: the workers of the Civilian Conservation Corps. During the Great Depression of the 1930s, hundreds of CCC men improved trails, fire lanes, and roads at the Blue Hills, just as they did at other parks throughout the region and the country. The CCC provided useful work, income, and vocational training for unemployed single men. Many CCC members were able to take high school and even college level courses in the camps. The organization was run on a semi-military basis by the War Department and assigned projects selected and supervised by the Departments of Agriculture and Interior. Living in barracks (the Blue Hill camp was near Randolph Avenue, at the upper-left corner of Map 41), the workers were organized into companies of about two hundred men. Base pay was $30 per month, and if a man's family at home was on relief, most of his wages were sent there. At its peak in 1935, the CCC had more than half a million men in over 2,600 camps working on forest and wildlife protection, flood control, soil conservation, and the development of federal, state, and local parks.

THE BLUE HILLS are almost entirely forested, yet as is typical for southern New England, the present-day stands of trees are mostly less than a hundred years old. The original timber was cut long before the Revolution to supply lumber for houses and for ships, to provide fuel for home and industry, or simply to clear the land for farming. By the middle of the nineteenth century, about three-quarters of southern New England was unforested.

By that time, however, the decline of New England farming had already set it. Even in the early 1700s, the productivity of tilled fields began to decline as the soil became depleted. Grain and other staples grown on better land in the Mid-Atlantic states competed with local foodstuffs. By the time of the Revolution, the agricultural landscape of New England had slowly changed into one dominated by pastures and

264

orchards. Beginning in the second quarter of the nineteenth century, many New England farms even reverted to woods as the Erie Canal and later the railroads brought all manner of cheap farm products from the Great Lakes region to the Eastern seaboard. Also, industrialization provided many New Englanders with alternative employment in mills. The new forests, however, were seldom left to themselves. Long before the trees matured, they were cut for cordwood or for slats to make crates for the packing industry. "It is not likely that a single acre of the reservation has escaped the woodcutter's axe," the Metropolitan Parks Commissioners reported in 1895, shortly after the Blue Hills were acquired for public use.

The brush and branches left from timber operations at the Blue Hills provided tinder for a series of major conflagrations. "The surface has been repeatedly burned," the commissioners said, "and frequently the brush, the sticks, and the poles are dead and falling in a tangled mass." So as to look on the bright side of things they added, "An unusually favorable opportunity is offered for the study of fires on different species of plants." Indeed, the effect of fires, set by careless visitors, vandals, and lightning, is still often evident. The trails pass charred clearings or dense thickets of new growth, from which rise a few blackened and branchless trunks of older trees. As a result of fire and other factors, including thin, dry, acidic soil and exposure to wind, some hilltops are dominated by lowbush blueberry and huckleberry. These windswept rises are among the most attractive areas in the reservation, providing views in all directions and a refreshing sense of exposure reminiscent of the treeless zones of far larger mountains.

In some places the exposed bedrock on the hilltops still has a sheen left by glacial scouring, despite millennia of weathering. In the oblique light of dawn and sunset, the polished rock surfaces show parallel grooves and scratches made by rocks dragged beneath the continental ice sheet that rode over the hills. Aligned northwesterly, the scratches show the direction from which the ice advanced.

≈      ≈      ≈      ≈

## AUTOMOBILE DIRECTIONS TO THE WESTERN BLUE HILLS:
This area is located mostly in Milton, 10 miles south of downtown Boston. (See •21b on **Map 1** on page 6, and also **Map 40** on page 259.) Two approaches are described below.

### To the western Blue Hills from Interstate 93 south of Boston:
Skirting the Blue Hills, this segment of I-93 (old

MAP 42 — Western Blue Hills

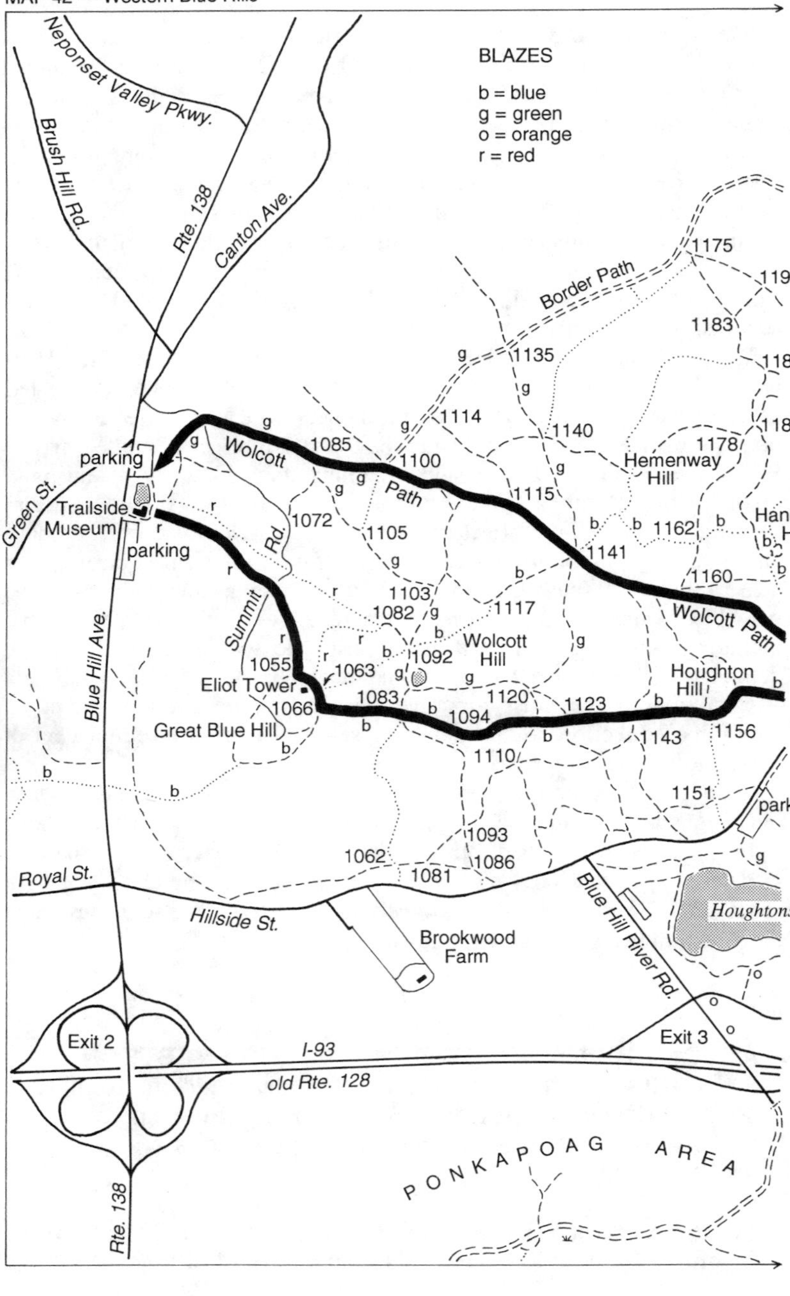

Neponset Valley Pkwy.

Brush Hill Rd.

Rte. 138

Canton Ave.

BLAZES

b = blue
g = green
o = orange
r = red

1175

1191

Border Path

1183

1135

1185

g

1114

1140

g

1180

Wolcott

1085

1100

1178

Hemenway
Hill

parking

g

Path

1115

g

Green St.

Trailside
Museum

r

1072

1105

1103

b

b

1162

b

Hancock
Hill

b

b

parking

Rd.

1082

1117

1141

b

1160

b

g

1103

Wolcott Path

b

Summit

r

b

1092

Wolcott
Hill

g

Blue Hill Ave.

1055

r

1063

g

1120

Houghton
Hill

b

Eliot Tower

1066

1083

1094

1123

1156

b

Great Blue Hill

b

1110

1143

b

b

b

1151

parking

Royal St.

b

1093

g

1062

1081

1086

Hillside St.

Blue Hill River Rd.

Houghtons

Brookwood
Farm

o

Exit 2

I-93

Exit 3

o

old Rte. 128

o

PONKAPOAG    AREA

Rte. 138

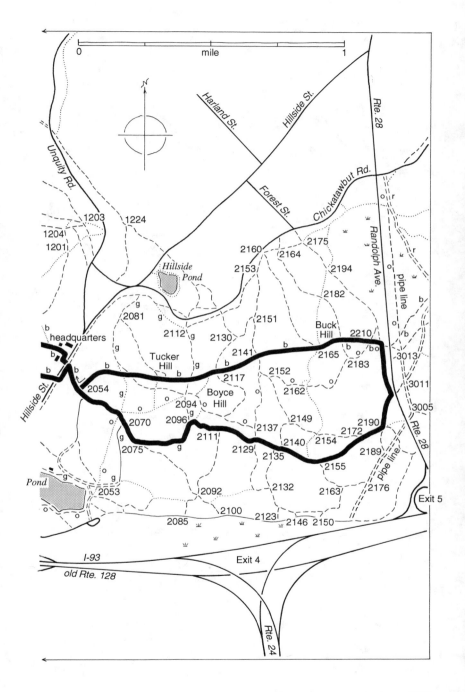

MAP 43 — Western Blue Hills: green-blazed loops

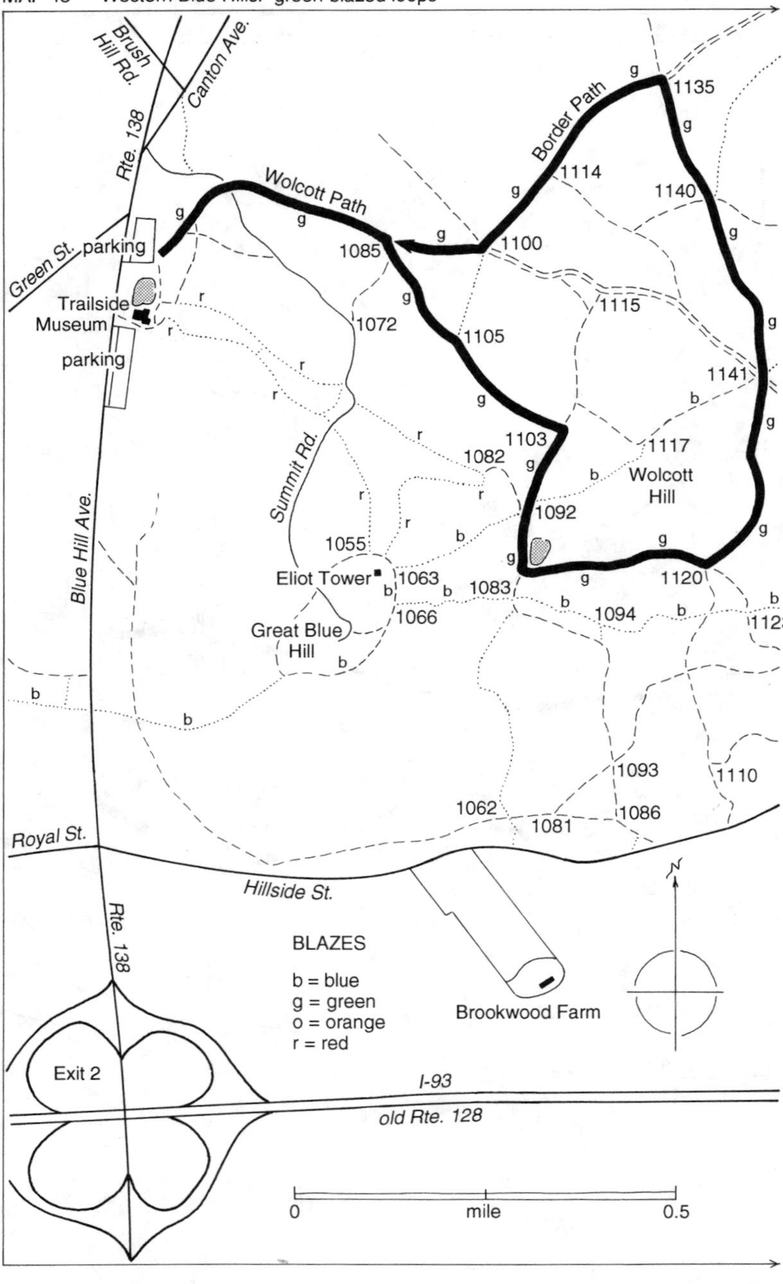

Brush Hill Rd.
Canton Ave.
Rte. 138
Green St. parking
Trailside Museum
parking
Blue Hill Ave.
Summit Rd.
Wolcott Path
Border Path
g 1135
g
1114
1140
g
1100
1085
g
1072
1105
1115
g
1141
b
1103
1082
1117
g
1092
b
Wolcott Hill
1055
r
1083
1120
g
Eliot Tower
1063
1066
1094
b
1123
Great Blue Hill
b
1093
1110
1062
1081
1086
Royal St.
Hillside St.

BLAZES

b = blue
g = green
o = orange
r = red

Brookwood Farm

Rte. 138

Exit 2
I-93
old Rte. 128

0          mile          0.5

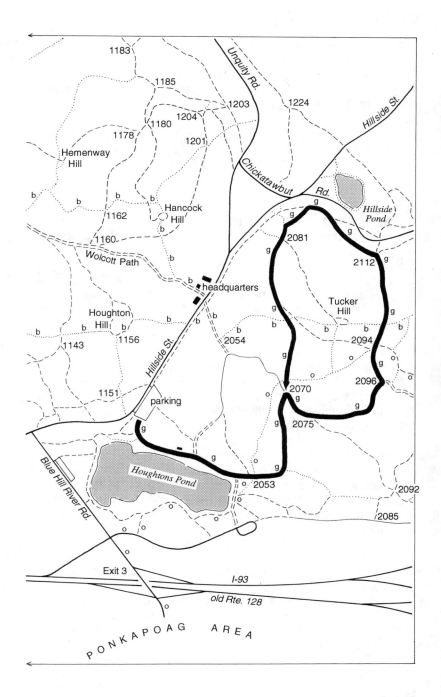

269

Route 128) runs east-west between the junctions with Interstate 95 and Route 3.

Leave I-93 at Exit 2B for Route 138 north toward Milton. Go about one mile to the parking lots for the Trailside Museum and Blue Hill Ski Area on the right.

**To the western Blue Hills from southernmost Boston and Milton:** Follow Route 138 south to the parking lots for the Trailside Museum and Blue Hill Ski Area on the left.

≈        ≈        ≈        ≈

**WALKING IN THE WESTERN BLUE HILLS:** Several specific routes, each with its own map, are described below.

**Map 42** on pages 266-267 shows a 6.5-mile route that alternates difficult and easy going. In part it follows the Skyline Trail from one summit to the next, and at other times it follows fire roads along the flanks of the hills. For a shorter excursion, this figure-eight route is easily cut in half by treating the parts west and east of Hillside Street as separate outings.

**Start your walk** by climbing Great Blue Hill. From the otter tank behind the Trailside Museum, follow the path marked by red blazes up through the woods and over bare patches of rock. Continue uphill past another red-blazed trail that intersects from the left. (It too leads to the summit.) Climb to a stone observation tower at the top of the hill.

From the observation tower, cross a stone footbridge commemorating Charles Eliot, a landscape architect who played a leading role in the creation of the Metropolitan District Commission, as discussed on pages 256-258. Follow the path 100 yards to a stone post on the left marking the South Skyline Trail. Turn left and follow the blue-blazed trail downhill, then eventually up again over Houghton Hill and back down to Hillside Street.

With caution, cross Hillside Street and follow it left for 130 yards on a bridle path. At a stone post marking the Skyline Trail, turn right onto a dirt path. When the blue-blazed trail goes left, continue straight. (You will return via the blue-blazed path later.) At an asphalt road, bear left and follow the road uphill. Pass though a parking area and continue on a dirt road where the asphalt drive curves right downhill. At first the trail is marked with green blazes, but after a quarter-mile, bear right where the green-blazed route turns sharply left. Follow the main track for a mile to Randolph Avenue, referring if necessary to the numbers posted at trail intersections and shown also on the map.

Without crossing Randolph Avenue, turn left and follow a wide path that runs through the woods parallel with the road. Go 370 yards. After another path intersects from the right, turn left to rejoin the blue-blazed Skyline Trail heading west. From here follow the blue-blazes for 1.5 miles up and down over Buck Hill and Tucker Hill and back to Hillside Street.

With caution, cross Hillside Street and follow a driveway to the right of a barn. Head straight into the woods past a gate to the left of a house (the park headquarters) where a stone post says *Wolcott Path.* About 60 yards past the gate, ignore the blue-blazes leading uphill to the right, unless you feel like more climbing. Instead, simply follow the main track all the way back to Blue Hill Avenue. When the trail meets an asphalt road, continue straight ahead through the woods to one of the parking lots by the Trailside Museum.

**Map 43** on pages 268-269 shows two easy loops through the woods. Both are about 3 miles long, and both are marked with green blazes. For a longer outing, it is an easy matter to link these two green-blazed routes by using some of the connecting trails shown on the map.

The more westerly of the two trails starts at the parking lot just north of the Trailside Museum, which is located on Route 138 a mile north of Exit 2B off Interstate 93. From the trailhead near the upper-back corner of the parking lot, the green-blazed route leads around Wolcott Hill.

The more easterly of the two trails shown on Map 43 starts at the parking lot for Houghton's Pond Beach, which is entered from Hillside Street 0.8 mile north of Exit 3 off Interstate 93. (This lot is entirely separate from the Houghton's Pond picnic sites and ball fields located only 0.2 mile north of Exit 3.)

From the right end of the parking lot, the green-blazed route leads past Houghton's Pond Beach and around Tucker Hill.

≈

≈    ≈    ≈    ≈

≈

## FOWL MEADOW

WETLANDS SUCH AS FOWL MEADOW are one of the most common elements of the New England landscape. For the most part, they are the work of continental glaciation. When the last ice sheet advanced over this region, it picked up vast quantities of earth and rock. Later, as the ice melted, its load of clay, sand, and gravel was dumped in an uneven blanket over the landscape, leaving a layer of stony soil called till or drift. Former river valleys were clogged. Streams were dammed to form new ponds and shallow natural reservoirs. Over thousands of years many of these have been filled with sediments and vegetation and so have changed into marshes, bogs, and low swampy woods. Since the time of European settlement, wetlands have often been drained or filled for farming and development.

Although wetlands appear to be wastelands as far as human activity is concerned, they lend valuable support to human enterprise. Marshes serve to replenish ground water that ultimately feeds wells for drinking, agriculture, and industry. Wetlands are also settling and filtering basins, collecting silt from upland erosion and reducing sedimentation in undesirable places, such as navigable rivers and harbors. Wetlands are often called natural sponges that absorb huge quantities of storm runoff, then release the water slowly over a period of weeks. In this way they prevent or moderate floods and also keep streams flowing throughout the year that otherwise would dry up after each rainfall like a southwestern arroyo. And apart from their direct value to humans, wetlands provide habitat for many species of animals.

Because of their importance, wetlands have been protected by a variety of state and federal laws and regulations established during the last few decades. The leading law in Massachusetts is the Wetlands Protection Act of 1972. It requires that a permit from the municipal conservation commission be obtained before an owner may fill or dredge a wetland. The conservation commissions are empowered to issue "orders of conditions" specifying what steps developers must take to avoid adverse effects on wetlands and the functions they perform. There are of course provisions for appeal from unsound orders. The areas affected by the law are defined by their plant communities. The Wetlands Act specifies that a marsh, for example, is an area characterized by button bush, cattails, duckweed, leatherleaf, rushes, sedges, and similar plants.

IN 1969 FOWL MEADOW was one of the battlefields in the plan to bring Interstate 95 north through Boston. If you walk all the way to the end of the dike trail as described below, you will in fact arrive at the stub of the proposed expressway, projecting into the woods from the interchange with Route 128. From there, the state's Department of Public Works wanted to run the highway through Fowl Meadow. The DPW, however, lacked the power to use eminent domain to take land already in public ownership without specific legislative approval. Consequently, the DPW, backed by Governor Francis Sargent, sought the cooperation of the Metropolitan District Commission, which controls Fowl Meadow. In what many people saw as a breach of trust, the MDC agreed to convey the proposed corridor to the DPW under a law allowing transfer of public land from one agency to another for highway purposes without legislative approval.

In *Robbins v. Department of Public Works*, opponents of the highway plan sued to prevent the transfer. The case eventually went to Massachusetts' top court, which ruled first that ordinary citizens had standing to challenge the transaction. Addressing the main issue, the Supreme Judicial Court then said:

> We think it is essential to the expression of plain and explicit authority to divert parklands . . . and kindred areas to new and inconsistent public uses that the legislature identify the land and that there appear in the legislation not only a statement of the new use but a statement or recital showing in some way legislative awareness of the existing public use. In short, the legislation should express not merely the public will for the new use but its willingness to surrender or forego the existing use.

When the proposed transfer of Fowl Meadow went to the legislature, the Department of Public Works was able to obtain approval, after extended debate, of the highway route it sought. The governor, however, reversed his position, stating that he would not permit the transfer of the reservation. Since then the principle of the court's decision has been incorporated into Article 49 of the Massachusetts Constitution, which provides for a two-thirds vote of both branches of the legislature before parkland can be used for other purposes.

As for Interstate 95 through Boston, after years of opposition to the expressway from neighborhoods along its route, the entire project was dropped. Not only has Fowl Meadow remained a public reservation, but also a *new* linear park was created along Boston's Southwest Corridor, where the Department of Public Works had acquired a right-of-way for the big road. The Southwest Corridor Park is featured in Chapter 17.

≈        ≈        ≈        ≈

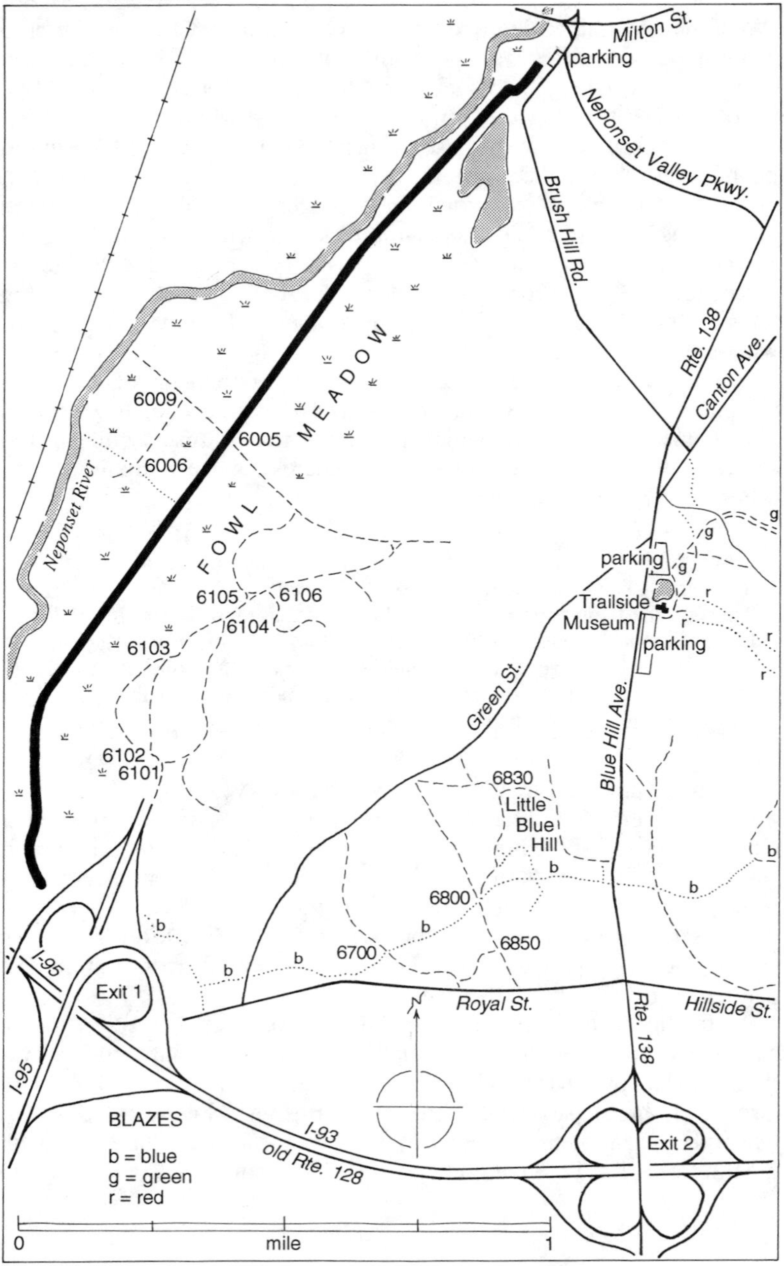

MAP 44 — Fowl Meadow

Milton St.

parking

Neponset Valley Pkwy.

Brush Hill Rd.

Rte. 138

Canton Ave.

F O W L   M E A D O W

Neponset River

6009

6005

6006

6105

6106

6104

6103

6102
6101

g

parking

g

Trailside
Museum

r

r

parking

r

r

g

Green St.

Blue Hill Ave.

6830

Little
Blue
Hill

b

b

b

6800

b

b

b

6700

6850

b

b

Royal St.

Hillside St.

Rte. 138

Exit 1

I-95

I-95

BLAZES

b = blue
g = green
r = red

I-93
old Rte. 128

Exit 2

0                         mile                         1

**AUTOMOBILE DIRECTIONS TO FOWL MEADOW:**
This area is located a half-mile west of Great Blue Hill. (See
•21c on **Map 1** on page 6, and also **Map 44** at left.

**To Fowl Meadow from Interstate 93 south of Boston:**
Skirting the Blue Hills, this segment of I-93 (old Route 128) runs
east-west between the junctions with Interstate 95 and Route 3.
   Leave I-93 at Exit 2B for Route 138 north toward Milton. Go
1.7 miles, then turn left onto the Neponset Valley Parkway.
After 0.6 mile, turn left into the parking lot at the intersection
with Brush Hill Road.

≈        ≈        ≈        ≈

**WALKING AT FOWL MEADOW: Map 44** at left shows a
route through Fowl Meadow. Dead level and nearly dead
straight, the dry, elevated path leads through marsh and
swampy woods that border the Neponset River. The round-
trip distance is 3.8 miles.

**To get started,** locate the trailhead to the left of the parking
area. The trail is marked by a stone post inscribed "Fowl
Meadow," from which a footpath and boardwalk lead a few
dozen yards to a wide track called by punsters the Berma Road.
Follow the Berma Road south to its end, then return the way
you came. There are also some side trails that you may want to
explore.

≈

≈        ≈        ≈        ≈

≈

## PONKAPOAG TRAIL

PONKAPOAG MEANS SWEETWATER. It is a very large pond south
of the Blue Hills to which the Neponset Indians withdrew after selling
their land in Dorchester to the Puritan settlers in 1630. Although
located south of Interstate 93 (old Route 128), the pond and nearly a
thousand acres of surrounding rocky woods are part of the Blue Hills
Reservation.
   A major attraction of a walk around Ponkapoag Pond is the quaking
bog at the northwestern shore. A spur from the main trail follows a

boardwalk out through wet deciduous woods, then past stands of Atlantic white-cedar. It continues across the thick, floating mat of sphagnum moss and leatherleaf shrubbery to the water's edge, where small trees sway when you jump. For a discussion of the process by which bogs are formed, see pages 31-33 in Chapter 3.

One peculiarity of bogs is that they are singularly deficient in plant nutrients. The carpet of sphagnum moss tends to retain rainwater, which has a very low mineral content. The sodden sphagnum also seals off the underlying pond water from the air, so that conditions low in oxygen develop. Decay of the vegetable debris below the surface of the water slows down, and so peat accumulates. The type of decay that does occur under these anaerobic bog conditions consumes nitrogen — an essential nutrient — and produces acid, which makes absorption of water difficult for most plants. Acid is also produced directly by the sphagnum, which has the property of absorbing bases and freeing acids. And the fallen needles of cedar and other bog trees release tannic acid as they steep in the water.

The result is a hostile environment for most plants. Those that survive show special adaptations. For example, the waxy, dry leaves of leatherleaf reflect its need to retain water, even though its roots are immersed in sodden moss. Pitcher plants and sundew, which are common bog plants, obtain nitrogen and other nutrients by trapping and digesting insects. As shown on page 280, pitcher plants are so named because of the shape of their leaves. Insects that enter the pitcher can't get out because downward-pointing bristles block the way. After they drop into the water within the pitcher, the insects are digested by enzymes.


DURING THE COLONIAL PERIOD, bogs and shallow ponds — and also low, wet woods that had once been ponds — were the primary source of iron ore, until the discovery of rock ore in western Connecticut about 1730. Leached from throughout the watershed by rain and snow, soluble ore is carried by streams to the basins of standing water, where the ore precipitates as the temperature rises during summer. Thick beds of brown, hydrous ferric oxide accumulate. Called limonite, the deposits range in consistency from earthy to solid chunks. At the many bogs, swamps, and ponds in coastal Massachusetts, the beds of ore were dug up with pick and shovel or pulled from the shallow water with long-handled scoops and tongs.

The first ironworks in New England was started in 1643 by John Winthrop, Jr., the enterprising son of Governor Winthrop of the Massachusetts Bay Colony. The younger Winthrop conducted a survey of bogs and ponds between Cape Elizabeth, Maine, and Marshfield in what was then the Plymouth Colony. With his samples, he went back to England to enroll investors in the Company of Undertakers of the Iron Works in New England. Returning to Massachusetts, Winthrop selected Braintree, just east of Ponkapoag Pond, as the site for his furnace because the nearby deposits of ore were the best that he found. Also, ample timber was available to make charcoal for fuel, and the coastal settlements provided laborers. The Braintree furnace smelted iron for only a few years before failing, but even as late as the Revolutionary War, most other ironworks in Massachusetts were concentrated in the former Plymouth Colony because of the numerous bogs and ponds.

Another site for iron making was a furnace and forge that the Company of Undertakers, with Richard Leader as manager, established about 1645 at Saugus north of Boston. This furnace produced eight to ten tons of iron per week before closing down in 1668. The reconstructed Saugus Iron Works are open to the public under the administration of the National Park Service, as discussed in Chapter 8.

≈     ≈     ≈     ≈

**AUTOMOBILE DIRECTIONS TO THE PONKAPOAG TRAIL:** The trail goes around Ponkapoag Pond, which is located in Canton and Randolph, 11 miles south of downtown Boston. (See •21d on **Map 1** on page 6, and also **Map 40** on page 259.)

You may have noticed while driving on Interstate 93 south of the Blue Hills that a highway sign declares access to the Ponkapoag Trail at Exit 3. You can park there if you want, but space is rather limited, so the directions below steer you to the far larger parking lot at the MDC's Ponkapoag Golf Course, where hikers may also park.

**To Ponkapoag Pond from Interstate 93 south of Boston:** Skirting the Blue Hills, this segment of I-93 (old Route 128) runs east-west between the junctions with Interstate 95 and Route 3.

Leave I-93 at Exit 2A for Route 138 south toward Stoughton. Go about 0.8 mile to the entrance to the MDC Ponkapoag Golf Course on the left (opposite an intersection with Washington Street).

≈     ≈     ≈     ≈

MAP 45 — Ponkapoag Pond

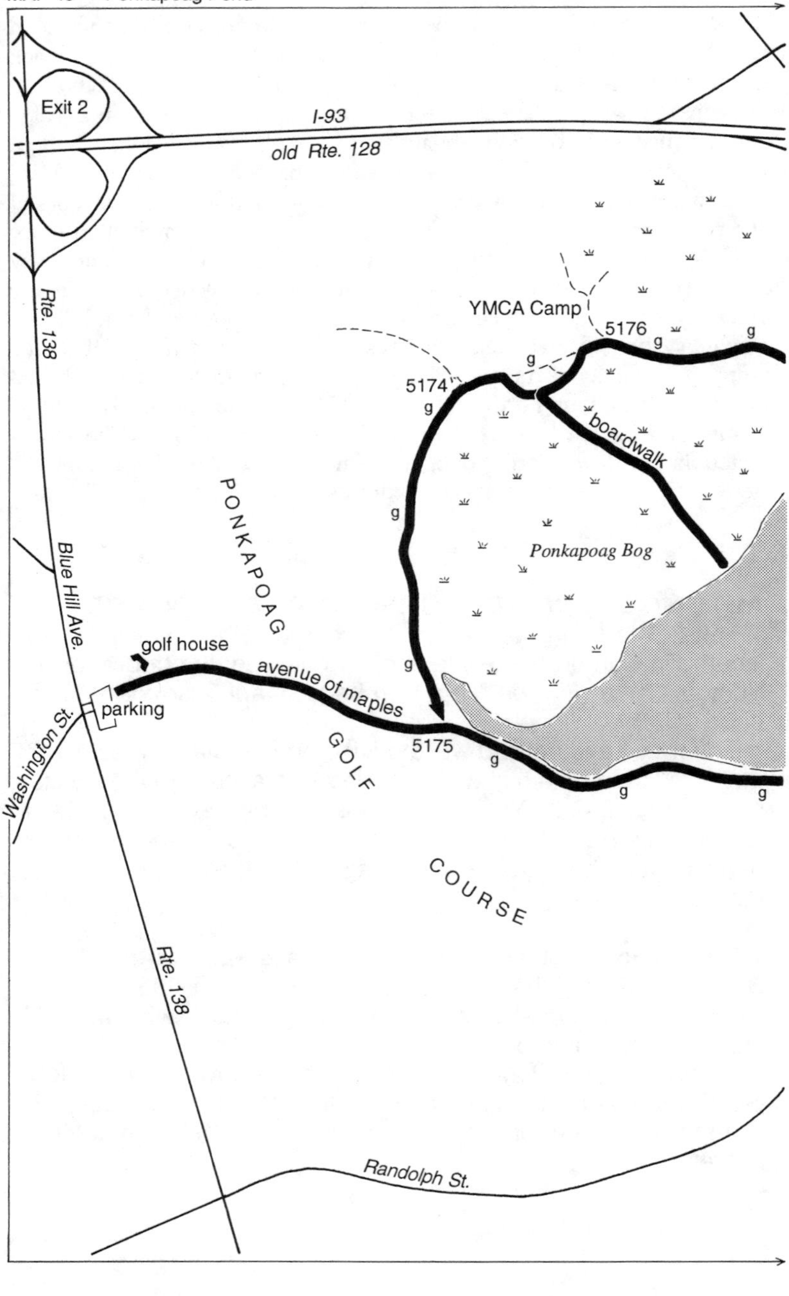

Exit 2

I-93

old Rte. 128

Rte. 138

YMCA Camp

5176  g  g

5174
g

boardwalk

g

Ponkapoag Bog

g

P O N K A P O A G

g

golf house

avenue of maples

parking

5175
g

g  g

Blue Hill Ave.

Washington St.

G O L F

C O U R S E

Rte. 138

Randolph St.

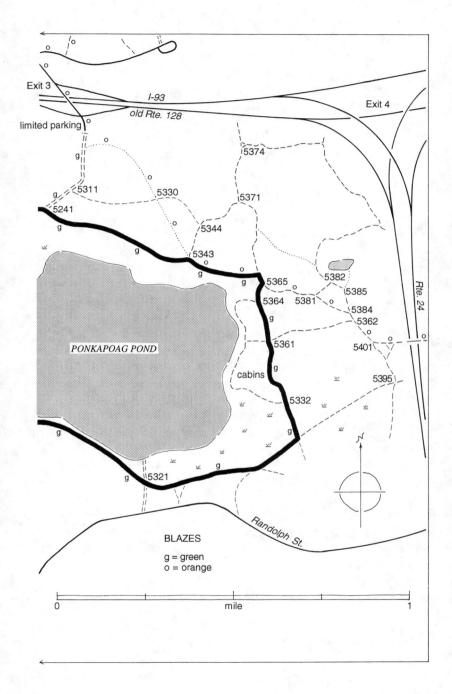

Exit 3

I-93

old Rte. 128

Exit 4

limited parking

5374

g

5311
5330
5371

5241
5344

g
5343

g
5365
5382

5364
5385

5381
5384

g
5362

PONKAPOAG POND
5361
5401

cabins
5395

g
5332

g

g
5321

Rte. 24

Randolph St.

BLAZES
g = green
o = orange

0                                    mile                                    1

279

**WALKING AT PONKAPOAG POND:   Map 45** on pages 278-279 shows a 5-mile loop around the pond.

**To get started** from the golf course parking lot, follow an avenue of sugar maples that leads to the right of the golf house and across the course.  Continue straight where the asphalt drive ends in order to follow the green-blazed trail counter-clockwise around the pond and back to the avenue of maples. If necessary, you can refer to the numbers posted at trail inter-sections and shown also on the map.

A highlight at Ponkapoag Pond is the Ponkapoag Bog Board-walk.  As shown on Map 45, this spur trail starts near the YMCA Ponkapoag Outdoor Center and leads a third of a mile across the bog to the edge of the pond.  To locate the boardwalk trail-head, fork left at the YMCA camp, then curve right through an open area until you spot a sign for the boardwalk.

# 22

# BROADMOOR WILDLIFE SANCTUARY

There are more than 9 miles (14.4 kilometers) of trails at Broad-moor Wildlife Sanctuary in Natick southwest of Boston. The trail system is shown on **Map 47** on page 293. This is a beautiful and varied area where you can enjoyably wander for hours.

The sanctuary trails are open Tuesday through Sunday from dawn to dusk. The trails are closed Monday (except Monday holidays), Thanksgiving, Christmas, and New Year's Day. An admission fee is charged. Dogs are prohibited.

The sanctuary's visitor center is open Tuesday through Friday from 9 A.M. to 5 P.M. and on weekends and Monday holidays from 10 to 5.

Broadmoor Wildlife Sanctuary is managed by the Massachusetts Audubon Society. For information on natural history programs, including courses, workshops, field trips, and camps, telephone (508) 655-2296 or (781) 235-3929.

For automobile directions to Broadmoor, please turn to page 290. Walking directions start on page 292.

---

WITH ITS WIDE RANGE OF HABITATS, including deciduous and coniferous woods, meadows, weedy fields, brush, freshwater marsh, swamp, ponds, and streams, the Broadmoor Wildlife Sanctuary is one of the better places near Boston to see a wide variety of birds at every season, although, of course, the periods of spring and fall migration are best.

Even for fledgling birders, identifying the approximately three hundred species that are seen regularly at the places discussed in this book is easier than might at first be thought. Shape, size, plumage, and other physical characteristics are distinguishing field marks. Range, season, habitat, song, and behavior are other useful keys to identifying birds.

Range is of primary importance for the simple reason that many birds are not found throughout North America or even the eastern United

States, and so can immediately be ruled highly unlikely when birding in eastern Massachusetts. For example, the cedar waxwing and Bohemian waxwing closely resemble each other, but the latter is rarely seen here. A good field guide provides range maps based on many years of reported sightings and bird counts. Of course, bird ranges are not static; some pioneering species, such as the glossy ibis and house finch, have extended their ranges during recent decades. Other birds, such as the ivory-billed woodpecker, have lost ground and died out. Although it is true that birds sometimes occur as "accidentals" far outside their normal ranges, it is best to be skeptical with yourself.

Season is related to range, since migratory birds appear in different parts of their ranges during different times of year. The five species of spot-breasted thrushes, for instance, are sometimes difficult to distinguish from each other, but if you see such a bird here in winter, it is almost certainly a hermit thrush, and in summer the odds strongly favor the wood thrush. Again, the maps in most field guides reflect this sort of information.

Habitat is important in identifying birds. Even before you sight a bird, the surroundings can tell you what species you are likely to see. Within its range a species usually appears only in certain preferred habitats, although during migration some species are less particular. (In many cases, birds show a degree of physical adaptation to their preferred environment.) As its name implies, the marsh wren is seldom found far from cattails, rushes, sedges, or tall marsh grasses. If a wren-like bird is seen in such a setting, it is unlikely to be a house wren, which is commonly found in thick underbrush or shrubbery. The area where two habitats join, called an *ecotone*, is a particularly good place to look for birds because species peculiar to either environment may be present. For example, both meadowlarks and wood warblers might be found where a grassy field abuts a forest. All good field guides provide information on habitat preferences that can help to locate a species or to assess the likelihood of a tentative identification. A bird list available at Broadmoor contains information on habitat preference and also seasonal occurrence.

Song announces the identity (or at least the location) of birds even before they are seen. Although some species, such as the red-winged blackbird, have only a few songs, others, such as the mockingbird, have an infinite variety. (Even so, mockingbird songs are characterized by the repetition of each phrase up to a half-dozen times, before moving on to another phrase.) Some birds, most notably thrushes, sing different songs in the morning and evening. In many species the songs vary somewhat among individuals and from one area to another, giving rise to regional "dialects." Nonetheless, the vocal repertory of most songbirds is sufficiently constant in timbre and pattern to identify each species simply by its songs.

Bird songs, as distinguished from calls, can be very complex. They are sung only by the male of most species, usually in spring and summer. The male arrives first at the breeding and nesting area after migration. He stakes out a territory for courting, mating, and nesting by singing at prominent points around the area's perimeter. This wards off intrusion by other males of his species and simultaneously attracts females. On the basis of the male's display and the desirability of his territory, the female selects her mate. Experiments suggest that female birds build nests faster and lay more eggs when exposed to the songs of males with a larger vocal repertory than others of their species, and the relative volume of their songs appears to be a way for males to establish status among themselves.

In a few species, including eastern bluebirds, northern orioles, cardinals, and white-throated sparrows, both sexes sing, although the males are more active in defending their breeding territory. Among mockingbirds, both sexes sing in fall and winter, but only males sing in spring and summer. Some birds, such as canaries, have different songs for different seasons.

Birds tend to heed the songs of their own kind and to ignore the songs of other species, which do not compete for females nor, in many cases, for the same type of nesting materials or food. In consequence, a single area includes the overlapping breeding territories of different species. From year to year such territories are bigger or smaller, depending on the food supply. Typically, most small songbirds require about half an acre from which others of their species are excluded.

Bird calls (as distinguished from songs) are short, simple, sometimes harsh, and used by both males and females at all times of year to communicate alarm, aggression, location, and existence of food. Nearly all birds have some form of call. Warning calls are often heeded by species other than the caller's. Some warning calls are thin, high-pitched whistles that are difficult to locate and so do not reveal the bird's location to predators. Birds also use mobbing calls to summon other birds, as chickadees and crows do when scolding and harassing owls and other unwanted visitors. Birds flying in flocks, like cedar waxwings, often call continuously. Such calls help birds migrating by night to stay together.

The study of bird dialects and experiments with birds that have been deafened or raised in isolation indicate that songs are genetically inherited only to a very crude extent. Although a few species, such as doves, sing well even when raised in isolation, most birds raised alone produce inferior, simplified songs. Generally, young songbirds learn their songs by listening to adult birds and by practice singing, called *subsong*. Even so, birds raised in isolation and exposed to many tape-recorded songs show an innate preference for the songs of their own species.

Probably the easiest way to learn bird songs is to listen repeatedly to recordings and to refer at the same time to a standard field guide. Most guides describe bird vocalizations with such terms as *harsh, nasal, flutelike, piercing, plaintive, wavering, twittering, buzzing, sneezy,* and *sputtering.* Although these terms are somewhat descriptive, they do not take on real meaning until you have heard the songs themselves on records or in the field. Incidentally, bird recordings that are played slowly demonstrate that the songs contain many more notes than the human ear ordinarily hears.

Shape is one of the first and most important aspects to notice once you actually see a bird. Most birds can at least be placed in the proper family and many species can be identified by shape or silhouette, without reference to other field marks. Some birds, such as kestrels, are distinctly stocky, big-headed, and powerful-looking, while others, such as catbirds and cuckoos, are elegantly long and slender. Kingfishers, blue jays, tufted titmice, waxwings, and cardinals are among the few birds with crests.

Bird bills frequently have distinctive shapes and, more than any other body part, show adaptation to food supply. The beak can be chunky, like that of a grosbeak, to crack seeds; thin and curved, like that of a creeper, to probe bark for insects; hooked, like that of a shrike, to tear at flesh; long and slender, like that of a hummingbird, to sip nectar from tubular flowers; or some other characteristic shape depending on the bird's food. Goatsuckers, swifts, flycatchers, and swallows, all of which catch flying insects, have widely hinged bills and gaping mouths. The long, thin bills of starlings and meadowlarks are suited to probing the ground. In the Galapagos Islands west of Ecuador, Charles Darwin noted fourteen species of finches, each of which had evolved a different type of beak or style of feeding that gave it a competitive advantage for a particular type of food. Many birds are nonetheless flexible about their diet, especially from season to season when food sources change or become scarce. For example, Tennessee warblers, which ordinarily glean insects from foliage, also take large amounts of nectar from tropical flowers when wintering in South and Central America.

In addition to beaks, nearly every other part of a bird's body is adapted to help exploit its environment. Feet of passerines, or songbirds, are adapted to perching, with three toes in front and one long toe behind; waterfowl have webbed or lobed feet for swimming; and raptors have talons for grasping prey.

Other key elements of body shape are the length and form of wings, tails, and legs. The wings may be long, pointed, and developed for swift, sustained flight, like those of falcons. Or the wings may be short and rounded for abrupt bursts of speed, like those of accipiters. The tail may have a deep fork like that of a barn swallow, a shallow notch like that of a tree swallow, or a square tip like that of a cliff swallow, or a round tip like that of a blue jay.

Size is difficult to estimate and therefore not very useful in identifying birds. The best approach is to bear in mind the relative sizes of different species and to use certain well-known birds like the chickadee, song sparrow, robin, kingfisher, and crow as standards for mental comparison. For example, if a bird resembles a song sparrow but looks unusually large, it might be a fox sparrow.

Plumage, whether plain or princely, muted or magnificent, is one of the most obvious keys to identification. Color can occur in remarkable combinations of spots, stripes, streaks, patches, and other patterns that make even supposedly drab birds a pleasure to see. In some instances, like the brown streaks of American bitterns and many other species, the plumage provides camouflage. Most vireos and warblers are various shades and combinations of yellow, green, brown, gray, and black, as one would expect from their forest environment. The black and white backs of woodpeckers help them to blend in with bark dappled with sunlight. The bold patterns of killdeers and some other plovers break up their outlines in much the same manner that warships used to be camouflaged before the invention of radar. Many shore birds display countershading: they are dark above and light below, a pattern that reduces the effect of shadows and makes the birds appear an inconspicuous monotone. Even some brightly colored birds have camouflaging plumages when they are young and least able to avoid predators.

For some species, it is important *not* to be camouflaged. Many sea birds are mostly white, which in all light conditions enables them to be seen at great distances against the water. Because flocks of sea birds spread out from their colonies to search for food, it is vital that a bird that has located food be visible to others after it has landed on the water to feed.

To organize the immense variation of plumages, focus on different body parts or areas and ask the following types of questions. Starting with the head, is it uniformly colored like that of the red-headed woodpecker? Is there a small patch on the crown, like that of Wilson's warbler and the ruby-crowned kinglet, or a larger cap on the front and top of the head, like that of the common redpoll and American goldfinch? Is the crown striped like the ovenbird's? Does a ring surround the eye, as with a Connecticut warbler, or are the rings perhaps even joined across the top of the bill to form spectacles, like those of a yellow-breasted chat? Is there a stripe over or through the eyes, like the red-breasted nuthatch's, or a conspicuous black mask across the eyes, like that of a common yellowthroat or loggerhead shrike? Such marks are not merely peculiar to this or that individual (as is the case with spotted horses) but rather are reliably characteristic of different bird species. From the head go on to the rest of the body, where distinctive colors and patterns can also mark a bird's bill, throat, breast, belly, back, sides, wings, rump, tail, and legs.

Finally, what a bird *does* is an important clue to its identity. Certain habits, postures, ways of searching for food, and other behavior characterize different species. Some passerines, such as larks, juncos, and towhees, are strictly ground feeders; other birds, including flycatchers and swallows, nab insects on the wing; and others, such as nuthatches and creepers, glean insects from the crevices in bark. Woodpeckers bore into the bark. Vireos and most warblers pick insects from the foliage of trees and brush.

All of these birds may be further distinguished by other habits of eating. For example, towhees scratch for insects and seeds by kicking backward with both feet together, whereas juncos rarely do, although both hop to move along the ground. Other ground feeders, such as meadowlarks, walk rather than hop. Despite the children's song, robins often run, not hop. Swallows catch insects while swooping and skimming in continuous flight, but flycatchers dart out from a limb, grab an insect (sometimes with an audible smack), and then return to their perch. Brown creepers have the curious habit of systematically searching for food by climbing trees in spirals, then flying back to the ground to climb again. Woodpeckers tend to hop upward, bracing themselves against the tree with their stiff tails. Nuthatches walk up, down, and around tree trunks and branches, seemingly without regard for gravity. Vireos are sluggish compared to the hyperactive, flitting warblers.

Many birds divide a food source into zones, an arrangement that apparently has evolved to ensure each species its own food supply. The short-legged green heron sits at the edge of the water or on a low overhanging branch, waiting for its prey to come close to shore. Medium-sized black-crowned and yellow-crowned night herons hunt in shallow water. The long-legged great blue heron stalks fish in water up to two feet deep. Swans, geese, and many ducks graze underwater on the stems and tubers of grassy plants, but the longer necks of swans and geese enable them to reach deeper plants. Similarly, different species of shore birds take food from the same mud flat by probing with their varied bills to different depths. Species of warblers that feed in the same tree are reported to concentrate in separate areas among the trunk, twig tips, and tree top.

Starlings and cowbirds feeding in flocks on the ground show another arrangement that provides an even distribution of food: birds in the rear fly ahead to the front, so that the flock rolls slowly across the field.

Different species also have different styles of flight. Soaring is typical of some big birds. Gulls float nearly motionless in the wind. Buteos and turkey vultures soar on updrafts in wide circles, although turkey vultures may be further distinguished by wings held in a shallow V. Some other large birds, such as accipiters, rarely soar but instead interrupt their wing beats with glides. Kestrels, terns, kingfishers, and ospreys can hover in one spot. Hummingbirds, like oversized dragonflies, can also hover and even fly backward. Slightly more erratic than the swooping, effortless flight of swallows is that of swifts, flitting with wing beats that appear to alternate from one side to the other (but do not). Still other birds, such as the American goldfinch and flickers, dip up and down in wavelike flight.


AND NOW for a few practice puzzlers to illustrate and apply some of the points discussed above.

At the wooded edge of a ponds in summer you observe a small bird that is all brown above and streaked with brown below. A long, pale-yellow stripe runs above each eye. As it walks the bird teeters and bobs. This is a . . . (I'm waiting for you to answer first) . . . a northern waterthrush, whose peculiar gait is shared by the somewhat larger spotted sandpiper, also seen near water.

Standing at the edge of thickets early in May, you hear a distinctive song: about eight buzzy notes ascending the chromatic scale, or that is, rising in a series of half tones. This song is enough to identify — what? Finally, you spot a small warbler with an olive back and yellow underparts, streaked black along the sides. The bird bobs its tail. It is the misnamed prairie warbler, which is common in bushy pastures, saplings, and low pines. The palm warbler also bobs its tail, but it is brown above and in spring has a chestnut cap. Yet other birds with idiosyncratic tail tics include the eastern phoebe, which regularly jerks its tail downward while perching, and wrens, which often cock their tails vertically.

Soaring overhead in big circles in spring is a bird with broad wings and a wide unbanded tail. It is probably a buteo, but which? Broad-winged hawks have wide white tail bands (i.e., equal in width to the intervening black bands); red-shouldered hawks have narrow white tail bands; mature red-tailed hawks have no tail bands, so this is your bird. Your identification is confirmed by a glimpse of red on the upper surface of the tail as the hawk banks in its flight. You might also see a harrier (or marsh hawk) at Broadmoor, flying low over a meadow with wings held in a shallow V as it veers from side to side, showing a white spot at the rump just above its long tail. Also present at Broadmoor are ospreys, soaring like buteos. From time to time, they hover and then plunge feet first into the water, from which they immediately emerge and fly off, interrupting their wing beats to shudder in mid-flight, like a dog shaking itself.

At Plum Island in July (see Chapter 2), you spot a large, dark, long-legged, long-necked wading bird in the marsh. It has a downward-curved bill. Of course, the vast majority of large, dark waders are great blue herons, but herons have straight bills. So your bird is probably a glossy ibis. The identification is confirmed when the creature flies off with its neck outstretched. Herons and egrets fly with their necks folded back. The whimbrel, too, has a downwardly curved bill and flies with its neck outstretched, but its neck and legs are visibly shorter than those of the glossy ibis.

≈      ≈      ≈      ≈

**AUTOMOBILE DIRECTIONS: Broadmoor Wildlife Sanctuary** is located 17 miles southwest of Boston in South Natick. (See •22 on **Map 1** on page 6, and also the upper panel of **Map 46** at right.) Four approaches are described below.

**To Broadmoor from Interstate 95 (Route 128):** Leave I-95 at Exit 21 for Route 16 west toward Wellesley. Go 3.1 miles and then — in the center of Wellesley — turn half-left to continue west on Route 16 for 1.9 miles to South Natick. At South Natick, continue on Route 16 (Eliot Street) for 1.8 miles to the entrance to Broadmoor Wildlife Sanctuary on the left.

**To Broadmoor via the Massachusetts Turnpike (Interstate 90)** *westbound* **from Boston:** Leave the turnpike at Exit 16 for Route 16 west toward Wellesley. At the end of a long U-shaped ramp, turn right and follow Route 16 west 4.9 miles and then — in the center of Wellesley — turn half-left to continue west on Route 16 for 1.9 miles to South Natick. At South Natick, continue on Route 16 (Eliot Street) for 1.8 miles to the entrance to Broadmoor Wildlife Sanctuary on the left.

MAP 46 — Broadmoor Wildlife Sanctuary

ORIENTATION showing automobile access

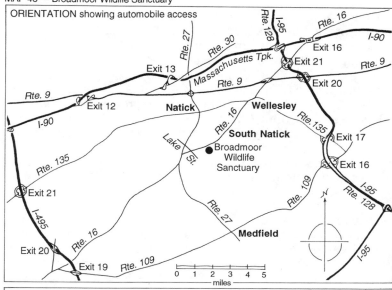

DETAIL showing route to mill sites

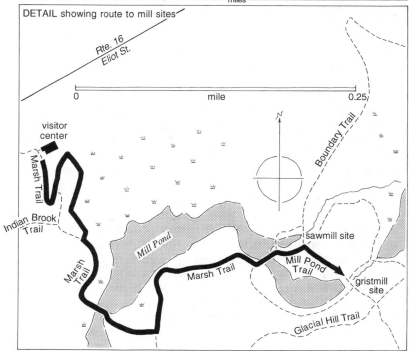

**To Broadmoor via the Massachusetts Turnpike (Interstate 90)** *eastbound* **from Framingham and beyond:** Leave the turnpike at Exit 13 for Route 30. After paying the toll, fork left for Route 30 east toward Natick and Wellesley. From the bottom of the ramp, follow Route 30 east 1.4 miles, then turn right onto Route 27 (Main Street). Follow Route 27 south for almost 5 miles, in the process crossing **Route 9** and **Route 135** in Natick, then bear left onto Lake Street toward Dover. (This obscure intersection occurs 0.8 mile after entering Sherborn.) Go 0.4 mile on Lake Street, then turn left onto Route 16 (Eliot Street). Follow Route 16 east for 1.1 miles to the entrance to Broadmoor Wildlife Sanctuary on the right.

**To Broadmoor from Interstate 495:** Leave I-495 at Exit 19 for Route 109. From the bottom of the ramp, follow Route 109 west toward Milford for 1 mile, then turn right onto Route 16 and follow it east for almost 12 miles through Holliston and Sherborn. The entrance to Broadmoor Wildlife Sanctuary is on the right, 0.5 mile after entering Natick.

≈      ≈      ≈      ≈

**WALKING:** The first thing to do at Broadmoor is to stop in at the visitor center to pay the sanctuary's entrance fee and to pick up their literature, including a bird list.

**Map 47** at right shows the trail system at **Broadmoor.** The paths are identified by signs posted at intersections. In addition, blue blazes lead away from the parking area; yellow blazes point the way back. White blazes mark paths that connect the trail network's three main arms, which lead east to the Charles River, south to Blueberry Swamp, and west to a doughnut-shaped glacial hill.

Near the visitor center are the sites of the two **Morse Mills,** discussed on pages 294-295. Centrally located, the mill sites are a good place to go first, before exploring the more distant trails. The way there is shown by the bold line on the lower panel of **Map 46** on page 291. Directions are as follows: to reach the mill sites, turn left out the door of the visitor center. Enter the woods on the Marsh Trail. Go 75 yards, then turn sharply left and continue straight to the marsh boardwalk. Follow the boardwalk right along the edge of the wetland.

MAP 47 — Broadmoor Wildlife Sanctuary

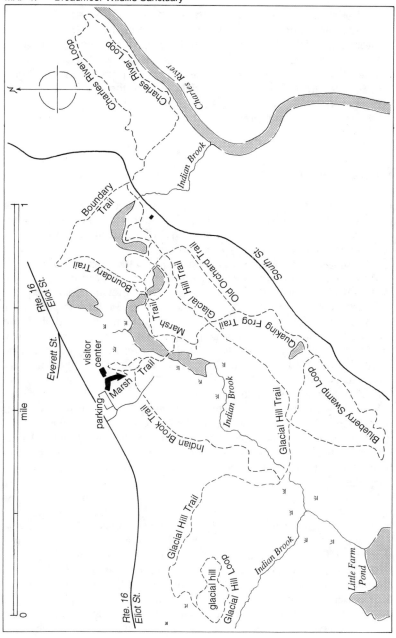

After again entering the woods, bear left. Cross another boardwalk, a knoll, and then yet another boardwalk. At a T-intersection (still the Marsh Trail), turn left. Eventually, turn left across a bridge on the Mill Pond Trail, then fork right on the far side. Pass the sawmill site. At a four-way intersection, turn right (i.e., away from the Boundary Trail). Follow the Mill Pond Trail to the gristmill site, where there are some buhrstones. The former wheel pit is visible below the dam.

≈    ≈    ≈    ≈

## MORSE MILLS

IN 1651 the Massachusetts General Court set aside six thousand acres for the Christianized Indians at Natick. With its own church and government, the village was the most successful of fourteen communities of "praying Indians" established by the Puritan missionary John Eliot. At Natick, only Indians could own land or reside in the town.

However, after growing weary of taking their corn and other grain to Watertown or Medfield to be ground, the Indians petitioned the Massachusetts General Court to allow Thomas Sawin, operator of a sawmill at Sherborn, to have fifty acres in their town, provided he would construct a gristmill. The legislature approved the arrangement, and so in about 1692 Sawin became the first English resident at Natick, where he built a gristmill and sawmill on Indian Brook. Now the sanctuary visitor center overlooks Sawin's mill pond, and his house on South Street is occupied by the sanctuary's director.

Sawin's gristmill was a custom or country mill, meaning that it served individual farmers and households on a fee-for-service basis, grinding grain as needed for cornmeal, flour, or animal feed. People brought in their grain and had it ground while they waited. The standard practice was for the miller to be compensated by keeping a part of what he ground, which he could then sell.

In 1858 Sawin's descendant, also named Thomas, sold the mills and sixteen acres of land to John Andrew Morse. Under Morse's ownership, mill operations continued into the twentieth century. Morse ground grain year-round, if there was enough water to power the mill. In a short memoir that is available at the Broadmoor office, Mrs. Marion Pfeiffer recalls that it was a common thing, when she was a child of ten or eleven, for her parents to send her to the Morse house to learn "if Mr. Morse were grinding that day." If so, she drove a horse and wagon loaded with five or six bushels of corn to be ground at the mill, where she might have to wait her turn. At night and at other times when the mill was not running, flashboards were dropped into slots at the dam, blocking the headrace and allowing the water to rise in the pond. When one or another of the mills was in use, the flashboards were removed, allowing water to flow into the race and over the wheel. The greatest flow of water was in spring, and it was then that Morse sawed logs into lumber. Customers sledded their logs to the sawmill during winter and left them in piles along Mill Lane (also known as Old Mill Road and now part of the Boundary Trail). After being cut in the spring, the finished lumber was stacked and left by the road to be picked up by the customers.

John Andrew Morse received help at the sawmill from his son Preston, a mechanic and tinkerer of considerable talent. Preston had a machine shop at the sawmill, where he generated electricity with his own dynamo. He designed and built chicken incubators, cranberry winnowers, machines for demagnetizing watch parts, and other devises. For his family he built a telephone connecting the house and the mills. As automobiles came into use toward the end of his life, he familiarized himself with internal combustion engines and turned to automobile repair.

The Morse sawmill burned in 1918, but by then neither it nor the gristmill was still running. Preston Morse died in 1929 after selling the mill tract to Carl S. Stillman, who tore down the gristmill. In 1968 the Stillman family gave the property to the Massachusetts Audubon Society.

# CARYL PARK
# NOANET WOODLANDS

Located next to each other in the town of Dover, **Caryl Park** and the **Noanet Woodlands** have more than ten miles of trails. **Map 48** on page 302 outlines a route of 4.5 miles (7.2 kilometers). It shows the area's chief attractions, including a chain of millponds created by the old Dover Union Iron Company. The trail also passes over Noanet Peak, from which there is a distant view of Boston.

One feature of Caryl Park is the **Benjamin Caryl House**, built in about 1777. During spring and fall, the Dover Historical Society opens the house to visitors each Saturday from 1 P.M. to 4 P.M.

Access to the Noanet Woodlands is through Caryl Park. Both properties are open daily from dawn to dusk. The park is owned by the town of Dover and the Noanet Woodlands by The Trustees of Reservations; telephone (781) 821-2977.

For automobile directions, please turn to page 301. Walking directions start on page 303.

---

CARYL PARK is named for the Reverend Benjamin Caryl, whose late-eighteenth century house fronts on Dedham Street near the park entrance. After graduating from Harvard in 1761 at age twenty-nine, Caryl prepared for the ministry by reading theology in Wrentham. While there he received an offer to become the minister of Dedham's Springfield Parish, which had been authorized in 1748 to have its own meetinghouse and minister. The congregation was served by numerous visiting preachers before it called on Caryl, by unanimous vote, to take the pastorate. Caryl deliberated for five months, then wrote to the parish that "after so much pain taken to know my duty, I am well satisfied with the clearness of my call to settle among you in the work of the ministry." With a large gathering present, including pastors and elders from neighboring churches, Caryl was ordained on November 10, 1762 in the new meetinghouse, which had been finished two years earlier.

Springfield Parish had 352 inhabitants living in 49 houses. The minister's salary was very modest: just £66 a year. Caryl may have had some money of his own, or he may have got some by his marriage, a month after coming to Dedham, to the widowed daughter of another Harvard-educated minister, the Reverend Henry Messinger of Wrentham. In any case, Caryl bought a farm and in 1777 built the rather substantial house that still stands in the present-day park. During the revolution, he relinquished a fifth of his annual salary and accepted payment of the balance in £4000 of the grossly depreciated Continental currency.

Caryl was a sincere, dedicated, and entirely orthodox Congregational minister. His sermons were the usual exposition of scripture intermixed with tidings of salvation for the righteous and warnings of fiery damnation for the sinful. He visited and prayed with the sick and the needy, and he sought also to reform those who were too often drunk or were indifferent to religion. He is said to have caused nearly every household in the parish to set up a family alter for prayer at home.

In addition to his duties as minister, Caryl worked his farm, served sometimes as schoolmaster, coached boys for Harvard, provided commonplace medicines to the ill, and served as parish scrivener, drawing up wills and contracts. One lawyer, perhaps peeved by the competition, said Caryl's library "consisted of a Bible, a Concordance, and an old jack-knife." Caryl's range of work was usual for the time. During his long pastorate, which ended with his death in 1811, he saw Springfield Parish become independent from Dedham as the District of Dover in 1784. For the last two years of his ministry, his duties were performed for him by an assistant hired by the appreciative parish.

The District of Dover was incorporated as a town in 1836. Since then, like so many towns near Boston, Dover has gradually changed from being an agricultural village to a well-heeled bedroom suburb. In the nineteenth and early twentieth centuries, the town had some industries along the Charles River and more than a few summer homes and gentlemen farms — some of which, including Mill Farm just to the east of the Caryl House, still survive.

IN THE NOANET WOODLANDS, which are located next to Caryl Park, there is a large masonry dam and a chain of attractive ponds along the valley of Noanet Brook. This was the location of the Dover Union Iron Company, incorporated in 1815 to construct and operate a rolling and slitting mill. The site was thought to be an improvement over an

existing mill at Charles River Village, where the fall of water was so little that only a low-powered undershot waterwheel was possible. At Noanet Brook the dam for the "New Mill" was high enough — and the wheel pit deep enough — for a huge overshot wheel thirty-six feet in diameter, which increased the speed of the rollers fourfold and consumed less water than the undershot wheel. The stone wheel pit, forty feet long, is still visible. It formerly was twenty feet deep, and from its bottom the water drained away through an underground tailrace that ran down the valley for a hundred yards. Because virtually all water from the brook was impounded for use, the mill completely interrupted the stream, which did not resume its natural course until the water flowed out the tailrace.

The chain of ponds above the dam was intended, of course, to store as much water as possible for the use of the mill. Controlled by a gate in the main dam, the water flowed through a wooden trough, or fleam, and fell into the buckets of the wheel. Farther upstream, smaller dams impounded other ponds. Each had its own control gate that was opened or shut to maintain the proper level in the next pond below. The largest reservoir, now a swamp, was three-quarters of a mile above the mill.

The rolling and slitting process started with iron bars imported from Norway. Heated red-hot in a furnace, the bars were passed repeatedly through pairs of heavy, water-cooled rollers to produce wide, flat lengths of rolled iron. The mill workers then fed the pieces through slitting rollers that cut the iron lengthwise into strips that were used to make barrel hoops or were sold to blacksmiths. Much of the output, however, was slit again into long, thin iron rods. These were used by a nail factory on the Charles River, owned by some of the same people who had invested in the New Mill. Daniel Chickering, one of the proprietors of the Dover Union Iron Company, had previously invented a machine that cut and headed nails at the same time — an innovation that increased efficiency and created greater demand for rolled and slit iron.

The New Mill, however, was a failure. Despite the elaborate system of ponds, experience proved that there was not enough water. After a few years of operation, the mill was abandoned and allowed to fall into ruin. In 1876 the dam collapsed, but it was rebuilt in 1954 under the direction of Roland Wells, who has previously excavated and reconstructed the Saugus Iron Works, featured in Chapter 8. In addition to the dam, wheel pit, and ponds, other relics of the mill include traces of the brick furnace base, the stone paved floor, and thick iron eyebolts fastened into the rock to anchor the wooden blocks that supported the main shaft of the waterwheel.

Excavation of the mill site was paid for by Amelia Peabody, who owned the woods. She lived at the adjacent Mill Farm, where she raised thoroughbred horses, white-faced Herefords, and Yorkshire pigs. "In my younger days," she recollected in 1976, "I took great pleasure in riding horseback through the wood roads, often lined with lady slippers." Upon her death in 1984, the Noanet Woodlands passed by her bequest to The Trustees of Reservations.

≈  ≈  ≈  ≈

**AUTOMOBILE DIRECTIONS: Caryl Park and the Noanet Woods Reservation** are located adjacent to each other in Dover, 14 miles southwest of Boston. (See •23 on **Map 1** on page 6, and also the corner panel of **Map 48** on page 302.) Two approaches are described below.

**To Caryl Park and Noanet Woods from Interstate 95 (Route 128):** Leave I-95 at Exit 17 for Route 135 west. After 0.8 mile, turn left onto South Street. Go 1 mile, in the process forking left to stay on South Street. At a crossroads with Chestnut Street, turn left and go 0.4 mile, then curve right and continue on Dedham Street 1.9 miles to the entrance to Caryl Park and Noanet Woodlands on the left. If the lot is full, there is another lot nearby at Chickering Fields opposite the Caryl House.

**To Caryl Park and Noanet Woods from Interstate 495:** You may want to refer to the upper panel of **Map 49** on page 308. That map shows the local roads that are referred to in the following directions.

Leave I-495 at Exit 19 for Route 109. Follow Route 109 east 9.7 miles to the intersection of **Route 109 and Route 27** in Medfield. From there, continue east on Route 109 just 0.2 mile, then turn left onto North Street at a traffic light. Go 4.9 miles, in the process forking right twice to stay on North Street, which changes names to Centre Street as it enters Dover. After passing through the village center, fork right onto Dedham Street and go 0.5 mile to an entrance on the right that serves *both* Caryl Park and Noanet Woodlands (i.e., 0.2 mile after another entrance serving just Caryl Park). There is yet a third lot at Chickering Fields opposite the Caryl House.

≈  ≈  ≈  ≈

MAP 48 — Caryl Park and Noanet Woodlands

parking

Dedham St.

Caryl House

parking

parking

Charles River

South St.

Chestnut St.

South St.

Rte. 135

Exit 17

Centre St.

Willow St.

Mill St.

Dedham St.

Caryl Park and
Noanet Woodlands

Dover

0        mile        1

Rte. 128

I-95

CARYL

PARK

33  32

r        r

31

r

30

39  38  29

r

28

mill
site

r

BLAZES

b = blue
r = red
y = yellow

NOANET

5

37

36

b

27
26

Brook

25

r

7        6

Noanet
Peak

24

r

8

footpath

23

r

narrow

9

22

r

21

r

35
34

WOODLANDS

19        20

b

Walpole St.

10

11

12  13

18

17

private

Powissett St.

14

15  16

N

0        mile        0.5

302

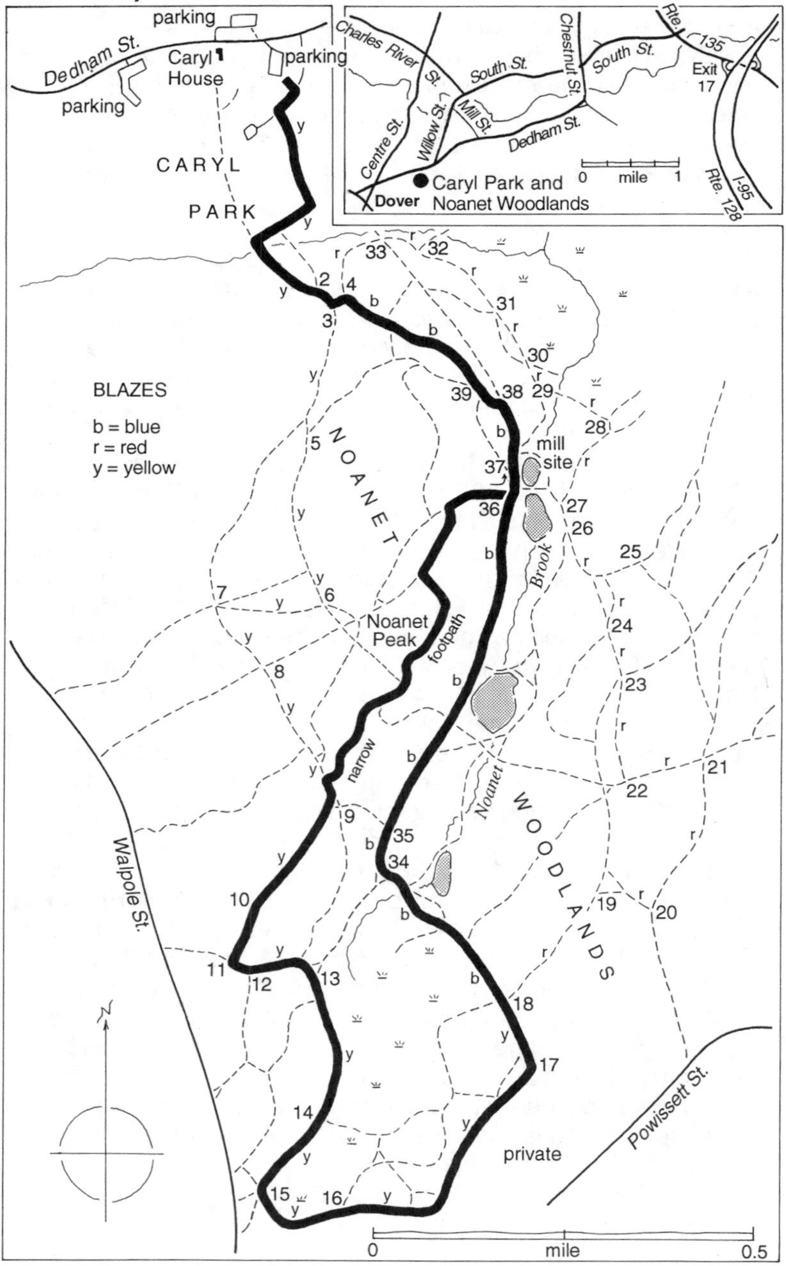

**WALKING: Map 48** at left outlines a 4.5-mile walk that links the best parts and most interesting features at **Caryl Park** and the **Noanet Woodlands**. As indicated on the map, some trails are marked with colored blazes, and many trail junctions are identified by numbers posted on trees.

Also at Caryl Park is the eighteenth-century **Benjamin Caryl House**, which is open to the public per the schedule noted on page 297. From the parking lot, the house is visible beyond the tennis courts.

**Start your walk** at the signboard near a shed at the back-left corner of the parking lot. Follow the trail into the woods, then bear right on a gravel road. After 100 yards, turn left to follow the yellow blazes. At junction 3, turn left off the yellow-blazed path and climb to junction 4, which is the trailhead for the blue and red paths.

At junction 4, turn right to follow the blue blazes on a wide path by several horse jumps and past trails diverging to either side. At junction 38, merge with a wide gravel track intersecting from the left-rear. Follow the blue blazes past a series of ponds on the left, eventually reaching junction 18, where the blue, red, and yellow trails all meet.

At junction 18, continue straight on the yellow-blazed trail. Within 20 yards of a steel gate, turn right to continue on the yellow trail past a farm on the left. Eventually, bear right at junction 15 near Walpole Street. Follow the yellow blazes through junctions 14, 13, and 12, then sharply right at junction 11. At junction 9, pass some trails ascending from the right, then immediately turn right, *leaving the yellow-blazed trail* in order to follow a rough, rocky, and eroded footpath steeply uphill.

Follow the footpath up along a ridge and past trails intersecting from either side. Cross the top of Noanet Peak, where there is a distant view of Boston, then descend gradually. At a T-intersection, turn right, then right again at the next junction.

At junction 36 at the foot of the hill, turn left onto the blue-blazed trail and follow it along the contour of the slope and straight past junction 37. At junction 38, bear left, then right to continue on the blue-blazed trail back to junction 4. Turn left, then right at junction 3 to follow the yellow blazes back to the parking lot.

# 24

# ROCKY WOODS and FORK FACTORY BROOK RESERVATIONS

Rocky Woods Reservation and the adjacent Fork Factory Brook Reservation are located in Medfield southwest of Boston. **Map 49** on page 308 shows the network of trails, altogether totaling more than 13 miles (20.8 kilometers) . As indicated on the map, trail intersections are identified by numbers that are posted on trees, and each trail is also identified by name. This exemplary system makes navigating easy, so that the two reservations are great places to wander without any preconceived route. The trails wind easily up and down the hills, occasionally passing ponds and rock outcrops.

Rocky Woods and Fork Factory Brook reservations are open daily from dawn to dusk. They are managed by The Trustees of Reservations; telephone (781) 821-2977. The name *Fork Factory*, incidentally, comes from a nineteenth-century foundry for the manufacture of pitchforks and other farm implements. Torn down in 1927, the factory was located where Route 109 crosses Mill Brook.

For automobile directions, please turn to page 307. Walking directions start on page 309.

---

ROCKY WOODS and the adjacent Fork Factory Brook Reservation are just two of many sites throughout Massachusetts held by The Trustees of Reservations, a nonprofit corporation founded in 1891 to preserve areas of outstanding scenic, historic, and ecological value. The Trustees was the first such land trust in the world. Four years after its creation, The National Trust was founded in England with a charter modeled on The Trustees. Now, numerous private land trusts are active around the globe. In the United States, these trusts operate at the municipal level (like the Lincoln Land Conservation Trust outlined in Chapter 15), at the state level (like The Trustees of Reservations itself), and at the national level (like The Nature Conservancy or the Trust for Public Land described in Chapter 1).

Creation of The Trustees of Reservations was primarily the work of one man: Charles Eliot. The son of the president of Harvard University, Eliot was a landscape architect who received his training in the Brookline office of Frederick Law Olmsted and eventually became one of his partners. In the early years of the parks movement during the 1870s and '80s, Boston was one of the few municipalities that acquired open space for public recreation. Most of the other towns in the region failed to act, either because they lacked funds or felt that parks established within their borders would benefit their city neighbors as much or more than themselves. As a result, many historic sites and scenic areas disappeared as urban and suburban development accelerated.

In response to this trend, Eliot proposed in 1890 to form "an incorporated association composed of citizens of all the Boston towns, and empowered by the State to hold small and well-distributed parcels of land free of taxes, just as the Public Library holds books and the Art Museum pictures — for the use and enjoyment of the public." Like Thoreau and the Transcendentalists, and also like his mentor Olmsted, Eliot believe that open space and the enjoyment of nature are necessary for good mental health and spiritual well-being. He wrote:

> The life history of Humanity has proved nothing more clearly than crowded populations, if they would live in health and happiness, must have space for air, for light, for exercise, for rest, and for the enjoyment of that peaceful beauty of nature which, because of the noisy ugliness of towns, is so wonderfully refreshing to the tired souls of townspeople.

After The Trustees of Public Reservations was created by act of the Massachusetts legislature, Eliot and The Trustees went on to play a leading part in the formation two years later of the Metropolitan Parks Commission, similarly empowered to buy land regardless of municipal boundaries, but having the additional advantages of public finance and the power of eminent domain.

Although The Trustees of Public Reservations dropped the word *public* from its name in 1954 (after all, the reservations are not publicly owned), the organization takes very seriously the objective of opening its sites for public use. It builds parking lots, develops trails, employs wardens and maintenance staff, and publishes maps and a comprehensive guide to more than eighty reservations altogether exceeding 21,000 acres. The sites of The Trustees of Reservations are at least as well publicized and managed as our state parks and forests.

The Trustees of Reservations also oversees a program of perpetual conservation restrictions. Typically, the restrictions are donated by owners who, because of long residence or other affiliation with the land, want to preserve their property in a natural condition while also receiving the income tax deductions, reduced property tax assessments, and inheritance tax savings that result from giving away the development rights. The Trustees of Reservations holds more than 170 such restrictions totaling nearly 12,000 acres. It tries to coordinate these conservation restrictions with the work of other organizations and with outright acquisition of sites in order to maintain historic landscapes over wide areas.

Yet another facet of The Trustees of Reservation is its Land Conservation Center, where owners can get advice regarding a wide variety of techniques for preserving valuable tracts, at least in part. For example, at a time when soaring values have made gifts of land increasingly unlikely, the Land Conservation Center counsels landowners on how they can obtain value by developing part of their property in a sensitive manner while protecting the rest by means of conservation restrictions. If done skillfully, the restrictions can greatly enhance the market price of the lots that are to be developed and also preserve unspoiled views for the enjoyment of the public.

In addition to the sites featured in this chapter, Boston-area properties of The Trustees include the Ward Reservation in Andover and North Andover (Chapter 3), Crane Beach in Ipswich (Chapter 6), Ravenswood Park and Coolidge Point on Cape Ann (Chapter 7), World's End and the Whitney and Thayer Woods in Hingham and Cohasset (Chapter 19), the Norris Reservation in Norwell (Chapter 20), and the Noanet Woodlands in Dover (Chapter 23). Support for these and other sites comes from membership dues, gifts, admission fees, endowment income, and grants. For information about the programs of The Trustees and what you can do to help, write or call The Trustees of Reservations, 572 Essex Street, Beverly, Massachusetts 01915-1530; telephone (508) 921-1944.

≈      ≈      ≈      ≈

## AUTOMOBILE DIRECTIONS: The Rocky Woods Reservation is located in Medfield 17 miles southeast of Boston. (See •24 on **Map 1** on page 6, and also the upper panel of **Map 49** on page 308.) The parking lots also serve the **Fork Factory Brook Reservation**, located across the road. Three approaches are described below.

### To Rocky Woods from Interstate 95 (Route 128):
Leave I-95 at Exit 16B for Route 109 west. Go about 5.6 miles, then turn very sharply right onto Hartford Street. Follow Hartford

MAP 49 — Rocky Woods Reservation and Fork Factory Brook Reservation

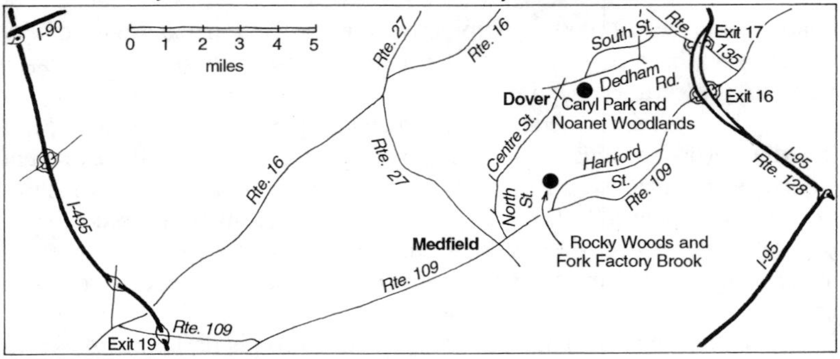

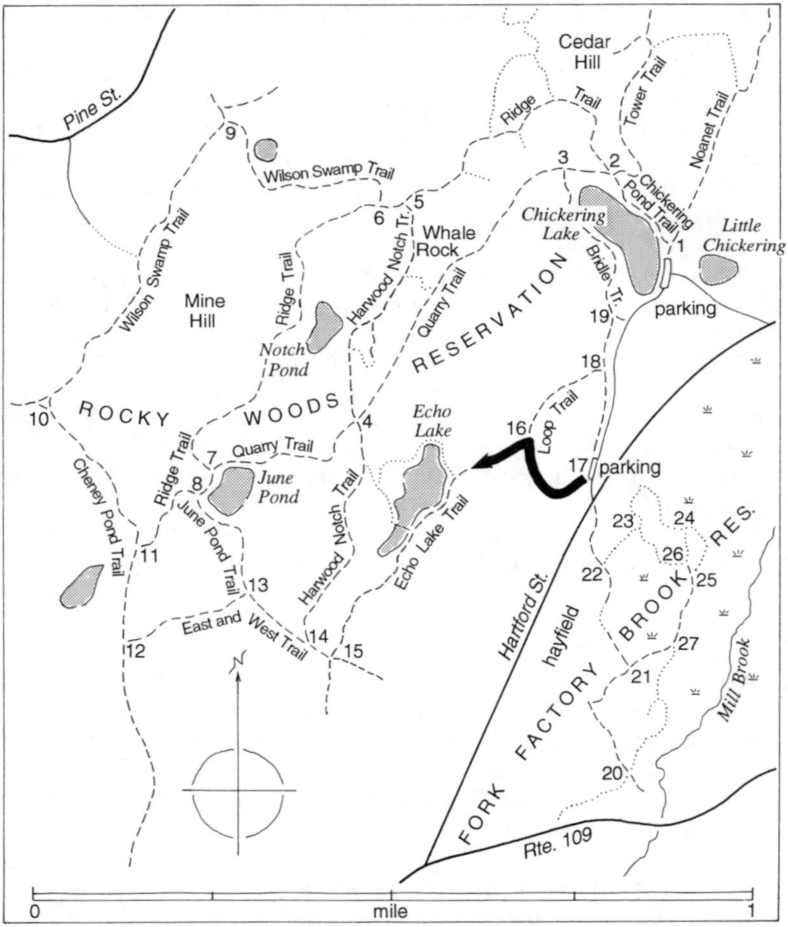

I-90

0 1 2 3 4 5
miles

Rte. 27
Rte. 16
South St.
Rte.
Exit 17
I-35
Dedham Rd.
Exit 16
**Dover**
Caryl Park and
Noanet Woodlands
Rte. 16
Rte. 27
Centre St.
Hartford St.
I-495
North St.
Rte. 109
I-95
Rte. 128
**Medfield**
Rocky Woods and
Fork Factory Brook
Rte. 109
Exit 19
I-95

Pine St.
Cedar Hill
Ridge Trail
Tower Trail
Noanet Trail
9
Wilson Swamp Trail
3
2
Chickering Pond Trail
Wilson Swamp Trail
5
6
Whale Rock
Chickering Lake
Little Chickering
1
Harwood Notch Tr.
Ridge Trail
Mine Hill
Notch Pond
Quarry Trail
RESERVATION
Birdle Tr.
19
parking
18
10
R O C K Y     W O O D S
Ridge Trail
4
Echo Lake
16
Loop Trail
17 parking
7
Quarry Trail
8
June Pond
Harwood Notch Trail
Echo Lake Trail
23
24
Cheney Pond Trail
11
26
22
25
13
Hartford St.
hayfield
27
East and West Trail
14
15
21
B R O O K   R E S.
F O R K   F A C T O R Y
12
20
Mill Brook
Rte. 109
N
0                              mile                              1

Street 0.6 mile to the entrance for Rocky Woods Reservation on the left. There are two parking lots; use the first one on the left, if there is room.

**To Rocky Woods from Interstate 495:** Leave I-495 at Exit 19 for Route 109. Follow Route 109 east 11.3 miles, then turn left onto Hartford Street. Follow Hartford Street 0.6 mile to the entrance for Rocky Woods Reservation on the left. There are two parking lots; use the first one on the left, if there is room.

**To Rocky Woods from the intersection of Route 109 and Route 27:** These two locally important roads cross in Medfield. Follow Route 109 east 1.7 miles, then turn left onto Hartford Street. Follow Hartford Street 0.6 mile to the entrance for Rocky Woods Reservation on the left. There are two parking lots; use the first one on the left, if there is room.

≈         ≈         ≈         ≈

**WALKING:** The lower panel of **Map 49** at left shows the trails at **Rocky Woods**. Most of the paths are identified by signs at junctions. In addition, each intersection has a number posted on a tree, corresponding to a number on the map. There are also paint blazes at junctions: blue indicates trails leading away from the parking lots; yellow indicates trails leading toward the parking lots. All these navigational aids make the reservation a great place to wander freely, picking out a route as you go. As shown on the map, there are more trails across Hartford Street in **Fork Factory Brook Reservation**.

I suggest that you begin at the parking lot near Hartford Street. From the left end of the lot, enter the woods at junction 17 on the Loop Trail. At junction 16, turn left onto Echo Lake Trail, which will get you started on any of several circuits through the woods.

# MOOSE HILL WILDLIFE SANCTUARY

There are about 12 miles (19.2 kilometers) of trails at the 2,200-acre Moose Hill Wildlife Sanctuary, which is located in Sharon south of Boston.

**Map 50** on pages 318-319 shows, by the bold line on the left, a loop of 3.8 miles (6 kilometers) through meadow and woods in the western part of the sanctuary. Part of the route passes along the top of high cliffs, from which there are distant views. Trail directions start on page 320.

Map 50 also shows, by the bold line on the right, a loop of 2 miles (3.2 kilometers) leading through the woods and past vernal pools in the sanctuary's northeastern sector. Trail directions are on page 321.

The trails are open daily from dawn to dusk. An admission fee is charged. Dogs are prohibited. The office and visitor center are open Tuesday through Saturday from 9 A.M. to 5 P.M. and on Sunday from 10 to 5.

Established in 1916, Moose Hill is the oldest of the wildlife sanctuaries of the Massachusetts Audubon Society. For information on natural-history programs, including field trips, a day camp, and maple sugar making in February and March, telephone (781) 784-5691. For automobile directions to Moose Hill, please turn to page 317.

---

WHAT ORNITHOLOGICAL DISTINCTION is shared by Philadelphia, Nashville, Savannah, and Ipswich, Massachusetts? They are the only U.S. municipalities whose names have been given to birds: the Philadelphia vireo, the Nashville warbler, and the Savannah and "Ipswich" sparrows. Perhaps Ipswich should be ousted from this select set, inasmuch as the American Ornithologists' Union has determined that the Ipswich bird is merely a pale race of the Savannah breed. And what about the Baltimore oriole, you ask? It and the city were both named for the Lords Baltimore, the colonial proprietors of Maryland. Mark Catesby, an eighteenth-century naturalist, called the oriole the "Balti-more-Bird" because its colors were the same as those of the Baltimores' heraldic flag.

Bird identification was the subject of Chapters 14 and 22. This chapter too is wholly bird talk, focusing on the rainy-day pastime of bird names. For example, as a word, *titmouse* is worth a little curiosity. Although a titmouse is easy to identify, how many birders know what the word means? Why is a petrel so called? And what about *killdeer, turnstone, nuthatch, knot*, and other peculiar bird names?

Although many American Indian place names were adopted by the Europeans, the settlers and early ornithologists made a clean sweep when it came to naming — or rather renaming — North American birds. In a few cases where the same species (brant, for instance) were found on both side of the Atlantic, use of the English name was a matter of course. More often, however, the settlers simply reused the names of Old World birds for similar-looking — but actually different — New World species. The English, for example, have given the name *robin* to various red-breasted birds in India, Australia, and North America. More often still, the use of general names like *wren* was extended to American birds, with the addition of qualifying words to identify individual species (house wren, Carolina wren, and so forth). However, scientific classifi-cation has sometimes placed whole categories of American birds in entirely different families than their European namesakes, as in the case of American warblers. The only North American birds in the same family as the European warblers are the gnatcatcher and kinglets — not at all what are called warblers here. Finally, in relatively rare instances, American birds have been given unique and colorful new names based on their behavior, appearance, and song, as, for instance, the yellow-bellied sapsucker, canvasback, and whip-poor-will.

Early American ornithologists seem to have been quite casual about naming birds. Alexander Wilson (1766-1813), author of the nine-volume *American Ornithology*, once shot a bird in a magnolia tree; hence, *magnolia warbler* for a bird whose preferred habitat is low, moist conifers. After Wilson's death his work was overshadowed by Audubon's superior, life-sized drawings, but Wilson was in many ways the greater pioneer, depicting 264 species of birds, of which 39 were not previously known. Usually Wilson named birds according to the locality where his specimens were collected. He named the Nashville warbler and the Savannah sparrow, but not the Philadelphia vireo. (It was named by naturalist Charles Lucien Jules Laurent Bonaparte, Prince of Canino and Musignano, a nephew of Napoleon Bonaparte and presumably an author-ity on names.)

Not surprisingly, many of the geographic names given to birds by early ornithologists bear no precise relation to the species' breeding territory or winter range. The Savannah sparrow, for example, is found throughout North America and might just as well have been named for Chicago or Seattle or even Anchorage. Among the Tennessee, Connecticut, and Kentucky warblers (all named by Wilson), only the last is at all likely to be found in its nominal state during the breeding season, and none winter north of Mexico. But probably the greatest geographical misnomer among bird names is our native turkey, after the supposed region of its origin. The name was first applied to the guinea cock, which was imported from Africa through Turkey into Europe and with which the American bird was for a time identified when it was first introduced to Europe in about 1530.

Some bird names, although seeming to refer to specific geographic areas, are actually far broader in their historical meaning. *Louisiana* in Louisiana heron refers to the vast territory of the Louisiana Purchase, even though the bird is usually found only in coastal areas. The species was first collected on the Louis and Clark expedition and was named by Wilson. *Arcadia*, as in Arcadian flycatcher, is an old French name for Nova Scotia, but the term was used generally to suggest a northern clime, as was also *boreal* in boreal chickadee, from the Greek god of the north wind, Boreas.

In addition to birds named *by* early ornithologists and explorers, there are birds named *for* them by contemporary and later admirers of their work. Wilson, for example, is memorialized in the name of a petrel, a phalarope, a plover, a warbler, and also a genus of warblers. Audubon is honored by Audubon's shearwater and "Audubon's" warbler, a form of the yellow-rumped warbler. There was a measure of reciprocity about this last bird name: in 1837 John Kirk Townsend, a Philadelphia ornithologist and bird collector, named "Audubon's" warbler, and a year or two later Audubon returned the favor with Townsend's solitaire. Then there are species named for ornithologists' wives, daughters, and relatives, as in Anna's hummingbird and Virginia's, Lucy's, and Grace's warblers. Some birds bear human names connected to no one in particular. Guillemot (French for "little William"), magpie (in part based on Margaret), martin ("little Mars"), and parakeet ("little Peter") are thought to be pet names or affectionate tags that have become attached to various species.

Color is probably the dominant theme in bird names. Plumages cover the spectrum, ranging from the red phalarope through the orange-crowned warbler, yellow rail, green heron, blue goose, indigo bunting, and violet-crowned hummingbird. For stripped-down straightforwardness there are names like bluebird and blackbird. For vividness there are color designations like scarlet tanager, vermilion flycatcher, lazuli bunting, and cerulean warbler. To improve our dictionary skills, there are color-based names like fulvous tree duck, ferruginous hawk, flammulated owl, and parula warbler. For unpoetry, there is hepatic tanager, so called because of the liver-colored, liver-shaped patch on each cheek. For meaningless-ness there is the clay-colored sparrow. (What color is that? Answer: buffy brown, at least on the rump.) Some bird names less obviously denote basic hues: vireo (green), oriole (golden), dunlin ("little dull-brown one"), canvasback (for its speckled gray and white back), brant (thought by some to mean "burnt," referring to the dusky black plumage), and waxwing (whose red-tipped secondary wing feathers recalled to someone the color and substance of sealing wax). A great many bird names pair color with some specific body part, as in redhead, goldeneye, yellowlegs, and so forth.

Shape or other distinctive features often are reflected in bird names. The profile of the bufflehead suggests an American buffalo or bison. The loggerhead shrike has a disproportionately large head. Shovelers have long, broad bills. The word *falcon* is derived from a Latin term for "sickle," suggesting the bird's curved talons. From head to toe, there is a body part that is some bird's nominal identity: tufted titmouse, horned lark, eared grebe (*grebe* itself may come from a Breton word for "crest"), ruffed grouse, pectoral sandpiper (for the air sack under its breast feathers), short-tailed hawk, stilt sandpiper (for its comparatively long legs), rough-legged hawk (for its feathered tarsi), sharp-shinned hawk (it has), semipalmated sandpiper (for its partially webbed feet), and Lapland longspur (for the elongated claw on the hind toe).

Some names indicate size, from *great* and *greater* to *little, lesser,* and *least.* Symmetry would seem to demand a *greatest,* but perhaps that need is filled by *king,* which occasionally refers to stature. The king rail, for example, is the largest of the rails. But sometimes *king* is simply a compliment to a bird's raiment or a reference to distinguishing plumage on its crown, as in the ruby-crowned and golden-crowned kinglets ("little kings"). *Gallinule* itself suggests size, being derived from Latin for "little hen." *Starling* is from the Anglo-Saxon word for bird; with the addition of the diminutive suffix *-ling,* it simply means "little bird." *Titmouse* similarly is a combination of Icelandic and Anglo-Saxon meaning "small bird." The base word *tit* for *bird* also appears in bushtit and wrentit.

A few names, like that of the gull-billed tern, make explicit com-parisons with other birds. The hawk owl has a long slender tail that gives this bird a falcon-like appearance. The lark bunting sings on the wing like a skylark, the curlew sandpiper has a downwardly curved, curlew-like bill. The swallow-tailed kite has a deeply forked tail like a

barn swallow. The turkey vulture has a head that somewhat resembles that of a turkey. And *cormorant* is derived from French for "sea crow."

Many bird names refer to distinctive behavior. Woodpeckers, sap-suckers, creepers, and wagtails all do what their names suggest. Turnstones do indeed turn over small stones and shells while searching for food. *Black skimmer* describes the bird's technique of sticking its lower bill into the water while flying just above the surface. *Shearwater* similarly suggests the bird's skimming flight. Frigatebirds (also called man-o'-war-birds) were named by sailors for the birds' piratical habit of pursuing and robbing other birds, as do also parasitic jaegers. *Duck* is derived from Anglo-Saxon for "diver." *Nuthatch* is from "nut hack," referring to the bird's technique of wedging a nut into a crevice and then hacking it into small pieces. *Vulture* is akin to Latin *vellere*, "to pluck or tear." Although many people associate *loon* with the bird's lunatic laugh, as in "crazy as a loon," more likely the word is derived from a Norse term for "lame," describing the bird's awkwardness on land — a result of its legs being very near its tail. There is, however, at least one North American bird that is named for its mental capacity: the booby. Seamen who raided the isolated colonies thought the birds stupid because they were unaccustomed to predators and inept at protecting themselves. The dotterel (whose name is related to "dolt" and "dotage") is another nominally foolish bird. Ernest A. Choate, in his fascinating *Dictionary of American Bird Names*, and Edward S. Gruson, in *Words for Birds*, discuss these and other names.

Some birds, such as the whooping crane, clapper rail, piping plover, laughing gull, mourning dove, warbling vireo, and chipping sparrow, are named for how they sound. Similarly, the comparative volume of their vocalizations is the theme that distinguishes between mute, whistling, and trumpeter swans. *Oldsquaw* suggests this duck's noisy, garrulous voice. The catbird mews and the grasshopper sparrow trills and buzzes like the insect. Gruson, however, says that the grasshopper sparrow is named for its diet, as are the goshawk (literally, "goosehawk") and oystercatchers, flycatchers, and gnatcatchers. The saw-whet owl is named for the bird's endlessly repeated note, which suggests a saw being sharpened with a whetstone — a sound now lost to history. The bittern, whose name ultimately is traceable to its call, has a colorful assortment of descriptive folk names, including "bog-bumper," "stake driver," "thunder pumper," and "water belcher." The evening grosbeak and vesper sparrow both tend to sing at dusk. Finally, of course, many birds' songs or calls are also the basis for their names, including the bobolink, bobwhite, bulbul, chachalaca, chickadee, chuck-will's-widow, chukar, crow, cuckoo, curlew, dickcissel, godwit, killdeer, kittiwake, owl, pewee, phoebe, pipits, towhee, veery, whip-poor-will, and willet. *Quail* (like "quack") and *raven* are thought originally to have been imitative of bird calls.

Habitat is a major theme of bird names, as with the surf scoter, sandpiper, seaside sparrow, waterthrush, marsh hawk, meadowlark, wood duck, mountain chickadee, and field, swamp, and tree sparrows. Then there is the *kind* of tree or shrub, as in spruce and sage grouse, willow ptarmigan, pinyon jay, cedar waxwing, myrtle warbler, pine siskin, and orchard oriole. The barn, cliff, cave, tree, and bank swallows are named for their preferred nesting sites. As noted in Chapter 22, however, *prairie warbler* is a misnomer; the bird is common east of the Mississippi and usually is found in brushy, scrubby areas.

Several bird names are associated with human figures. Knots, which frequent shores and tidal flats, are said to be named for Canute (or Cnut), King of the Danes. To demonstrate to the sycophants of his court that he was not omnipotent, Canute vainly ordered the tide to stop rising. Petrels are thought to be named for Saint Peter, who walked on the water at Lake Gennesaret. When landing in the water, petrels dangle their feet and hesitate for an instant, thus appearing to stand on the waves. Cardinals, of course, are named for the red robes and hats of the churchmen. Similarly, prothonotory warblers have the golden raiment of ecclesiastical prothonotories. The bizarre and contrasting pattern of the harlequin duck suggests the traditional costume of Italian pantomime.

Finally, there is the ovenbird, almost unique among North American birds for being named after the appearance of its nest, which is built on the forest floor and resembles a miniature, domed brick oven. "Basketbird" and "hangnest" are folk names referring to the pendulous nests of orioles.

≈　　　≈　　　≈　　　≈

**AUTOMOBILE DIRECTIONS: The Moose Hill Wildlife Sanctuary** is located 20 miles south of Boston in the town of Sharon. (See •25 on **Map 1** on page 6, and also the corner panel of **Map 50** on page 318.) The refuge is easily reached from Interstate 95 about 5 miles south of the juncture with Interstate 93, or 7 miles north of the crossing with Interstate 495. Two approaches — one from the north and one from the south — are described below.

**To Moose Hill Wildlife Sanctuary from the north via Interstate 95:** Leave I-95 at Exit 10. At the top of the ramp, turn left toward Route 27. Go 0.3 mile, then turn right onto Route 27 northbound (High Plain Street). After 0.6 mile, turn

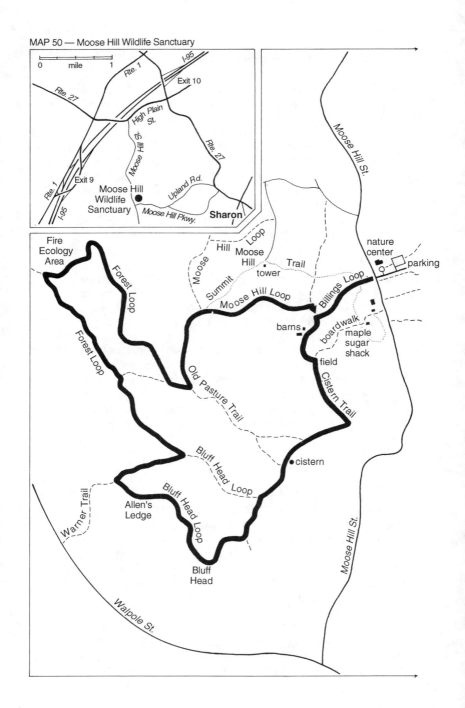

MAP 50 — Moose Hill Wildlife Sanctuary

318

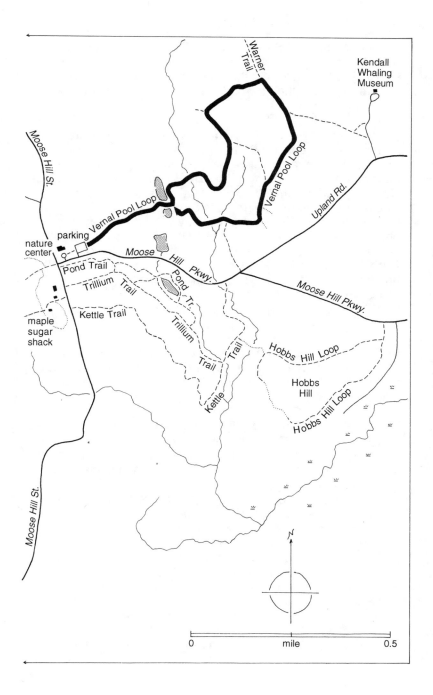

Map labels: Warner Trail, Kendall Whaling Museum, Vernal Pool Loop, Moose Hill St., Upland Rd., parking, nature center, Moose Hill Pkwy., Pond Trail, Pond Tr., Trillium Trail, Moose Hill Pkwy., Kettle Trail, Trillium Trail, Kettle Trail, Hobbs Hill Loop, Hobbs Hill, Hobbs Hill Loop, maple sugar shack, Moose Hill St.

0   mile   0.5

N

319

left onto Moose Hill Street and go 1.3 miles to an intersection with Moose Hill Parkway. If the parking lot just beyond the intersection is still in use, park there. If not, turn left and go about a hundred yards to the new parking lot on the left, just beyond the nature center.

**To Moose Hill Wildlife Sanctuary from the south via Interstate 95:** Leave I-95 at Exit 9 for Route 1 and Route 27. At the top of the ramp, curve left for Route 1 (i.e., don't exit right back onto I-95). Cross over the expressway, then bear right for Route 1 north toward Route 27. At a crossroads, turn right onto Route 27 southbound (High Plain Street). Go 0.4 mile (in the process passing over the expressway yet again), then turn right onto Moose Hill Street. Follow Moose Hill Street 1.3 miles to an intersection with Moose Hill Parkway. If the parking lot just beyond the intersection is still in use, park there. If not, turn left and go about a hundred yards to the new parking lot on the left, just beyond the nature center.

≈      ≈      ≈      ≈

**WALKING:** **Map 50** on pages 318-319 shows the trail system at **Moose Hill Wildlife Sanctuary**, with some overlap down the middle. The bold lines indicate two routes that are discussed below.

A 3.8-mile route on **the Bluff Head Loop and the Forest Loop** occupies the left half of **Map 50**. For a shorter outing, just make a circuit to the Bluff Head, where there is a sweeping view. This is a good spot for hawk watching during fall.

**To get started**, enter the woods on a wide path (the Billings Loop) between stone gateposts at the intersection of Moose Hill Street and Moose Hill Parkway. Pass a field on the right, then turn left at a slightly skewed T-intersection. After passing two small barns, curve left gradually to an intersection with the Cistern Trail. Turn right and follow the upper edge of the meadow, then re-enter the woods. Continue as the trail turns ninety degrees right, then bear left at the next junction. After passing a cistern where the town of Sharon formerly stored its drinking water, fork left twice to follow the Bluff Head Loop clockwise to the Bluff Head itself.

From the Bluff Head, continue around the loop to Allens

Ledge, where there are more views and also a chimney. At the next intersection, turn right uphill.

Leave the Bluff Head Loop by turning left toward the Forest Loop at a junction next to a stone wall. Bear left again at the next intersection in order to circle clockwise around the Forest Loop. Turn right at the northwest extremity of the Forest Loop and pass the Fire Ecology Area, where the woods are intentionally burned at long intervals. At the next intersection, bear left toward the Old Pasture Trail, then turn left again at a T-intersection with the Old Pasture Trail itself. Continue through the woods. Bear right at two intersections at the foot of Moose Hill. With a stone wall on the right and the hill on the left, continue to a T-intersection in front of a meadow, and there turn sharply right toward the Billings Loop. Go 70 yards, then turn left to reach the trailhead at the intersection of Moose Hill Street and Moose Hill Parkway.

The 2-mile **Vernal Pool Loop** is shown in the upper-right part of **Map 50**. As its name indicates, the trail leads past several seasonal ponds and damp hollows.

**To get started**, locate the trailhead at the new parking lot. Descend into the woods. When you reach a trail junction, turn left to follow the loop clockwise. (Take a good look at the intersection so that you will recognize it when you complete the circuit.) Pass trails joining from right and left. At a T-intersection with a woods road, turn right, then bear right again at the next trail junction. Pass a trail intersecting from the right-rear, then fork right at a series of intersections. When you complete the loop, bear left to return to the parking lot.

**26**

# BORDERLAND STATE PARK

Borderland State Park is located south of Boston on the boundary between Easton and Sharon.  An easy circuit of 4 miles (6.4 kilometers) is outlined on **Map 51** on page 332.  The route follows unpaved roads around the large ponds and through woods and meadows at the center of the park.  This is Borderland's most scenic section, but you may also enjoy the system of foot trails that crisscross the rocky hills in the park's northern half.

Borderland is open daily from sunrise to sunset.  Dogs must be leashed.  Call beforehand for information on a variety of programs, especially tours of the **Ames Mansion**, built in the style of an Elizabethan manor house.  Tours are conducted on the third Friday and Sunday of each month, April through November.  Reservations are recommended.

Borderland is managed by the Massachusetts Department of Environmental Management; telephone (508) 238-6566.  For automobile directions to the park, please turn to page 331.  Walking directions start on page 333.

---

BORDERLAND was formerly the country estate of Oakes and Blanche Ames.  Oakes Ames was a professor of botany at Harvard University and a specialist in orchids.  As a young man with the time and money to travel around the world, he assembled an outstanding collection of live orchids — the most complete in the United States — and in 1906 donated it to the New York Botanical Garden.  In 1938 he gave Harvard his privately-financed orchid herbarium consisting of dried specimens of 64,000 species, including more than a thousand new types first described by him.  In addition to his enthusiasm for orchids, he was a pioneer in the field of economic botany.  He assembled a herbarium of 14,000 plants useful or important in human culture, plus a library of 16,000 cross-referenced books and pamphlets.  All this he also gave to Harvard.  Over the course of his long career at the university, he was the director

323

of the Botanical Garden, chairman of the division of biology, supervisor of the Arnold Arboretum, and director of the Botanical Museum.

According to Oakes Ames' daughter Pauline, who edited his letters and diary for a book called *Oakes Ames— Jottings of a Harvard Botanist*, he was shy, reserved, and austere, alternating between charm and silence. His interests included book collecting, gardening, tennis, golf, and other sports. In a letter to Pauline in 1930, Oakes Ames described himself as he worked at home:

> Picture to yourself a lank, lean, old man (I guess) sitting before a manu-
> script that was begun in 1923, trying to produce a classic on the orchid
> flora of Spanish Honduras. For a while the ink flows freely from a
> turquoise-blue fountain pen. Then there is a pause — a cigarette is inserted
> in a prodigiously long amber holder, a miniature match gives a tiny flame.
> The trusty brassie [a golf club] is taken in hand from the chaise lounge and
> promptly thirty-six golf balls, one after the other, with hardly a failure,
> and not a perceptible slice, fly toward the new tree. Then, accompanied by
> three dogs, Tragus, the Great Dane, and . . . Zilla, this strange creature I am
> describing walks briskly to the tree, and soon all the balls are back again,
> and the turquoise-blue fountain pen begins once more the task of putting
> little words on big paper.

Most of Oakes Ames' numerous books and articles on orchids and other plants were illustrated by his wife Blanche, a 1899 Smith graduate with degrees from both the College and the School of Art. In contrast to her moody and sometimes melancholy husband, she was gay and out-going. She also delighted in controversy. Her daughter recalls an occa-sion when Prince Saluddin Aga Kahn was visiting at Borderland: "My mother proceeded to point out to him, vigorously, the deficiencies of Islam as compared with Unitarianism." Blanche's maiden name was Ames, but she was not related to her husband. She was known not only as a botanical illustrator but also as a portraitist who accepted commis-sions from prominent men and women throughout New England. Concerned with the accurate representation of colors, she developed with her brother a system for matching and duplicating 4,000 hues. In 1914 she became an officer in the Massachusetts Equal Suffrage League, and for a few years her biting political cartoons in support of women's suffrage appeared in national publications. In 1916 she co-founded the Birth Control League of Massachusetts and served as its first president. Because disseminating birth control devices was illegal, she devised ways for women to make their own. During World War II she patented a system for ensnaring low-flying aircraft in snarls of string, but nothing came of the idea despite a demonstration at Borderland using an old plane that she had bought. At age eighty she wrote a biography of her father, Major General Adelbert Ames, in order to set the record straight after

John F. Kennedy, in *Profiles in Courage*, derogated Ames' administration of Mississippi during Reconstruction.

Oakes and Blanche Ames were married in 1900. Six years later they bought the first of several tracts of farmland, woods, and ponds that eventually comprised their 1250-acre estate. On Mountain Street at the eastern edge of the property, they renovated a farmhouse, adding a servants' wing and piazza, plus vegetable and flower gardens and an orchard. Then in 1910 they built the Tudor gothic mansion that stands near the park's western entrance. As large as it is, the new house was only half the size of one designed for them by an architect whose plans the Ameses rejected as too grandiose and expensive. Instead, Blanche devised her own design with help from the contractor and a few books on architecture. Built of stone with concrete floors, the fire-proof house included a large, two-storied library in the north wing. This was Oakes Ames' room, where he spent most of his time as he got older. Often he left the dinner table early in order to return to the library, where he could be heard recounting the mealtime conversation to his dogs. For Ames' botanical research, there was a basement laboratory below the library, opening onto a sunken rock garden located within the foundation of an old barn.

Although the Ameses had other houses in Boston, Gloucester, and Ormond Beach, Florida, they and their four children lived mostly at Borderland. Oakes commuted to work in Cambridge by chauffeur-driven car. At times he and his wife employed as many as forty people, including a resident superintendent, farm hands, laborers, and house servants. The Ameses cultivated part of the estate and at one time or another raised chickens, turkeys, pheasants, and cattle. By constructing dams and dikes, they enlarged ponds and created new ones. They also built the carriage roads followed in part by the route shown on Map 51. Fond of tennis, Oakes and Blanche had two courts, one grass and the other hard-surfaced, and won many trophies in North Shore tennis tournaments for mixed doubles. Eventually they built a spring-fed swimming pool near the house. Now filled in, it was made from large stone blocks that were taken from a family-owned factory when it was torn down. In addition to tennis and swimming, the Ameses enjoyed walking, birding, hunting, horseback riding, canoeing, fishing, and ice skating. Their daughter Pauline wrote, "I can remember the grown-ups carrying a victrola out onto the ice of Pud's Pond and skating the waltz." In a typical diary entry for an autumn day in 1906, Oakes Ames wrote,

A dense fog veiled the landscape when I awoke. At 8:30 it had partly faded away, leaving a smoky film over the trees and low meadows. After breakfast I rode on my bike to North Easton and remained there till noon. Dinner was served by the time I reached Borderland. In the early afternoon

I gave my time and attention to matters of importance about the place. At 3:30 Blanche joined me and we took our shot guns with us to the woods. Although we passed through places where earlier in the season partridges were rather common, we saw but one. Throughout the afternoon not a shot was fired. We had our sport, however, in anticipation and in a thorough enjoyment of woodland scenery.

Oakes Ames died in 1950 and Blanche in 1969. In 1971 the Ames family sold Borderland — including the house and its furnishings, paintings, and Ames memorabilia — to the Commonwealth of Massachusetts for the bargain price of $1.2 million. Through gifts and additional purchases, the park is now about 1800 acres.

THE WEALTH of the Ames family originated with a shovel factory established at Easton in 1803 by Oakes Ames' great-grandfather, Oliver Ames. His sons, also named Oakes and Oliver Ames, grew rich by manufacturing not only shovels but also plows and other tools for the expanding nation. The California gold rush in 1849, the construction of railroads during the 1850s, the settlement of thousands of western farms annually, and the demand for equipment during the Civil War made the firm worth $8 million by 1865. Two years later the company sold more than a million shovels, one of every two manufactured in the United States.

His fortune made, Oakes Ames — grandfather of the botanist — helped to organize the new Republican party in Massachusetts. During the bloody conflict between pro- and anti-slavery forces in Kansas, he gave $10,000 to the Emigrant Aid Society to send Free Soil men to the contested territory. During the Civil War, he recruited and equipped two regiments at his own expense. From 1862 to 1873 he served in Congress, where construction of the transcontinental railway became his chief project. Oakes eventually became a major shareholder and director of the Union Pacific Railroad. His brother Oliver also invested heavily in the project and served as the railroad's president from 1866 to '68. By securing government land grants and loans, by pouring in his own fortune, and by scrounging indefatigably for cash from skeptical investors, Oakes Ames did more than any other individual to finance the colossal undertaking. He and his brother headed the faction, centered in Boston, that looked not to graft or stock manipulation for a quick payoff, but to the railroad's completion and profitable operation. Together, the Ames brothers were commemorated in 1881 by construction of the Ames monument near Sherman, Wyoming.

There is, however, more to the story. Oakes Ames and other insiders at the Union Pacific also controlled Credit Mobilier of America, a

construction company by which they contracted with themselves to build the line's last 667 miles. This in itself was not unusual; at that time other railroads did the same thing. It was a way for major backers to receive a return on their investment during the construction phase of the project. For example, various insiders got contracts to supply ties, axles, wheels, and other items made by firms in which they had interests. Later the matter blew up into a huge scandal involving charges of bloated profits and extravagant dividends. Most troublesome of all was the fact that Oakes Ames sold shares of Credit Mobilier to members of Congress at low prices — in some cases for no cash down. The obvious inference was that the shares were intended to quash unfavorable legislation and to forestall investigation into alleged profiteering by Credit Mobilier. Occurring in part during the presidential election of 1872, the scandal was trumpeted by the opposition press as yet another egregious example of corruption during Grant's first term of office — and so it has been remembered ever since.

The facts, however, were far more complex than the newspapers and two investigatory committees of Congress appreciated. The costs of construction were exceptionally high in large part because the conditions were exceptionally difficult. There was also much wasted effort due to false starts, disputes among the directors, lack of capital, expensive stop-gap loans, and the extremely speculative nature of the whole venture. Moreover, the dividends paid by Credit Mobilier were mostly in the form of Union Pacific shares and bonds, which for years had been worth little. The securities rose in value only as the railroad neared completion. Ames said that in his search for capital he tried to peddle Credit Mobilier stock to all his friends. He had made firm offers to sell shares when the price was low, and he felt compelled to adhere to that price later when his influential colleagues in Congress clamored for shares as the price soared. At most, he said, he wished to create a "general favorable feeling" for a great public project. His chief offenses, Oakes said, were that "I have risked reputation, fortune, everything, in an enterprise of incalculable benefit to the Government, from which the capital of the world shrank; . . . [and] that I have had friends, some of them in official life, with whom I have been willing to share advantageous opportunities of investment." His defense, however, was not helped by old letters that became public. In the correspondence he told a railroad associate that he had placed the shares of Credit Mobilier "where they will do most good to us," and that it was hard to get his congressional colleagues to familiarize themselves with the railroad's needs "unless they have an interest to do so." In February of 1873 Ames was censured by the House of Representatives, and later that year he died of a stroke. Of the nine representative and two senators who had bought shares, only one —

James Brooks of New York — was similarly censured, and he too died within a few weeks.

Other members of the Ames family also had noteworthy careers. The congressman's son — yet another Oliver Ames, the father of Oakes Ames the botanist — was first a partner in the family shovel firm, then he too turned to railroad building. But unlike his father, whose finances were deranged by constructing the Union Pacific, the young Oliver made a fortune as a railroad promoter. In 1873 he went to Kansas to build the Central Branch of the Union Pacific. He told the *Boston Globe* in 1895 that "I traveled in stage coaches all along the proposed route of the road, secured right-of-way grants and got town aid. . . . It was all done in three years, and I had made myself independent. That was my greatest business success." He was also a canny speculator in land and stocks and at one point got the better of Jay Gould in a deal that brought him more than a million dollars. Using his fortune, Ames entered politics and eventually became governor of Massachusetts from 1887 to 1890. His ultimate goal, never reached, was to be elected to Congress, where he hoped to push through a resolution reversing the censure of his father. He and his brothers did, however, build the Oakes Ames Memorial Hall at Easton, and Oliver also gave funds for the town's school and library.

On his way to the governorship, Oliver Ames was lieutenant governor under Benjamin Butler, the maternal grandfather of Blanche Ames. During the Civil War, Butler was in command of the Union forces that occupied New Orleans. There he became notorious for his order that any lady who insulted his officers or troops should be regarded as "a woman of the town plying her avocation." His highhanded rule earned him the moniker "Beast" Butler. Eventually he was removed from his position and put in charge of the Army of the James, but he did poorly and was relieved of command. After the war (but before being elected governor of Massachusetts) he was one of the House managers who conducted the impeachment trial against President Andrew Johnson. He was also a staunch defender of his Massachusetts colleague Oakes Ames. Regarded by many as an opportunistic demagogue who was at first a Democrat and then a radical Republican, Butler concluded his political career by running for president in 1884 on the Antimonopoly and Greenback ticket.

Butler's son-in-law (Blanche Ames' father) was Major General Adelbert Ames, a West Pointer who was the academy's first recipient of the Congressional Medal of Honor. After the Civil War, Adelbert served as the Union's military commander in Mississippi, then as a Reconstruction senator and finally as Mississippi's governor. Trying unsuccessfully to stop the systematic intimidation of black voters, Ames was impeached by the resurgent southern Democrats. Rather than face a trial

with a preordained outcome, he retired. Eventually, he settled in Tewksbury, Massachusetts, where he made a sizable fortune in real estate, textiles, and the invention and manufacture of pencil sharpeners and other devices. When the Spanish-American wore broke out in 1898, Ames returned to service as a brigadier general and participated in the siege of Santiago and the battle of San Juan Hill. When he died in 1933, he was the last surviving Civil War general.

Finally, there are the distinguished children and grandchildren of Oakes and Blanche Ames, including Amyas Ames (governor of the New York Stock Exchange and chairman of the board of the Lincoln Center for the Performing Arts and the New York Philharmonic Symphony), Oakes Ames (president of Connecticut College), and George Ames Plimpton, writer and editor.

≈     ≈     ≈     ≈

**AUTOMOBILE DIRECTIONS: Borderland State Park** straddles the boundary of Sharon and Easton 23 miles south of Boston. (See •26 on **Map 1** on page 6, and also the corner panel of **Map 51** on page 332.) Three approaches are described below.

**To Borderland State Park from Route 24:** Route 24 is the expressway that serves Brockton. It links Exit 4 on **Interstate 93** (old Route 128) and Exit 7A on **Interstate 495**.

Leave Route 24 at Exit 16B for Route 106 west. Follow Route 106 west 4.7 miles, then turn right onto Poquanticut Avenue. After 1.3 miles, turn left onto Massapoag Avenue and go 2.1 miles to the park entrance on the right. Immediately after entering, turn left to the visitor center.

**To Borderland State Park from Interstate 495:** Leave I-495 at Exit 10 for Route 123. Follow Route 123 toward Easton 3.1 miles, then turn right at a T-intersection onto Route 106 east (also called Route 123 east). Go only 0.5 mile, then turn left onto Poquanticut Avenue. After 1.3 miles, turn left onto Massapoag Avenue and go 2.1 miles to the park entrance on the right. Immediately after entering, turn left to the visitor center.

**To Borderland State Park from Route 1:** This approach is also good from Exit 10 off **Interstate 95 *southbound*.**

MAP 51 — Borderland State Park

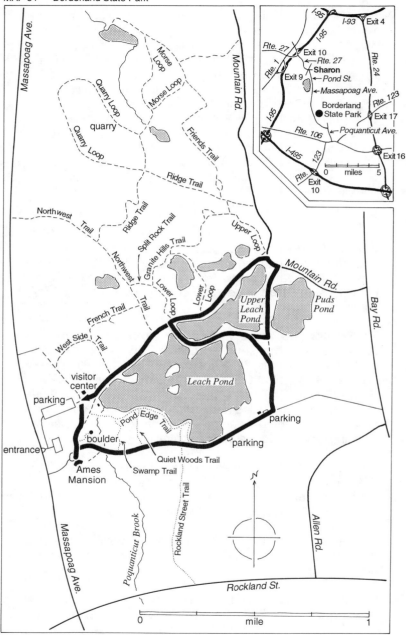

From the intersection with Route 1 or from Exit 10 off I-95, follow Route 27 south about 3 miles. At a traffic light in the center of Sharon, leave Route 27 (it turns left here) by continuing straight across Main Street, then *immediately* turn right onto Pond Street. Go 4.5 miles as the road passes Massapoag Lake and changes names to Massapoag Avenue. Turn left into the park and then left again to the visitor center.

≈    ≈    ≈    ≈

**WALKING: Map 51** at left outlines a 4-mile figure eight around Leach Pond and Upper Leach Pond at **Borderland State Park**. Carriage roads and farm lanes provide easy walking and vicarious enjoyment of the wealth that created this landscape. For a longer outing, you can also explore a system of footpaths through rocky, wooded hills north of the ponds.

**Start your walk** by going to the **Ames Mansion**, which is worth seeing even if only from the outside. (Occasions for touring the house are noted in the introduction to this chapter.) To reach the mansion from the parking lot, turn right at the four-way intersection of paths near the visitor center and follow a gravel track to the stone house visible across the lawn.

The figure-eight route shown on Map 51 continues from the front of the Ames Mansion. Facing the house, locate a gravel carriage road that descends to the left across the lawn and into the woods. Eventually, after passing Leach Pond and a gate, continue on a gravel road used occasionally by cars.

After passing a small farmhouse and a parking area, turn left by a gate and follow a worn path along the edge of a meadow, where signs point toward Upper Leach Pond and Puds Pond. Midway across another meadow, fork left onto a narrow track that leads to a dike separating Upper and Lower Leach Pond.

After crossing a small bridge below a spillway, turn right at a T-intersection. Eventually, fork right past the north end of Upper Leach Pond. With caution, follow a paved road right for 80 yards, then turn right at a gate .

After passing a spillway at Puds Pond, continue a few dozen yards to a meadow. Turn right along the edge of the grass, then descend into the woods. Once again, follow the dike that separates Upper and Lower Leach Pond, then turn left at the T-intersection just beyond the bridge. At a stone lodge, fork right uphill to return to the visitor center and parking lot.

# 27

# DUXBURY BEACH

Located south of Boston about half-way to Cape Cod, Duxbury Beach is so fascinating on a map that it compels investigation. Separating Massachusetts Bay from Duxbury Bay, the long, narrow spit links the mainland with Gurnet Point, as shown on **Map 52** on page 338. A walk down the spit and back totals about 7 miles (11.2 kilometers) and provides ample opportunity to enjoy the bleak and pleasant ambiance of the surf, beach, and low dunes. The spit's southern end, which is located in the town of Plymouth, is private.

The beach is open daily from dawn to dusk. During the swimming season, an entrance fee is charged. In winter, you can have the beach virtually to yourself — although sometimes the lot is closed because of ice, snow, or storms. For information, telephone Duxbury Beach Park at (781) 837-3112. In winter, the number is disconnected.

For automobile directions to the beach, please turn to page 336. Walking directions start on page 339.

---

THE REMARKABLE LANDFORM that includes Duxbury Beach, Gurnet Point, Saquish Neck, and Saquish Head (all shown together on Map 52) is the result of several processes, some of them discussed in Chapter 2 on Plum Island. At Duxbury Beach, the growth of the spit has been fed in part by sediments supplied by nearby rivers, chiefly the Back River and the Green Harbor River, both shown on the map's corner panel. The eroding headland at Brant Rock is another source of sand and gravel. Under the influence of northeasterly storms, the materials trail southward from the rivers and headland to form the long, narrow spit of Duxbury Beach.

At the southern end of the spit, the glacial hills at Gurnet Point and Saquish Head are other sources of sand and gravel that contribute to the growth of the barrier. Incoming waves have eroded the ocean side of

Gurnet Point, which may once have been several times its present size, and from there the sand and gravel have been washed westward to link with Saquish Head and Duxbury Beach.

Taken altogether, the hills (which once were islands) and the spit are a special kind of bay barrier called a *tombolo*. Tombolos attach one or more islands, usually of glacial or volcanic origin, to the mainland. In a tombolo, the island not only feeds the spit but also anchors its outer end, as does Gurnet Point, which is "armored" around the shore by cobbles and boulders left by erosion of the clay bluff in which the rocks were formerly imbedded. (To some extent, this rip-rap has been supplemented by human effort.)

Tombolos are common along the coast of New England. Nahant and Hull at the mouth of Boston Harbor are tombolos, showing much the same form as Duxbury Beach. The hills at the outer ends are drumlins, laid down throughout the Boston region and even off the present-day coast by the last continental glacier. The ice sheet impounded so much water that sea level was as much as three hundred feet lower than now. Isolated and eroded by the rising ocean as the ice melted, the drumlins became islands and tombolos. In the future, erosion and rising water will alter and eradicate many of these formations, but others will be created as the sea spreads inland. After Gurnet Point has been destroyed by erosion, Duxbury Beach (if it still exists) will probably retreat westward to Clarks Island, which for a time will anchor a much altered tombolo.

≈      ≈      ≈      ≈

**AUTOMOBILE DIRECTIONS: Duxbury Beach** is located on the south shore of Massachusetts Bay, about 30 miles from Boston. (See •27 on **Map 1** on page 6, and also the corner panel of **Map 52** on page 338.)

**To Duxbury Beach from the juncture of Route 3 and Interstate 93 in Quincy:** Follow Route 3 south toward Cape Cod for 20 miles, then leave Route 3 at Exit 11 for Route 14. Follow Route 14 east toward Duxbury 0.7 mile, then continue straight on Route 139 "west" (so say the signs) where Route 14 forks off to the right. Follow Route 139 for 3 miles — in the process crossing **Route 3A** — then fork right toward Duxbury Beach on Canal Street. Follow Canal Street 1.7 miles to the big parking lot at the northern end of Duxbury Beach.

≈      ≈      ≈      ≈

MAP 52 — Duxbury Beach

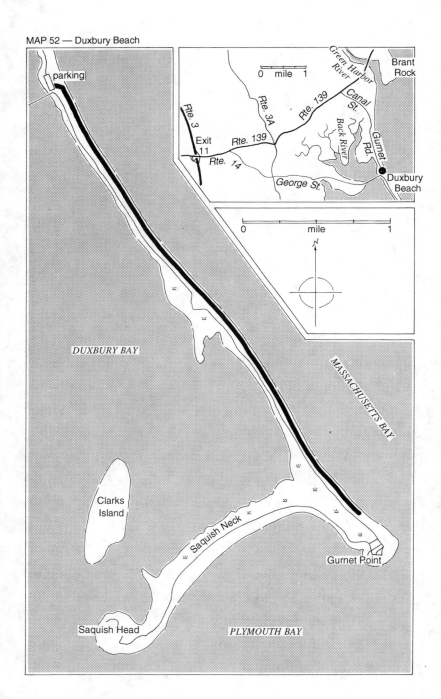

338

**WALKING:** As shown on **Map 52** at left, **Duxbury Beach** is a long, narrow barrier linking the mainland with the far-offshore demi-island of Gurnet Point. A walk along Duxbury Beach to Gurnet Point and back totals 7 miles. Although the beach is public, hikers are not entitled to continue up onto the headland at Gurnet Point, which is a private community of summer cottages. Saquish Neck and Saquish Head to the east are also private.

**To get started,** descend from the parking lot to Duxbury Beach and turn right along the shore. With the ocean on the left, follow the beach south as far as you care to go, then return the way you came. Signs posted at Gurnet Point mark the southern limit of the public beach. On weekdays in winter, when there is little traffic, you may for the sake of variety want to return north via the gravel road that runs along the eastern side of the spit, overlooking Duxbury Bay.

**28**

# MYLES STANDISH STATE FOREST

Located in Plymouth southeast of Boston, the immense Myles
Standish State Forest shares much with the landscape of Cape
Cod.  Its sandy hills are covered with pines, scrub oak, and blueberry heath dotted with many ponds and abrupt depressions.
Crisscrossing the forest are dozens of miles of foot trails, paved
hike-bike paths, and dirt roads, as shown on **Map 53** on page
347.  Four routes of different lengths are described below.

The left panel of **Map 54** on page 349 shows a circuit of 2.5
miles (4 kilometers) around East Head Reservoir.  The right panel
of Map 54 traces a route of 5.6 miles (9 kilometers) via paved
paths.

**Map 55** on page 351 shows two routes that follow dirt roads
and paved hike-bike paths.  The eastern route on the right side of
the map is 8 miles (12.8 kilometers) and the western route on the
left is 6.3 miles (10 kilometers).  On the maps, the straight roads
may appear to be boring, but that is far from the case in actuality.
Transecting the landscape, the roads accentuate the area's
irregular topography.

Myles Standish State Park is open daily from sunrise to sunset.
It is administered by the Massachusetts Department of Environmental Management; telephone (508) 866-2526 for information.
Please note that **hunting** occurs mid-October to December, and
during that period trails may be closed on Saturdays and other
occasions.

For automobile directions to the trailhead at the forest headquarters, please turn to page 346.  Directions to the several walks
are on pages 348 and 350.

---

MYLES STANDISH STATE FOREST is like no other place featured in
this book.  It consists of nearly twenty-three square miles of irregular
hills and hollows.  Like an immense sandbox soaking up the rain, it has

almost no streams. Nor does the terrain show the usual branching system of valleys, ravines, and swales gnawing into the upland. Instead, the surface is peculiarly random, unaffected even by the deeply-buried bedrock. What follows is a brief discussion of the glacial processes that account for this intriguing landscape.

Glaciers, of course, are simply the result of the accumulation of snow over many years, as frequently occurs at higher elevations and higher latitudes, where the total annual fall of snow exceeds what melts or evaporates. As the snow thaws during the day and refreezes at night, it packs down and becomes granular and then turns to ice. When the ice reaches a thickness of about one hundred feet, it becomes plastic under its own weight and is able to flow, typically only a few inches or feet per day, although sometimes the rate is much faster. The surface, however, remains brittle so that large cracks or *crevasses* develop as the plastic ice below moves under the force of gravity.

Photographs of Alaska, the Alps, and other mountainous regions have made familiar to everyone the image of glaciers flowing like rivers of ice down mountainsides and along broad valleys. As big as they are, these glaciers are small compared to *continental glaciers*, which develop when snow and ice accumulate over a large area and build to a thickness of one or two miles. For example, even at the present time, the Greenland ice sheet occupies 670,000 square miles and is about 10,000 feet thick at the center; the larger Antarctic ice sheet is about one and a half times as big as the United States and reaches a thickness of 2.5 miles. Spreading from the center, or *zone of accumulation*, a continental glacier flows outward in all directions, like pancake batter spooned onto a griddle. At first tongues of ice advance down valleys and spread out across the lowlands, but as the glacier thickens it overrides hills and even mountains.

At the beginning of the Pleistocene epoch (or Ice Age) in North America about one million years ago, when the world climate was somewhat cooler than at present, snow accumulated in Labrador and northwestern Canada, and from there the ice sheets spread radially until they merged and covered all of Canada and most of the United States north of New Jersey, Pennsylvania, and the Ohio and Missouri Rivers. At the same time, continental glaciers also spread from other, similar zones of accumulation in Scandinavia, Siberia, and Antarctica. In fact, in Europe the first Pleistocene glacier appears to have occurred about two million years ago.

Corresponding to the zone of accumulation at the center of the ice sheet is the *zone of wastage* at the perimeter. The wastage is caused by melting and evaporation (together called *ablation*) and by the *calving* of icebergs where the glacier meets the ocean. If the rate at which the glacier moves forward is greater than the rate of wastage, then on balance the ice sheet advances. If the ice front melts as fast as the glacier moves, the perimeter is stationary. And if the ice front melts faster than the rate of advance, the glacier recedes. Of course, as continental glaciers spread toward the equator, they eventually reach a standstill in warmer latitudes.

Glaciers act as huge earth scrapers and conveyor belts combined into one ponderous process. As it moves, the ice strips away the soil and grinds down the bedrock of the vast area over which the frozen mass advances. The immense weight of the ice even depresses the crust of the earth, so that the land surface beneath the glacier sinks (but later rises, or rebounds, after the ice melts). Boulders, rock fragments, sand, and a huge amount of finely pulverized stone called *rock flour* become imbedded in the bottom few meters of the glacier and constitute its *load*, which is carried forward by the ice sheet and deposited when the glacier melts, if not sooner. Often the bottom layer becomes so overloaded with material that the debris is simply smeared forward for a few miles before dropping out. As boulders are dragged and scraped along the surface beneath the glacier, they sometimes leave scratches or *striations* in the bedrock that show (after the ice sheet melts) the direction from which the glacier advanced. Although the flow near Boston was generally from northwest to southeast, the orientation of scratches may differ greatly from one place to another depending on the local topography that influenced the glacier's movement.

During the Pleistocene epoch, there were four distinct periods of continental glaciation in North America. Most recently the ice advanced about 70,000 years ago and retreated from New England starting about 12,000 years ago. The retreat was spasmodic; periods of steady withdrawal alternated with periods during which the ice front was at a standstill or even advanced again for short distances. In each case the earth materials carried by the glacier were deposited to create characteristic landforms. One common assemblage of deposits is that of an *end moraine* (or *terminal moraine*) fronted by an *outwash plain* and backed by a *ground moraine*.

An end moraine occurs where the ice front is stationary for a time. The glacier continues to flow forward, carrying its load of debris with it, but the rate of flow is more or less matched by the rate of wastage, so that the earth material is dumped in a line along the ice front. Pushed from behind, the advancing glacier ascends the accumulating debris, heaping the deposits higher and higher as the dirt-laden ice melts. The result is a range of irregular hills composed of unsorted clay, sand, small rocks, and boulders that together are called *glacial till* or *boulder clay*. The surface of the end moraine is described as *knob and kettle* topography, consisting of randomly distributed mounds and hollows. The

343

range of hills may be one or two miles wide and scores of miles long. Some outstanding examples of end moraines in the Midwest and in Europe are many hundreds of miles long. They may be interrupted by gaps carved by subsequent erosion, including erosion from meltwater pouring out of temporary lakes that were impounded between the moraines and the retreating ice front. In coastal Massachusetts, large sections of moraines have been obliterated by the rise of sea level, but some fragments survive.

The process of withdrawal sometimes followed a scenario called "stagnation zone retreat." For example, in New England the southern margin of the glacier often consisted of a narrow band of stagnant ice. Because of ablation, ice in the stagnation zone was no longer thick enough to flow. Active ice to the north rode up over the motionless mass, melting as it came and adding more and more gravel, sand, and silt. Streams pouring out from the glacier carried the material forward and deposited it in thick beds sometimes underlain by the stagnant ice. Of course, after the buried ice melted, the layered material settled and slumped to form an irregular surface that some writers call a *kame moraine*.

There is also evidence to support another model for glacial retreat: that of *regional* stagnation. As the climate changed and the ice sheet thinned, large units of the glacier may have stopped moving, perhaps because they lay to the south of highlands that were no longer surmountable by the diminished mass of ice flowing from the north. The heights that separate one preglacial watershed from another were no obstacle for the waxing ice sheet, but as the glacier waned, even modest ridges may have blocked and redirected the movement of ice. According to this theory, ice to the south of such barriers stagnated in huge units.

In front of the end moraine — or that is, in the direction toward which the ice advanced — is the *outwash plain*. Here numerous meltwater streams that were loaded with sediments deposited *alluvial fans* or *outwash fans*. Over time the alluvium spread and coalesced to form a continuous apron sloping gently away from the end moraine. Because the energy of the meltwater dissipated as the streams fanned out, the deposits are graded. Gravel and coarse sand were dropped close to the moraine, finer sand farther out, and rock flour (which gives glacial streams their characteristic milky appearance) was often carried all the way to the sea. Near the end moraine the outwash plain may be pitted with *kettleholes* that once were filled with isolated blocks of ice. The blocks were buried in the outwash debris, but after they finally melted, the earth collapsed to form steep-sided holes which frequently are occupied by ponds and marshes. Sometimes, curiously, the outwash plain now stands higher than the moraine where it originated. This anomaly occurs where the moraine was previously supported at a correspondingly high elevation by a foundation of stagnant ice that eventually melted, allowing the morainic deposits to collapse.

In back of the end moraine — that is, on the side from which the ice advanced — is the *ground moraine.* As already noted, the ice at the bottom of a glacier may become so thick with clay, sand, and rocks that some of this material drops out even as the glacier continues to move over it. When the ice sheet recedes steadily by melting, additional debris is left behind, so that a vast area is blanketed. The material often clogs former river channels, producing undrained or poorly-drained flats. There may also be scattered *drumlins* (smooth oval hills shaped by the ice) and *eskers* (sinuous ridges that previously were the beds of streams that flowed in tunnels within the ice).

In reality these landforms — end moraine, outwash plain, and ground moraine — are not always distinct. Frequently they grade into each other and may even obscure one another, overlapping like shingles as the glacier retreats. Also, successive end moraines that in some places are far apart may in other areas merge because the glacier did not retreat at the same rate along the entire ice front.

Southeastern Massachusetts shows a series of moraines and outwash plains, each with its characteristic features. The hills along the north coast of Nantucket and Martha's Vineyard are remnants of an end moraine that marks the farthest advance of the last continental ice sheet in New England. Here the ice front stood still for awhile before starting its withdrawal. In front of the moraine is an outwash plain sloping gently toward the southern coast of each island. The moraine reappears to the west as Block Island and the hilly spine of Long Island. A subsequent moraine lies along the southern shore of Cape Cod Bay and the eastern shore of Buzzard's Bay. It continues west as the Elizabeth Islands and the Rhode Island shore west of Narragansett Bay, Fishers Island, and the north coast of Long Island. Still farther north is yet another morainic complex running through Myles Standish State Forest. From Great South Pond, shown at the top of Map 53 on page 347, one arm (the Ellisville Moraine) runs southeast and the other arm (the Hog Rock Moraine) runs southwest. Between the two arms is the Wareham Pitted Plain. With its many kettleholes and other collapsed deposits associated with buried ice, the "plain" is flat only in some sections. One characteristic of all the morainic systems of southeastern Massachusetts is their parallel, festoon-like arrangement on a map, reflecting successive pauses during the gradual retreat of the glacier's several adjacent lobes.

≈      ≈      ≈      ≈

**AUTOMOBILE DIRECTIONS:** Myles Standish State Forest is located 45 miles southeast of Boston in the town of
Plymouth. (See •28 on **Map 1** on page 6, and also the corner
panel of **Map 53** at right.) Three approaches are described
below.

**To Myles Standish State Forest from the juncture of
Route 3 and Interstate 93 in Quincy:** Follow Route 3
south toward Cape Cod for 29 miles, then leave Route 3 at Exit
5 for Long Pond Road. At the bottom of the ramp, turn right and
follow Long Pond Road 3.7 miles, then turn right into Myles
Standish State Forest on Alden Road. After 1.8 miles, turn left
onto Upper College Pond Road toward the forest headquarters.
Go 2.1 miles (in the process passing a parking lot on the right),
then turn right at a crossroads with Halfway Pond Road. After
0.7 mile, fork left and continue 1.1 miles to the big parking lot on
the left at the forest headquarters.

**To Myles Standish State Forest from the south via
Route 3:** This approach is useful only if you are coming from
Cape Cod or southern Plymouth.
   Leave Route 3 at Exit 3 and follow Clark Road 0.5 mile to a T-
intersection with Long Pond Road. Turn right and go 1.9 miles,
then turn left into Myles Standish State Forest on Alden Road.
After 1.8 miles, turn left onto Upper College Pond Road toward
the forest headquarters. Go 2.1 miles (in the process passing a
parking lot on the right), then turn right at a crossroads with
Halfway Pond Road. After 0.7 mile, fork left and continue 1.1
miles to the big parking lot on the left at the forest headquarters.

**To Myles Standish State Forest from Interstate 495:**
Leave I-495 at Exit 2 for Route 58. (This is the first exit north of
the interchange with **Interstate 195**.) Follow Route 58 north
2.4 miles, then continue straight where Route 58 bears left.
After just 0.8 mile, turn right onto Cranberry Road and follow it
2.7 miles. At an intersection, continue straight a few dozen
yards, then turn left into the headquarters parking lot.

≈       ≈       ≈       ≈

**WALKING: Map 53** at right provides an overview of **Myles
Standish State Forest.** This is a small version of the map
that is available at the headquarters building in a larger format.

MAP 53 — Overview of Myles Standish State Forest

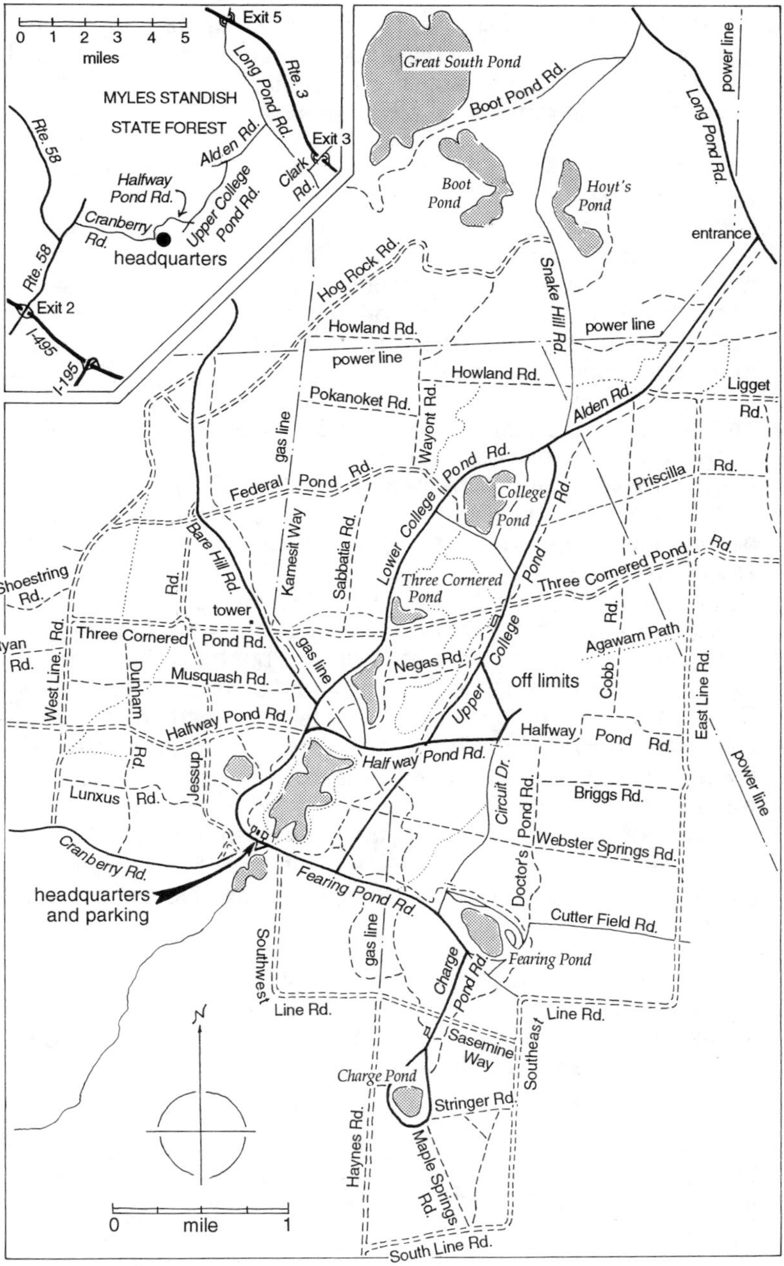

The other maps in this chapter outline four specific routes in greater detail. Each is discussed below, and each makes use of trails that are fairly well maintained — or, at least, that are well-traveled and therefore kept free of brush.*

The left panel of **Map 54** shows a 2.5-mile loop around East Head Reservoir.

**To start**, turn left out the headquarters parking lot and follow Fearing Pond Road across a small bridge. Fifty yards beyond the bridge, bear left into the woods on the blue-blazed East-head Nature Trail. Continue around the pond. At one point, the trail follows the shoulder of a road for about a hundred yards before diving back into the woods.

The right panel of **Map 54** shows a 5.6-mile route through the woods via paved hike-bike paths.

**To start**, turn left out the headquarters parking lot and follow Fearing Pond Road across a small bridge. About 260 yards beyond the bridge, turn left into the woods on the paved hike-bike path.

At the first intersection, bear right. Cross Upper College Pond Road, then turn right at the next intersection. Cross Fearing Pond Road. At a T-intersection with another hike-bike path, turn right. Pass through a parking lot and across Charge Pond Road, then continue uphill to a T-intersection with another hike-bike path. Turn left and follow the path across three paved roads. (The last — Circuit Drive — is closed to cars.) At a four-way intersection of hike-bike paths, turn right and continue to Upper College Pond Road. On the far side, turn left at a T-intersection and follow the hike-bike path back to your starting point, in the process passing two paved paths intersecting from the left.

The right half of **Map 55** on page 351 shows an 8-mile circuit that starts and ends on the paved hike-bike path, but that mostly follows rutted fire roads through piney woods and broad open areas of lowbush blueberry.

---

* Not discussed here is a hiking circuit that is reached from the parking lot on Upper College Pond Road. Overgrown with brush on occasions when I have visited the forest, it may be in good condition when you are there.

MAP 54 — East Head Reservoir Loop (left panel) and hike-bike loop (right panel)

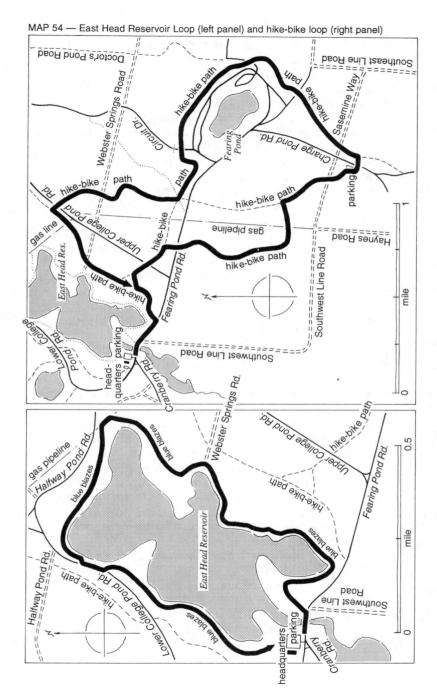

349

**To start**, turn left out the headquarters parking lot and follow Fearing Pond Road across a small bridge. About 260 yards beyond the bridge, turn left into the woods on the paved hike-bike path. After passing two paved trails intersecting from the right, turn right at a somewhat skewed four-way intersection with a rutted woods road. This is Webster Springs Road. Follow it east nearly 2 miles to its end at a T-intersection. (In the process, you will cross a paved road, a gas pipeline right-of-way, a paved hike-bike path, a narrow track, an old asphalt road, and intersections with other trails and roads.)

At the end of Webster Spring Road, turn left onto East Line Road. Go another 2 miles, passing various trails and roads intersecting from the left. At the first cross roads, turn left onto Three Cornered Pond Road and follow it about a mile to a paved road. (This is Upper College Pond Road.) On the far side, turn left onto a paved hike-bike path and follow it back to your starting point, in the process passing several other hike-bike paths intersecting from the left.

The left half of **Map 55** shows a circuit of 6.3-miles. Like the previous excursion, it too begins and ends on a paved hike-bike path, but it mostly follows unpaved fire roads through the hill-and-hollow landscape created by the glacier.

**To start**, go to the staff parking lot on the upper side of the headquarters building. Enter the woods on a paved hike-bike path and follow it uphill past a gate and along the slope above East Head Reservoir. At intervals, cross two paved roads.

After crossing unpaved Three Cornered Pond Road and a gas pipeline right-of-way called Kamesit Way, continue on the hike-bike path past a fire tower on the left. At the next cross-roads, turn left onto unpaved Federal Pond Road and follow it across paved Bare Hill Road. Continue straight through the woods for half a mile, then turn left at a T-intersection with unpaved West Line Road.

Follow West Line Road through the woods 1.3 miles, in the process passing two roads on the right, Three Cornered Pond Road on the left, Ryan Road on the right, and Musquash Road on the left. At a four-way intersection atop a slight rise, turn left onto unpaved Halfway Pond Road. Go another 1.3 miles, then turn right at an intersection with the paved hike-bike path and follow it back to the forest headquarters.

MAP 55 — Myles Standish State Forest: two loops via fire roads and hike-bike paths

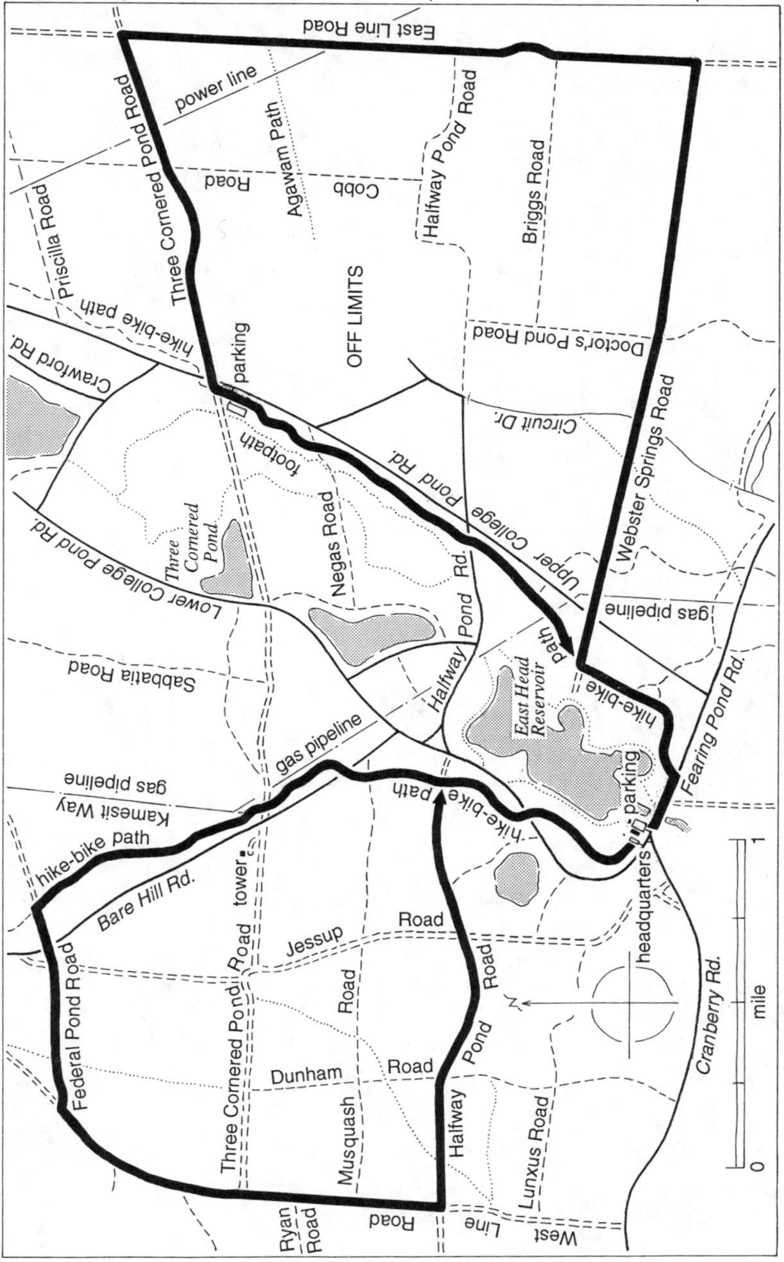

East Line Road

power line

Three Cornered Pond Road

Priscilla Road

hike-bike path

Crawford Rd.

Agawam Path

Cobb Road

Halfway Pond Road

Briggs Road

OFF LIMITS

Doctor's Pond Road

Circuit Dr.

Webster Springs Road

parking

footpath

Three Cornered Pond

Lower College Pond Rd.

Negas Road

Upper College Pond Rd.

Halfway Pond Rd.

gas pipeline

Sabbatia Road

East Head Reservoir

hike-bike path

Fearing Pond Rd.

gas pipeline

Kamesit Way

hike-bike path

Bare Hill Rd.

tower

hike-bike path

parking

headquarters

Federal Pond Road

Three Cornered Pond Road

Jessup Road

Road

Halfway Pond Road

Cranberry Rd.

Dunham Road

Musquash Road

Ryan Road

West Line Road

Lunxus Road

1

mile

0

351

# 29

# CAPE COD CANAL

As shown on **Map 56** on page 357, both banks of the Cape Cod Canal are bordered by a wide, paved path stretching from one end of the waterway to the other. Each hike-bike path is about 7 miles long (11.2 kilometers). Although you may have crossed the canal hundreds of times on the high bridges, the waterside paths are by far the best way to view the canal and to appreciate the immensity of this engineering project.

The canal paths are open daily from dawn to dusk. Dogs must be kept on a short leash to avoid accidents with cyclists. In turn, cyclists should ride single file and yield as necessary.

**Scusset Beach State Reservation** is located at the eastern end of the canal on the north bank. Lifeguards are on duty during the summer.

The **Cape Cod Canal Field Office** is open to the public weekdays from 9 A.M. to 5 P.M. It is located on Academy Drive at the canal's western end (north bank).

The Cape Cod Canal is administered by the U.S. Army Corps of Engineers; telephone (508) 759-4431, extension 20 for information on scheduled walks and programs, including a slide show on the construction and operation of the waterway.

For automobile directions to the canal, please turn to page 356. Walking directions are on page 359.

---

THE IDEA FOR A CANAL across the isthmus where Cape Cod joins the rest of Massachusetts goes back to the first years of European settlement. Myles Standish, military commander of the Plymouth Colony, saw the potential benefit of a waterway connecting Cape Cod Bay and Buzzards Bay, but of course nothing came of the matter. Later, as the colonies of the Atlantic seaboard grew and established trade among themselves, a canal at Cape Cod was envisioned as an obvious aid to coastal navigation. Such a waterway would not only save as much as

150 miles of travel but would also (and more importantly) avoid the dangerous shoals off Martha's Vineyard, Nantucket, and the cape's outer banks, which were becoming a graveyard for ships.  During the Revolutionary War, George Washington regarded a canal at Cape Cod as a way for shippers to evade British raiders operating offshore.  Acting on Washington's order, Thomas Machin, an engineer with the Continental Army, investigated the feasibility of a canal.  His report, which concluded that a man-made waterway was both possible and desirable, is the first known survey for a canal at Cape Cod.

During the nineteenth century, a succession of companies were chartered to build a toll canal.  Some even began construction, but none made significant progress.  Then in 1899 the Boston, Cape Cod, and New York Canal Company acquired a charter.  Five years later the investment banker August Perry Belmont bought the company, reorganized it, and hired William Barclay Parsons as Chief Engineer. After Parsons submitted a favorable report, Belmont determined to go ahead with the project.  At the ceremonial groundbreaking on June 22, 1909, he vowed "not to desert the task until the last shovelful has been dug." Although there was obviously no relation with the far larger Panama Canal, on which construction had started in 1907, Belmont announced that he wanted to finish his canal first.

According to the plan, the waterway would follow a low trough, nowhere more than thirty feet above sea level.  This trough had been created about ten thousand years earlier by a torrent of glacial meltwater flowing from the stagnant lobe of ice in what is now Cape Cod Bay. Caught between the ice mass to the north and the terminal moraine at Cape Cod, the water rose until it found an outlet across the cape to Buzzards Bay.  The outpouring of water carved the trough that subsequently was occupied and deepened by Scusset River, which flows northeast into Cape Cod Bay, and by Manament (or Monument) River, flowing southwest into Buzzards Bay.  A low sandy barrier separated the headwaters of the two streams.

Construction of the canal started at both ends and proceeded toward the middle.  At the eastern end, the first step was building jetties to prevent shoaling where the channel approached shore.  Schooners sailing from quarries in Maine brought in granite blocks, which were then transferred to lighters and dropped into place.  Meanwhile, dredging began on a long and sinuous channel approaching the western end from Buzzard's Bay. Not much was accomplished the first year, but by 1910 twenty-six vessels, including ten dredges, were working at the waterway's western end. The Buzzard's Bay railroad bridge was completed that year, and the Bourne and Sagamore highway bridges in 1911 and 1912.  These bridges were not those that exist now.  Rather, they were drawbridges, close to the water, with navigational openings only 140 feet wide.

Excavation went more slowly than expected. The crews encountered clusters of huge boulders, some of them the size of locomotives, and these had to be blasted into pieces. If the boulders were underwater, divers had to go down, place the charges, withdraw, detonate the explosives, then go down again, over and over. To make faster progress, the canal company brought in steam shovels to dig in the middle of the isthmus. Workers laid down railroad tracks so that the earth could be carried off and dumped in low areas bordering the canal. Frequently the tracks were moved as the men and machines dug the cut wider and deeper.

In August 1912, two large dipper dredges went into operation, digging toward each other from the ends of the canal. With a derrick and huge, proboscis-like boom in front, each dredge had been built on the spot, one at Sagamore and the other at Buzzards Bay, by the American Locomotive Company of Patterson, New Jersey. After Belmont ceremoniously blended bottles of water from Cape Cod Bay and Buzzards Bay, the last barrier of earth between the two canal sections was removed in April 1914. A parade of ships (including Belmont's 81-foot yacht, the *Scout*, and the destroyer *McDougall* carrying Assistant Secretary of the Navy Franklin Delano Roosevelt, officially opened the canal on July 29, seventeen days before inauguration of the Panama Canal.

When the canal opened, the channel's depth was only 15 feet rather than the 25 feet required by the company's charter, so dredging continued. As the canal was deepened, the number of vessels passing through the waterway increased, and so too did tolls, but traffic and revenue never reached the level anticipated by the investors. In 1915, when the canal was 20 feet deep, Belmont tried without success to sell the problematic waterway to the federal government. Troubles included swift tidal currents, narrow bridge openings, shoaling, and the sharply curved approach at the western end. Because of its narrow width, the waterway was open in only one direction at a time. When boats approached the bridges, they often had to wait for the spans to lift, but as the vessels slowed they risked losing steerage. Collisions with the bridges caused long canal closures. Many vessels simply avoided the waterway.

Finally, under the authority of the Rivers and Harbors Act of 1927, the federal government bought the Cape Cod Canal in 1928 for $11.5 million. Congress directed the U.S. Army Corps of Engineers to operate and improve the waterway. Immediately the toll was eliminated. The high bridges seen today, each with a vertical clearance of 135 feet and a horizontal clearance of 480 feet, were designed by the Corps of Engineers and built as projects of the National Industrial Recovery Act of 1933, providing employment to about seven hundred workers during the Great Depression. All three bridges opened to traffic in 1935. That same year, work began on enlarging the entire 17.4 mile channel to a uniform width of 480 feet and a depth of 32 feet. Based on tests using a large hydraulic model built by the Massachusetts Institute of Technology, the western approach was straightened. After work was completed in 1940, the wider, deeper, two-way canal attracted far more vessels than before. By the 1960s, tonnage had increased tenfold. To cope with the rise in traffic, the Corps of Engineers designed and installed a system of radar scanners and closed-circuit television cameras during the 1970s and '80s to monitor ships in the canal. Sitting at a computer console that displays the location, speed, and heading of all vessels, a controller communicates with the ships by radio. The control center is located at the canal headquarters in the town of Buzzards Bay and is an interesting place to stop by for a quick tour and a look at a model of the canal.

≈        ≈        ≈        ≈

**AUTOMOBILE DIRECTIONS: The Cape Cod Canal** is located 50 miles southeast of Boston. (See •29 on **Map 1** on page 6.) There are two waterside paths, one on the north side of the canal and another on the south side. There are also two main approaches: Route 3 and Interstate 495. Directions from each of these highways to both of the canal trails are provided below.

**To the Cape Cod Canal** *northside trail* **via Route 3:** Route 3, of course, joins **Interstate 93** in Quincy, a few miles south of Boston. Follow Route 3 south toward Cape Cod for 42 miles.

Go to a traffic circle just before the high Sagamore Bridge over the Cape Cod Canal. *Do not cross the bridge.* Instead, go slightly more than half way around the rotary, then turn right onto Canal Road and follow it downhill 0.2 mile to the parking lot for the **Sagamore Recreation Area** next to the canal. Or, if you prefer, you can go three-quarters of the way around the rotary to a road that leads 1.4 miles to **Scusset Beach State Reservation** at the eastern end of the canal path.

**To the Cape Cod Canal** *southside trail* **via Route 3:** Route 3, of course, joins **Interstate 93** in Quincy, a few miles south of Boston. Follow Route 3 south 42 miles to Cape Cod.

Immediately after crossing the high Sagamore Bridge over the Cape Cod Canal, take Exit 1 for Route 6A. At the bottom of the hill, turn right and follow Route 6A east 1.5 miles, then turn left onto Tupper Road toward the Cape Cod Canal. After 0.8 mile,

MAP 56 — Cape Cod Canal

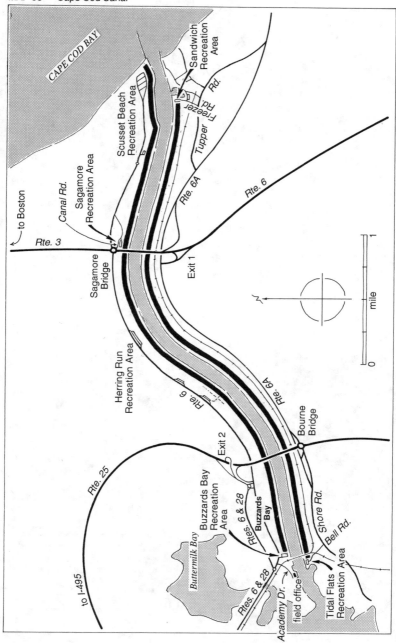

357

turn left onto Freezer Road. which leads 0.2 mile to the parking lot for the **Sandwich Recreation Area**, located at the eastern end of the canal path.

**To the Cape Cod Canal *northside trail* from Interstate 495:** Follow I-495 south to its end at the juncture with Interstate 195 (Exit 1). Without exiting, continue east on Route 25. Eventually, leave Route 25 at Exit 2 for Route 6. At the end of the ramp, bear right for Route 6 west (aka Route 28 north) toward Wareham. Go 1.2 miles, then circle three-quarters of the way around a traffic rotary in order to take the exit for Buzzards Bay and the Massachusetts Maritime Academy. After leaving the rotary, go only 0.1 mile, then turn right just beyond a traffic light and an old train station (now the local chamber of commerce). Follow the entrance road 0.2 mile to the large parking lot for the **Buzzards Bay Recreation Area** next to the Cape Cod Canal.

**To the Cape Cod Canal *southside trail* from Interstate 495:** Follow I-495 south to its end at the juncture with Interstate 195 (Exit 1). Without exiting, continue east on Route 25 to and across the high Bourne Bridge. At the traffic circle on the south side of the bridge, turn right (west) toward Bourne Village, Mashnee Village, and Gray Gables. Go straight 1.2 miles, then turn right onto Bell Road and follow it 0.3 mile to the parking lot for the **Tidal Flats Recreation Area** next to the Cape Cod Canal.

   **To reach the path,** start with the canal on your left. With caution, cross the railroad tracks at the end of the high lift bridge, then continue east on the paved trail.

≈     ≈     ≈     ≈

**WALKING: Map 56** on page 357 shows the **Cape Cod Canal** and its bordering hike-bike paths. Once you are on the paved paths, the way is self-evident.

# INDEX OF FEATURED SITES

IF YOU LIKE THIS BOOK, you might also enjoy some of the other guidebooks listed below. All follow the same format. These guides are widely available at bookstores, nature stores, and outfitters, and also from online booksellers.

## DAY TRIPS IN DELMARVA

The Delmarva Peninsula, which consists of southern Delaware and the Eastern Shore of Maryland and Virginia (hence Del-Mar-Va, in local parlance) is one of the most fascinating vacation areas on the East Coast. *Day Trips in Delmarva* emphasizes the region's historic towns, scenic back roads, wildlife refuges, undeveloped beaches, and routes for car touring, hiking, and bicycling.

"The best organized, best written, most comprehensive and practical guide to the Delmarva Peninsula" — *The Easton Star Democrat* • "An infinitely enjoyable book" — *Baltimore Magazine*

## COUNTRY WALKS NEAR WASHINGTON

Dozens of outings explore national, state, and local parks and hike-bike trails located within an hour's drive of the U.S. capital. Each chapter includes an overview, detailed directions, one or more maps (there are sixty in all), and extensive commentary.

"Cream of the local outdoors-guide crop" — *Washington Post* • "The happy union between a utilitarian and historically informative guide" — *Washington Times*

## COUNTRY WALKS & BIKEWAYS
## IN THE PHILADELPHIA REGION

This guidebook explores the Delaware Valley's parks, wildlife refuges, and trail networks, including eighty-five miles of canal trails along the Delaware River.

## COUNTRY WALKS NEAR BALTIMORE

"Fisher's books, with his own photos illustrating them, are models of pith and practicality. . . . The maps for '*Country Walks*' excel." — *Baltimore Sun*

## COUNTRY WALKS NEAR CHICAGO

"A handy guide. . . . The general information sections — which, if combined, constitute three-fourths of the book — are excellent." — *Chicago Tribune*